Excel 2007

BEYOND
THE MANUAL

D1455922

Receive a $10 rebate on this book!

Visit www.apress.com/promo for rebate details and form.

ISBN-13: 978-1-59059-798-9
ISBN-10: 1-59059-798-2

53999

9 781590 597989

Valid for U.S. and Canadian residents on the first printing of this book.
For complete terms and details, see www.apress.com/promo.

Excel 2007

2007

BEYOND THE MANUAL

Helen Dixon

Apress®

Excel 2007: Beyond the Manual

Copyright © 2007 by Helen Dixon

ISBN-13 (pbk): 978-1-59059-798-9

ISBN-10 (pbk): 1-59059-798-2

Printed and bound in the United States of America 9 8 7 6 5 4 3 2 1

Lead Editor: Jonathan Hassell
Technical Reviewer: Judith Myerson
Editorial Board: Steve Anglin, Ewan Buckingham, Gary Cornell, Jason Gilmore, Jonathan Gennick, Jonathan Hassell, James Huddleston, Chris Mills, Matthew Moodie, Jeff Pepper, Paul Sarknas, Dominic Shakeshaft, Jim Sumser, Matt Wade
Project Manager: Richard Dal Porto
Copy Edit Manager: Nicole Flores
Copy Editor: Liz Welch
Assistant Production Director: Kari Brooks-Copony
Production Editor: Laura Esterman
Compositor: Dina Quan
Proofreaders: Elizabeth Berry and Lori Bring
Indexer: Valerie Perry
Artist: April Milne
Cover Designer: Kurt Krames
Manufacturing Director: Tom Debolski

Distributed to the book trade worldwide by Springer-Verlag New York, Inc., 233 Spring Street, 6th Floor, New York, NY 10013. Phone 1-800-SPRINGER, fax 201-348-4505, e-mail orders-ny@springer-sbm.com, or visit http://www.springeronline.com.

For information on translations, please contact Apress directly at 2560 Ninth Street, Suite 219, Berkeley, CA 94710. Phone 510-549-5930, fax 510-549-5939, e-mail info@apress.com, or visit http://www.apress.com.

The source code for this book is available to readers at http://www.apress.com in the Source Code/Download section.

In memory of my father, Brian McGarry

Contents at a Glance

Contents

CHAPTER 11

Charts 231

CHAPTER 12

Adding Graphics to a Worksheet 251

CHAPTER 13

Preventing and Correcting Errors

About the Author

**HELEN DIXON** has been working as an IT trainer for almost ten years, specializing in Microsoft Excel. She currently works for Queen's University in Belfast, training staff and students in IT and providing a consultancy service for staff. Her qualifications include a Bachelor's (with Honors) in Business Studies and a Master's in Computing and Information Systems and various IT qualifications, including MOS Excel 2002 Expert and ECDL Advanced Spreadsheets. She is currently studying for a PhD in Electronic Commerce at the University of Ulster.

About the Technical Reviewer

JUDITH M. MYERSON is a systems architect and engineer. Her areas of interest include middleware technologies, enterprise-wide systems, database technologies, application development, web development, web services, object-oriented engineering, software engineering, network management, servers, security management, information assurance, standards, RFID technologies, and project management. Judith holds a Master of Science degree in engineering, as well as several certificates, and is a member of the IEEE organization. She has reviewed/edited a number of Apress books, including *Hardening Linux*, *Creating Client Extranets with SharePoint 2003*, and *Microsoft SharePoint: Building Office 2003 Solutions*.

Acknowledgments

I would like to thank everyone who has been involved in the production of this book, especially Jonathan Hassell, Jim Sumser, Richard Dal Porto, Liz Welch, Laura Esterman, and Judith Myerson for all their input. Hugs and thanks to my husband, DJ, and children, Ella and Daniel, for their patience and love, and also to my mother, Isobel McGarry, and all my family (not forgetting the in-laws) for their continued support. Thanks also to my colleagues Martin Reid, Maureen McKee, and Paddy Brannigan at Queen's University, Belfast. Finally, a special thank-you goes to the excellent Helen Glackin, Lorna McGivern, and Margaret Kane for always being available for coffee and a chat when I need some time out.

Introduction

The latest version of Microsoft Office brings with it some of the most notable enhancements to this popular suite of applications in years. *Excel 2007: Beyond the Manual* will help you to quickly adjust to the reconstructed interface of Microsoft Excel, directing you to the features that you have become accustomed to in previous versions of the software, as well as introducing you to more advanced components that you may not have tried yet and the new tools available with this release. Advanced techniques like consolidation, what-if analysis, PivotTable and PivotChart reports, and data validation are concisely described in straightforward steps, allowing you to quickly become confident with some of Excel's most powerful tools. The book also includes information on working with external data connections and a chapter on SharePoint and Excel Services to reflect the growing need for organizations to distribute information or provide access to spreadsheet models while maintaining control. Throughout the book I have included screenshots and examples to illustrate these features in operation along with timesaving shortcuts and tips to help you to increase your efficiency at producing professional-looking spreadsheets.

Who This Book Is For

This book is aimed at spreadsheet users who already have some familiarity with previous versions of Microsoft Excel and who want an overview of the modifications and new features being introduced with Microsoft Office 2007. The book is also intended to be a practical guide to anyone wishing to update their Excel skills and progress to the more advanced features of this essential spreadsheet application.

How This Book Is Structured

Excel 2007: Beyond the Manual can be used as a roadmap to becoming a power user in Excel or as handy reference to be called upon when required. Here is an outline of each chapter:

- Chapter 1, "What's New in Excel 2007?": The opening chapter of the book provides you with an overview of the modifications and enhancements you can expect to find in the latest version of Excel. The most notable difference when upgrading to Excel 2007 is the revamped interface, and this chapter will help to ease your transition from the traditional menus and toolbars to the new Ribbon. Advice is provided on how to work your way around the enlarged grid and where to find the tools and commands that you have become accustomed to in previous versions.

- Chapter 2, "Customizing Excel": You can save yourself a lot of time by customizing features of Excel to match any personal preferences or requirements. In this chapter, you will learn how to customize the Quick Access toolbar and Status bar and store custom views. Useful techniques like freezing and splitting panes and organizing multiple windows are also covered.

- Chapter 3, "Excel Essentials": This chapter covers some of the basic yet fundamental features of Excel that every user should be aware of. Data entry techniques like AutoFill and Custom Lists are covered here, along with the different ways you can paste data. You will also have an opportunity to become familiar with the new Name Manager for working with defined names. Finally, techniques for working with multiple worksheets are discussed, including how to enter and format data simultaneously on different worksheets.

- Chapter 4, "Styles and Formatting": This chapter looks at the different ways you can format the data on a worksheet, starting with the new document themes and cell and table styles. The formatting of numerical data is equally important, and the chapter includes comprehensive instructions on how to use the built-in number formats and create your own custom formats. You will also learn about the advances made to conditional formatting with the introduction of the new color scales, data bars, and icon sets.

- Chapter 5, "Sorting and Filtering": The increased functionality of the sort and filter features is discussed in this chapter. You will learn how to sort and filter by cell color or icon and discover how much easier it is to sort and filter by multiple items. The new easy-to-use date, text, and number filters are introduced, and for those who prefer something more complex, advanced filtering is also included.

- Chapter 6, "Analyzing Data Using Subtotals, Consolidations, and Tables": There are various tools in Excel that can help you organize, structure, and summarize your data. This chapter covers the ways you can group and outline data and insert subtotals. It also explains how you can summarize data across different worksheets by consolidating by position, category, or formula. The section on tables will bring you up to speed with the advances made to the feature previously known as Excel Lists, allowing you to effectively work with data in tabular form.

- Chapter 7, "Creating PivotTables and PivotCharts": As the title suggests, this chapter discusses how you can summarize and analyze data using a PivotTable or PivotChart report. Excel 2007 has made these versatile tools much more user-friendly, so if you haven't tried them before, now's your chance.

- Chapter 8, "Editing PivotTables and PivotCharts": Following on from Chapter 7, this chapter will show you how to manipulate PivotTables and PivotCharts to summarize your data exactly how you want it. Topics covered include sorting and filtering data in PivotTables and PivotCharts, changing field settings, creating calculated fields and calculated items, and using PivotTable options.

- Chapter 9, "What-If Analysis": Excel has a number of tools that can be used to answer what-if questions, including data tables, scenarios, Goal Seek, and Solver. This chapter shows you how you can make use of these tools to help you explore possible outcomes and make informed decisions.

- Chapter 10, "Formulas and Functions": This chapter outlines the fundamentals of constructing formulas in Excel 2007, including the new Formula AutoComplete feature. It also examines some of the more commonly used functions in Excel and includes examples of financial, text, statistical, math and trigonometry, lookup and reference, and database functions.

- Chapter 11, "Charts": Excel's ability to graphically represent data using a gamut of chart types is a key feature of the application. This chapter takes you through the different stages of producing a chart, from choosing the appropriate type to editing and formatting the chart and adding analysis features.

- Chapter 12, "Adding Graphics to a Worksheet": Microsoft Office 2007 introduces a new family of graphics for producing diagrams and lists known as SmartArt. Its use within Excel, along with the familiar graphics like AutoShapes, clip art, and WordArt, are the topic of this chapter.

- Chapter 13, "Preventing and Correcting Errors": This chapter looks at how you can use data validation to prevent errors by controlling what can be entered in a cell. It also discusses the different types of errors that can occur in formulas and how you can use formula auditing to check and correct formulas.

- Chapter 14, "Protection and Security": The different ways that you can protect worksheets and workbooks are discussed in this chapter. Adding digital signatures and changing security settings in the new Trust Center are also covered here.

- Chapter 15, "Getting Data from External Sources": Excel data can come from various sources, including Microsoft Access, text files, or web pages. This chapter examines how you can import data from other sources and manage external data connections, allowing you access to data that is always up-to-date.

- Chapter 16, "Sharing, Reviewing and Distributing Data": As workbooks are often the work of more than one user, this chapter examines how you can share a workbook, add comments for other users, and track the changes that have been made. It will also look at how you can prepare a document for printing or for distribution to others.

- Chapter 17, "SharePoint and Excel Services": No book on Excel 2007 would be complete without mentioning Excel Services, the new technology that enables the distribution of workbooks via a browser using Microsoft Office SharePoint Server 2007. The final chapter provides you with an introduction to Excel Services and explores how it can be used to facilitate managed, secure access to organizational data.

CHAPTER 1

What's New in Excel 2007?

Microsoft Office 2007 heralds the most significant changes to the Office suite for years. The user interface across the main applications has been given a new image aimed at improving usability as well as modernizing the overall look of the software. The regenerated appearance penetrates down to the documents with the introduction of new Office styles and themes and a new family of SmartArt graphics intended to give your creations an increased depth of professionalism. But the improvements are not simply aesthetic. Behind the contemporary façade lie some important enhancements that will allow you to experience more flexibility and functionality than ever before with Excel from the new XML file formats to improved analysis tools, although some critics may feel that many potential improvements have been omitted in this release.

This chapter will provide you with an overview of the most consequential modifications to Excel and will help you to settle into the new surroundings. First I will look at how Excel has been expanded both in size and in data-handling capability. I will then discuss its new image for 2007 and the features available that will allow you to produce an attractive and consistent look for your documents. Following a quick outline of the increased functionality of Excel's analysis tools, I will identify the file formats that can be used when saving work as well as the new ways you can share your worksheets with others and how Excel 2007 facilitates the management of external connections. By the time you have finished this chapter, you will know that we are not in Excel 2003 anymore!

From Excel to XXL

Microsoft has certainly pushed the limits with Excel 2007, making this version capable of handling more data more quickly than ever before. Excel users who need to store large amounts of data will be pleased to see that they can now enter over 16,000 columns and 1 million rows into a worksheet—a total of over 17 billion cells! To some this may seem cumbersome and unnecessary, but for those who analyze thousands of items or record data at small intervals this will be a welcome expansion. For example, if you are using Excel to keep a record of readings taken every minute, this will now allow almost two years of data to be stored in rows, or just over 11 days if stored by columns. If you record daily data in columns, your worksheet can now span almost 45 years!

> **NOTE** The last column is now XFD, which means that Excel 2007 may not accept some of the named ranges in workbooks created in previous versions. For example, names like DAY21 or TAX2007 can no longer be used, as these will now be cell references.

The size of the grid is not the only feature that has been augmented in Excel 2007. Excel can now support up to 4.3 billion colors (32-bit) and unlimited format types, and the number of cell references per cell is limited only by available memory. Excel 2007 also supports dual processors and multithreaded chipsets, and the amount of PC memory that it can use is limited only by the maximum allowed by Windows, thereby improving its overall performance. Table 1-1 lists some of the increases to limits that have been incorporated in Excel 2007.

Table 1-1. Excel 2007 Limits

Item	Excel 2003 Limit	Excel 2007 Limit
Columns	256	16,384
Rows	65,536	1,048,576
PC memory that Excel can use	1GB	Maximum allowed by Windows
Unique colors in a workbook	56 (indexed color)	4.3 billion (32-bit color)
Unique cell formats/cell styles	4000	64,000
Conditional formats in a cell	3	Limited by available memory
Levels of sorting in a table or range	3	64
Items in AutoFilter dropdown list	1,000	10,000
Characters that can be displayed in a cell	1,024 (255 when formatted as text)	32,768
Characters that can be printed in a cell	1,024	32,768
Cell styles in a workbook	4,096	65,536
Characters in a formula	1,024	8,192
Levels of nesting in a formula	7	64

Item	Excel 2003 Limit	Excel 2007 Limit
Arguments in a function	30	255
Items that can be found with Find All	~65,000	~1 million
Columns in a PivotTable	255	16,384
Items in a Pivot field	32,768	~1 million
Number of fields in a PivotTable	255	16,384

If you don't already use shortcut keys for navigating around your worksheet, you may find that now is a good time to start getting the hang of them. Table 1-2 lists some key combinations that could save you a lot of time scrolling around the super-sized grid.

Table 1-2. Shortcut Keys for Navigating in Excel

To Go To...	Press
Cell A1	Ctrl+Home
Column A of the current row	Home
Last used cell in a worksheet (even if it is currently blank)	Ctrl+End
First row of the data (provided there are no blank cells)	Ctrl+Up arrow
Last row of the data (provided there are no blank cells)	Ctrl+Down arrow
First column of the data (provided there are no blank cells)	Ctrl+Left arrow
Last column of the data (provided there are no blank cells)	Ctrl+Right arrow
Next worksheet	Ctrl+Page Down
Previous worksheet	Ctrl+Page Up

TIP Using the Shift key along with the key combinations in Table 1-2 will select the range of cells; e.g., pressing Ctrl+Shift+Home will select all the cells from cell A1 to the active cell. To select the current region (i.e., the contiguous range of cells surrounding the active cell that contain data), press Ctrl+* (use the * in the numeric keypad or Ctrl+Shift+* on a laptop).

Table 1-3 contains some more tips for quickly selecting, inserting, deleting, hiding, and unhiding rows and columns.

Table 1-3. Shortcut Keys for Selecting, Inserting, Deleting, Hiding, and Unhiding in Excel

To Do This...	Press
Select the column or columns for the active cell or cells	Ctrl+Spacebar
Select the row or rows for the active cell or cells	Shift+Spacebar
Insert a row in a table or a cell, row, or column in a range	Ctrl++ (plus sign)
Insert a column in a table or range	Ctrl+Spacebar, then Ctrl++
Delete a row in a table or a cell, row, or column in a range	Ctrl+- (hyphen)
Delete a column in a table or range	Ctrl+Spacebar, then Ctrl+-
Hide the column or columns for the active cell or cells	Ctrl+0
Unhide the column or columns between the selected cells	Ctrl+Shift+0
Hide the row or rows for the active cell or cells	Ctrl+9
Unhide the row or rows between the selected cells	Ctrl+Shift+9

You can also use the Name box to quickly go to a cell, select a range, or copy a formula or text to a large number of cells. To go to a cell, you simply type the cell reference in the Name box and press Enter; to select the range starting from the active cell to the cell reference you have typed in the Name box, press Shift+Enter. The same process can be used to paste copied data into a range: copy the data to be pasted, select the first cell in the range, type the cell reference of the last cell in the range in the Name box, press Shift+Enter to select the range, and then press Enter again to paste the data.

TIP To copy a cell down the length of a column (as far as there is data in an adjacent column), select the cell and move the mouse pointer over the bottom-right corner of the cell; when the pointer changes to the Fill Handle (black cross), double-click.

Excel Gets a Makeover

Even veteran users of Excel will probably find that they have lost their bearings when they look at Excel 2007 for the first time. The traditional menu bar and Standard and Formatting toolbars have now been rendered obsolete, replaced by what is referred to as the Ribbon, a display of larger icons that spans the top of the window where the menu bar and toolbars used to be. The big difference with the Ribbon is that it is contextual and updates in accordance with the tasks that you are currently carrying out. The Ribbon also features in the new versions of Microsoft Word, Access, and PowerPoint.

However, the Ribbon is not the only method of accessing commands in the new version of Microsoft Office. The Quick Access toolbar, Microsoft Office Button, and access keys are all new features intended to improve usability. Excel also now benefits from the addition of a Page Layout view, allowing you to see how the printed worksheet will appear as you edit your data.

The Ribbon

Probably the most significant change to the user interface is the demise of menus and toolbars and the introduction of the Ribbon (see Figure 1-1). Running across the top of the screen, the Ribbon groups together related commands and features into different tabs and will adapt depending on the task you are completing. So, for example, if you want to insert an object you can select the Insert tab to see the range of objects that can be included in your worksheet and the related commands. If you are working with a table, the Ribbon will feature additional tabs that include the tools that are relevant to tables. Consequently, users can see at a glance the various commands that are available related to the task they are currently completing rather than having to search through an ever-increasing menu system.

Figure 1-1. On the Ribbon, each tab contains groups of related commands for the different activity areas.

The Ribbon is made up of a variety of content, including dialog boxes, galleries, and many of the familiar toolbar buttons. The contents of the Ribbon will vary for each Office application, but across applications it is composed of similar components:

- *Tabs*, placed along the top of the ribbon, which identify different activity areas. The standard tabs are Home, Insert, Page Layout, Formulas, Data, Review, and View, but additional tabs may become available for specific tasks. For example, if you have any active application add-ins, the Add-Ins tab will also be displayed. The default tab is the Home tab; to select a different tab, click on it with your mouse.

- *Groups* within each tab; for example, on the Home tab the groups include Clipboard, Font, and Alignment. These are sets of related commands used to carry out the various tasks.

- *Commands* can take the form of boxes, menus, or buttons and are arranged together within groups.

As well as the standard tabs, there are two other types of tabs that may appear on the Ribbon when they are relevant to the current task. *Contextual tabs* will appear when you work with a particular object like SmartArt, a chart, or table. For example, additional Design, Layout, and Format tabs will appear under a *Chart Tools* label when a chart is selected. These contextual tabs house further commands appropriate for working with charts. When the object is deselected, the contextual tabs will be hidden again. *Program tabs* replace the standard tabs when you are using certain authoring modes or views. For example, when you switch to Print Preview by selecting it from the Print command in the Microsoft Office Button, the standard tabs are replaced by a Print Preview tab. There is also a Developer tab, which you can opt to display by selecting the appropriate checkbox in the Personalize section of Excel Options (see the following section on the Microsoft Office Button). This contains commands for carrying out tasks like recording macros and features related to XML (see information on new file formats in the "Finishing Touches" section later in this chapter).

In some groups on the Ribbon (for example, Clipboard, Font, Alignment, and Number in Figure 1-1), you will see a small icon at the bottom-right corner of the group; this icon is known as a Dialog Box Launcher. As the name suggests, clicking this icon will open the relevant dialog box or task pane for that group of commands, allowing you to select further options.

> **TIP** To collapse the Ribbon and reveal more of the grid, double-click on any of the tabs. The tabs will still be visible and you can view the Ribbon temporarily by clicking a tab, enabling you to still select commands. To restore the Ribbon again, double-click any tab.

The Microsoft Office Button

The Microsoft Office button is a feature that you will now discover in Word, Power-Point, and Access as well as Excel. It is a circular button positioned at the top-left corner of the screen and is used to access many of the common functions that were previously available from the File menu or the Standard toolbar, like Open, Save, Close, and Print (see Figure 1-2). Two new features that are listed are Prepare and Publish.

Prepare provides quick access to tools that may be required to check and secure finished documents, including checking a workbook for hidden metadata or for features that are not supported by earlier versions of Excel. You can also set document properties and permissions, make a document read-only, and add a digital signature within the Prepare option.

When you have finalized the settings for the finished documents, you can then use the Publish command to distribute it to other people. You can distribute a document in various ways, including through Excel Services (a web-based data exploration and reporting system for Excel workbooks), by using a document management server, or by creating a document workspace using SharePoint (see the information on new ways to share data in the "Finishing Touches" section and in Chapters 16 and 17).

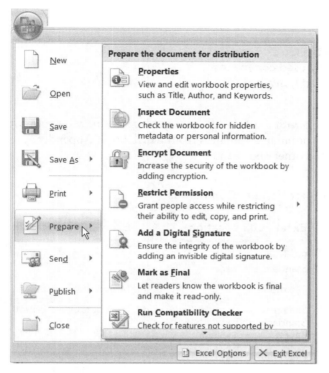

Figure 1-2. The contents of the Microsoft Office Button in Excel 2007. The Prepare option allows you to carry out a variety of tasks to check and secure finished documents.

Also in the Microsoft Office Button you will find Excel Options (see Figure 1-2), which allows you to customize many of the features within Excel (see Chapter 2 for more on this). Here you will find most of the commands that were traditionally located within the Options command of the Tools menu.

The Quick Access Toolbar

As the commands available on the Ribbon will update as you perform different tasks, Excel provides a toolbar where you can store frequently used commands regardless of the Ribbon tab being displayed. The Quick Access toolbar (see Figure 1-3) appears above the Ribbon and by default contains the Save, Undo, and Redo icons (the Undo and Redo icons will be grayed out when they are not available). You can customize the Quick Access toolbar to display commands of your choice so that your favorite commands are permanently on view (see Chapter 2).

Figure 1-3. You can use the Quick Access toolbar to store frequently used commands so that they are always readily available.

Table 1-4 provides you with a quick reference guide to the new locations in Excel 2007 of some of the most popular commands from Excel 2003. Appendix A provides the location of most of the other commands.

Table 1-4. New Locations for Popular Commands

Command	Excel 2003 Location	Excel 2007 Location
New, Open, Print	File menu Standard toolbar	Microsoft Office Button
Close, Exit, Save As	File menu	Microsoft Office Button
Save	File menu Standard toolbar Quick Access toolbar	Microsoft Office Button
Page Setup Print Area, Set Print Area, Clear Print Area	File menu	Page Layout tab, Page Setup group Page Layout tab, Sheet Options group (Dialog Box Launcher)
Print Preview	File menu Standard toolbar	Microsoft Office Button, Print, Print Preview
Undo, Redo	Edit menu Standard toolbar	Quick Access toolbar
Cut, Copy, Paste	Edit menu Standard toolbar	Home tab, Clipboard group
Delete	Edit menu	Home tab, Cells group
Delete Sheet	Edit menu	Home tab, Cells group, Delete
Move or Copy Sheet	Edit menu	Home tab, Cells group, Format
Find, Replace, Go To	Edit menu	Home tab, Editing group, Find & Select
Header and Footer	View menu	Insert tab, Text group
Cells, Rows, Columns, Worksheet	Insert menu	Home tab, Cells group, Insert
Chart	Insert menu Standard toolbar	Insert tab, Charts group
Function	Insert menu	Formulas tab, Function Library group

Command	Excel 2003 Location	Excel 2007 Location
Name	Insert menu	Formulas tab, Defined Names group
Cells, Rows, Columns Sheets—Rename, Hide, Unhide, Tab Color	Format menu	Home tab, Cells group, Format
Options	Tools menu	Microsoft Office Button, Excel Options
Sort, Filter	Data menu	Home tab, Editing group, Sort & Filter Data tab, Sort & Filter group
Font, Font Size, Bold, Italic, Underline, Border, Fill Color, Font Color	Formatting toolbar	Home tab, Font group
Align Left, Align Center, Align Right, Merge and Center, Increase Indent, Decrease Indent	Formatting toolbar	Home tab, Alignment group
Currency, Percent Style, Comma Style, Increase Decimal, Decrease Decimal	Formatting toolbar	Home tab, Number group

> **TIP** If you can't find an Excel 2003 command on the Ribbon, you may be able to locate it and add it to the Quick Access toolbar using the Customize category of Excel Options in the Microsoft Office Button (see Chapter 2). If you can't find it there, use the Help facility to find out how to complete the task that you would have used the command to do.

Access Keys

Access keys allow you to access the Ribbon, Microsoft Office Button, and Quick Access toolbar using the keyboard, rather like keyboard shortcuts. To switch to command mode to use the access keys, you need to press the Alt key on the keyboard. This will reveal small boxes containing *key tips*, indicating the key you need to press in order to access a feature of the screen (see Figure 1-4). Every command on the Ribbon, Microsoft Office Button, and Quick Access toolbar has an access key. So, for example, pressing Alt and then F will access the Microsoft Office Button, with further key tips then being displayed for each of the commands within it. To use access keys to execute a command on any tab on the Ribbon, you must select the key for the appropriate tab first.

> **NOTE** Keyboard shortcuts, like Ctrl+C for Copy, have remained largely unaffected by Excel 2007.

Figure 1-4. Key tips for the Insert tab. To view key tips for a tab, press the Alt key and then select the access key for the tab.

Only one layer of key tips is displayed at a time, so you must select the access key for a particular tab before the key tips for the commands on that tab are revealed. As you only see the key tips for the active tab, a particular key can relate to different commands, depending on the tab that is displayed. For example, when you turn on the access keys, the H key will access the Home tab. Once on the Home tab, pressing the H key will access the Fill Color command, but if you had selected the Insert tab, the H key would refer to the Header & Footer command. If a dialog box is open, its key tips will take precedence over key tips on the Ribbon.

When you are in command mode, you can also use the arrow keys and Tab key to move around the Ribbon (although the access keys are probably a much more efficient method) as follows:

- Use the left and right arrows to move between the tabs.
- Use the down arrow to activate a tab and then all the arrows to move through the groups and commands.
- From the tabs, use the up arrow to move to the Quick Access toolbar.
- From the Quick Access toolbar, use the left arrow to move along the toolbar and then to the Microsoft Office Button.
- Use the down arrow to access the Microsoft Office Button and use all the arrows to move around the commands.
- Use the Tab key to move through each command in each group of the active tab in turn from left to right. Once you reach the last command of the last group, the Tab key will take you through the Help button, the Microsoft Office Button, and the Quick Access toolbar. Use Shift+Tab to move backward from right to left.
- Use the Enter key to select the highlighted command.

Once you start to use the arrows to navigate around the screen, the key tips will disappear. You will need to press the Alt key twice to display the key tips again. To remove the key tips and return to text entry mode, press the Alt key again.

If you use an old keyboard shortcut that begins with Alt, like Alt+E to open the Edit menu, a message will appear to say that you are using an Office 2003 access key. If you know the key sequence you want to use, you can continue to type it or press Esc to cancel.

Enhanced ScreenTips

Another enhancement to the user interface of Excel 2007 is the augmented capabilities of the ToolTip feature. Now, when you hover your mouse over a command on the Ribbon, not only will its name be displayed but you will also be provided with additional details, such as the shortcut key for the command (where available), what the command does, and when it would typically be used. Where appropriate there may be graphics illustrating what the command does or showing a dialog box that can be opened to access further options.

This embellishing of ToolTips with feature descriptions has led to them being renamed as Enhanced ScreenTips, or Super ToolTips. The main benefit is that you can gain a quick overview about the particular command (see Figure 1-5) and what it is generally used for without having to search through reference guides or use the Help facility. If you do require further information, you can still press F1 to open the Help facility.

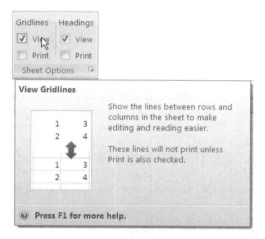

Figure 1-5. The Enhanced ScreenTip for View Gridlines. These new Super ToolTips, as they are known, provide more detail than their predecessors.

> **TIP** If you are not impressed and want to get rid of the Super ToolTips, you can change the setting by clicking the Microsoft Office Button, clicking Excel Options, and selecting the Popular category. Under "Top options for working with Excel," click the down arrow beside the ScreenTip Style box and select "Don't show feature descriptions in ScreenTips" to display the 2003-style ToolTips, or select "Don't show ScreenTips" to remove ToolTips altogether.

Page Layout View

In Excel 2007, Microsoft has added a Page Layout view to the Normal and Page Break Preview views that were already available. This allows you to see how your printouts will appear as you create and edit your worksheets. Using Page Layout view, you can carry out a range of tasks—such as inserting headers and footers, changing margins, or rearranging objects—and see exactly how these alterations will impact your printed document. Page Layout view can be accessed from the Workbook Views group on the View tab or by clicking the Page Layout View icon on the Status bar at the bottom of the screen.

> **TIP** You can now configure the Status bar to show a Zoom slider and to display various statistics about selected data like Average, Count, Sum, etc., as well as the different views. Just right-click on the Status bar and select the items that you want to be displayed.

Better-Looking Documents

In addition to revamping the user interface, Microsoft has provided Office 2007 with various new features that allow you to produce superior documents that can have a consistent look across your applications. New document themes can be applied to all your Microsoft Office documents while Excel styles can be used to format specific items like charts, tables, PivotTables, shapes, diagrams, and so forth, thus maintaining a uniform look within your workbooks. There is also a wider range of templates available with Excel 2007, and you can quickly access more through Microsoft Office Online.

The conditional formatting feature has been greatly enhanced to include a variety of methods of highlighting cells based on criteria. Excel 2007 sees the introduction of new visual features like icon sets, color scales, and data bars. SmartArt, another new graphical concept making its debut with this version, can be used to create diagrams that will convey the message behind your data in a visually appealing manner. Like styles, SmartArt is based on the document themes, ensuring that the consistent appearance of your documents is upheld.

Themes and Styles

Document themes are predefined sets of fonts, colors, lines, and fill effects that can be applied to an entire workbook and shared between different types of Office documents. You can even create custom themes by specifying your own settings for any or all of the theme components to add your own personal touch to your finished work.

Styles are based on the current theme and can be applied to Excel tables, Pivot-Tables, charts, diagrams, and shapes. A nice touch is the Live Preview feature, which automatically shows you what your object will look like as you move your mouse over each style, helping you to choose a suitable style (see Figure 1-6).

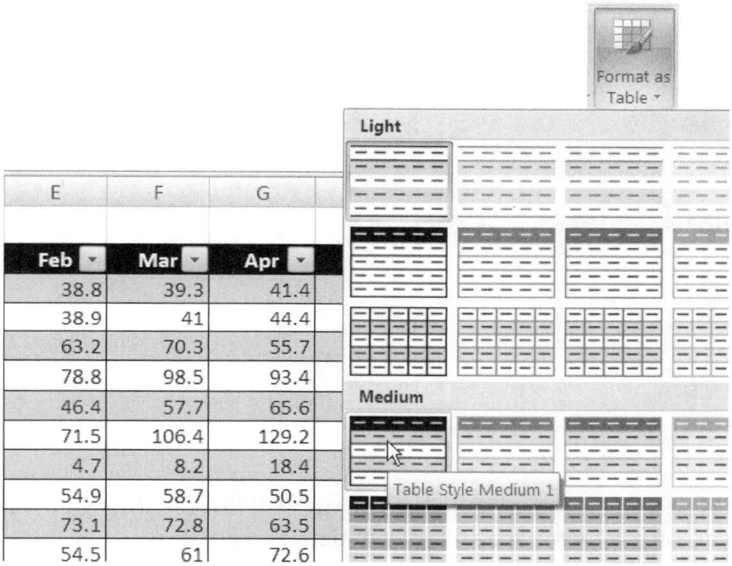

Figure 1-6. As you move the mouse pointer over a style in the gallery in Live Preview, the selected table will temporarily take on the features of that style, allowing you to preview the style.

If you decide that none of the built-in styles are suitable, you can create your own, although you cannot create your own chart style. Excel 2007 also includes pre-defined cell styles that can be applied to individual cells or ranges, and many of these are independent of the document theme. Again, if you want to, you can create your own custom cell styles.

More Templates

Microsoft Excel 2007 is installed with a variety of built-in templates that you can use to base your new worksheets on, covering a range of purposes from balance sheets to a blood pressure tracker. If none of these are appropriate, you can search Microsoft Office Online for a much wider selection of templates, which are divided into various categories:

- Agendas
- Budgets
- Calendars
- Expense Reports
- Forms
- Inventories
- Invoices
- Lists
- Planners
- Plans
- Purchase Orders
- Receipts
- Reports
- Schedules
- Statements
- Stationery
- Timesheets

Of course, as with themes and styles, if you are still not satisfied you can create your own templates to suit your specific type of data and analysis.

SmartArt

SmartArt (or OfficeArt as it is sometimes referred to) is another new concept being offered to Excel users with the intention of giving documents a more professional design. Basically, SmartArt provides you with a range of diagrams or captions that you can use to highlight information or convey points from your data. Suggested uses would be to create high-impact lists or to illustrate a process, cycle, hierarchy, or relationship. Available layouts include horizontal and vertical lists, organization charts, pyramids, Venn diagrams, and radial diagrams. Figure 1-7 shows some examples of the SmartArt graphics available in Microsoft Office 2007.

Once you have selected a SmartArt layout that you want to use, it is easy to add and edit text, to resize or format the graphic, and to switch to a different layout. SmartArt graphics are built on the document themes and will adopt colors and styles appropriate to your chosen theme; however, you can customize most of the elements if you want to, including shape fills, line styles, and 3D effects. The finished result is graphics that look like they have just stepped out of a designer's studio.

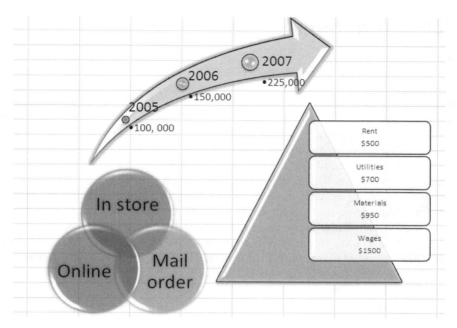

Figure 1-7. Use SmartArt graphics to add a professional touch to lists and diagrams.

Easier Analysis

Although these aesthetic enhancements are mostly welcome, you are probably wondering what the "real changes" are and how Excel 2007 will make your working life easier. Microsoft has made a variety of improvements to existing features in Excel that are intended to streamline the processes involved in some of the traditional analytical procedures and to make more complex data-management activities not as daunting for less experienced users.

Conditional Formatting (available from the Styles group on the Home tab) and Sorting and Filtering (located in the Editing group on the Home tab or the Sort & Filter group on the Data tab) are all fundamental features of Excel that have been expanded in this new version to include more functionality and to allow you to display your data in a more comprehensible manner. The feature formerly known as Lists has been given a polish and renamed as Excel Tables, and PivotTables and charts have benefited from some attention from the Microsoft developers as well. Finally, an attempt has also been made to make formula writing easier, and Online Analysis Processing (OLAP) formulas and Cube functions have been introduced to the application.

Rich Conditional Formatting

The Conditional Formatting feature has been taken to new levels with Excel 2007 with the introduction of novel tools like Color Scales, Icon Sets, and Data Bars to allow you to visualize your data in a more interpretable manner. Depending on a cell's position within a range of values, you can allocate it a different color, a particular icon, or a varying length of shaded data bar. Each of these new tools allows you to convey a certain degree of meaning along with your data from within the actual cell.

Excel 2007 also provides you with various types of common rules to make it easier to create your conditional formats. These rules are divided into Highlight Cells Rules and Top/Bottom Rules. With Highlight Cells Rules, you can select from a range of rules to highlight specific data, including rules to identify values that are greater than, less than, or equal to a set value, or indicate dates that occur within a given range. Top/Bottom Rules allow you to identify the top or bottom percentage or number of items or to indicate those cells that are above or below the average. Figure 1-8 shows the options available with these two new sets of conditional formatting rules.

Figure 1-8. Highlight Cells Rules and Top/Bottom Rules. Use one of these predefined rules to create conditional formats or select More Rules to create a new formatting rule.

Another important advancement in conditional formatting is the removal of the restriction on the number of conditional formats that can be applied to a range of cells. Instead of only being able to identify three criteria, the number of conditional formats that can be specified is now unlimited (within the bounds of available memory). To help you keep track of these potentially numerous formatting rules, Excel 2007 provides you with the Conditional Formatting Rules Manager (which you open by clicking Manage Rules in a Conditional Formatting dropdown list) to look after the various chores that may be associated with rules, including creating, editing, and deleting rules and controlling the rule precedence.

Although a fairly comprehensive selection of built-in rules is available, conditional formats are also customizable, enabling you to define your own rules or formats. This allows you to control the technicalities, like exactly how the range is partitioned when allocating icons or colors, as well as the specific formatting features, like the color of the data bars or border and fill effects.

Excel Tables

Within Excel 2007 you can easily create, format, and expand an Excel table (or Excel List as it was known back in 2003) to organize your data in a manner more suited for analysis. Along with the name change Microsoft has improved the functionality of tables to include features like

- Headers that can be switched on and off
- Calculated columns that automatically expand to include additional rows
- An Automatic Filter button in each header cell for quick sorting and filtering
- Structured references that allow you to use column heading names and special item specifiers in formulas instead of cell references
- Total rows that can use custom formulas and text entries
- Table styles to add coordinated formatting that will update automatically as rows are added or removed

PivotTables and PivotCharts

PivotTables have long been a fundamental analysis tool in Excel, so the improvements to the design of the interface and the enhanced capabilities will probably be welcome by most Excel users (although they may not go as far as some users would have liked). Many users who have not experimented with PivotTables to any great extent may be more encouraged to do so now that the creation process has been streamlined and made more approachable. For example, checkboxes and new drop zones in the PivotTable Field List make adding and removing fields to and from a PivotTable or PivotChart report easier. Other features that will make summarizing data with PivotTables more efficient include

- The ability to undo actions taken on a PivotTable
- Plus and minus drilldown indicators that make it clear whether data can be expanded or collapsed
- Simpler sorting and filtering of PivotTable data
- The ability to apply conditional formats to cells within a PivotTable
- PivotTable styles for quickly formatting a PivotTable
- PivotCharts that are easier to create (also, chart formatting is preserved when changes are applied to a PivotChart)

- PivotChart styles that can be applied in a similar fashion to regular charts
- The ability to easily convert a PivotTable linked to an OLAP cube to formulas

Sorting and Filtering

Sorting and filtering have been enhanced with some useful features in Excel 2007 to allow you to arrange your data quickly in a meaningful way according to your current needs. You can now sort data by anything up to 64 levels, and you can also sort by cell color, font color, or cell icon as well as cell value. The actual wording of the Sort command will change depending on the data being sorted: if the cells contain text, you can choose either Sort A to Z or Sort Z to A; if you are sorting dates you can select Sort Oldest to Newest or Sort Newest to Oldest; if the data consists of numbers, the options will be Sort Smallest to Largest or Sort Largest to Smallest.

AutoFilter (or Filter as it is often now referred to) has been augmented to facilitate more complex and dynamic filtering by providing a range of Date, Number, and Text filters that will reflect your data type. For example, for numerical data, available filters include Equals, Greater Than, Above Average, Top 10, and so forth. If the column selected contains text, you can select filters such as Begins With, Ends With, and Contains. If the data you are filtering contains dates, filters like Tomorrow, This Week, Last Month, Next Quarter, This Year, and so forth can be applied, allowing dynamic filtering of dates to be carried out simply. The capabilities of AutoFilter have also been expanded; the AutoFilter list will now display up to 10,000 items, and you can also filter by multiple items within a column. Like the Sorting tool, AutoFilter accommodates the new conditional formats that can be applied to cells and allows data to be filtered by value, cell color, font color, or cell icon. A Reapply command has also been added to enable you to reapply all sort and filter conditions on a table.

Changes to Charts

Like tables and other objects, charts in Excel will have their formatting founded on the document theme. The new look for charts will also include special effects such as soft edges, shadows, beveling, and 3D effects, as illustrated in Figure 1-9. The intention is obviously to make the charts more visually appealing, though some users may feel that such embellishments will detract from the message the chart is supposed to convey. Other useful features include the ability to switch between charting the data in the rows and the data in the columns of the worksheet with one click and to save the formatting and layout of a chart as a template that can be applied to future charts.

A major change being implemented with Office 2007 is that the chart engine for Excel will also now be used for Word 2007 and PowerPoint 2007, therefore eliminating the need to use Microsoft Graph. As an Excel worksheet is now used as the chart datasheet for Word and PowerPoint, these applications can take advantage of the increased functionality provided by Excel—including the use of formulas, filtering, sorting, and the ability to link the chart to external data sources like SQL Server Analysis Services. The Excel data worksheet can be embedded in the Word document or PowerPoint presentation, or it can remain in a separate file to minimize file size.

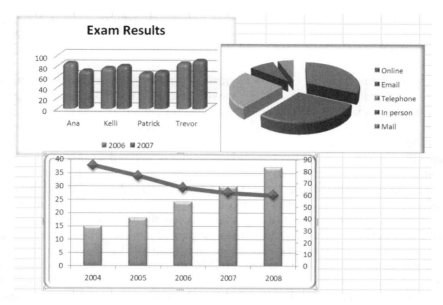

Figure 1-9. Excel 2007 lets you choose from a wide range of chart styles and apply features like glow and bevel effects to charts.

Simplified Formula Writing

Excel 2007 has attempted to expedite the task of formula writing, particularly if you need to write long and complex formulas. First, the formula bar can now be resized to accommodate long formulas without overlapping onto the worksheet and covering the headings or data. You can now include over 8,000 characters and up to 64 levels of nesting in a formula, compared to just 1,000 characters and 7 levels in Excel 2003. The number of arguments that a function can hold has also been increased from 30 to 255.

The Formulas tab on the Ribbon provides quick reference to the commands you may require when creating and auditing formulas. It also includes an easy-to-use Function Library, which displays the main function categories and lets you quickly select your required function. The familiar AutoSum button is also there and operates in a similar way as before, facilitating immediate access to a dropdown list and allowing you to select from the popular Sum, Average, Count Numbers, Max, and Min functions. If you prefer to enter a function by launching the traditional Insert Function dialog box, then you can click the Insert Function button. Finally, the Calculation Options button in the Calculation group allows you to control when formulas are calculated.

Formula AutoComplete is a new feature that will help you to remember the exact name of a function and enter the formula syntax correctly. As you begin to type in a formula, Excel will display a list of functions (and named ranges and table references where appropriate) that match what you type; once you detect the formula (or name or reference) that you want to use, you can select it using the Tab key or the mouse.

Excel will then help you to enter the right number of arguments and will suggest defined names or structured references where appropriate. A ToolTip will appear for each formula to help you to select the correct one without having to refer to the Help facility.

Defining names has long been recognized as a way of simplifying formula construction and readability. Excel 2007 provides us with the Name Manager, a new interface to accommodate the general housekeeping duties associated with creating, viewing, editing, and deleting names. Prominently positioned on the Formulas tab of the Ribbon, the Name Manager and other commands within the Defined Names group will allow you to create and update your list of defined names more efficiently than in Excel 2003. The ability to add comments to defined names has been included, enabling you to provide a description that will be displayed as a ToolTip in Formula AutoComplete. The Name box can also now be resized to display long names.

A further useful innovation in Excel 2007 is the ability to incorporate structured references (where you can reference a table or part of a table directly by name rather than cell references) in formulas. For example, to sum all the values in a table called Table1 you can enter the formula **=SUM(Table1)**; to sum all the values in the Sales column of that table, you would enter the formula **=SUM(Table1[Sales])**. Table names (and subsequently column names) will appear in Formula AutoComplete where appropriate.

> **TIP** Formulas can still be entered by typing them straight in and ignoring Formula AutoComplete. If you really dislike the feature, Formula AutoComplete can be turned off in the Formulas category of Excel Options.

More Functions

The function library within Excel has been expanded to include a set of seven new Cube functions to allow the extraction of information from SQL Server Analysis Services, and the Analysis ToolPak functions have now been integrated into the main function library (the Engineering functions category is now available as standard). Microsoft has also added the following general functions, specifically requested by users:

- *IFERROR (Logical)*: To identify formula errors rather than using IF and ISERROR
- *AVERAGEIF (Statistical)*: To conditionally average a range in a similar manner to SUMIF and COUNTIF
- *SUMIFS (Math & Trig)*: Similar to SUMIF but for multiple criteria
- *COUNTIFS (Statistical)*: Similar to COUNTIF but for multiple criteria
- *AVERAGEIFS (Statistical)*: Similar to AVERAGEIF but for multiple criteria

If you work with multidimensional databases (like SQL Server Analysis Services) in Excel 2007 you can use OLAP formulas to build complex, free-form, OLAP data-bound reports. Seven new Cube functions have been added to Excel to accommodate the extraction of data from SQL Services Analysis Services (2000 and 2005), including any member, set, aggregated value, property, or Key Performance Indicator (KPI) from the OLAP cube. This data can then be placed anywhere within the spreadsheet and integrated with other calculations or within other formulas. These new Cube functions are

- *CUBEMEMBER*: Fetches the defined member or tuple from the cube
- *CUBEVALUE*: Fetches the aggregated value from the cube filtered by various arguments
- *CUBESET*: Fetches the defined set of members or tuples
- *CUBESETCOUNT*: Returns the number of items in a set
- *CUBERANKEDMEMBER*: Returns the *n*th ranked member from a set
- *CUBEMEMBERPROPERTY*: Returns the value of a member property from the cube
- *CUBEKPIMEMBER*: Returns a KPI property from the cube and displays the KPI name in the cell

If you have a PivotTable connected to an OLAP cube, you can convert the PivotTable to a set of formulas, where each formula will use one of the Cube functions. This will allow you to modify your work by inserting rows or columns or adding calculations, using the converted PivotTable as a starting point.

Finishing Touches

With a growing emphasis on sharing data and producing information that can be viewed and analyzed by multiple users, Excel 2007 brings with it important enhancements to much of its importing and exporting functionality. This includes streamlining the process for connecting to external sources and distributing data through Excel Services. Microsoft has also introduced some new file formats to improve the transferability of Office documents, and it is also much easier to save workbooks in alternative formats, thus increasing the transferability of information from Excel workbooks.

External Connections

The Get External Data group on the Data tab of the Ribbon renders the task of importing data from external sources much less daunting. The Existing Connections command provides you with quick access to connections in the current workbook, as well as to connection files on your computer or network. The other commands in the Get External Data group allow you to easily import data from Access, the Web, and text files, or to create new connections to other sources.

Managing external connections should be easier with Excel 2007 thanks to the Connections group on the Data tab. If you have a workbook that is connected to an external data source, for example, an Access or Oracle database or an Analysis Services cube, you can see a list of the connections in your workbook and where they are used, and change the properties of the connections. This ability to view and manage all of the connections in a workbook in a central location is a significant shift from the way connection information was stored with the object that used the connection in previous versions. This will make updating and sharing connections easier, especially with the introduction of Cube functions where the connection to a particular OLAP cube must be specified with each function.

New File Formats

Microsoft Office 2007 sees the inauguration of new file formats for Excel, Word, and PowerPoint known as XML formats. The purpose of XML file formats is to ease integration with external data sources, to reduce file size, and to improve data recovery. The default format for an Excel 2007 workbook will now be the XML-based file format (.xlsx). Other XML-based formats that will also be available for Excel 2007 are the XML-based and macro-enabled workbook format (.xlsm), the format for an Excel template (.xltx), the macro-enabled template (.xltm), and the macro-enabled add-in (.xlam).

In addition to the new XML file formats, Excel 2007 introduces a new non-XML binary file format for large or complex workbooks. This binary version of the segmented compressed file format or BIFF12 file format (.xlsb) will allow optimal performance and backward compatibility. Excel 2007 spreadsheets can also be saved as XPS (XML Paper Specification) format or exported to PDF without needing to have a PDF writer installed.

When you open an Excel file that was created in an earlier version, it will automatically open in Compatibility mode. In this mode, new or enhanced 2007 features are not available, preventing any loss of data or fidelity when the workbook is opened in an earlier version again. When the file is saved, it will be saved using the Excel 97–2003 file format (.xls) and not the new XML file format. If you want to upgrade the workbook to the current 2007 file format, you can convert it using the Convert command in the Microsoft Office Button, which will replace the original file with the new XML file. If you want to retain a copy of the original file format, you can save it to XML format, which will create a new copy of the file with the .xlsx extension.

TIP Check your Excel 2007 workbooks to see if they contain any formatting or other features that are not compatible with earlier versions of Excel so that you can make any necessary changes. You can do this by running the Compatibility Checker in Compatibility mode by clicking the Microsoft Office Button, pointing to Prepare, and then clicking Run Compatibility Checker. The Compatibility Checker will run automatically if you save a workbook that is in the Excel 97–2003 file format. Updates and converters can be installed in earlier versions to allow Excel 2007 workbooks to be opened, updated, and saved without losing any of their Excel 2007–specific functionality.

New Ways to Share Data

With Excel 2007 you can distribute worksheets to others in various ways. If you need to share your worksheets with other users within your organization and have access to Excel Services (a new server technology available as part of Microsoft Office SharePoint Server 2007 that allows browser-based access to Excel spreadsheets), you can save your workbook to Excel Services using the Publish option in the Microsoft Office Button. You can then specify the worksheet data (for example, sheets or items like charts or tables) that you want others to be able to see. The other users can then use Microsoft Excel Web Access to carry out tasks like viewing, analyzing, extracting, and saving this data, or they can take a static snapshot of the data at regular intervals or when required. The main advantages that Excel Services will bring are the ability to provide controlled access to data via a browser and the ability to avoid having more than one "version of the truth" (i.e., multiple copies of a spreadsheet that are inconsistent with one another).

Excel Services is optimized for organizations where multiple users are accessing the same spreadsheets and consists of three parts: Excel Web Access, Excel Calculation Services, and Excel Web Services. Excel Web Access is used to display a spreadsheet in a browser and permits users to perform various Excel activities, including scrolling, sorting, filtering, viewing charts, and using drilldown in PivotTables. If they have the correct permissions, they can even open the workbook in Excel 2007 (if they have it installed on their own computer), enabling them to take advantage of the full functionality of Excel to analyze the data. Excel Calculation Services is the component that loads the spreadsheets, performs the calculations on them, and manages the sessions. Excel Web Services provides programmatic access, allowing you to automate the update of Excel spreadsheets and to develop custom applications that incorporate calculation.

To make a workbook available to other users from a central location, you can use the Publish command to save it to a document management server, enabling you to automate workflows and share document libraries. If you want to allow users to collaborate on a workbook while maintaining a local copy synchronized with any changes, you can save it to a Document Workspace site hosted by Windows SharePoint Services 3.0. A *Document Workspace site* is a SharePoint site that incorporates tools to help users share and update files while keeping everyone informed of changes. Other advantages of a Document Workspace site include the ability to allocate tasks and to receive email alerts when changes are made to a document or task (see Chapters 16 and 17 for more information on sharing data and Excel Services).

This chapter has given you an overview of the main enhancements that have been introduced with Microsoft Excel 2007. The remainder of this book will guide you through these and the many other useful features of this versatile application.

CHAPTER 2

Customizing Excel

It is always worthwhile taking some time to get to know an application and to adjust elements of it to suit your own preferences and requirements. Whether you are an ad hoc user or your job revolves around spreadsheets, by creating a personalized workspace within the Excel environment you can make sure that your workbooks are displayed the way you want them and that commands you repeatedly use are always near at hand.

The new Ribbon feature of Excel 2007 is not customizable in the same way that the toolbars in earlier versions are; however, you *can* decide which commands appear on the Quick Access toolbar. Many of the traditional ways of personalizing your Excel environment that were previously accessible through the Options command on the Tools menu are still available in Excel 2007—they have just been relocated to Excel Options, which can be accessed from the Microsoft Office Button. The Window group in the View tab of the Ribbon is similar to the old Window menu and facilitates working with multiple windows. It also allows you to save your window arrangement as a workspace so that you can retrieve it at a later date.

This chapter will direct you to the familiar customizable options while introducing you to some new features that you can adapt to improve your working experience with Excel 2007. You will discover how you can easily customize the Status bar and the new Quick Access toolbar to improve your efficiency at creating and editing spreadsheets. You will also learn how to use custom views and how to customize Excel windows, enabling you to add your own personal touches to your latest version of Excel.

Excel Options

Excel's default settings are generally the most appropriate or the most secure for the majority of users, although there may be occasions when you need to deviate from the norm or you just want to personalize certain features. To set your preferences for a wide range of Excel settings, including those for editing, calculations, and display, click the Microsoft Office Button and then click the Excel Options button. The options available for Excel are divided into different categories, which are listed on the left of the screen.

Figure 2-1 shows an image of the Popular category, which you can use to change settings, such as whether to display the Mini toolbar when you have selected text, or which ScreenTip scheme to use. You can use this screen to set the username, and to specify things like the language, the color scheme, how many worksheets should be in a new workbook, and the default font. If you want to create or edit a custom list for use in fill sequences, you can do that here too.

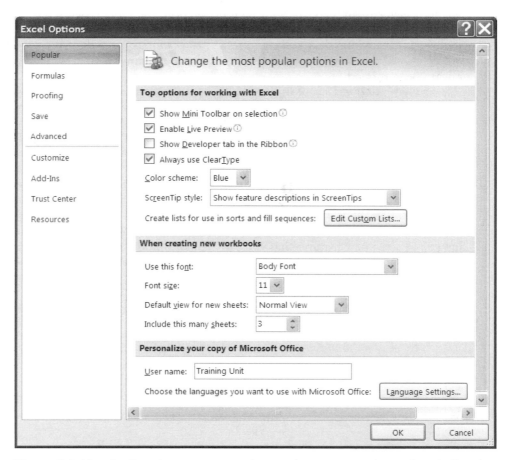

Figure 2-1. Use the Popular category to change the most popular options in Excel.

The Formulas category allows you to change the default settings that control how Excel performs calculations. For example, you can switch between automatic and manual calculation, or enable iterative calculation and change the settings for it. You can also customize settings for working with formulas and choose which rules Excel should use for error checking. The Proofing category can be used to change options for AutoCorrect, AutoFormat, and Smart Tags. This category is also used to select options for spelling correction and to manage custom dictionaries.

In Excel Options you can use the Save category to adjust your Save and Auto-Recover settings. This is where you can specify the default file location for saving and opening files, a feature that was previously located on the General tab of the Options dialog box. You can also choose where to save drafts for document management server files and what colors will be seen if the workbook is opened in a previous version of Excel.

To customize the display of your Excel workbook or worksheets, you can adjust a variety of settings using the Advanced category of Excel Options (see Figure 2-2). For example, you can decide whether to show or hide particular features, such as row and column headings, gridlines, scroll bars, sheet tabs, comments, and formulas. You can also select or deselect features, such as allowing editing directly in cells or enabling AutoComplete or automatic percent entry. If you want to automatically open certain files at startup, you can specify these here. Additionally, you can choose settings for Lotus compatibility. To customize the commands displayed on the Quick Access toolbar on the Excel user interface, use the Customization category in Excel Options, as described in the next section.

As you'd expect, the Add-Ins category allows you to view and manage add-ins, and the Trust Center category provides information about privacy and security and allows you to adjust security settings for features like macros, add-ins, ActiveX controls, and external content. You can also specify trusted publishers and trusted locations from which content and documents can be safely downloaded. Both of these categories are discussed in detail in Chapter 14.

Finally, the Resources category allows you to access resources and features provided by Microsoft. From here you can download updates for Microsoft Office, run Microsoft Office Diagnostics to diagnose and repair problems, contact Microsoft for support, and access Microsoft Office Online to obtain further help and updates.

NOTE There are too many customizable aspects of the Excel environment to look at all of them in detail here; however, some of the more important features will be discussed in this chapter and other Excel Options will be highlighted throughout the book as appropriate.

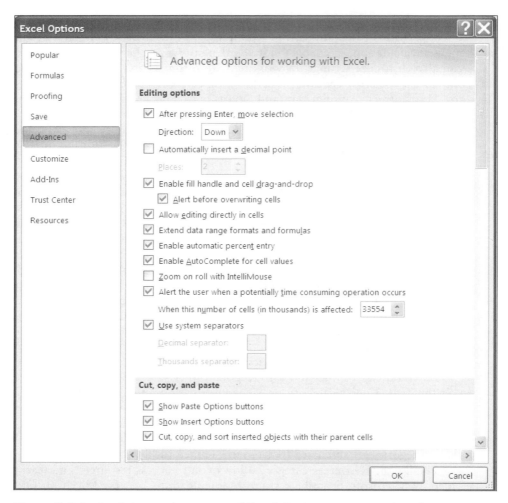

Figure 2-2. In the Advanced category of Excel Options, you can select from a variety of advanced options.

Customizing the Quick Access Toolbar

The Quick Access toolbar (see Figure 2-3) is a small toolbar that usually is positioned above the Ribbon beside the Microsoft Office Button. It contains shortcuts for commands independent of the Ribbon tab that is currently displayed and can be used to give you easy access to frequently used commands. This will be particularly useful if you are finding it difficult to navigate around the new Ribbon. You can choose which shortcuts to add to the Quick Access toolbar, and you can also select one of two locations to display it: above or below the Ribbon.

Figure 2-3. The Quick Access toolbar

> **TIP** To quickly add a command to the Quick Access toolbar, right-click the command on the Ribbon and select Add to Quick Access Toolbar.

Customizing the Quick Access toolbar so that it hosts your most commonly accessed commands could prove much more efficient than jumping between tabs on the Ribbon. You can change the commands that appear on the Quick Access toolbar or change its position by using the Customization category within Excel Options:

1. Click the Microsoft Office Button and then click the Excel Options button to open the Excel Options dialog box.
2. Select Customization from the menu. A screen similar to Figure 2-4 will be displayed.

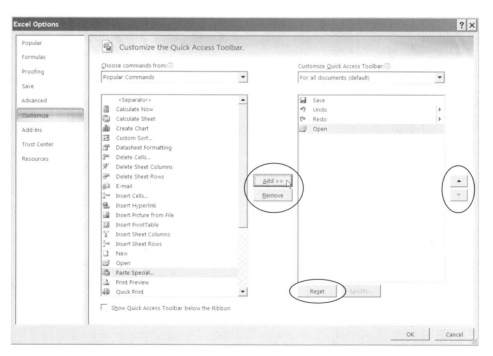

Figure 2-4. Use the Customization screen to customize or move the Quick Access toolbar.

3. Select a category from the "Choose commands from" dropdown list to display a list of related commands in the box below it. For example, you can view commands from a particular tab or commands not on the Ribbon.

4. Choose the command you would like to appear on the Quick Access toolbar from the list and click the Add button. You can add as many commands as you like using separators (select <Separator> at the top of the list of commands) to divide commands into related groups.

5. To reposition a command on the Quick Access toolbar, select the command from the list on the right and use the up and down arrows to the right of the list to reorder the commands.

6. To remove a command from the Quick Access toolbar, select the command from the list on the right and click the Remove button.

7. Under Customize Quick Access Toolbar, select whether you want the new settings to apply to all documents (the default) or just to the selected workbook.

8. To reset the Quick Access toolbar to the default settings, click the Reset button.

9. To position the toolbar below the Ribbon, check the "Show Quick Access Toolbar below the Ribbon" option.

10. When you have finished adjusting the Quick Access toolbar, click OK.

You can also use the Customize Quick Access Toolbar button (see Figure 2-5) to add or remove popular commands from the Quick Access toolbar, to open the Excel Options dialog box at the Customization category, or to move the toolbar.

1. Click the down arrow to the right of the Quick Access toolbar to display the Customize Quick Access Toolbar context menu.

2. Select or deselect commands to add or remove them from the Quick Access toolbar.

3. To open the Customization category in Excel Options and view all the commands that can be added to the Quick Access toolbar, click More Commands.

4. To move the toolbar, click Show Below the Ribbon. The toolbar will move to beneath the Ribbon.

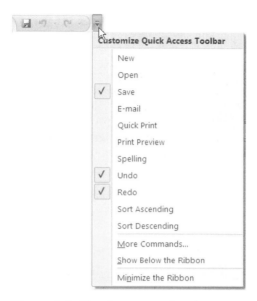

Figure 2-5. The Customize Quick Access Toolbar menu

Customizing the Status Bar

In Excel 2007 you have some control over what is displayed in the Status bar at the bottom of the Excel window (see Figure 2-6). For example, you can use the Status bar to indicate if features like Caps Lock, Num Lock, Permissions, and Signatures are turned on or off. You can also use the Status bar to switch views, change the zoom level, or record a macro by clicking the appropriate icon. When you're selecting cells, the Status bar can provide a count of the cells selected, and if the cells contain numerical values, information like the maximum, minimum, average, and sum values can be displayed. To customize the Status bar, follow these steps:

1. Right-click the Status bar. A list of all the features on the Status bar will be displayed.
2. Select or deselect features by clicking them.
3. Click outside of the list to finish.

Figure 2-6. Right-click the Status bar to select what you want to be displayed on it.

Custom Views

When working with Excel, you may find that you use different display and print settings for different purposes. For example, the settings you use for editing may not be the same as the settings you like to use when analyzing data. Also, if different people need to work with the same file, each may have their own preferences for how the data appears or is printed. Excel lets you store multiple settings for printing and display as custom views so that you can switch between views as required. Settings that can be stored in custom views include

- The view that the document is displayed in, such as Normal, Page Layout view, Page Break Preview
- Margins, Orientation, Breaks
- Print Area and Print Titles
- Ruler, Gridlines, Formula Bar, Headings
- Zoom
- Window Arrangements and Splits

You can create several views based on different settings for each worksheet in a workbook.

1. Select the worksheet that you want the view to apply to.
2. Adjust all the appropriate settings to display or print the worksheet the way you want it using the Page Layout tab or the View tab.
3. On the View tab, click Custom Views in the Workbook Views group. The Custom Views dialog box will open.
4. Click the Add button to create a new view. The Add View dialog box will open (see Figure 2-7).

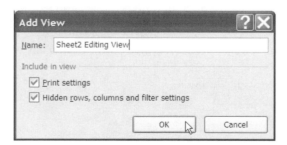

Figure 2-7. In the Add View dialog box, enter a name for your custom view and select the settings to be included.

5. In the Name box, type a name for the current view settings.

6. Use the checkboxes to select whether to include print settings and hidden rows, columns, and filter settings.

7. Click OK when you have finished.

Once you have created your custom views, you can quickly apply the required one to display the appropriate worksheet using the stored settings.

1. On the View tab, click Custom Views in the Workbook Views group. The Custom Views dialog box will open (see Figure 2-8).

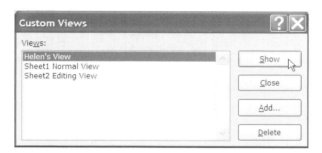

Figure 2-8. In the Custom Views dialog box, select the view you want to use and click Show.

2. From the Views list, select the view whose settings you wish to use.

3. Click the Show button. The worksheet associated with the selected view will be displayed with the stored display and print settings.

If you no longer have any use for a custom view, you can delete it by doing the following:

1. On the View tab, click Custom Views in the Workbook Views group. The Custom Views dialog box will open (Figure 2-8).

2. From the Views list, select the view that you wish to delete.

3. Click the Delete button. A box will appear asking you to confirm that you wish to delete the selected view.

4. Click Yes to confirm the deletion. The selected view will be removed from the Views list.

5. Click the Close button to close the Custom Views dialog box.

Customizing Your Excel Windows

If you work with particularly large spreadsheets, you may want to view different parts of a worksheet at the same time, or occasionally you may need to compare different workbooks on screen. The Window menu in previous versions of Excel provides commands that allow users to display different sections of a worksheet or different workbooks simultaneously. These facilities are now located in the Window group of the View tab in Excel 2007.

Freezing Panes

Excel allows you to freeze panes to lock rows and columns so that they will remain in view as you scroll through a worksheet. This is particularly beneficial when working with large worksheets as it allows you to display the row and column headings that you have entered in the first rows or columns at all times as you scroll down and across, thus making entering, editing, and analyzing your data much easier.

To freeze only the first row or the first column, complete the following steps:

1. Select the View tab on the Ribbon.

2. In the Window group, click Freeze Panes. You will be provided with three options, as shown in Figure 2-9.

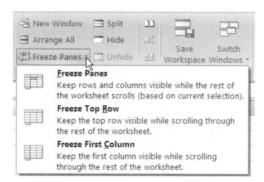

Figure 2-9. Select the appropriate Freeze Panes option to keep rows and/or columns visible while scrolling through a worksheet.

3. Select either Freeze Top Row or Freeze First Column as appropriate.

To freeze more than one row or column or to freeze both rows and columns:

1. Select the cell *below* the last row you want to freeze and to the *right* of the last column you want to freeze. For example, if you want to freeze the first row and the first column, select cell B2.
2. Select the View tab on the Ribbon.
3. In the Window group, click Freeze Panes.
4. Select the Freeze Panes option.

> **NOTE** A black line will appear below the last row that has been locked and to the right of the last column that has been locked.

To unlock the rows and/or columns again so that the worksheet will scroll normally:

1. Click Freeze Panes in the Window group of the View tab.
2. Select Unfreeze Panes. Any locked rows or columns will now be unlocked.

Splitting Panes

Another way of viewing different parts of a worksheet simultaneously is by splitting panes. When you use Freeze Panes, only the unlocked part of the worksheet can be scrolled; when you use Split Panes, each pane can be scrolled individually. You can split a window into either two or four panes, allowing you to view up to four different sections of your worksheet at a time.

1. Before you split a window into separate panes, you must select where you want the split to appear. Do one of the following:
   - To split a window into two panes horizontally, select the first cell in the row *below* where you want the split to appear.
   - To split a window into two panes vertically, select the first cell in the column to the *right* of where you want the split to appear.
   - To split a window into four panes, select the cell *below* the row and to the *right* of the column where you want the split to appear.
2. Click Split in the Window group of the View tab. A gray split bar will appear horizontally and/or vertically in the location of the split, dividing the window into two or four sections. Figure 2-10 shows an Excel window split into four panes. Note that there are now two scroll bars on the right and two scroll bars on the bottom of the window, allowing each half of the window to be scrolled without changing the other half. When you move the mouse pointer over a split bar, it will change to a *split pointer*; you can use this to move the split bar and adjust the size of the panes.
3. To remove a split, click the Split command again.

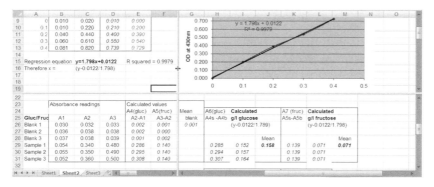

	A	B	C	D	E	F
9	0	0.010	0.020	0.010	0.000	
10	0.1	0.010	0.220	0.210	0.200	
11	0.2	0.040	0.440	0.400	0.390	
12	0.3	0.060	0.610	0.550	0.540	
13	0.4	0.081	0.820	0.739	0.729	

Chart: $y = 1.798x + 0.0122$, $R^2 = 0.9979$, OD at 430nm

15	Regression equation	y=1.798x+0.0122			R squared = 0.9979
16	Therefore x =		(y-0.0122/1.798)		

	Absorbance readings				Calculated values		Mean	A6(gluc) Calculated		A7 (fruc) Calculated	
23/24					A4(gluc)	A5(fruc)	Mean	A6(gluc) Calculated		A7 (fruc) Calculated	
25	Gluc/Fruc	A1	A2	A3	A2-A1	A3-A2	blank	A4s -A4b g/l glucose (y-0.0122/1.789)		A5s-A5b g/l fructose (y-0.0122/1.798)	
26 Blank 1	0.030	0.032	0.033	0.002	0.001	0.001			
27 Blank 2	0.036	0.038	0.038	0.002	0.000				
28 Blank 3	0.037	0.038	0.039	0.001	0.002		Mean	Mean
29 Sample 1	0.054	0.340	0.480	0.286	0.140	0.285	0.152	**0.158**	0.139	0.071	**0.071**
30 Sample 2	0.055	0.350	0.490	0.295	0.140	0.294	0.157		0.139	0.071
31 Sample 3	0.052	0.360	0.500	0.308	0.140	0.307	0.164		0.139	0.071

Sheet1 Sheet2 Sheet3

Figure 2-10. Use the Split command in the Window group to divide a window into separate sections.

You can also quickly split a window into panes by using the Split box at the top of the vertical scroll bar or to the right of the horizontal scroll bar (see Figure 2-11).

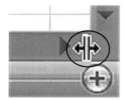

Figure 2-11. When you move the mouse pointer over the Split box, it will change to a split pointer.

1. Position the mouse pointer over the Split box until it changes to a split pointer (see Figure 2-11).

2. Use the split pointer to drag the split box on the vertical scroll bar down or the split box on the horizontal scroll bar to the left.

3. To remove a split, double-click on any part of the split bar that divides the panes.

Working with Multiple Windows

If you want two separate views of the current workbook, you can open a second copy in a new window. This will allow you to look at the same worksheet using different views or to view different worksheets in the same workbook simultaneously. Any changes made to the document in one window will be replicated in the other.

1. To open a new window containing a view of the current document, click New Window in the Window group of the View tab. Excel opens a second copy of the workbook in a separate window.

2. To arrange the layout of all the open windows, click Arrange All in the Window group of the View tab. The Arrange Windows dialog box will open (see Figure 2-12).

Figure 2-12. In the Arrange Windows dialog box, select the layout that you want to use to display open windows.

3. Select one of the four options—Tiled, Horizontal, Vertical, or Cascade—to arrange the open windows as required.

> **NOTE** When you arrange windows, all open windows in the application will be displayed. To view only the windows containing the active workbook, check the "Windows of active workbook" option in the Arrange Windows dialog box (see Figure 2-12).

4. You can move a window by dragging its title bar to the new position, or you can adjust the size of a window by dragging the edge of the window with the mouse.

5. To temporarily remove a window from view, make the window the active window and click Hide in the Window group.

6. To display a hidden window again, click Unhide in the Window group to open the Unhide box. Select the window that you want to bring back again from the list (if more than one window is hidden) and click OK.

7. If you want to retain the layout of your windows to use again the next time you are working with the same workbooks, you can save it as a workspace by clicking Save Workspace in the Window group.

To close all the open windows for the active workbook, click the Microsoft Office Button and select Close. To close the active window but leave other windows for the same workbook open, click the Close button at the top of the window.

Comparing Windows Side by Side

The Window group on the View tab also provides the facility to compare two windows side by side so that two versions of a document or two different worksheets can be viewed and contrasted. To compare two worksheets, you must have both open in separate windows.

1. To compare the active workbook with another open workbook, click the View Side by Side icon button in the Window group (see Figure 2-13) to open the Compare Side by Side box.

Figure 2-13. View Side by Side, Synchronous Scrolling, and Reset Window Position icon buttons

2. Select a workbook from the list in the Compare Side by Side box and click OK. Both workbooks will be displayed horizontally, although you can change the arrangement if you wish by using the Arrange All command.

3. By default, synchronous scrolling will be switched on allowing you to scroll both workbooks simultaneously. To turn off synchronous scrolling and scroll one workbook independently of the other, click the Synchronous Scrolling icon button (see Figure 2-13).

4. If you have moved or adjusted the size of the windows, you can use the Reset Window Position icon button (see Figure 2-13) to reposition them evenly on the screen again.

5. To turn off the View Side by Side feature and return to your original view of the windows, click the View Side by Side icon button again.

CHAPTER 3

Excel Essentials

Excel is often misconstrued, by those who are not familiar with it, as being a glorified calculator or an alternative to creating a table in Microsoft Word. Those who take the time to become acquainted with the application soon realize that Excel has much more to offer, and with a few fundamental techniques, users can easily create purposeful and flexible worksheet models. Excel is used by corporations and individuals worldwide for a gamut of purposes, from statistical analysis of numerical results to sorting and filtering lists of data. With each new version, Microsoft has streamlined and enhanced the multitude of worksheet operations that can be carried out in Excel to help users make the most of this versatile application.

This chapter takes a look at some of the features of Excel that every user should be aware of, especially if they want to save valuable time. If you are an experienced Excel user, most of these features will probably already be familiar to you as they were introduced with earlier versions of Excel. However, because they have been relocated in 2007 and are integral to the efficient use of Excel, it would be negligent not to mention them.

The chapter begins by briefly looking at how you can enter and edit worksheet data. I'll introduce the AutoCorrect and AutoFill features, which can reduce the amount of time you need to spend typing. I'll also discuss the Custom Lists and Series tools and show you how you can quickly enter a defined list or a series of numerical values.

The section "Working with Paste" will make you rethink the way you copy and paste in Excel and show you just what's so special about Paste Special. You may find that the Paste options available to you can save you a lot of time and effort in formatting and formula construction. There are numerous occasions when you can use Paste Special once you realize how versatile it is.

Defining names is an important aspect of efficient Excel usage, particularly when it comes to constructing formulas and functions. If you are not already in the habit of naming cells and ranges, I will convince you of the benefits of it in this section. You will also get an opportunity to become acquainted with the Name Manager, the new interface for creating and managing defined names for cells, ranges, constants, and formulas.

Most Excel workbooks consist of more than one worksheet, and the worksheets are often laid out in a similar manner. The final section of this chapter will show you how to insert, rename, move, copy, and delete worksheets. I will also furnish you with some tips on working with multiple worksheets, including how to enter data into and format several worksheets simultaneously.

Entering and Editing Data

Excel 2007's new supersized grid will allow you to store and analyze more data than ever before. Each of the 17 billion cells can contain a numerical value, a piece of text, or a formula—that's a lot of data! Naturally you will want to make the data entry process as straightforward and efficient as possible. The most obvious way to enter data is to type the number, text, or formula directly into the relevant cell. You can then press the Tab key to move to the cell to the right or press Enter to move down a cell.

> **TIP** To enter the same data in multiple cells simultaneously, select the cells, type the data, and press Ctrl+Enter.

Numerical values can be positive or negative (use a minus sign or parentheses to indicate a negative value) and can include different types of numbers, such as decimals, fractions, percentages, monetary values, and so on. When entering a number with a fraction, leave a space between the whole number and the fraction. For example, to enter 1¼ you would type **1 1/4** (although the formula bar will display 1.25). If there is only a fraction and no whole number, use 0; for example to enter ¾, type **0 3/4**.

Dates and times are stored by Excel as serial numbers starting with January 1, 1900, which is represented as 1. Times are stored as a fraction of a day starting at midnight; therefore, noon on January 1, 2007, is represented by 39083.5. Generally, Excel will recognize a date or time when you enter it and will format it accordingly— use a slash (/) or hyphen (-) to separate the different parts of a date and a colon (:) to separate the different parts of a time. Chapter 4 will show you how to use the built-in formats and how to create custom formats for numbers, dates, and times to control how they are displayed.

> **TIP** Press Ctrl+; (semicolon) to enter the current date or Ctrl+Shift+; to enter the current time in a cell.

Like numerical data, text can be typed directly into a cell. Each cell in Excel now hold over 32,000 characters, which should be ample for most purposes. If you want to enter a line break in a cell, press Alt+Enter. Text may be used as labels or comments as well as the actual data in the spreadsheet. If you want Excel to treat a number or date as text—for example, if it is a label—you can precede it by an apostrophe ('). To illustrate, if you enter a code as **12-5**, Excel will normally interpret and display this as December 5, but if you enter it as **'12-5**, Excel will interpret the code as text.

When you have entered your data in a worksheet, you can use formulas to manipulate the data and perform calculations, thus creating sophisticated worksheet models. Formulas always begin with an equals sign (=) and can involve quite simple addition, multiplication, division, and subtraction, or they can incorporate any of the built-in functions and be used for more complex data analysis. When you enter a formula, like **=A1+B2**, in a cell, the result will be displayed (in this case, the total of the contents of cell A1 and cell B2). If you change the value in any cell referred to by a formula, it will recalculate automatically. Chapter 10 will discuss using formulas and functions in more detail.

As you enter data, you may need to insert additional cells, rows, or columns. You can do so easily by using the Cells group on the Home tab. Just select the cell where you want to insert or delete a cell, row, or column; click the down arrow to the right of the Insert or Delete command in the Cells group; and choose the correct option from the menu that appears. The cells in the worksheet will move to accommodate the insertion or deletion.

To replace the contents of a cell at any time, simply select the cell and type in the new data. If you only want to edit part of a cell's contents, double-click the cell or select the cell and press F2 to switch to edit mode. You can also edit the selected cell's contents using the formula bar. If you want to erase the contents of a cell, select the cell and press Delete. Alternatively you can use the Clear icon in the Editing group on the Home tab to control exactly what gets deleted as follows (see Figure 3-1):

- Select Clear All to remove everything from the cell.
- Select Clear Formats to remove the formatting while leaving the number, text, or formula intact.
- Select Clear Contents to remove the contents of the cell but leave the formatting intact.
- Select Clear Comments to remove any comments attached to the cell.

Figure 3-1. Use the Clear command to control exactly what is cleared from a cell.

To help speed up the chore of data entry, Excel provides us with a few handy features, including AutoCorrect and AutoFill. As you enter data in a column, Auto-Correct will prompt you with a suggested entry, based on text that you have already entered. If you type the first few letters of a name that you have previously entered in the same contiguous column, Excel will complete the word for you—to accept its suggestion, just press Enter. It will even keep the case of the entry consistent with the previous entry. This can help simplify your data entry significantly if you repeatedly have to enter the same text in cells in a column. However, if you want to turn the feature off you can—just deselect the "Enable AutoComplete for cell values" option in the Advanced category of Excel Options.

AutoFill can also quicken the data entry process by allowing you to copy data or a formula from one cell or range of cells to another cell or multiple cells by using the Fill Handle. The Fill Handle is the small square in the bottom-right corner of the selected cell or range. When you move the mouse pointer over the Fill Handle, it changes to a black cross. If you click and drag the black cross, the contents of the selected cell will be copied to the cells that you drag over. The Fill Handle can also be used to continue a series—for example, a series of numbers or dates—or to enter a custom list (as discussed in the following section). For example, if you enter **Quarter 1** in a cell and use the Fill Handle to fill this to the next three cells, the series Quarter 2, Quarter 3, and Quarter 4 will be entered automatically. You can even use the Fill Handle to quickly delete data by dragging the Fill Handle of an empty cell over cells containing data.

Custom Lists

Many users find that they continually use the same lists of labels for rows or columns in their spreadsheets—for example, the departments within the organization or the names of colleagues. Custom lists can save you time entering data by allowing you to enter one item from a list into a cell and then using the AutoFill feature to continue the series in adjacent cells in the specified order. You can also use custom lists to control the sort order of items if you want a list to be sorted in a particular way instead of alphabetically.

Excel already has predefined fill series for the days of the week and months of the year, which most users have probably used at some stage. You can create your own lists to use in fill series or when sorting by using the Popular category of the Excel Options box. This can be done by typing list entries directly or by selecting a list you have already created in your worksheet.

1. Click the Microsoft Office Button and then click the Excel Options button to open the Excel Options box.
2. Select Popular from the menu. Click the Edit Custom Lists button to open the Custom Lists dialog box (see Figure 3-2).

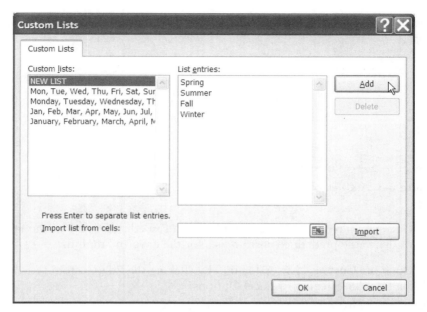

Figure 3-2. To create a new list, edit list entries, or import a list from cells in the worksheet, use this dialog box.

3. To type the list in directly, type each item into the List entries box, using the Enter key to separate each entry. When you have typed all the entries for the list, click Add.

4. To import a list from the worksheet, click in the "Import list from cells" box and enter the cell references for your list by typing the references in or by selecting the cells from your worksheet. Click Import to import the cell contents as a list.

5. When you have finished adding custom lists, click OK. To try out the feature, type an entry from your list into a cell and use the Fill Handle to continue the series across the row or down the column.

When you use AutoFill, Excel will display the AutoFill Options icon beside the filled cells. If you click this icon, a list of options will be displayed that lets you control how Excel fills the series—for example, Fill Without Formatting (see Figure 3-3). If you have created a series of dates, you can select options like Fill Weekdays (to omit Saturdays and Sundays) or Fill Months (to increment the cells by months rather than days).

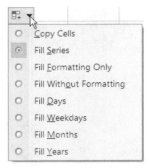

Figure 3-3. AutoFill options

Once you have created a custom list, you can edit or delete it, though you can't edit or delete the predefined custom lists for the days and months.

1. Open the Custom Lists dialog box by clicking the Edit Custom Lists button in the Popular category of Excel Options.

2. Select the list that you want to edit or delete.

3. Make the required changes to the list in the List entries box and then click Add, or click Delete to delete the entire list.

4. Click OK when you have finished.

Creating a Series

The Series dialog box, which can be opened by clicking Fill in the Editing group on the Home tab, offers an alternative to the Fill Handle for entering a series. The options in the Series dialog box allow you to exert more control over how a series is incremented and when it will stop. The following steps outline how you can use the Series dialog box to define a series:

1. Enter the starting value for the series in a cell and, if necessary, enter values in enough cells to establish the pattern for the series.

2. Select the entire range that you want to be filled by the series and select the Home tab.

3. Click the Fill icon button (blue down arrow) in the Editing group and select Series from the menu that appears. The Series dialog box will open (see Figure 3-4).

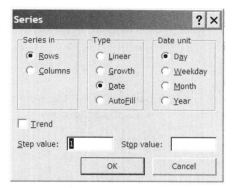

Figure 3-4. Use the Series dialog box to create a series.

4. Under Series in, click either Rows or Columns as appropriate.

5. Under Type, select one of the following:

- Linear, to calculate the next series value by adding the step value to the preceding value

- Growth, to calculate the next value by multiplying the step value to the preceding value

- Data, to create a series of dates—you will need to select Day, Weekday, Month, or Year under Date unit to indicate how the date should be incremented

- AutoFill, to continue a series of numbers or text in the same way as dragging the Fill Handle

6. If you have selected either a Linear or a Growth type, you can select the Trend option to calculate a line-of-best-fit for a Linear series or a geometric curve for a Growth series.

7. If you have selected Linear, Growth, or Date as the type, enter the value that you want to use as the increment for the series in the Step value box.

8. If you want to impose a limit on the series, enter a value in the Stop value box. Any remaining cells in the selection will remain blank if the Stop value is reached before all the cells are filled.

9. Click OK to close the Series dialog box and enter the series in the selected cells.

Working with Paste

All experienced Microsoft Office users will be familiar with the Clipboard facility and the Cut, Copy, and Paste commands. Microsoft Excel offers some variations on the standard Paste feature to accommodate the different types of data that may be contained within cells in a worksheet. Paste Special and Paste Options can save you a lot of time readjusting the formatting of pasted cells and can help you avoid the frustration and false results of cells updating when you don't want them to—or not updating when you do!

> **TIP** To open the Office Clipboard in the task pane, click the Clipboard Dialog Box Launcher in the bottom-right corner of the Clipboard group.

Paste Special

When you use Copy and Paste to copy cell contents, you may find that when you paste the cells to the new location the result is not quite what you had anticipated. For example, if you copy a cell containing a formula and paste it to a new worksheet, quite often you will encounter a #REF! error as the cell references in the formula will no longer be applicable. To overcome problems like this, you may need to use Paste Special rather than the straightforward Paste command to specify exactly what it is you want to appear in the destination cell(s). Using Paste Values, for instance, will allow you to remove a formula from a cell without removing the result. Paste Special also allows you to carry out a mathematical operation (add, subtract, multiply, or divide) using the copied value(s) and the destination values, replacing the values in the destination cells with the results.

1. To use Paste Special, copy the selected cell(s) by clicking the Copy icon in the Clipboard group (see Figure 3-5) on the Home tab or by pressing Ctrl+C on the keyboard.

Figure 3-5. You can access the Paste, Cut, Copy, and Format Painter commands from the Clipboard group on the Home tab.

2. Right-click the destination cell and select Paste Special. You can also find Paste Special by clicking Paste in the Clipboard group (see Figure 3-5).

3. Choose the appropriate option from the Paste Special dialog box (see Figure 3-6) and click OK, or click the Paste Link button to create a link between the source cell(s) and the destination cell(s). Table 3-1 explains the purpose of the various options in the Paste Special dialog box.

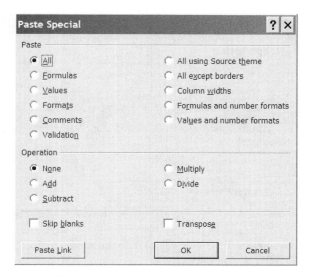

Figure 3-6. The Paste Special dialog box

NOTE Cells can be linked between two open workbooks using Paste Link. The linked cells will update automatically as changes are made to the original cells.

Table 3-1. Paste Special Options

Paste Special Option	Description
Paste Options	
All	Paste the cell contents along with formatting information.
Formulas	Paste the formulas.
Values	Paste the values (formula results).
Formats	Paste cell formatting information only.
Comments	Paste cell comments.
Validation	Paste the data validation rules for the copied range.
All using Source theme	Paste the cell contents using the same theme formatting as the source cells.
All except borders	Paste cell contents and all formatting information except for cell borders.
Column widths	Paste the cell contents using the same column width as the copied range.

Continued

Table 3-1. Continued

Paste Special Option	Description
Paste Options	
Formulas and number formats	Paste formulas along with the number formats.
Values and number formats	Paste the values (formula results) along with the number formats.
Operation Options	
None	Do not perform any operation.
Add	Add the copied values to the contents of the destination cell(s).
Subtract	Subtract the copied values from the contents of the destination cell(s).
Multiply	Multiply the copied values by the contents of the destination cell(s).
Divide	Divide the contents of the destination cell(s) by the copied values.
Other Options	
Skip Blanks	Do not replace values in the destination area when blank cells occur within the copied data.
Transpose	Transpose columns to rows or rows to columns.
Paste Link	Paste a link to the source cells so that the destination cells will automatically update if the source cells change.

Paste Options

Paste Options is similar to Paste Special in that it gives you control over how the data is pasted; however, it has less functionality than Paste Special. The Paste Options icon will appear when you paste a cell or cells to allow you to quickly select what you want to paste without having to use the Paste Special command. To use Paste Options, copy and paste the cells as normal. The Paste Options icon (see Figure 3-7) will appear beside the pasted cells.

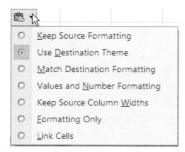

Figure 3-7. Click the Paste Options icon to select how you want the copied data to be pasted.

Click the Paste Options icon and select the appropriate option from the list that appears. Table 3-2 explains the various options within Paste Options—the range of commands available will depend on the type of data that you paste.

Table 3-2. Paste Options

Paste Options	Description
Keep Source Formatting	Paste the cell contents (including formulas) using the same formatting as the source cells.
Use Destination Theme	Paste the cell contents using the same theme as the destination cells.
Match Destination Formatting	Paste the cell contents using the same formatting as the destination cells.
Values Only	Paste the cell values (formula results)—only appears when the pasted data contains formulas.
Values and Number Formatting	Paste the values (formula results) along with the number formatting—text formatting is removed.
Values and Source Formatting	Paste the values (formula results) using the same formatting as the source cells.
Keep Source Column Widths	Paste the cell contents using the same column width as the copied range—preserves all formulas and formatting.
Formatting Only	Paste cell formatting information only.
Link Cells	Paste a link to the source cells so that the destination cells will update automatically—all formulas and formatting are removed.

If you find the Paste Options feature annoying, you can turn it off by deselecting "Show Paste Options buttons" in the "Cut, copy, and paste" section of the Advanced category in Excel Options.

Defining Names

Excel users have long recognized the advantages of defining names for items like cells, constants, or formulas, particularly when authoring formulas. When you have entered data into your worksheet, you'll find it worthwhile to examine it to identify cells or ranges that may be used later in formulas and assign meaningful names to them. Having created names, you can go on to construct stable formulas that are more comprehensible by referring to these names rather than cell references. A defined name like **Total_Cost** is much more user-friendly, and much less likely to be mistyped, than a reference like **J213**. Furthermore, formulas and functions that incorporate names, for example **=Total_Profit-Total_Expenses** or **=AVERAGE(MonthlySales)**, certainly convey a clearer impression of what the result will mean than formulas or functions that only use cell references.

> **NOTE** Excel will sometimes create a name for you, for example when you set a Print Area. Also, when you create a table, Excel will automatically allocate a name in the format of Table1, Table 2, etc.; however, you can change these names to make them more meaningful.

The easiest way to create a name for a cell or range is to select the cell or cells and type the name directly into the Name box to the left of the formula bar (see Figure 3-8) and press Enter. You can also use the Name box to go directly to a named cell or range by selecting the name from the dropdown list that appears when you click the down arrow to the right of the Name box.

Figure 3-8. You can use the Name box to quickly create and navigate to named cells or ranges. If the selected cell has not been named, the Name box will display the reference of the cell.

> **NOTE** Names can be up to 255 characters in length and should begin with a letter, underscore, or backslash. They cannot be the same as cell references and should not contain spaces or hyphens (use periods or underscores instead). Names are not case sensitive; therefore, Excel will regard Total and TOTAL as the same name.

Excel 2007 has acknowledged the importance of defining names, especially when inputting formulas, by including a Defined Names group in the center of the Formulas tab on the Ribbon. Commands for naming ranges and creating names from selected cells are prominently positioned there (instead of being hidden in the Insert menu as before) and the tasks of creating, finding, editing, and deleting names can now be facilitated in a much more convenient manner by using the Name Manager.

Defining a Name

The Name Manager in Excel 2007 provides you with an alternative interface for viewing and managing the names in a workbook. You can use the Name Manager to simplify naming chores like editing or renaming names or deleting multiple names. You can even add comments to clarify the purpose of a name.

1. Choose the Formulas tab on the Ribbon. In the Defined Names group, click Name Manager (see Figure 3-9).

Figure 3-9. Click Name Manager to create, view, edit, and delete defined names.

2. The Name Manager dialog box will appear, listing any names that have already been defined in the current workbook (see Figure 3-10).

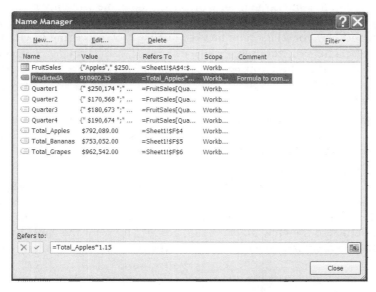

Figure 3-10. Use the Name Manager to create a new name or select an existing one to edit or delete.

3. Click New to open the New Name dialog box (see Figure 3-11). You can also open the New Name dialog box directly from the worksheet by clicking Define Name in the Defined Names group.

Figure 3-11. Enter the appropriate details for the new name and click OK.

4. Enter a name in the Name box (or use the name that Excel suggests if appropriate). Excel will automatically insert any text that appears in a cell to the left or above the selected cell or range in the Name box.

5. Select the Scope setting for the name (either to a specific worksheet or to the entire workbook). The scope of a name defines where the name can be used without being qualified and is either local (a worksheet) or global (a workbook). If the scope of a name is the local worksheet, the name will only be recognized within that worksheet. To use a defined name whose scope is the local worksheet in another worksheet, you need to qualify it by preceding it with the worksheet name. For example, if the name Start_Date is restricted to Sheet1, to use it in another sheet you will need to enter **Sheet1!Start_Date**. If the scope for the name Start_Date is the workbook, it can be used in any worksheet in the same workbook.

6. Add a description or explanation for the name in the Comment box if appropriate. Text entered in the Comment box will appear as the ScreenTip for the name in the Formula AutoComplete box.

7. By default, the selected cell or range will be the reference in the Refers to box. If you want to enter a different reference, click the Collapse Dialog icon on the right. The "New Name—Refers to" dialog box will appear, allowing you to select the cell or range on the worksheet. Click the Expand Dialog icon on the right to return to the New Name dialog box. If you want the name to refer to a constant or a formula, type = followed by the constant or formula in the Refers to box.

8. Click OK to return to the Name Manager; your new name will be listed in the Name Manager. (If you opened the New Name box by clicking Define Name in the Defined Names group, you will be returned to the worksheet when you click OK in the New Name box.)

9. Continue to define any other names you want to create or click Close to close the Name Manager dialog box.

> **NOTE** Each new name you create must be unique within its scope, although you can use the same name several times within one workbook as long as each instance has a different scope. For example, you can create a name Total_Cost scoped to Sheet1 and another name Total_Cost scoped to Sheet2 within the same workbook. You can even have a third Total_Cost scoped to the global workbook as this is a separate scope—although this could cause a name conflict, in which case the local worksheet level will take precedence.

Managing Names

Once you have defined names in your workbook, you can use the Name Manager to help you manage them. To sort the names in the Name Manager, click the column heading that you want to sort the names by. To filter the names (for example, to display only the names whose scope is a particular worksheet), click the Filter button and select the appropriate option. If you want to edit a name, select it and click Edit to open the Edit Name dialog box (which is similar to the New Name dialog box). Finally, to delete one or more names, select the name or names and click Delete. A dialog box will appear asking you to confirm the deletion.

> **NOTE** The Name Manager will not display hidden names (where the Visible property is set to false) or names defined in Visual Basic for Applications (VBA).

Creating a Name from a Selection

If you already have existing row or column labels, you can use these to quickly create names for multiple cells. Select the range of cells that you want to name along with the labels (which should be in the row above or below or the column to the left or to the right). Click Create from Selection in the Defined Names group of the Formulas tab. In the Create Names from Selection dialog box, select the location of the text you want to use as the names and click OK. Each cell will be named individually using its corresponding label. You can check this by selecting any of the cells and looking in the Name box to the left of the formula bar. Excel will insert an underscore at the start of the name if the label begins with a number and it will replace any spaces in the label with an underscore.

Creating a Dynamic Range

Spreadsheets often do not remain a fixed size; the number of rows will increase and decrease as records are added or deleted. This can cause problems if it affects a named range that is used in subsequent formulas. To avoid having to edit your named ranges every time you add or remove a row or column, you can create what is known as a *dynamic range*. A dynamic range is a named range that uses a dynamic reference so that it will expand automatically as new items are added to the range, therefore giving any formulas dependent on it more flexibility. You can create a dynamic range by using the OFFSET function that defines the range size based on the number of items in the column, which is calculated using a COUNT or COUNTA function.

1. Open the New Name dialog box by clicking Name a Range in the Defined Names group or by clicking New in the Name Manager dialog box.

2. Enter a name for the range in the Name box, select a scope in the Scope box, and add a description in the Comment box as appropriate.

3. In the Refers to box, enter a dynamic reference using the following format as a guide:

   =OFFSET(Sheet1!$A$1,0,0,COUNTA($A:$A),1)

   where the list is on Sheet1 starting at cell A1 and the arguments are

   - Reference cell: **Sheet1!$A$1**
   - Rows to offset: **0**
   - Columns to offset: **0**
   - Number of rows: **COUNTA($A:$A)**
   - Number of columns: **1**

NOTE If you want the number of columns to be dynamic, replace **1** with **COUNTA($1$1)**.

Working with Multiple Worksheets

By default, each new workbook in Excel has three worksheets (although you can change this setting in the Personalize category of Excel Options) named Sheet1, Sheet2, and Sheet3. You can insert and delete worksheets as necessary, or you can move, copy, and rename them. New worksheets can be based on a template that you have created or obtained from Office Online.

You can move between worksheets by clicking the direction arrows to the left of the sheet tabs at the bottom of the screen (see Figure 3-12). To quickly go to a particular worksheet, right-click any of the direction arrows at the bottom of the screen and select the worksheet you want from the list that appears. You can also use Ctrl+Page Down to move to the next worksheet and Ctrl+Page Up to move to the previous worksheet.

Figure 3-12. You can view a different worksheet by clicking its sheet tab, by using the direction arrows, or by right-clicking these arrows and selecting the sheet from a list.

Inserting Worksheets

The number of new worksheets that you can insert into a workbook is limited only by available memory. There are different ways to insert new worksheets into a workbook. To insert a new worksheet at the end of the existing worksheets, you can simply click the Insert Worksheet tab to the right of the sheet tabs at the bottom of the screen (see Figure 3-12).

To insert a new worksheet before an existing worksheet, right-click the worksheet tab and select Insert. Select Worksheet (or whichever option is appropriate) on the General tab of the Insert dialog box or click the Spreadsheet Solutions tab to choose one of the custom templates. Alternatively, you can go to the Home tab on the Ribbon and, in the Cells group, click the down arrow to the right of Insert (see Figure 3-13) and select Insert Sheet.

Figure 3-13. Use the Cells group to insert, delete, and format worksheets.

You can also insert multiple worksheets simultaneously. Using the Shift key, select the same number of existing worksheet tabs as worksheets you want to insert. Then, click the down arrow to the right of Insert in the Cells group of the Home tab and select Insert Sheet.

Renaming Worksheets

It makes sense to rename your worksheets to something more meaningful than Sheet1, Sheet2, Sheet3, etc., especially if you are planning to include the sheet name in the header or footer when printing. To rename a worksheet, double-click the tab of the worksheet you want to rename (or right-click the tab and select Rename). This will select the current name on the tab. With the tab selected, enter the new name for the worksheet. The original name will be replaced as you type.

If you have a lot of worksheets, you might find it useful to categorize them by applying colors to the sheet tabs. You can do this by right-clicking the tab, pointing to

Tab Color, and then clicking your selected color. You can also rename a worksheet or change the tab color by clicking Format in the Cells group (see Figure 3-13) and selecting Rename Sheet or Tab Color under Organize Sheets.

Deleting Worksheets

It is a good idea to remove any worksheets that you no longer require from your workbook. You can delete unused or redundant worksheets, either singly or together, by selecting the tab(s) of the worksheet(s) to be deleted and clicking the down arrow to the right of Delete in the Cells group of the Home tab (see Figure 3-13) and selecting Delete Sheet. (Or you can right-click the sheet tab and select Delete.) A dialog box will appear warning you that data may exist in the selected sheet(s) and requesting you to confirm the deletion. Click Delete to continue to delete the selected sheet(s).

> **CAUTION** Be careful when deleting worksheets as you cannot undo the deletion.

Moving and Copying Worksheets

At times you may want to move a worksheet to another location within the current workbook, to another open workbook or to a new workbook. You can also create a second copy of a worksheet and position it within the same workbook, another workbook, or a new workbook.

1. Right-click the tab of the worksheet that you want to copy or move and select Move or Copy. The Move or Copy dialog box will open (see Figure 3-14).

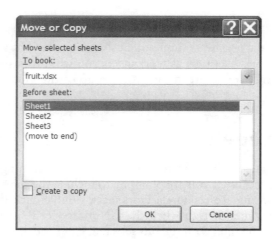

Figure 3-14. Select the workbook and position where you want the moved or copied worksheet to appear.

2. From the To book list, select the book that you want to move or copy the sheet to, or select (new book) to create a new book for the sheet. If you want to move or copy the sheet to another existing workbook, you must have that workbook already opened.

3. Select the worksheet that you want the moved/copied worksheet to be positioned before from the Before sheet area.

4. If you want to create a copy of the worksheet rather than move the original, select "Create a copy" and click OK.

NOTE You can also move or copy a worksheet by clicking Format in the Cells group and selecting Move or Copy Sheet.

Entering and Formatting Data in Multiple Worksheets Simultaneously

Quite often an Excel workbook will contain several worksheets that are structured in a common way to hold similar information, such as worksheets analyzing weekly sales. Consequently, situations can often arise where you need to enter identical data in the same position in multiple worksheets within the same workbook—for example, when entering headings or constant values. In addition, you may want to format related worksheets in the same way. Excel allows you to group worksheets together so that you only need to enter the data or apply formatting on one sheet and the same data or formatting will automatically be applied to the other worksheets in the group. If you have a workbook containing 52 weekly sales sheets, this can save you a significant amount of time!

To group sheets together so that you can enter data in all of them or format them simultaneously, select all the worksheets that you want to group by holding down the Ctrl key as you click each of the worksheet tabs (or to select a number of consecutive sheets, click the tab for the first sheet, and hold down the Shift key as you click the tab for the last sheet). When the worksheets are grouped together the word [Group] appears in the title bar. Enter the data or formulas or format the cells in the worksheet as required in the usual way. The same data or formatting will be entered in the same cells in the other worksheets in the group. You can apply most types of formatting to grouped cells although you cannot use the Format as a Table feature or apply conditional formatting. To ungroup the worksheets again, click the tab of any worksheet not in the group or right-click the tab of a grouped worksheet and select Ungroup Sheets.

CAUTION Make sure you ungroup the worksheets after you have finished or you could end up unintentionally replacing data in the other worksheets.

CHAPTER 4

Styles and Formatting

For most Excel users who take pride in their creations, factors like the consistency and professional presentation of the finished document are almost as important as the validity of the data contained within it, particularly when the spreadsheet is intended to be viewed by others. The AutoFormat feature in previous versions of Excel automated at least part of the process of formatting lists and tables but had limited adaptability and, frankly, had begun to look rather dated. Excel 2007 has taken worksheet formatting to new lengths by providing a large selection of built-in styles for both individual cells and entire tables. Furthermore, if your spreadsheet is part of a range of documents, you can apply one of Microsoft Office's document themes to ensure ultimate consistency and coordination across your spreadsheets, word processing documents, and presentations.

In addition to making your worksheets more aesthetically pleasing, formatting can be used to highlight noteworthy data or make a range of cells stand out from the rest of the sheet. There are various ways you can apply formatting effects to change the appearance of your Excel worksheets. This chapter will look at the ways you can manually format cells as well as how you can automatically format your data using cell and table styles and document themes. It also looks at how you can customize these styles and themes to suit your document design criteria.

As the formatting of numerical data can be particularly important in a spreadsheet, Excel has several built-in number formats to control how numbers are displayed and therefore how they are ultimately interpreted. These formats can dictate features like the number of decimal places and any symbol that should be displayed along with the value. This chapter will look at how you can apply a predefined number format to cells and how to create a custom number or date format to give you a high level of control over how numbers and dates appear in your worksheets.

The conditional formatting feature has always been a useful tool in Excel because it allows you to automatically format cells whose values satisfy certain conditions, thus making them instantly identifiable. Its serviceability has now been further enhanced to allow you to visualize data by using icon sets, data bars, and color scales so that you can add meaning to cell values or indicate a value's position within the overall range of values. The final section in this chapter looks at the conditional formatting feature.

Document Themes

Document themes have been introduced with Microsoft Office 2007 and allow you to quickly and uniformly format an entire document using a collection of formatting settings that includes theme colors, fonts (body and heading fonts), and effects (such as line and fill effects). When you apply a document theme, elements like headings, text, charts, tables, and effects will adopt settings that will complement each other and give your document a professional and coordinated look. The styles that you can apply to cells and tables in your worksheet will be affected by your choice of document theme. If you want to, you can customize document themes to suit your own color schemes, corporate colors, or formatting preferences. Document themes can also be shared across Microsoft Office programs, allowing all your documents to boast a consistent appearance.

Applying a Document Theme

You can change the default Office theme for a workbook by selecting another theme from the predefined themes available. To choose a new theme, select the Page Layout tab on the Ribbon and click Themes in the Themes group (see Figure 4-1).

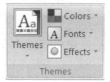

Figure 4-1. Click Themes to open the gallery showing the available Office themes.

Select the theme that you want to apply to your document by clicking it. If you cannot find the theme that you want in the gallery, click Browse for Themes to search for it on your computer or network. To search for a document theme on Microsoft Office Online, click More Themes on Microsoft Office Online. A browser window will open at the Microsoft Office Online website where you can download new themes.

Customizing a Document Theme

If none of the predefined document themes are suitable for your needs, you can create your own theme by customizing aspects of an existing theme. To create a custom document theme, you need to start by altering the colors, fonts, or effects that are used. Once you have finished changing the formatting elements that you want to customize, you can then save the settings collectively as your own custom document theme.

In each group of theme colors there are four text and background colors, six accent colors, and two hyperlink colors. To change any or all of these, use the following steps:

1. On the Page Layout tab, click Colors in the Themes group (see Figure 4-1). (If you have reduced the size of the window, click the Theme Colors icon.) The names of all the predefined sets of theme colors will be displayed. The colors that are displayed next to the name of each set of theme colors are the accent and hyperlink colors for that theme.

2. Click Create New Theme Colors. The Create New Theme Colors dialog box will open (see Figure 4-2).

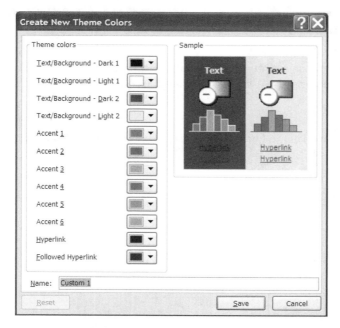

Figure 4-2. Click a theme color element to change the selected color for that element.

3. Under Theme colors, click the button for the theme color element that you want to change.

4. Select a new color for the theme element. The display in the Sample area will update to reflect your changes.

5. Continue changing elements of the theme colors until you are satisfied with the range of selected colors.

6. Enter a name for your custom theme colors in the Name box and click the Save button when you have finished. Your new theme will be listed under Custom when you click Colors in the Themes group.

> **TIP** You can cancel all your changes and revert to the preset colors by clicking the Reset button before you click Save.

Each theme fonts set contains a heading font and a body text font. To change either or both of these, do the following:

1. On the Page Layout tab, click Fonts in the Themes group (see Figure 4-2). (If you have reduced the size of the window, click the Theme Fonts icon.) The various theme fonts will be displayed indicating the names of the heading font and the body text font.

> **TIP** Move the mouse pointer over any of the theme fonts to see the name; the data on your worksheet will be displayed using the theme fonts you are pointing at.

2. Click Create New Theme Fonts. The Create New Theme Fonts dialog box will open (see Figure 4-3).

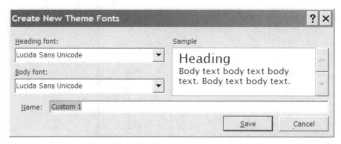

Figure 4-3. The Create New Theme Fonts dialog box

3. Select a Heading font and/or a Body font using the dropdown lists. The display in the Sample area will update to reflect your changes.

4. Enter a name for your custom theme fonts in the Name box and click the Save button when you have finished. Your new theme fonts will be listed under Custom when you click Fonts or the Theme Fonts icon in the Themes group.

Theme effects include specifications for items like lines, fill effects, SmartArt, and shapes. Although you can't create customized theme effects, you can select which set to use with your document theme. To do this, click Effects in the Themes group (see Figure 4-2). (If you have reduced the size of the window, click the Theme Effects icon.) The names of all the predefined sets of theme effects will be displayed along with an illustration representing the style of each group of theme effects. Click the theme effect that you want to use.

When you have finished making changes to the theme colors, fonts, and effects, you can save your settings as a new document theme that can be applied to other documents in the future. To do this, select the Page Layout tab on the Ribbon and click Themes in the Themes group. Select Save Current Theme to open the Save Current Theme dialog box. Enter a name for your theme in the File name box and click Save. Your custom document theme will be saved to the Document Themes folder and will appear under Custom when you click Themes in the Themes group.

Cell Styles

Cell styles are used to apply predefined characteristics like font, border, and shading styles to selected cells, thus allowing you to quickly and consistently format your data. You can use predefined cell styles to instantly highlight selected cells—for example, to identify the cells that require user input or that contain the results. Excel 2007 has a range of coordinated styles that can be used as they are or modified to suit your own tastes or corporate colors. The built-in cell styles are dependent on the current document theme and are arranged into categories, including Themed, Titles and Headings, and Data and Model. If you are feeling particularly creative, you can even design your own styles entirely.

Applying a Cell Style

To apply a cell style to the selected cell(s), click the Home tab on the Ribbon and select Cell Styles from the Styles group. The Cell Styles gallery will open (see Figure 4-4).

Figure 4-4. Select a cell style from the gallery to apply it to the selected cells.

As you move the mouse pointer over a style in the gallery, the selected cell(s) will take on the style's attributes, allowing you to preview the style with your data. Apply the style that you want by clicking it.

Modifying a Cell Style

Not entirely happy with a cell style? You can tweak a predefined style by adapting the individual attributes of it, like the color or font style. The new settings will then be applied to all cells already formatted to that style in the current workbook. To modify a cell style, follow these steps:

1. Select Cell Styles from the Styles group on the Home tab of the Ribbon.
2. Right-click the style that you wish to change and select Modify. The Style dialog box will open (see Figure 4-5).

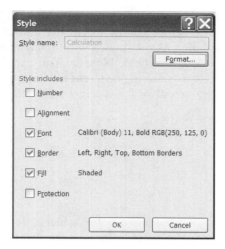

Figure 4-5. Use the Style dialog box to select the formatting attributes that you want to be included in the new style.

3. Click the Format button and use the tabs of the Format Cells dialog box to alter the various settings for the style.

4. When you have finished choosing the format settings, click OK.

5. Select or deselect the checkboxes in the Style dialog box to specify the formatting attributes that are to be included in the style.

6. Click OK when you have finished.

Creating a Custom Cell Style

Rather than adapting an existing style, you may want to create an entirely new cell style. If none of the built-in cell styles are suitable for your needs, you can create a custom style as follows:

1. Select Cell Styles from the Styles group on the Home tab of the Ribbon.

2. Click New Cell Style. The Style dialog box will open with a name for the new style in the Style name box—for example, Style 1.

3. If you want to change the name of the style, enter the new name in the Style name box.

4. Click the Format button and use the tabs of the Format Cells dialog box to alter the various settings for the style.

5. When you have finished choosing the format settings, click OK.

6. Select or deselect the checkboxes in the Style dialog box to specify the formatting attributes that are to be included in the style.

7. Click OK when you have finished. New cell styles will be listed under the heading Custom in the Cell Style gallery.

If you want to customize an existing style without overriding the original style, you need to create a duplicate of the style before you modify it by right-clicking the style and selecting Duplicate. The Style dialog box will open with a new name for the duplicate style in the Style name box—for example, Note 2. You can then click the Format button and customize the style by selecting different formatting attributes as described earlier. Any duplicate cell styles will be listed under the heading Custom in the Cell Style gallery.

Table Styles

Excel 2007 provides you with a range of predefined color schemes to enable the speedy formatting of tables. These work in a similar fashion to the AutoFormat feature in previous versions but with enhanced styles and options. These table quick styles, as they are sometimes referred to, can be adjusted to include header and total rows as well as special formatting for first and last columns, or to display banded rows or columns. If you have very specific formatting needs, you can even create and apply customized table styles.

Applying a Table Style

Once you have entered data in rows and columns, you can format it as a table and incorporate elements like header and total rows. Excel has 60 predefined table styles arranged under the headings Light, Medium, and Dark.

1. Click within (or select) the cells you want to format as a table.

2. Select Format as Table from the Styles group on the Home tab of the Ribbon to view the gallery of table styles (see Figure 4-6).

3. Choose a table style from the gallery for your table by clicking a style. The Format as Table dialog box will appear.

4. Enter the correct cell range in the "Where is the data for your table?" box (if Excel's guess is incorrect) and select the "My table has headers" option if appropriate.

5. Click OK to apply the table style to your data. This will display Table Tools on the Ribbon and add a Design tab (see Figure 4-7).

6. Use the Table Style Options group on the Design tab to select or deselect particular formatting features for your table. If you select Header Row, the header row will be displayed with special formatting. If you select Total Row, a total row will be added to the bottom of the table. Selecting the First Column or Last Column option will apply special formatting to the appropriate column and selecting Banded Rows or Banded Columns will format even rows or columns differently from odd rows or columns to make the table easier to read, provided you have selected a table style that accommodates this.

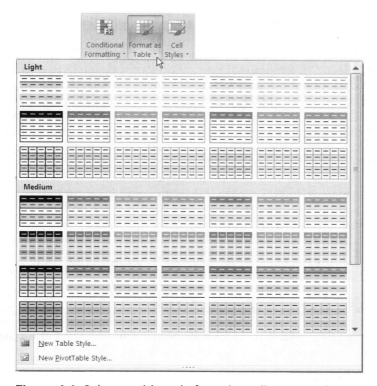

Figure 4-6. Select a table style from the gallery to apply it to the selected cells.

Figure 4-7. Use the Design tab in Table Tools to alter features of your table.

To set a particular table quick style as the default for the current workbook, right-click the style in the gallery and select Set As Default. If you have already applied some formatting to your data before applying a table quick style, you can opt to maintain or to clear this formatting when you apply the table style. Instead of clicking with the left mouse button to select the style, right-click the style and select Apply and Clear Formatting to remove any previous formatting or select Apply (and Maintain Formatting) to preserve the original formatting.

Changing or Removing a Table Style

Once you have formatted a range as a table, you can change the table style by selecting a different style from the Design tab. First, click within the table to select it and choose a different style from the Table Styles group on the Design tab (see Figure 4-7) and then click the up and down arrows to the right of the Table Styles group to scroll through the Table Styles gallery. Click the More arrow button at the bottom-right corner of the Table Styles group to open the Table Styles gallery and view all the available styles. If the Excel window is reduced in size, the table styles can be accessed by clicking Quick Styles in the Table Styles group.

As you move the mouse pointer over a table style, the formatting will be applied to your table, allowing you to preview the style with your actual data. The name of the style will also appear beside the style as a ToolTip. Click the style that you want to apply or click None to remove the formatting from your table.

> **NOTE** The other features of Excel tables will be discussed in Chapter 6.

Creating a Custom Table Style

It is possible to design your own table quick style, which can then be set as the default table style for your document. To create a custom table style, do the following:

1. On the Home tab, select Format as Table from the Styles group.
2. Select New Table Style to open the New Table Quick Style dialog box.
3. Enter a name for your new table style in the Name box.
4. Select an element of your table style that you want to format from the Table Element list and click the Format button.
5. Use the Font, Border, and Fill tabs of the Format Cells dialog box to specify the font settings for that element of your new table style. Click OK when you have finished choosing settings for that element.
6. Continue selecting Font, Border, and Fill settings for each table element that you wish to format.
7. If you want to make your new table style the default style for any new tables you insert in the current document, select the "Set as default table quick style for this document" checkbox in the New Table Quick Style dialog box.
8. Click OK when you have finished.

> **NOTE** Any table styles that you create will be displayed under Custom in the Table Styles gallery.

If you like certain elements of an existing table style but not others, you can use the existing style to base a custom table style on; however, you must create a duplicate first by right-clicking the table style that you want to base your custom style on and selecting Duplicate. The Modify Table Quick Style dialog box (which is similar to the New Table Quick Style dialog box) will open. You can then specify formatting attributes for each element of the table style as described earlier. To remove the existing formatting for an element, select the element and click the Clear button.

Manually Formatting Worksheets

If you prefer to format your worksheet in the traditional way, the Home tab on the Ribbon contains most of the commonly used formatting commands that were previously available on the Formatting toolbar (see Figure 4-8). These buttons and dropdown lists are combined into related groups and allow you to apply a combination of formatting effects to the selected cells or their contents.

Figure 4-8. The Font, Alignment, and Number groups on the Home tab

The Font group includes the familiar Font and Font Size dropdown lists for changing the font or size of the selected characters, or you can use the Increase Font Size or Decrease Font Size button to incrementally change the size of the font. The Bold, Italics, and Underline commands are also in this group, and the Double Underline command can be easily accessed by clicking the down arrow to the right of the Underline button. You can click the dropdown arrow beside the Borders button to reveal various options for applying borders to the selected cell or range. Dropdown controls are also there to facilitate the selection of a fill color for cells or a font color for cell contents.

The Alignment group allows you to quickly change the vertical or horizontal alignment of text within cells, and clicking the Orientation button will reveal options for the direction of the text—for example, you may want to display text diagonally or vertically. The Decrease Indent and Increase Indent buttons are located here, along with the Wrap Text command, which enables you to wrap text within the cell so that it is displayed on more than one line. The Merge and Center command is also in this group, allowing you to merge selected cells and center the contents in the new, merged cell (a popular feature for headings). Clicking the down arrow to the right of the Merge and Center button will reveal a menu with other options.

The Number group on the Home tab houses the formatting options specific to numerical data. Clicking the down arrow for the Number Format dropdown menu will allow you to choose from the various built-in number formats available (these are explained in the next section). The Accounting Number Format button will display values using the default currency format, or you can click the down arrow to select another currency. Use the Percent Style button to display the value as a percentage or the Comma Style button to include a thousands separator. Finally, the Increase Decimal and Decrease Decimal buttons will allow you to quickly change the number of decimal places that the selected cells display.

If you cannot find the formatting option you require on the Home tab, clicking the Dialog Box Launcher in the Font, Alignment, or Number group will open the Format Cells dialog box, allowing you to access further options. The Format Cells dialog box contains tabs for Number, Alignment, Font, Border, Fill, and Protection where you can access most available formatting options for numbers, fonts, and cells.

While having the main formatting commands available together on the Home tab of the Ribbon makes them easy to locate, it can be inconvenient if you wish to format text as you are working with the other tabs. To avoid having to switch back to the Home tab each time you want to make formatting changes, Office 2007 has introduced the Mini toolbar, which appears when you select data within a cell (see Figure 4-9).

Figure 4-9. The Mini toolbar appears
when you select data in a cell.

The Mini toolbar provides instant access to a few popular formatting options, allowing you to quickly format the selected text regardless of the current tab displayed on the Ribbon. To display the Mini toolbar, double-click a cell containing data to switch to edit mode and then select the data that you want to format by clicking and dragging over it with the mouse (or select the data in the formula bar). The Mini toolbar will appear very faintly at first, but will become clearer as you move the mouse pointer over it. If you prefer not to see the Mini toolbar when you select data in a cell, deselect the "Show Mini Toolbar on selection" option in the Popular category of Excel Options.

Formatting Numbers

When it comes to numerical data, accuracy is extremely important, not just in how the data is entered but also in how it is displayed. The way a number is formatted can influence its meaning and how it is interpreted by others viewing the data. Excel lets you apply a wide range of formats to numerical data to reflect the various types of numerical data that spreadsheets are used to analyze. For example, if a number refers to a monetary amount, you will probably wish to display it to two decimal places and with a currency symbol, or you may prefer dates to be displayed in a long format rather than a short format. Excel provides us with built-in number formats, such as Currency, Percentage, Short Date, or Long Date, that can be applied by clicking the down arrow in the Number Format box in the Number group of the Home tab (see Figure 4-10). You can change the formatting of the numbers in the selected cells by choosing a number format from the menu, using the example provided below each format as a guide to how the number will appear.

Figure 4-10. Number formats

Changing the format of a number will not alter its value but only how it is displayed in the cell. Table 4-1 explains the purpose of each of the predefined number formats and illustrates how the value 1234.5 would be displayed by each.

Table 4-1. Number Formats

Number Format	Description
General	This is the default number format and normally displays the number the way it is typed or using scientific notation for numbers with more than 12 digits, e.g., 1234.5.
Number	This format allows you to control how negative numbers are displayed, to specify the number of decimal places, and to include a thousands separator, e.g., 1234.50.

Continued

Table 4-1. *Continued*

Number Format	Description
Currency	Use this format for monetary values and to display the default currency symbol. You can also control how negative numbers are displayed, specify the number of decimal places, and indicate whether you want to use a thousands separator, e.g., $1234.50.
Accounting	This format is similar to Currency but it also aligns currency symbols and decimal points in a column, e.g., $1234.50.
Short Date	Use this format to interpret the value as a date and time serial number and display the date value in digits, e.g., 5/18/1903.
Long Date	Use this format to interpret the value as a date and time serial number and display the date value with the day and month in words, e.g., Monday, May 18, 1903.
Time	Use this format to interpret the value as a date and time serial number and display the time value, e.g., 12:00:00 PM.
Percentage	This format multiplies the value by 100, displays a percent sign, and allows you to specify the number of decimal places, e.g., 12350.00%.
Fraction	This format displays the value as a fraction, e.g., 1234 1/2.
Scientific	Use this format to display the value in scientific (exponential) notation using the specified number of decimal places, e.g., 1.23E+03 (1.23 times 10 to the third power).
Text	Use this format to display the number as text, exactly as you typed it, e.g., 1234.5.

If none of the listed number formats are suitable, select More Number Formats to open the Format Cells dialog box at the Number tab (see Figure 4-11). Here you change attributes for some of the formats, like the number of decimal places, the type of fraction, or the currency symbol used. You can also select one of the formats available in the Special category, like Zip Code, Social Security Number, or Phone Number. If you are still unable to find an appropriate format, you can select the Custom category and create your own, as described in the next section.

> **TIP** Changing how a number is formatted will not generally affect its actual value. If you want to permanently change all the values in a worksheet to their displayed values, go to the Advanced category of Excel Options and select "Set precision as displayed" in the "When calculating this workbook" section. You will be asked to confirm the change. Once you click OK, all the values will be irreversibly changed to the displayed values.

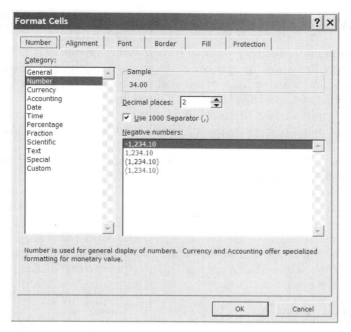

Figure 4-11. The Number tab in the Format Cells dialog box

Custom Number and Date Formats

If Excel's built-in number and date formats don't cover all your requirements, you can create your own custom number or date format. For example, you may need to display numerical data with a set number of significant digits or lead zeros, or you may want the decimal point to align down a column of numbers regardless of the number of decimals. If you are entering a date, you may want to include the day of the week at the end or use a different symbol to separate the parts of the date. The Custom category in the Number tab of the Format Cells dialog box allows you to design your own formats using varying combinations of format codes.

Creating Custom Number Formats

By creating a custom number format, you can have greater control over how your numerical data appears, including the number of decimal places, the number of lead zeros, symbols, colors, and the alignment of decimal points. This can be particularly useful if you are entering, say, customer identification numbers or telephone numbers, or if you want to add units of measurement, like kg or cm. You can create between 200 and 250 custom number formats depending on the language version of Excel that has been installed.

Excel custom number formats use a combination of symbols to represent the formatted digits. Separate formats can be specified for positive numbers, negative numbers, zero values, and text, in that order, with each section being separated by a semicolon. If no format is specified for zero values, they will be formatted in the same way as positive values. If no format is specified for text, entered text will not be affected by the format. For example, the following number format will display positive values in green, with a thousands separator, and to one decimal place; negative values in red, with a minus sign and a thousands separator, and to two decimal places; zeros in blue; and text in cyan:

```
[Green]#,##0.0;[Red]-#,##0.00;[Blue];[Cyan]
```

To create a custom number format to control how a number is displayed, use the following procedure:

1. Select the cells containing the numerical data that you wish to format.

2. From the Home tab of the Ribbon, click the Dialog Box Launcher in the bottom-right corner of the Number group. The Format Cells dialog box will open.

3. Make sure that the Number tab is selected and choose the Custom category. The existing format codes are displayed in the Type list (see Figure 4-12). These format codes can be used as they are or they can be modified to suit your own requirements.

Figure 4-12. To create a custom number format, enter a number format code or modify an existing code.

4. To use an existing format code, click the code in the Type list to select it. In the Sample box you will see how your data will appear using the selected code.

5. To modify an existing format, click it and adjust it in the Type box by adding or removing format codes as necessary.

6. To create your own format code, delete the contents of the Type box and enter the new code. Make sure you separate each section of the format with a semicolon (;). The Sample box will provide an indication of how the formatted data will appear.

7. When you have finished, click OK to close the Format Cells dialog box.

Table 4-2 describes the function of the various symbols that are used in number formats and shows examples of how the formatted data would appear.

Table 4-2. Custom Number Format Codes

Symbol	Description	Format Code	Cell Contents	Result
0	Displays insignificant zeros if there are fewer digits in the number than zeros in the format.	0.00 00.0	1 .123	1.00 00.1
#	Displays only significant digits, not insignificant zeros.	#,###.# #.##	1,234.56 .103	1,234.6 .1
?	Adds spaces at the end so that decimal points will line up.	0.??	21.5 12.54	21.5 12.54 (with aligned decimals)
/	Displays a number as a fraction.	# ???/???	1.0125 2.375	1 1/80 2 3/8 (with aligned fractions)
, (comma)	Displays the thousands separator (,) or scales a number by a multiple of one thousand.	#,### #, #,, #.#,	1234567	1,234,567 1,235 1 1234.6
$, £, +, /, (,), :, ^, &, ', ~, {}, <, >, =, !, space	Inserts that symbol in the number at the same position as in the number format.	$#,##0.00 ##~##	1234 123	$1,234.00 1~23
%	Makes the number a percentage.	0.00%	0.25	25.00%
E-, E+, e-, e+	Displays the number in scientific format using exponent codes. E- or e- will insert a – sign for negative exponents but will not insert a sign for positive exponents. E+ or e+ will insert the appropriate sign for both positive and negative exponents.	0.0E+0 0.00E+00 0.00E+0 0.00E-0 0.00E-00	1234567 -123456 -0.00123 12345678 0.012345	1.2E+6 -1.23E+05 -1.23E-3 1.23E7 1.23E-02

Symbol	Description	Format Code	Cell Contents	Result
" "	Includes the text entered between the quotes in the number format.	$0.00 " Over"; $-0.00 " Under"	12.34 -12.34	$12.34 Over $-12.34 Under
\	Used to insert single characters. Includes the character following the backslash in the number format.	\b0.00	12.34	b12.34
@	Displays any text entered into a formatted cell – if @ is omitted any text within the cells will not be displayed.	0;-0.0;"Nil";"Text " @ 0;-0.0;"Nil";"Text"	Unknown Unknown	Text Unknown Text
_ (underscore)	Inserts a space the width of the character following it. Usually used to line up positive and negative numbers.	0.00_);(0.00)	12.01 -12.01	12.01 (12.01) A space the same width as) will be inserted after the positive numbers
*	Repeats the next character as many times as required to fill the column width.	*0#,##0	12345	000000012,345
[Black], [Blue], [Cyan], [Green], [Magenta], [Red], [White], [Yellow]	Displays the section of the format in the specified color.	[Black];[Red];[Blue]; [Green]		Will display positive numbers in black, negative numbers in red, zeros in blue, and text in green.

NOTE You can also apply conditions to a format by enclosing the condition in square brackets. For example, [Green][<=50]; [Red][>50] will display numbers less than or equal to 50 in a green font and numbers greater than 50 in a red font.

Creating Custom Date and Time Formats

As dates and times are stored as numbers in Excel, they can be formatted in a similar way to numerical data. Excel has several existing formats for dates and times, or you can create custom formats to display them in the manner you require, using separate codes to display the day, month, year, hours, minutes, and seconds. For example, the following custom format will display May 7, 2007, as May 07, 2007 (Monday): mmm dd, yyy (dddd).

To create your own custom date format to display dates or times in a specific manner, use the following steps:

1. Select the cells containing the dates or times that you wish to format.
2. From the Home tab of the Ribbon, click the Dialog Box Launcher in the Number group. The Format Cells dialog box will open.
3. Make sure the Number tab is selected and choose the Custom category. Scroll through the existing format codes displayed in the Type list to see the codes that apply to dates and times. You can use these format codes as they are, or you can modify them to suit your own requirements.
4. To use an existing format code, click it to select it. In the Sample box you will see how your date or time will appear using the selected code.
5. To modify an existing format, click it and adjust it in the Type box by adding or removing format codes as necessary.
6. To create your own custom date or time format, delete the contents of the Type box and enter the new code. The Sample box will provide an indication of how the formatted date or time will appear.
7. When you have finished, click OK to close the Format Cells dialog box.

Table 4-3 describes the function of the various symbols that are used in date and time formats and shows examples of how the formatted data would appear.

Table 4-3. Custom Date and Time Formats

To Display . . .	Format Code	Result
Months	m mm mmm mmmm	1–12 01–12 Jan–Dec January–December
Day	d dd ddd dddd	1–31 01–31 Sun–Sat Sunday–Saturday
Year	yy yyyy	00–99 1900–9999
Hours	h hh	0–23 00–23
Minutes	m mm	0–59 00–59
Seconds	s ss	0–59 00–59
AM/PM	h AM/PM h:mm AM/PM h:mm:ss A/P h:mm:ss.00	1 AM 2:34 PM 5:59:12 A 3:45:56.75
Elapsed time	[h]::mm [mm]:ss [ss].00	1:23 (hours and minutes) 67:09 (minutes and seconds) 8901.23 (seconds and hundredths)

NOTE To display minutes, the m or mm code must appear immediately after an hour code or immediately before a seconds code; otherwise, it will be displayed as a month.

Deleting a Custom Number or Date Format

If you no longer have any use for a custom format that you have created, you can delete it; however, you cannot delete any of the predefined custom formats that were installed with Excel. When you delete a custom format, any cells formatted with it will revert to the General number format. To remove an obsolete custom format, click the Dialog Box Launcher in the Number group to open the Format Cells dialog box. Make sure that the Number tab is selected and choose the Custom category. Scroll through the custom format codes in the Type list until you find the code that you wish to delete. Click the custom format to select it and then click the Delete button to remove the custom format. Click OK to close the Format Cells dialog box.

Conditional Formatting

Conditional formatting allows you to communicate meaning with your data by emphasizing cells that meet certain conditions or fall within particular ranges. To achieve this, you use specified color formats or one of Excel 2007's new features: color scales, icon sets, or data bars. Conditional formatting works by evaluating the contents of a cell or a range using specified criteria; if the cell or range meets the criteria, it will adopt the formatting defined. For example, you can allocate different colors to different value ranges or display a particular icon depending on whether a cell's value is above or below a set threshold. Data bars can be used to indicate the value of a cell in relation to other cells—the longer the bar, the higher the value of the cell.

Unlike manual formatting, conditional formatting is dynamic and will update to take into account changes to the contents of a cell. Once you apply a conditional format to a range of cells, any alteration to your data that changes which cells satisfy the condition will result in automatic changes in the formatting to reflect this. In addition, the conditional formats, including color scales, data bars, and icon sets, are all customizable, allowing you to create your own rules and set your own formats. The overall result is the ability to quickly produce sophisticated-looking worksheets that can convey a certain degree of significance with the data.

> **TIP** If you copy and paste, fill, or copy formatting using the Format Painter from cells that have conditional formats applied to them, the conditional format rules will be applied to the destination cells as well.

Highlight Cells Rules

Highlight Cells Rules is probably the simplest type of conditional formatting and basically involves formatting cells that satisfy the specified condition in a defined way. This is an effective way of attracting attention to values that are, for example, within a particular range, or to indicate cells that contain a given text string. There are various types of value-based highlight rules that you can create, including

- Greater Than
- Less Than
- Between
- Equal To
- Text That Contains
- A Date Occurring
- Duplicate Values

The first five rules all work in a similar manner and allow you to compare the contents of a cell with an entered value or text string, the contents of another cell, or the result of a formula.

If the data that you want to evaluate is composed of dates, you can use A Date Occurring to create a condition using dynamic ranges like Yesterday, This Week, or Next Month. For example, you could use this rule to highlight contracts that will expire next week. Each week the records that satisfy this condition will vary and consequently the formatting will change each week. This ensures that your conditional format is always current and removes the need to update it regularly. If you want to create static conditions that compare cells with specified dates, use one of the first four rules instead.

The Duplicate Values rule can be used to quickly highlight cells that are either duplicated or unique. This can be useful for validating your data entry and identifying duplicated records or exclusive values.

To use any of these rules, follow these steps:

1. Select the cells that you want to evaluate.

2. Click Conditional Formatting in the Styles group of the Home tab.

3. Point to Highlight Cells Rules and select Greater Than, Less Than, Between, Equal To, Text That Contains, A Date Occurring, or Duplicate Values from the fly-out menu that appears. The appropriate dialog box for the selected rule, similar to the one shown in Figure 4-13, will open.

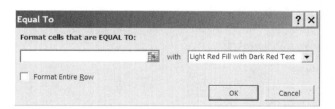

Figure 4-13. The Equal To dialog box

4. Enter the value, text, cell reference, timeframe, or formula that you want to compare the selected cell or cells with in the first box. If you have selected the Between rule, you will have to enter two values, references, or formulas. If you have selected Duplicate Values, you can choose between Duplicate or Unique. As you enter the criteria, Excel will apply the default formatting to any relevant cells in your worksheet, thus allowing you to preview the conditional format with your actual data.

5. Select a predefined format from the last dropdown list, or select Custom Format to open the Format Cells dialog box and choose your own format settings. The cells in the selected range that meet the criteria will update to show the selected formatting.

6. If you want the entire row of any cells that satisfy the condition to be formatted, check the Format Entire Row option.

7. When you have finished creating the conditional format, click OK to commit it.

Top/Bottom Rules

Top/Bottom rules allow you to format those cells that occur within the top or bottom specified number or percent. These rules enable you to identify the largest or smallest values within the data. The Top 10 Items, Top 10%, Bottom 10 Items, and Bottom 10% rules all work in a similar manner and allow you to select a top or bottom number or percentage of items to highlight. The number or percentage does not have to be 10; you can select any integer that you want. The Above Average and Below Average rules calculate the average for the selected cells and highlight any whose value is either above or below the average as appropriate (values equal to the average will not be highlighted). Use the following steps to create a conditional format based on the average or the top or bottom number or percent for the selection:

1. Select the range of cells that you want to evaluate.

2. Click Conditional Formatting in the Styles group of the Home tab.

3. Point to Top/Bottom Rules and select Top 10 Items, Top 10%, Bottom 10 Items, Bottom 10%, Above Average, or Below Average as required from the fly-out menu that appears. The appropriate dialog box, similar to the one shown in Figure 4-14, will open.

Figure 4-14. Use Top 10 Items to identify the top number that you specify.

4. If you selected Top 10 Items, Top 10%, Bottom 10 Items, or Bottom 10%, select the number or percentage of values that you want to highlight in the first box. As you select the number or percentage, Excel will apply the formatting to any relevant cells in your worksheet, thus allowing you to preview the conditional format with your actual data. If the number of cells you have selected is less than or equal to the number of items you want to format, all the selected cells will be formatted.

5. Select a predefined format from the second dropdown list, or select Custom Format to open the Format Cells dialog box and choose your own format settings. As you change the formatting, any cells within the selected range that meet the criteria will update to show the selected formatting.

6. When you have finished creating the conditional format, click OK to commit it.

Data Bars

The Data Bars feature is a new concept in Excel 2007 that enables you to conditionally format data to display a graphical representation of the value of the cell in relation to the other selected cells. The length of the colored bar provides an indication of the relative value of the cell—the longer the bar, the greater the value. The data bar for the highest value in the range will be almost as wide as the cell. The end result will resemble an integrated bar chart within the actual cells.

To add data bars to a group of cells, select the range of cells that you want to evaluate. Click Conditional Formatting in the Styles group of the Home tab, point to Data Bars and select the color for your data bars from the fly-out gallery that appears. Data bars of varying length based on the cell value will be added to each of the cells.

If you want, you can choose to show only the data bar in the cell. To do this, click Conditional Formatting in the Styles group, point to Data Bars, and select More Rules. In the New Formatting Rule dialog box, select the Show Bar Only option in the "Edit the Rule Description" area.

Color Scales and Icon Sets

Color scales are another new feature within Excel that you can use to visualize your data using color. When you apply a color scale to a range of cells, a two- or three-color gradient will be displayed within the range with the shade of the cell indicating its relative value.

To apply a color scale to a group of cells, select the range of cells that you want to evaluate. Click Conditional Formatting in the Styles group of the Home tab, point to Color Scales and select either a two-color or a three-color gradient from the fly-out gallery that appears using the images provided as a guide. The color displayed at the top of each image indicates the color that the cells containing the highest values will adopt, and the color at the bottom of the image indicates the color that the cells containing the lowest values will adopt.

Icon sets are the third new conditional formatting feature that you can employ to convey a visual interpretation with your data. Excel 2007 has a range of built-in icon sets containing three, four, or five icons that you can apply to a cell range (see Figure 4-15). Each cell will feature a particular icon depending on its value.

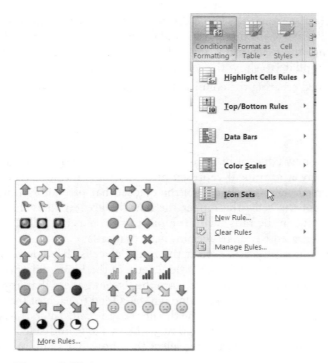

Figure 4-15. Icon sets

To use an icon set with a group of cells, select the range of cells that you want to evaluate. Click Conditional Formatting in the Styles group of the Home tab. Point to Icon Sets and select a group of icons from the fly-out gallery that appears to apply to your data. The first icon within each set indicates the color that the cells containing the highest values will adopt, and the last icon within each set indicates the color that the cells containing the lowest values will adopt.

Creating Custom Rules

If none of the predefined formatting rules are appropriate for your needs or you want to customize the colors and formats that are applied, you can create a new rule. For example, you can change the default values that are used to determine which icon to apply within a set, or you can create a rule to format those cells whose values are a specified number of standard deviations above or below the average. The options are too numerous to cover them all here, so experiment and see the effect.

1. Select the range of cells that you want to evaluate.
2. Click Conditional Formatting in the Styles group of the Home tab.
3. Select New Rule to open the New Formatting Rule dialog box (see Figure 4-16).

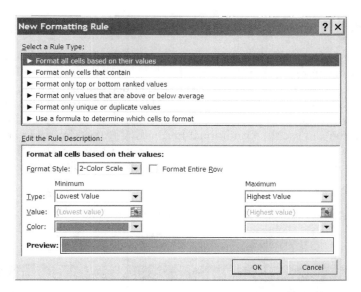

Figure 4-16. Use the New Formatting Rule dialog box to create your own conditional formatting rules and formats.

4. Select a rule type from the list available (see Figure 4-16). The Edit the Rule Description section will change to reflect your selection.

5. Enter the condition(s) for your rule and set colors or formats for the cells that meet the condition(s).

6. Look at the Preview area to see how your formatting will appear when the rule is applied.

7. When you have finished creating your new rule, click OK to apply it to the selected data.

TIP You can also open the New Formatting Rule dialog box by selecting More Rules in the fly-out menus for the other options in the Conditional Formatting menu.

Removing Conditional Formats

If you no longer want to conditionally format your data, you can remove any rules applied to it and return it to its original format. To remove conditional formats from the selected cells, sheet, table, or PivotTable, click Conditional Formatting in the Styles group of the Home tab. Point to the Clear Rules option and select the appropriate option from the fly-out menu.

Managing Conditional Formatting Rules

With all the new types of conditional formatting rules available, it is likely that the feature will become more popular than ever. The Conditional Formatting Rules Manager is a user interface that allows you to view, edit, or delete existing formatting rules and create new rules. You can also use the Rules Manager to rearrange the precedence of rules, change their scope, or apply a Stop If True condition to stop evaluation at a particular rule. You can use the Conditional Formatting Rules Manager to easily perform general housekeeping on the formatting rules you have created. To view the conditional formatting rules for a selected area or worksheet, follow these steps:

1. Click Conditional Formatting in the Styles group of the Home tab.
2. Select Manage Rules to open the Conditional Formatting Rules Manager (see Figure 4-17).

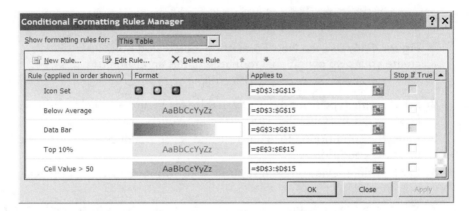

Figure 4-17. Use the Conditional Formatting Rules Manager to manage existing formatting rules and to create new rules.

3. Select the appropriate option from the "Show formatting rules for" list to display all the rules for the selected area or a particular worksheet.
4. To create a rule, click New Rule to open the New Formatting Rule dialog box.
5. To edit a rule, click it to select it and click the Edit Rule button to open the Edit Formatting Rule dialog box, which is similar to the New Formatting Rule dialog box.
6. To change the cell range that a rule is applied to, amend the entry in the Applies to box.
7. To delete a rule, click it to select it and click the Delete Rule button.

When more than one conditional formatting rule applies to a range of cells, they are evaluated in the order that they appear in the Conditional Formatting Rules Manager— that is, rules higher in the list have greater precedence than rules lower in the list.

New rules are always added to the top of the list, but you can change the order of precedence by rearranging the position of the rules using the move up and move down arrows.

When more than one rule relating to a range of cells evaluates to true, all the formatting is applied unless there is a conflict. For example, if one rule formats a cell with green font and another rule formats it in bold, both can be applied because there is no conflict: the cell will be formatted in bold and green. However, if one rule specifies a green font and another rule specifies a red font, there is a conflict. In situations like this, the rule that is higher in precedence will be applied. Conditional formatting rules will also take precedence over manual formats.

To change the precedence of a formatting rule, select the rule whose precedence you want to change (you can only select one rule at a time) and use the blue up or down arrows to change the rule's position. To stop rule evaluation at a particular rule, select the Stop If True checkbox for that rule.

5

Sorting and Filtering

T
o make the data in your spreadsheet easier to work with, you may need to display the data in a particular order or view only those records that meet specified conditions. Sorting and filtering are the most basic types of analysis carried out on data, and Excel 2007 has built on the functionality of previous versions to allow you to carry out more complex sorting and filtering. This includes revising these tools to accommodate the new sophisticated conditional formats described in Chapter 4, such as the ability to sort and filter by cell color or cell icon. Excel 2007 has also expanded the sorting and filtering features to make them more versatile, in particular making it easier to sort and filter by multiple items. This chapter will look at how you can use sorting and filtering to display the data you require, arranged in the order you want to view it. It will also introduce you to Advanced Filtering in Excel, a powerful tool that is worth understanding if you need to create more sophisticated filters to sift through your data.

Sorting Data

Sorting data in Excel using a single column is still as simple as before: place the insertion point in the column and click the Sort & Filter command (see Figure 5-1), which is now more prominently positioned in the Editing group on the Home tab of the Ribbon. You can then choose whether to sort the data in ascending or descending order. With Excel 2007, the actual commands will change depending on the type of data you are analyzing, that is, Sort Oldest to Newest or Sort Newest to Oldest for dates, Sort A to Z or Sort Z to A for text, and Sort Smallest to Largest or Sort Largest to Smallest for numerical data. Alternatively, there are Sort Ascending and Sort Descending buttons in the Sort & Filter group on the Data tab.

Figure 5-1. The commands in the Sort & Filter menu will change depending on the type of data.

> **TIP** When creating your list or table, you may want to add an extra field (for example, Record Number) where you can add consecutive numbers as you enter each new record. This will allow you to return your list to the original order the records were entered in at any stage.

To perform more complicated sorts, you need to use the Custom Sort option that is available from the Sort & Filter button. Not only does Custom Sort allow you to sort by more than one column (Excel 2007 can sort by up to 64 columns), it also allows you to sort on values, cell color, font color, or cell icon. The cell color and font color can be applied manually or by using conditional formatting (see Chapter 4). In addition to sorting in ascending or descending order, you can choose to sort your data using a different sort order by creating a custom list (see Chapter 3).

1. To sort by more than one column, click Sort & Filter on the Home tab and select Custom Sort. The Sort dialog box will open (see Figure 5-2).

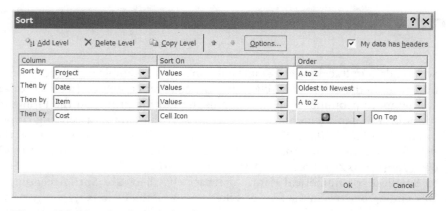

Figure 5-2. Use the Sort dialog box to create more complex sorts.

2. Select a field heading from the Sort by dropdown list.

3. From the Sort On dropdown list, select Values, Cell Color, Font Color, or Cell Icon.

4. Choose the appropriate option from the Order dropdown list. If you want to use a custom list to determine the sort order, select the Custom List option and choose the list from those available or create a new custom list.

5. Click Add Level to insert another sort level, if necessary.

6. Enter subsequent sort criteria in the rows below, adding more sort levels as required. If you want, you can click Copy Level to insert a copy of the selected level and adjust it accordingly. If you need to remove a level, select it and click Delete Level. You can also reorder the conditions using the up and down arrow buttons.

7. Click Options to open the Sort Options dialog box and specify the sort orientation (i.e., left to right or top to bottom) and whether the sort should be case sensitive.

8. When you have finished specifying all the sort conditions, click OK.

The filter buttons beside the column headings on your worksheet will indicate the sort status for each column, as shown in Figure 5-3. An up arrow indicates that the column has been sorted in ascending order, and a down arrow indicates that the column has been sorted in descending order.

Figure 5-3. Filter buttons indicate the sort status of each column.

Filtering Data

Filtering allows you to view a subset of records that satisfy specified criteria and can be used with any range of data that has column headings in its first row. By filtering records, you can make a large table of data much more manageable by temporarily hiding the data that is not relevant to your current requirements. For example, you can use filtering to view only the details of customers who live in a particular region and who have purchased a particular product.

Previous users of Excel will already be familiar with filtering using the AutoFilter tool. Excel 2007 now refers to this as Filter, although the shortened name has been more than compensated for in increased functionality. Advances include allowing multiple items to be included in the filter and more complex filtering using filter options based on the type of data in the column.

Despite the augmentation of AutoFilter, for many users it is still limited in its filtering capabilities. In this section we will also look at Advanced Filtering, which can be used to create quite complex filters using multiple criteria and criteria containing formulas. Advanced Filtering also allows you to copy the filtered list to another location, leaving the original list intact, rather than simply filtering in place.

> **TIP** If you need to filter more than one dataset on a sheet, you will need to use tables. Tables also have the advantage of remembering their own sort conditions. See Chapter 6 for more on using the new Tables feature in Excel.

Using Filter

Excel's Filter tool allows you to quickly apply filters to one or more columns to filter your data in place. To filter a list by selecting a value or values, click Sort & Filter in the Editing group of the Home tab and select Filter. Alternatively, you can click Filter in the Sort & Filter group on the Data tab. A filter arrow (dropdown arrow) will be displayed next to each field name. (If your data is formatted as a table, the filter arrows will already be visible.) Then, click the filter arrow beside the name of the first field to be used in the filter to reveal the list of values (up to 10,000 values can be displayed), as shown in Figure 5-4. Deselect the (Select All) option and select the checkboxes beside each of the items that you want to be included in the filter.

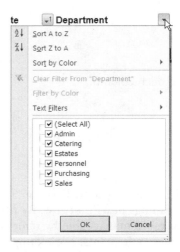

Figure 5-4. When you click a filter button, a dropdown menu appears.

When you click OK, your list will be filtered to display only those records that contain one of the selected items in that column. Check the Status bar at the bottom of the screen for a quick count of the number of records found. You can narrow your list even further by applying filters to other columns.

TIP If you copy and paste a filtered list, only the displayed records will be copied. However, if you cut and paste a filtered list, all records between the first and last records in the filtered list will be cut.

When you have applied a filter to a column, the Filter button beside the column heading will display a filter icon to indicate that the column has a filter applied. If you hover the mouse over this icon, a ToolTip will be displayed indicating the nature of the filter, as illustrated in Figure 5-5.

Figure 5-5. Hover the mouse pointer over the Filter button to see how the column has been filtered.

The dropdown list for dates allows you to group data hierarchically by year, month, and day rather than selecting from a flat list of entered dates. You can click the expand button (plus sign) beside the year to reveal the months available, and months can also be expanded to show the actual dates if necessary (see Figure 5-6). This allows you to select all records for March 7, 2006, all records for March 2006, or all records for 2006, for example.

Figure 5-6. When filtering dates, you can select days, months, or years.

> **TIP** If you want to ungroup the dates so that they appear as a flat list, click the Microsoft Office Button and click Excel Options. Select the Advanced category and, under "Display options for this workbook," select a workbook and clear the "Group dates in the AutoFilter menu" option.

Excel 2007 makes more complex and dynamic filtering much simpler by providing filtering options based on the type of data within the column being filtered (i.e., date filters, number filters, and text filters commands). You can use these filtering commands to create criteria for your filters. As already mentioned, Excel 2007 also allows you to filter by color: cell color, font color, or cell icon.

Date Filters

If the column you are filtering by contains dates, you can filter the records to various date ranges using common filters based on comparison operator commands: Equals, Before, After, or Between. Alternatively, you can choose one of the predefined dynamic filters like This Week, Last Week, This Month, Next Month, and so forth. As the dynamic filters are dependent on the current date, they may change each time they are reapplied. You can also select All Dates in the Period to choose a particular month or quarter. These filters will filter by the period regardless of the year, so they can be used to compare months or quarters across several years.

1. To apply a filter to a list of dates, click the filter arrow beside the column heading and select Date Filters. A fly-out menu of date filters will appear (see Figure 5-7).

Figure 5-7. Select a date to filter by or use one of the dynamic date filters.

2. Select one of the predefined date commands to filter for that date range, or click one of the comparison commands (Equals, Before, After, Between) or Custom Filter to open the Custom AutoFilter dialog box (see Figure 5-8).

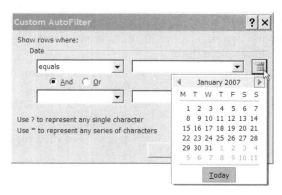

Figure 5-8. Use the Custom AutoFilter dialog box to create customized filters.

3. If you selected a comparison command, the appropriate comparison operator will be in the box on the left in the Custom AutoFilter dialog box. If you selected Custom Filter, choose the required operator by clicking the dropdown arrow in the box on the left.

4. Choose a value from the box on the right. For dates, you can click the Date Picker icon to the right of the box to display a calendar.

5. If you want, you can filter by a second criterion by using the second row of boxes. Select And if both criteria must be true, or select Or if either criterion must be true. Click OK when you have finished to apply the filter.

TIP To filter by the day of the week regardless of date (for example, to display all records for Wednesday), format the date to display the day of the week and use the TEXT function to convert the cells to text. You can then use a Text Filter to select the day.

Text and Number Filters

For textual data, comparison conditions that can be applied include Begins With, Ends With, Contains, and Does Not Contain. For numerical data, you can select comparison filtering options like Smaller Than, Larger Than, Between, Above Average, and Below Average. The Top 10 option allows you to enter a number (it doesn't have to be 10!) and display its equivalent Top or Bottom items or Top or Bottom percent within a field.

If none of the available options are suitable, there is also a Custom Filter option to enable you to enter up to two criteria joined by either an And or an Or. To apply one of the text or number filters, or a custom filter, to a column, do the following:

1. Click the filter arrow beside the column heading and select Text Filters or Number Filters as appropriate.

2. Select one of the comparison commands or Custom Filter from the fly-out menu to open the Custom AutoFilter dialog box.

3. If you selected a comparison command, the appropriate comparison operator will be in the box on the left in the Custom AutoFilter dialog box. If you selected Custom Filter, choose the required operator by clicking the dropdown arrow.

4. Enter the text or number that you want to use in the filter in the box on the right (or select an entry from the list).

> **TIP** Use wildcard characters to search for text that shares some characters but not others. Use a ? to replace a single character or an * to replace more than one character. For example, Sm?th will find Smith and Smyth; J*n will find John, Jean, Jon, etc.

5. Add a second criterion to the row below if required, joining the two criteria with either And or Or. When you have finished, click OK to apply the filter.

> **CAUTION** Avoid mixing data types within a column as only one type of filter command is available for each column. If a column does contain different data types—for example, 10 cells contain text and 12 cells contain numbers—the command that will be displayed will be for the data type that occurs most frequently (in this case, Number Filters). If the cells are divided equally between data types—for example, 10 cells contain text and 10 cells contain numbers—the Text Filters command will be displayed. If the column contains an equal split between numbers and dates, the Number Filters command will be displayed.

Filter by Selection

You can quickly filter a list using the value, color, font color, or icon of the selected cell as the criterion. Filter by Selection allows you to display those records whose corresponding cell matches the chosen attribute of the selected cell. To filter a column by selection, right-click the cell whose value, color, font color, or icon you wish to use to create a filter. Then, point to Filter on the menu that appears and select the appropriate option from the context menu, as shown in Figure 5-9.

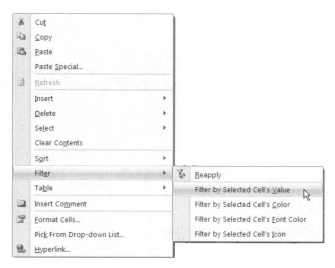

Figure 5-9. Filter by Selection

Reapplying and Clearing Filters

Data in spreadsheets often does not remain static. If you need to reapply a filter—for example, if you add records to a table—simply do one of the following:

- Right-click any cell in the filtered list, point to Filter in the menu that appears, and select Reapply.
- Select the Home tab and, in the Editing group, click Sort & Filter and choose Reapply from the list that appears.
- Select the Data tab and, in the Sort & Filter group, click Reapply.

When clearing filters from your data, you can remove the filter applied to a particular column or you can remove all the filters applied to the data range. To remove the sort state and filter from the current data range, do either of the following:

- Select the Home tab and, in the Editing group, click Sort & Filter and choose Clear from the list that appears.
- Select the Data tab and, in the Sort & Filter group, click Clear.

If you just want to remove the filter for a particular column without removing the sort order, click the filter arrow on the column heading and select Clear Filter from "Field Name". Only the filter applied to the current column will be cleared; any other filters on the data range and any sort states will remain intact.

Advanced Filtering

The Advanced Filter command allows you to create more complex queries to filter your data. You will now find Advanced Filter in the Sort & Filter group on the Data tab (see Figure 5-10). The functionality of Advanced Filtering remains basically the same as in Excel 2003.

Figure 5-10. The Sort & Filter group on the Data tab

For an advanced filter, you need to have an area in your worksheet (usually directly above the data) where you can specify the criteria for your filter. Excel will use this criteria range as the source for the advanced filter criteria. To create the criteria range, insert at least three rows above the data range and enter at least one column heading in the top row. There should be at least one blank row between the criteria range and the data range. You can use multiple criteria in an advanced filter: entering criteria on the same row is like using the Boolean AND operator; entering criteria on separate rows is like using the Boolean OR.

The following steps describe how to use an advanced filter with a list in Excel 2007:

1. Make sure that no filters are currently applied to the worksheet.

2. Insert four blank rows above the data range.

3. Copy the first row of your data range, containing the field names, and paste it to the top row of your criteria range. This is where you will enter criteria for any of the fields.

> **CAUTION** Do not create your criteria in the same rows as any of your data as these rows may be hidden when the filter is applied.

4. Enter the criteria below the appropriate column heading(s) in the criteria range as illustrated in Figure 5-11.

	A	B	C	D	E
1	Date	Department	Project	Item	Cost
2		Sales			>50
3		Personnel			>40
4					
5	Date	Department	Project	Item	Cost
6	2/1/2006	Catering	DA1	Coffee	$ 8.75
7	2/2/2006	Catering	DA1	Coffee	$ 4.50

Figure 5-11. Enter the criteria below the appropriate heading(s) in the criteria range. This example will return those records where the Department is Sales and the Cost is greater than 50 OR where the Department is Personnel and the Cost is greater than 40.

5. Click any cell within the list range (not the criteria range) and select Advanced from the Sort & Filter group on the Data tab. The Advanced Filter dialog box will open with the references for the List range (i.e., the dataset) already entered (see Figure 5-12).

Figure 5-12. Enter the cell references for your list range and criteria range in the Advanced Filter dialog box.

6. In the Criteria range box, enter the reference for the range where you have entered the filter criteria (A1:E3 in our example).

7. Choose "Filter the list, in-place" or "Copy to another location". If you select another location, enter the reference of the cell where you want the filtered list to start in the Copy to box or click in the Copy to box and click the cell. When copying a filtered list to another location, make sure that you won't accidentally overwrite any data!

> **TIP** If you name your criteria range Criteria, your data range Database, and the area where you want to paste the filtered list Extract, these ranges will appear automatically in the appropriate boxes in the Advanced Filter dialog box.

8. If you want only unique records returned, select the "Unique records only" option. Click OK to apply the filter.

If you are copying the filtered rows to another location, you can specify which columns to include in the filtered list. To do this, copy the column labels that you want included to the first row of the area where you want the filtered list to appear. When you carry out the filter, enter the reference to the copied column labels in the Copy to box and only the columns for which you copied the labels will be pasted.

Entering Advanced Criteria

To enter multiple criteria for one column, enter each criterion in a separate row below the column heading, as shown here. The filter shown is entered on two rows and will return all the records that contain Production **or** Marketing in the Department column.

Project Name	Department	Start Date
	Production	
	Marketing	

To enter multiple criteria in different columns where all the criteria must be met, enter all the criteria on the same row, as shown here. The filter shown will display those records with Production in the Department column and a Start Date greater than 01/01/2007.

Project Name	Department	Start Date
	Production	>01/01/2007

To enter multiple criteria in different columns where any of the criteria must be met, enter the criteria on separate rows. The filter shown will return those records that have Production in the Department column or a Start Date greater than 01/01/2007.

Project Name	Department	Start Date
	Production	
		>01/01/2007

To search for records that contain Production in the Department column and a Start Date before 01/01/2007 OR records that contain Sales in the Department column and a Start Date after 01/01/2007, the criteria would be entered as shown.

Project Name	Department	Start Date
	Production	<01/01/2007
	Marketing	>01/01/2007

If you wish to enter multiple criteria for the same column, you can add another column heading so that records must meet both conditions, as shown here. This filter will return those records where the Start Date is greater than 01/01/2006 and less than 01/01/2007.

Project Name	Department	Start Date	Start Date
		>01/01/2006	<01/01/2007

> **NOTE** When entering the criteria range in the Advanced Filter dialog box, make sure you include all the rows containing criteria but do not include any blank rows or the filter will not work correctly.

When entering criteria for numerical data you can use any of the comparison operators: = (equal to), <> (not equal to), < (less than), > (greater than), <= (less than or equal to), and >= (greater than or equal to). You can also use the equal to and the not equal to comparison operators with text. Table 5-1 lists examples of text criteria that can be entered into an advanced filter.

Table 5-1. Text Criteria for Advanced Filters

Entering This Criteria . . .	Will Select Records That . . .
A	Start with the character A
Brown	Start with the word Brown
="=C" '=C	Only contain the character C
="=David" '=David	Only contain the text David
="=e?f" '=e?f	Contain text that begins with e, has one other character, and then the letter f (may be more than three characters long)
="=g*h" '=g*h	Contain text that begins with g, has one or more other characters, and then the letter h
=	Contain a blank
<>	Contain any nonblank entry
<>J*	Contain any text except text that begins with J
<>*k	Contain any text except text that ends with k
'=???	Contain exactly three characters
<>????	Do not contain exactly four characters

| **NOTE** Text filters are not case sensitive.

Computed Criteria

Computed criteria (or formula criteria) use calculations that refer to one or more list fields or cells outside the list and will return either TRUE or FALSE. Those records that evaluate to TRUE will be displayed in the filtered list. For example, you could use computed criteria to filter a list to display only those products where the sales for January is greater than the sales for February. Use the following steps as a guideline to creating computed criteria:

1. Add a column to the criteria range using a different name from the other criteria fields (or leave the column heading field blank).

2. Enter the calculation in the criteria range using the first row of data in the list for any references—for example, **=A5=C5** will return those records where the value in column A equals the value in column C or **=A5>AVERAGE(A:A)** will return those records where the value in column A is greater than the average for column A. Use absolute referencing for any cells outside the list but relative referencing for cells within the list (unless you want to test a single reference that does not change).

3. Use AND, NOT, and OR to create compound computed criteria—for example, =AND(A5>AVERAGE(A5:A25), A5<100) will find those records where the value in column A is greater than the average for A5:A25 and less than 100.

4. Add any further criteria that you require. You can use more than one computed criterion in a filter, and you can use computed criteria along with ordinary criteria.

5. Apply the advanced filter as normal (remembering to include the additional column in the criteria range). Ignore any value returned in the criteria range—this will only refer to the first row of the list.

> **TIP** You can use the label for the list column in the computed criteria formula instead of a cell reference to test each cell in that column. For example, to find those records where the value in the Hours column is less than 20, you could enter **=Hours<20**. The cell in the criteria range containing the computed criteria formula will return a #NAME? error when the filter is applied, but the computed criteria will work in the same way.

By using advanced and computed criteria, you can create quite sophisticated filters. The best way to learn, of course, is to experiment and see!

CHAPTER 6

Analyzing Data Using Subtotals, Consolidations, and Tables

More important than its ability to record and display data are Excel's analytical capabilities. When you use Excel to store related information in an organized structure, you can make full use of its various tools for analysis, as we have already seen when we looked at sorting and filtering in the previous chapter. This chapter discusses some of the other ways you can summarize and manage your data when it is arranged as a list or table.

By grouping together related data in your worksheet, you can create an outline that will provide you with the ability to quickly hide or display levels or individual groups within the data. You can also use these groupings to summarize the data in your worksheet by inserting a summary function like Sum or Average. If flexibility is required, you can create an outline yourself or, if speed is paramount, use Excel's Subtotal feature to ameliorate the process of grouping data and inserting the summary rows.

Excel's Consolidation tool allows you to amalgamate facts and create summaries of data taken from different worksheets, not only from the same workbook but from other workbooks. You can consolidate data by matching the data according to its position in a range or by using row or column labels. You can also construct formulas that reference cells in different worksheets or use 3D references to create consolidations.

Excel tables are the successor of the Excel Lists feature in previous versions of the software. By creating a table, you can manage it, and the data stored within it, independently of the data in the rest of the worksheet. This includes formatting it using one of the new table styles, filtering or sorting it, or adding rows or columns. You can include headers, totals rows, and calculated columns in a table, and you can use structured references to refer to the table or sections of it in formulas or when creating charts or PivotTables from it. If you decide that you no longer need the table, you can convert it back to a range of data or delete it entirely.

Inserting Subtotals and Outlining Data

One of the simplest ways to analyze the data in your worksheet is to create an outline. This generally involves grouping data together so that you can summarize it, usually by inserting subtotals. Excel's Subtotal tool automates the process of grouping data and inserting rows with appropriate functions to display the subtotals for each group. You can even choose from 11 different functions to use in the calculations that summarize your data.

In addition to the automatic grouping outline that Excel creates when you use the Subtotal command, you can manually create multiple vertical and horizontal outlines in order to divide your data into different levels, thus producing a hierarchical structure. Each inner level in the outline will contain the detail for the outer level preceding it; outer levels will summarize and group the inner-level detail. You can then control how much detail is displayed by deciding whether to show or hide a level.

> **TIP** Before grouping your data or inserting subtotals, you should make sure that it is laid out in a suitable format for outlining. Each column should have a label in the first row (or each row should have a label in the first column if you will be creating an outline of columns) and should contain similar data. There should also be no blank rows or columns within the range. You cannot use the Subtotal or Outline tool on data formatted as a table.

Calculating Subtotals

The most convenient way to create an outline for your worksheet data and to insert subtotals is to use the Subtotal command, which is now situated in the Outline group of the Data tab. You can then select the column that contains the groups that you want to base your calculations on (for example, at every change of value in the Department column), the actual calculation that you want to be carried out (you can choose from a range of functions, not just Sum), and the column or columns that contain the values that you want to summarize. Excel will then define groups within the data and insert additional rows to display the subtotal values for each group along with the grand total for all the data. If your worksheet is set to calculate formulas automatically, Excel will recalculate the subtotals and grand total each time you edit the data.

To create automatic subtotals, follow these steps:

1. Sort the data by the column that you want to base your calculation on (this will allow Excel to group the data correctly). If you want to display subtotals for a filtered list, make sure that you filter the list before you sort it.

2. Click the Subtotal command in the Outline group on the Data tab. The Subtotal dialog box will open (see Figure 6-1).

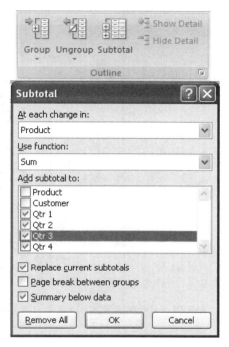

Figure 6-1. Click the Subtotal command in the Outline group to open the Subtotal dialog box.

3. Select the column that you want to base the summary calculations on from the "At each change in" dropdown list.

4. Select the function that you want to use for the summary calculation from the Use function dropdown list. You can choose from Sum, Count, Average, Max, Min, Product, Count Numbers StdDev, StdDevp, Var, or Varp.

5. From the "Add subtotal to" list, select the columns for which you want to include summary calculations.

6. Select or deselect the "Replace current subtotals," "Page break between groups," and "Summary below data" options as appropriate. If you deselect the "Summary below data" option, the subtotals will appear above their respective groups, with the grand total at the top of the data.

7. When you have finished making your selections, click OK. Excel will outline your data according to the values in the specified column and will insert the appropriate subtotals and grand total into your worksheet, as illustrated in Figure 6-2.

NOTE Grand totals are calculated using the detail data not the values in the subtotals. For example, if you use Average as your summary function, the value in the Grand Average row will be derived from the average of all the detail rows and not from the average of the values in the subtotal rows.

	A Sales Rep	B Product	C Customer	D Qtr 1	E Qtr 2	F Qtr 3	G Qtr 4
2	Ahmed	Apples	Anderson	$ 1,112.00	$ 1,702.00	$ 1,687.00	$ 1,175.00
3	Ahmed	Bananas	Anderson	$ 1,231.00	$ 1,165.60	$ 1,060.00	$ 1,183.35
4	Ahmed	Grapes	Anderson	$ 1,423.24	$ 1,231.50	$ 1,842.00	$ 1,215.00
5	Ahmed	Oranges	Anderson	$ 1,250.00	$ 1,586.50	$ 1,680.00	$ 1,996.50
6	Ahmed	Strawberries	Anderson	$ 2,115.20	$ 1,587.75	$ 1,237.60	$ 2,112.50
7	**Ahmed Total**			$ 7,131.44	$ 7,273.35	$ 7,506.60	$ 7,682.35
8	Jian	Apples	Croskery	$ 1,420.00	$ 1,593.75	$ 1,063.00	$ 1,055.20
9	Jian	Bananas	Croskery	$ 1,346.80	$ 1,110.01	$ 1,060.00	$ 1,183.35
10	Jian	Grapes	Croskery	$ 1,313.20	$ 1,423.14	$ 1,877.50	$ 1,294.00
11	Jian	Oranges	Croskery	$ 1,390.00	$ 2,560.00	$ 1,612.00	$ 1,395.10
12	Jian	Strawberries	Loughlin	$ 1,240.00	$ 1,835.20	$ 1,202.08	$ 1,887.40
13	**Jian Total**			$ 6,710.00	$ 8,522.10	$ 6,814.58	$ 6,815.05
14	Mary	Apples	Peoples	$ 1,294.00	$ 2,104.00	$ 4,900.00	$ 1,789.75
15	Mary	Bananas	Daly	$ 1,240.00	$ 1,877.50	$ 1,772.80	$ 1,736.00
16	Mary	Grapes	Daly	$ 1,346.80	$ 1,110.01	$ 1,300.00	$ 1,204.75
17	Mary	Oranges	Daly	$ 1,012.94	$ 1,052.11	$ 3,380.00	$ 2,317.00
18	Mary	Strawberries	Daly	$ 1,027.00	$ 2,093.50	$ 1,842.88	$ 1,625.00
19	**Mary Total**			$ 5,920.74	$ 8,237.12	$ 13,195.68	$ 8,672.50
20	**Grand Total**			$ 19,762.18	$ 24,032.57	$ 27,516.86	$ 23,169.90

Figure 6-2. Excel creates the groups and inserts the appropriate subtotals and grand total.

For each group you can include more than one subtotal so that you can summarize your data in different ways. For example, you may wish to display the Count or Average for each group as well as the Sum. To insert an additional subtotal, repeat the earlier procedure using the same field in the "At each change in" box but a different function in the Use function box. This time deselect the "Replace current subtotals" option to make sure that both subtotals are displayed. Excel will insert the new subtotals and grand total into your worksheet.

To include even more detail in your datasheet, you can insert a subtotal within a subtotaled group (known as *nesting* subtotals). If you are planning to nest subtotals, make sure that you include the columns that the nested subtotals will be based on when you first sort the data. Your data should be sorted by the column that the outermost subtotal is based on, then by the column that the first nested subtotal is based on, and so on. Nested subtotals are created using similar steps to creating the first subtotal, except this time you need to select a different field in the "At each change in" box. Again, deselect the "Replace current subtotals" option to make sure that all subtotals are displayed. Excel will insert the new groups and subtotals within the existing groups in your worksheet.

Removing Subtotals

You can easily remove all the subtotals you have added to your data by clicking Subtotal in the Outline group of the Data tab and clicking the Remove All button in the Subtotal dialog box (see Figure 6-1). Any subtotals you have added to your data will be removed, along with the grouping levels, and your data will revert to its original state.

Outlining Data

To allow you even more flexibility in viewing and working with your data, you can create your own outline levels either horizontally or vertically. This is particularly useful if you want to group your data in ways other than by each change in a column or if you want to combine other groups together. You can also use this method to group columns together instead of rows. For example, you may want to group monthly data into quarters. Excel allows you to create up to eight levels both horizontally and vertically within your data.

Creating an Outline of Rows or Columns

To create an outline of rows or columns follow these steps:

1. Sort the columns or rows that you want to use in your outline groups.

> **TIP** To sort a row, select the row and click Sort & Filter in the Editing group on the Home tab and select Custom Sort. A warning will appear asking if you want to expand your selection. Select "Continue with the current selection" and click the Sort button. Click the Options button in the Sort dialog box, select "Sort left to right" in the Sort Options box, and click OK. Make the appropriate selections from the Row, Sort on, and Order dropdown lists and click OK.

2. Insert summary rows immediately above or below each group of detail rows or summary columns immediately to the left or to the right of each group of detail columns. When manually creating groups, you need to insert summary rows or columns to mark the boundary between where one group ends and another group begins; otherwise, the rows or columns for the second group will be included in the first group. These summary rows or columns should contain appropriate formulas that reference each of the detail rows or columns for that group. When you use the Subtotal command to create groups automatically, the subtotal row that is inserted for each group forms this boundary.

3. Click the Dialog Box Launcher in the bottom-right corner of the Outline group on the Data tab to open the Settings dialog box. Select or deselect the "Summary rows below detail" or "Summary columns to right of detail" option as appropriate to indicate the position of the summary rows or columns.

4. Click the Create button in the Settings dialog box to create the outline groups.

> **TIP** If you do not need to change the default setting for the location of the summary rows (i.e., your summary rows are below the data), you can click the down arrow on the Group button in the Outline group and select Auto Outline to automatically create your outline without opening the Settings dialog box.

Grouping Rows or Columns Manually

If you want to create your outline manually by selecting and grouping each set of rows or columns—for example, if you need to group together rows or columns that belong to more than one category—do the following:

1. Make sure that you have all your data displayed to avoid grouping rows or columns incorrectly.

2. Select the rows or columns that you want to group together (including any subordinate summary rows or columns but not the summary row or column for the entire group).

3. Click the Group command in the Outline group on the Data tab. A new level will be added to your outline and the grouped rows or columns will be indicated by a level bar at the left of or above the worksheet. You can expand or collapse this new level in the same way as the levels created by Excel.

4. Continue to group rows or columns together until you have the outline structure that you require.

Showing and Hiding Outlined Data

When you group rows or columns, an outline section will appear on your worksheet that contains controls for hiding or displaying the groups of data. The outline section for grouped rows will be to the left of the worksheet, and the outline section for grouped columns will be above the worksheet. Figure 6-3 shows a worksheet that has both vertical and horizontal outline levels.

> **TIP** If the outline section is not displayed when you create an outline, click the Microsoft Office Button, click Excel Options, and select the Advanced category. Under the "Display options for this worksheet" section, select the worksheet and select the "Show outline symbols if an outline is applied" option.

In the example in Figure 6-3, you can see that all the sales rows for each Sales Rep have been grouped together and subtotals using the Sum and Max functions have been created for each. Nested within this level are the subtotals using the Sum function for each product. Although they are not visible in Figure 6-3, a Grand Total and Grand Max for all the Sales Reps are also included at the bottom of the data.

Vertically, the six months have been grouped and a summary column has been inserted containing appropriate Sum functions to provide the total for the half year (H1). Within this level are nested subtotals for each quarter (Q1 and Q2).

	Sales Rep	Product	Jan	Feb	Mar	Q1	Apr	May	Jun	Q2	H1
1	Sales Rep	Product	Jan	Feb	Mar	Q1	Apr	May	Jun	Q2	H1
2	Ahmed	Apples	$ 338	$ 702	$ 479	$ 1,519	$ 576	$ 546	$ 772	$ 1,894	$ 3,413
3	Ahmed	Apples	$ 365	$ 300	$ 235	$ 900	$ 546	$ 401	$ 330	$ 1,277	$ 2,177
4	Ahmed	Apples	$ 392	$ 300	$ 300	$ 992	$ 562	$ 401	$ 330	$ 1,293	$ 2,285
5		**Apples Total**				$ 3,411				$ 4,465	$ 7,875
6	Ahmed	Grapes	$ 303	$ 321	$ 340	$ 964	$ 359	$ 377	$ 353	$ 1,090	$ 2,053
7		**Grapes Total**				$ 964				$ 1,090	$ 2,053
8	Ahmed	Oranges	$ 298	$ 321	$ 340	$ 959	$ 327	$ 327	$ 327	$ 982	$ 1,941
9		**Oranges Total**				$ 959				$ 982	$ 1,941
10	Ahmed	Strawberries	$ 153	$ 587	$ 340	$ 1,080	$ 327	$ 327	$ 645	$ 1,300	$ 2,379
11	Ahmed	Strawberries	$ 736	$ 340	$ 340	$ 1,416	$ 327	$ 810	$ 897	$ 2,034	$ 3,450
12		**Strawberries Total**				$ 2,496				$ 3,334	$ 5,829
13	**Ahmed Max**					$ 1,519				$ 2,034	$ 3,450
14	*Ahmed Total*					$ 7,829				$ 9,870	$ 17,699
15	Jian	Apples	$ 462	$ 562	$ 340	$ 1,364	$ 327	$ 369	$ 290	$ 986	$ 2,350
16		**Apples Total**				$ 1,364				$ 986	$ 2,350
17	Jian	Bananas	$ 62	$ 263	$ 340	$ 666	$ 327	$ 69	$ 290	$ 686	$ 1,351
18	Jian	Bananas	$ 62	$ 263	$ 340	$ 666	$ 55	$ 69	$ 121	$ 245	$ 911
19		**Bananas Total**				$ 1,332				$ 930	$ 2,262
20	Jian	Grapes	$ 62	$ 263	$ 612	$ 938	$ 55	$ 69	$ 121	$ 245	$ 1,183
21	Jian	Grapes	$ 110	$ 110	$ 110	$ 330	$ 55	$ 69	$ 121	$ 245	$ 575
22		**Grapes Total**				$ 1,268				$ 490	$ 1,758

Figure 6-3. The vertical and horizontal outline sections contain controls to allow you to expand or collapse each outline level.

In the outline sections to the left and at the top of the screen, you can use the outline controls to specify how much detail you want to display.

- To hide (collapse) the rows or columns for a group, click the button showing a minus sign (-) beside that group. You can also click the level bar connected to the button showing a minus sign that indicates the rows or columns that are grouped together to hide the details for that group.

- To show (expand) the rows or columns for a group that is hidden, click the button showing a plus sign (+) beside the subtotal row or column for the hidden group.

- Use the numbered level buttons (1, 2, 3, 4, etc.) to hide all levels of detail below the number you have clicked. Clicking level 1 will hide all the detail data, and clicking the highest level will show all the detail data. For example, in the example in Figure 6-3, using the row level buttons: level 1 will leave only the Grand Total and Grand Max visible; level 2 will show the Grand Total and Grand Max rows and the subtotal rows for each Sales Rep; level 3 will display all the rows shown in level 2 plus the maximum for each Sales Rep; level 4 will display all the rows shown in level 3 along with the nested subtotals for each product; and level 5 will display all the subtotals and detail rows.

Figure 6-4 illustrates how the data would look if we select level 2 in the column-level buttons and level 4 in the row-level buttons.

	A	B	F	J	K
1	Sales Rep	Product	Q1	Q2	H1
5		Apples Total	$ 3,411	$ 4,465	$ 7,875
7		Grapes Total	$ 964	$ 1,090	$ 2,053
9		Oranges Total	$ 959	$ 982	$ 1,941
12		Strawberries Total	$ 2,496	$ 3,334	$ 5,829
13	Ahmed Max		$ 1,519	$ 2,034	$ 3,450
14	*Ahmed Total*		$ 7,829	$ 9,870	$ 17,699
16		Apples Total	$ 1,364	$ 986	$ 2,350
19		Bananas Total	$ 1,332	$ 930	$ 2,262
22		Grapes Total	$ 1,268	$ 490	$ 1,758
25		Strawberries Total	$ 2,215	$ 2,493	$ 4,708
26	Jian Max		$ 1,927	$ 1,482	$ 2,938
27	*Jian Total*		$ 6,178	$ 4,899	$ 11,077
30		Apples Total	$ 5,974	$ 2,246	$ 8,220
33		Bananas Total	$ 2,966	$ 2,197	$ 5,163
36		Grapes Total	$ 4,251	$ 3,444	$ 7,694
39		Oranges Total	$ 2,253	$ 2,837	$ 5,090
40	Mary Max		$ 4,262	$ 1,722	$ 5,556
41	*Mary Total*		$ 15,444	$ 10,724	$ 26,168
42		Grand Total			
43	Grand Max		$ 4,262	$ 2,034	$ 5,556
44	Grand Total		$ 29,452	$ 25,492	$ 54,944

Figure 6-4. You can hide the detail rows and columns to display a summary of your data.

Applying Automatic Styles to an Outline

If you want, you can apply automatic styles to outlined rows and columns in order to differentiate summary rows and columns. These styles use bold, italic, and other formatting but can be customized in the same way as other cell styles and will update to reflect changes to the overall document theme. They are referred to as RowLevel_1, RowLevel_2, ColLevel_1, ColLevel_2, and so on.

You can apply automatic styles to an outline when you create it by selecting the Automatic styles option in the Settings dialog box when you are specifying the location of the summary rows or columns. To apply automatic styles to an outline that has already been created, select the cells that you want to apply outline styles to, click the Dialog Box Launcher in the bottom-right corner of the Outline group on the Data tab to open the Settings dialog box, select the Automatic styles option, and click the Apply Styles button. Once you have applied automatic styles, you can modify them to suit your own preferences—see Chapter 4 for information on customizing cell styles.

Copying Outlined Data

If you want to copy and paste a summary of your data without all the detail, you can use the outline levels along with the Go To Special feature, as explained in the following steps:

1. Use the level buttons or outline symbols to hide the detail data that you do not want to copy.
2. Select the range of data that you want to copy.
3. Select the Home tab and, in the Editing group, click Find & Select.
4. Choose Go To Special from the menu that appears.
5. In the Go To Special dialog box, select "Visible cells only" and click OK.
6. Copy and paste the cells as normal.

Creating a Chart from Outlined Data

Once you have designed a summary report by hiding the detail data, you can easily create a chart to display the totals by doing the following:

1. Use the level buttons or outline symbols to hide the detail data that you do not want to chart.
2. Select the range of data that you want to chart.
3. Select the Insert tab and, from the Charts group, select the type of chart that you want to use to display your data. An embedded chart will appear on your worksheet.
4. Use the tabs for the Design, Layout, and Format under Chart Tools to alter features of the chart as necessary (see Chapter 11 for more information on charts).

Ungrouping Rows or Columns

To ungroup rows or columns that you have grouped together, select the rows or columns that you want to ungroup again (to select all the detail rows or columns in a group, hold down the Shift key while you click the Hide Detail or Show Detail button for the group). With the rows or columns selected, click Ungroup in the Outline group of the Data tab. The rows and columns will no longer be grouped. Once all groups within a level have been removed, the level bar will also disappear from the outline.

> **NOTE** If you ungroup an outline while the detail rows (or columns) are hidden, the detail rows (or columns) may remain hidden. To reveal the rows (or columns) again, select the rows above and below (or the columns to the right and to the left of) the hidden data, right-click, and select Unhide from the context menu.

Consolidating Data

To create a report that summarizes data from multiple worksheets, you can consolidate the data from separate worksheets into a master worksheet. For example, if you have a workbook that contains separate worksheets displaying data for various periods, you may want to create a summary worksheet that displays the aggregate data for the year. When using the Consolidate tool to summarize data, you can choose from 11 different functions, including Sum, Count, and Average. You can also consolidate worksheets from the same workbook or from different workbooks. There are three main ways that you can consolidate data: by position, by category, or by formula.

If you want to consolidate data that is arranged in the same position within the range (although not necessarily in the same cells) on each of the worksheets, you can consolidate by position. If you want to consolidate data that uses the same row and column labels even if it is arranged in different positions on each of the worksheets, you can consolidate by category. The steps to consolidate by either of these methods are similar and are outlined here:

1. Make sure that each range of data to be consolidated has a similar format and layout. Each column should have a heading in the first row and should contain similar data, and there should be no blank rows or columns within the range. Each range should be on a separate worksheet, but there should be no range on the worksheet where you want the consolidation to appear.

2. Name each range using the Defined Names group on the Formulas tab or the Name box (see Chapter 3 for more on naming ranges).

3. Select the cell in the top-left corner of the range where you want the consolidation to appear (making sure that you will not overwrite any important data on the worksheet).

4. Select the Data tab and, in the Data Tools group, click Consolidate (if you have reduced the size of your window, click the Consolidate icon). The Consolidate dialog box (see Figure 6-5) will appear.

5. Select the summary function that you want to use in the consolidation from the Function dropdown list. You can choose from Sum, Count, Average, Max, Min, Product, Count Numbers StdDev, StdDevp, Var, or Varp.

6. Enter the name of the first range in the Reference box and click Add. If the range is on another worksheet, click Browse first, and select the worksheet. The name of the worksheet will be entered in the Reference box followed by an exclamation mark (!). Type the name of the range after the exclamation mark and click Add.

7. Continue adding the names of the rest of the ranges.

8. To consolidate by position, leave the boxes in the "Use labels in" section blank so that Excel will consolidate the data according to its position. You can add labels to the summary manually when you have finished. To consolidate by category, select either the Top row and/or the Left column option in the "Use labels in" section to indicate the position of the labels in the source ranges.

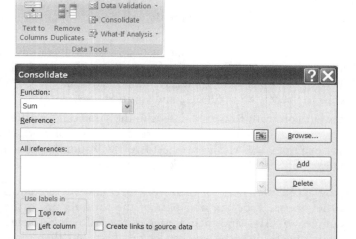

Figure 6-5. Click Consolidate in the Data Tools group to open the Consolidate dialog box.

9. If you want the consolidation to update automatically if you change the contents of any of the cells in the source ranges, select the "Create links to source data" option. If you select the "Create links to source data" checkbox, you will not be able to change the cells or ranges included in the consolidation.

10. Click OK when you have finished. The consolidation will appear on the worksheet, starting from the selected cell.

> **TIP** When you are consolidating by category, any labels that do not match labels in other worksheets will result in separate rows or columns. Therefore, if you do not want to consolidate certain data, make sure that it has a unique row or column label.

Consolidating by Formula

If you do not have a consistent position or category to base your consolidation on, or you only want to consolidate certain cells, you can use formulas to consolidate cells. This involves entering a formula that contains cell references for other worksheets or a 3D reference to reference the same cell in a range of worksheets, as shown in the next steps:

1. Enter the row or column labels that you want to use for the consolidated data on the summary worksheet.

2. Select the cell where you want the consolidated data to appear.

3. Enter a formula that contains cell references to the source cells on each worksheet or a 3D reference containing the data that you want to consolidate using the following guidelines:

- If the data that you want to consolidate is in different cells on different worksheets, enter a formula with cell references to each individual worksheet—for example, =SUM(Sheet1!A4,Sheet2!B5,Sheet3!C6) will sum cells A4 in Sheet1, B5 in Sheet2, and C6 in Sheet3.

- If the data that you want to consolidate is in the same cell on different worksheets, enter a 3D reference that references a range of worksheet names—for example, =SUM(Sheet1:Sheet4!A5) will sum the value in cell A5 on each of Sheet1, Sheet2, Sheet3, and Sheet4.

Instead of typing in cell references for each worksheet and 3D references, you can enter them using the mouse. Type the first part of the formula up to the first cell reference—for example, =SUM(—and then do one of the following: to enter cell references for each worksheet, click the worksheet tab first and then click the cell, separating each reference with a comma (,); or to enter a 3D reference, click the first worksheet tab, hold down the Shift key and click the last worksheet tab, and then click the cell. Type the remainder of the formula as normal. If your workbook is set to automatically calculate formulas, a consolidation by formula will update automatically when any changes are made to the data in the source worksheets.

Editing a Data Consolidation

After creating a data consolidation, you may wish to alter it to add or remove worksheets or to change the cells that are included. To make changes to a data consolidation by position or category, select the top-left cell in the consolidated data and click Consolidate (or the Consolidate icon) in the Data Tools group of the Data tab. In the Consolidate dialog box, make the changes required to the consolidation and click OK. You can make changes to a data consolidation by formula by directly altering the formula or function or by changing the cell references or 3D reference. To quickly add a worksheet to a 3D reference without using the Consolidate dialog box, drag the worksheet tab into the range of tabs that the 3D reference refers to.

NOTE If you selected the "Create links to source data" option when you first created the consolidation, you will not be able to edit it but will have to create a new consolidation instead.

Excel Tables

Excel tables simplify the analysis of rows and columns of related data by allowing you to manage the data in the table independently of the other rows and columns of the worksheet. When you create a table, it will include a header row, using either the headings included in your data or default headers used by Excel. Filter icons are automatically displayed beside each header, allowing easy filtering and sorting of the data within the table. You can insert more than one table on the same worksheet and format or analyze each independently.

The new table styles available in Excel 2007 enable you to quickly format a table by selecting one of a range of coordinated predefined styles. You can also select from various quick style options to include features like header and total rows or to apply banding to rows and columns. These table styles provide dynamic formatting that will update as your table expands or contracts. You can also create your own custom table styles to add your own touch or to accommodate your corporate requirements.

As well as one-click formatting, working with data as a table instead of a range allows you to use features like totals rows, calculated columns, and structured references. Totals rows include a dropdown list of relevant functions like Average, Count, Max, and Min that can be used to analyze the data. Calculated columns use a single formula that adjusts for each row of the table and will expand to include additional rows as they are added. Structured references allow you use table names rather than cell references in formulas.

If you have access to a SharePoint Services site and have the correct permissions, you can use it to share a table with other users. Tables exported to a SharePoint list can be viewed, edited, and updated by other users, and you can also synchronize your table to keep changes to the data up-to-date (see Chapter 17 for more on exporting tables to SharePoint).

Creating a Table

You can create a table either before or after you enter the data into the worksheet using the following steps:

1. Select the range of cells that you want to convert to a table.

2. Select the Insert tab and click Table in the Tables group. The Create Table dialog box will appear.

3. If the range that you have selected includes headers for your table, select the "My table has headers" option. If you do not select this checkbox, table headers using default names (for example, Column1, Column2, etc.) will be created (although these can be changed later). When you click OK, the range of cells will be converted into a table and the default formatting will be applied.

4. Use the commands on the Design tab under Table Tools (see Figure 6-6) to quickly name, edit, and format your table as required.

TIP A quick way to create a table is to use the Ctrl+L shortcut key. You can also select Format As Table in the Styles group of the Home tab and select a table style from the gallery.

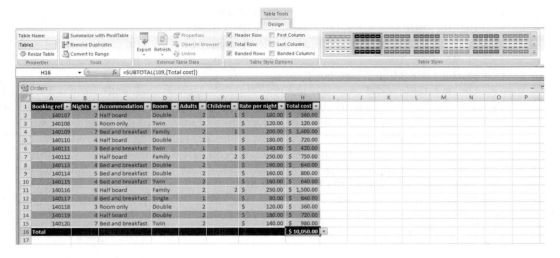

Figure 6-6. Use the Design tab under Table Tools to name, edit, and format a table.

> **NOTE** For more information on formatting a table, see the "Table Styles" section in Chapter 4.

Turning On and Off Header Rows

Table headers are automatically displayed when you create a table, using the first row of your data or default headers if you have not specified a header row. As you scroll down through your table, the table headers will replace the worksheet headers so that they remain visible (as long as the active cell is in the table). If you insert a new column in a table where the headers are following a series (for example, months), the appropriate header will be applied to the new column based on the headers in the adjacent columns.

You can turn off table headers if you do not want to display them by deselecting the Header Row checkbox in the Table Style Options group on the Design tab. When you turn off the header row, the column headings will disappear and any filters applied to the table will be removed. If table headers are not displayed when you insert a new column, Excel will not be able to determine the header for the new column based on the adjacent columns and so the new column will adopt a default header.

> **CAUTION** Turning off table headers may cause formulas that refer to those cells to return unexpected results.

Displaying a Total Row in a Table

A handy feature of Excel tables is the ability to add a Total row to the bottom of the table and quickly insert functions to summarize the data in the table as shown in the following steps:

1. Click anywhere in the table to display Table Tools.
2. Select the Design tab and, in the Table Style Options group, select the Total Row checkbox. A new row will be added to the bottom of your table with the title Total in the first column. You can also display or hide a Totals row by right-clicking the table, pointing to Table in the menu that appears, and clicking Totals Row.

> **NOTE** Excel may automatically insert a function in the last cell—you can delete or change this if it is incorrect.

3. Click a cell in the Total row where you want to insert a calculation. A dropdown arrow will appear in the cell.
4. Click the dropdown arrow and select the function you require from the list that appears (see Figure 6-7) or select More Functions to open the Insert Function dialog box.

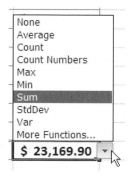

Figure 6-7. Select a function for the Total row.

5. Insert functions or text into the other cells of the Total row as required.
6. To hide the Total row, deselect the Total Row option in the Table Style Options group. Any text or functions that have been entered will be "remembered" until you turn the Total Row option back on again.

There are different ways you can quickly select a row or a column in an Excel table. Some of these are outlined in Table 6-1.

Table 6-1. Select Rows and Columns in a Table

To Select . . .	Do This . . .
Table column data	Click the column header when the mouse pointer changes to a down arrow; or Select a cell in the column and press Ctrl+Spacebar.
Entire table column	Click twice on the column header when the mouse pointer changes to a down arrow; or Select a cell in the column and press Ctrl+Spacebar twice.
Table row	Click on the left border of the table row when the mouse pointer changes to a right-pointing arrow; or Select a cell in the row and press Shift+Spacebar.
All table data	Click in the top-left corner of the table when the mouse pointer changes to an arrow pointing diagonally to the bottom right of the table; or Select a cell in the table and press Ctrl+A.
All table rows and columns	Click twice in the top-left corner of the table when the mouse pointer changes to an arrow pointing diagonally to the bottom right of the table; or Select a cell in the table and press Ctrl+A twice.

Adding and Removing Table Rows and Columns

Excel tables can easily be expanded to incorporate additional rows or columns, and the features of the table will be extended to the new cells. If you need to remove data you can delete rows or columns from a table without affecting the rest of the worksheet. You can even have Excel check your data for duplicate records and remove them accordingly.

To add a new blank row to the end of a table, press the Tab key when in the last cell of the last row (excluding the Totals row). If a Totals row is displayed, it will move down to accommodate the new row. If you do not have a Totals row displayed, you can append a new row by simply entering data in the row immediately below the table. You can also add a column to a table by entering data in a cell in the column immediately to the right of a table. When you add a new row or column to a table, the appropriate formatting will be applied and the border around the table will be adjusted.

A new feature of Excel tables is the concept of *stickiness*. Basically this means that, if you apply a feature like conditional formatting or data validation to a column, Excel will assume that this feature should always apply to the entire column. As new rows are added to the end of the table (or inserted in the middle) or rows are deleted,

Excel will expand or contract the feature as appropriate. In addition, if new rows or columns are added to a table, they will be picked up by objects like charts or Pivot-Tables.

> **TIP** If you enter data in the row below or the column to the right of the table and it is automatically included in the table but you do not want it to become part of the table, click the AutoCorrect Options button and select Undo Table AutoExpansion.

Resizing a Table

To adjust the range for a table, you can use the Properties group on the Tools tab as follows:

1. Select a cell in the table to display Table Tools.
2. Select the Design tab and click Resize Table in the Properties group. The Resize Table dialog box will appear (see Figure 6-8).

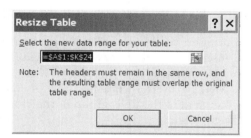

Figure 6-8. Enter a new range for the table in the Resize Table dialog box.

3. Click the Collapse Dialog icon beside the field in the Resize Table dialog box to select the new range for your table from the worksheet (or enter the new data range for your table in the field). The new range for the table should overlap the current range.
4. Click the Collapse Dialog icon again to return to the Resize Table dialog box and click OK.

> **TIP** You can also resize a table by dragging the resize handle at the bottom-right corner of the table up, down, left, or right.

Inserting Table Rows or Columns

You can use the Insert command in the Cells group of the Home tab to insert rows or columns within a table as follows:

- To insert a row in a table, select a cell in the row that you want to be below the new row and click Insert in the Cells group of the Home tab.
- To insert a column in a table, select two or more cells in the column that you want to be on the right of the new column and click Insert in the Cells group of the Home tab.

You can also insert one or more rows or columns by selecting the equivalent number of existing rows or columns in the table and clicking the arrow beside the Insert command. To insert several table rows, select the same number of rows in the table as you want to insert and that are positioned below where you want the new rows to appear. Click the down arrow beside Insert in the Cells group of the Home tab and select Insert Table Rows Above. If you select the last row, you can insert a row above or below the selected row.

To insert several table columns, select the same number of columns in the table as you want to insert and that are positioned to the right of where you want the new columns to appear. Click the down arrow beside Insert in the Cells group of the Home tab and select Insert Table Columns to the Left. If you select the last column, you can insert a column to the right or to the left of the selected column. You can also insert table rows or columns by right-clicking the selected cells and clicking Insert in the menu that appears. You can then select whether you want to insert rows or columns.

Excel also gives you the option to insert worksheet rows and columns as well as table rows and columns. When you insert a table row or column, it will not displace other data outside of the table whereas inserting a worksheet row or column will adjust the layout of the entire worksheet. To insert a worksheet row or column, click the down arrow next to the Insert command in the Cells group of the Home tab and select Insert Sheet Rows or Insert Sheet Columns.

Deleting Table Rows or Columns

To remove rows or columns from a table, select the rows or columns that you want to remove (you can select one or more cells in the rows or columns) and click the down arrow beside the Delete command in the Cells group of the Home tab. Select Delete Table Rows or Delete Table Columns as appropriate. The selected rows or columns of the table will be deleted without affecting the rest of the worksheet. You can also delete table rows or columns by right-clicking the selected cells and clicking Delete in the context menu. You can then select whether you want to delete rows or columns.

Excel also gives you the option to delete worksheet rows and columns as well as table rows and columns. When you delete a worksheet row or column, it will adjust the layout of the entire worksheet and remove any data positioned within that row or column both inside the table and from the worksheet surrounding the table. To delete a worksheet row or column, click the down arrow next to the Delete command in the Cells group of the Home tab and select Delete Sheet Rows or Delete Sheet Columns.

Removing Duplicates

In some cases you may wish to check the data within your table to identify and remove any duplicated records (for example, if a customer's details have been entered more than once). To delete any duplicated data from your table, do the following:

1. Click any cell in the table to display Table Tools and select the Design tab.

2. In the Tools group, select Remove Duplicates. The Remove Duplicates dialog box will appear (see Figure 6-9).

> **TIP** You can also select Remove Duplicates in the Data Tools group of the Data tab.

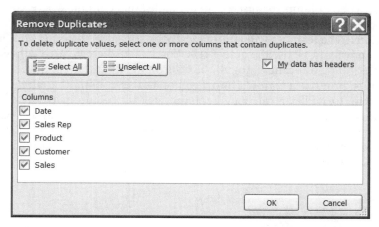

Figure 6-9. Select the columns that you want to examine for duplicated data.

3. If you want to check all the columns for duplicated data, click the Select All button (if all the columns are not already selected). If you only want to check certain columns, click the Unselect All button and then use the checkboxes to select the columns that you want to check.

4. Select or deselect the "My data has headers" option as appropriate and click OK.

5. A box will appear indicating how many duplicate values have been found and removed and how many unique values remain. Click OK.

> **CAUTION** Removing duplicates will delete data from your table! If you inadvertently delete data that you need, click Undo on the Quick Access toolbar to restore it.

Using Calculated Columns in a Table

In an Excel 2007 table you can easily insert what is known as a *calculated* column. A calculated column uses a single formula that automatically updates for each row in the column. If rows are added to the table, the calculated column will expand to include calculations for the new rows. With a calculated column you only need to enter the formula once; you do not need to use Fill or Copy. If you enter additional formulas (or other data) in a calculated column as exceptions, Excel will notify you of any inconsistencies so that they can be resolved.

Creating a Calculated Column

To create a calculated column, click in a cell of a blank table column that you want to make a calculated column (or insert a new blank table column where you want the calculated column to be). Then, type the formula that you want to use into the cell and press Enter. The formula will automatically be copied to the other cells in the column, both above and below the active cell. You can also create a calculated column by copying or filling a formula into all the cells of a blank table column.

If you type or move a formula into a cell of a table column that already contains data other than formulas, a calculated column will not be automatically created, but the AutoCorrect Options icon will appear beside the column, providing you with the option to overwrite the existing data and create a calculated column (see Figure 6-10). If you copy a formula into a cell of a table column that already contains data, you do not have this option.

Figure 6-10. Use the AutoCorrect Options button to overwrite data in a column.

At times you may not want a formula to be copied to the other cells in a column. You can use the Undo button on the Quick Access toolbar to undo a calculated column if you only want the formula to appear in one cell.

Creating Exceptions in a Calculated Column

In some situations you may want a cell in a calculated column to contain something different from the formula the other cells hold. Calculated column exceptions are indicated in the table column by a small green marker in the top-left corner of the cell so that inconsistencies can be identified and corrected if necessary. There are various ways you can create exceptions in a calculated column, including the following:

- Entering data other than the formula into a calculated column cell
- Entering a formula into a calculated column cell and clicking Undo on the Quick Access toolbar so that the new formula is only applied to one cell

- Entering a new formula into a calculated column cell that already contains exceptions
- Copying data into a calculated column that does not match the formula used in it (if the copied data is a formula, this formula will overwrite the existing data in the calculated column and you will need to click Undo)
- Deleting or moving a cell in another part of the worksheet that is referenced by one of the rows in the calculated column
- Deleting a formula from a calculated column cell (this exception will not be marked)

When you move the mouse pointer over a cell displaying an error indicator, the Error Checking button will appear beside the cell. If you click this button, a menu will be displayed, providing you with options to help you resolve the inconsistency (see Figure 6-11).

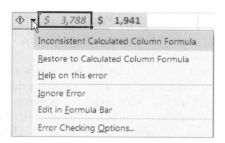

Figure 6-11. Click the Error Checking button to reveal options to help you resolve an exception in a calculated column.

Editing a Calculated Column

If your calculated column does not contain any exceptions, you can edit it by doing either of the following:

- Clicking in any cell in the calculated column and editing the formula
- Copying a new formula into any cell in the calculated column

> **NOTE** If you copy more than one formula, the calculated column will not be updated, but any inconsistencies will be identified so that they can be resolved.

If there already are exceptions in your calculated column, Excel will not automatically propagate changes to a cell to the rest of the column to avoid overwriting custom values. If you do want to update the entire column with a modified formula, click in any cell in the calculated column and enter the new formula. As there are exceptions, Excel will only update the active cell. To apply the changes to the rest of the column, click the AutoCorrect Options icon that will appear beside the column and select the "Overwrite all cells in this column with this formula" option. A calculated column will be created using the modified formula.

You can delete a calculated column in the same way you delete any column in a table: select the column and click Delete in the Cells group on the Home tab. If you just want to delete the contents of the column, select the column and press the Delete key.

Using Structured References in a Table

Structured references can be used in a similar way to named ranges when referring to a table, or to sections of it, in a formula. Like named ranges, structured references can make formula construction much simpler, and the result is more comprehensible formulas that will adjust as table ranges change. For example, if a table named Sales has a column labeled Jan in cells B2:B33, you could use the formula =SUM(Sales[Jan]), which is easier to understand and much more flexible than =SUM(B2:B33). Table references are not limited to formula creation—they can also be used when entering references in some dialog boxes, including dialog boxes for PivotTables, Charts, Defining Names, and Page Setup.

A major difference between named ranges and structured references is that the names that can be referenced in tables are automatically generated when you create the table, including the name of the table itself. If a table expands or shrinks, the names will adjust, and if a table is deleted, the names will be removed. Also, if you rename a table or a column, Excel will automatically update any structured references that use that table or column header. This can save you a lot of time, not only when initially entering formulas but also by lessening the need to alter formulas as your table is edited and rows or columns are added or deleted.

Structured references can take many different forms depending on whether you are referring to the whole table or a subsection of it. The structured reference =Sales[[#Totals],[Jan]] refers to the value in the Totals row of the Jan column of the Sales table and is made up of several components as outlined here:

- A *table name (Sales)*: Used to reference the table data (excluding header and totals rows). For example, you could use the formula =SUM(Sales) to return the sum of all the data in the Sales table. When you insert a table into a worksheet, Excel automatically assigns it a default name (Table1, Table2, etc.). You can change this default name to something more meaningful by changing the entry in the Table Name box in the Properties group of the Design tab.
- A *column specifier ([Jan])*: Taken from the column header, enclosed in square brackets, and used to reference the column data (excluding header and totals rows). For example, the formula =SUM(Sales[Jan]) will return the sum of the data in the Jan column of the Sales table.

- A *special item specifier ([#Totals])*: Refers to a particular section of the table—for example, the Totals row—and is enclosed in square brackets and indicated by #. For example, the formula =SUM(Sales[#Totals]) will return the sum of the Totals row of the Sales table.

- A *table specifier ([[#Totals],[Jan]])*: The outer portion of a structured reference that is enclosed in square brackets following the table name.

When entering structured references, you can make use of Formula AutoComplete to help ensure you use the correct syntax (see Figure 6-12). The names of the available tables, columns, and special item specifiers will appear in the Formula AutoComplete list, and you can select them using the Tab key or the mouse. See Chapter 10 for more information about using Formula AutoComplete.

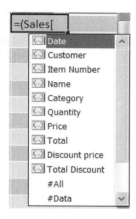

Figure 6-12. You can use Formula AutoComplete to help you enter structured references.

Table names must follow the same rules as defined names. They can be up to 255 characters in length and should begin with a letter, underscore, or backslash. They cannot be the same as cell references and should not contain spaces or hyphens (use periods or underscores instead). Table names are not case sensitive; therefore, Excel will regard Sales and SALES as the same name. Table names are globally unique to a workbook and therefore do not require a sheet reference. As table names exist along with defined names, you cannot use the same name for a named range and a table. Column names must be unique within the table.

> **TIP** If you enter a formula by selecting the cells, by default Excel will enter the structured reference in the formula rather than the cell references. If you want to turn this feature off so that the cell references are displayed, click the Microsoft Office Button and select Excel Options. Choose the Formulas category and, in the Working with formulas section, deselect the "Use table names in formulas" option.

Reference Operators

If you need to refer to more than one column in a structured reference, you can use the following reference operators to combine column specifiers:

- Range operator (colon) to refer to all of the cells in two or more adjacent columns—for example, =Table1[Column2]:[Column4] would refer to Column2, Column3, and Column4.
- Union operator (comma) to refer to a combination of two or more columns—for example, =Table1[Column2],Table1[Column4] would refer to Column2 and Column4.
- Intersection operator (space) to refer to the intersection of two or more columns—for example, =Table1[Column1]:[Column3] Table1[Column2]:[Column4] would refer to Column2 and Column3.

Special Item Specifiers

To allow you even more flexibility, you can use special item specifiers (for example, =Table1[#Totals]) to refer to specific portions of the table as outlined here:

- *#All*: The entire table, including column headers and totals
- *#Data*: Only the data (excludes headers and totals)
- *#Headers*: Only the headers row (turning off the Header Row will not affect structured references that use headers)
- *#Totals*: Only the Totals row (returns null if there is no Totals row)
- *#ThisRow*: Only the intersection of the columns with the current row (cannot be combined with any other special item specifier)

Qualifying Structured References in Calculated Columns

When creating calculated columns, you may find that you are often using structured references in the formulas. Usually these references can be unqualified or fully qualified. An example of unqualified structured references being used in a formula would be =[Column1]*[Column2], which would multiply the corresponding values from the current row.

Generally, when using structured references within the table, as when you are creating a calculated column, you can use unqualified structured references. However, if you are using structured references outside of the table, you should use fully qualified structured references in order to identify the table that the column refers to. An example of fully qualified structured references being used would be =AVERAGE(Table1[Column1])*AVERAGE(Table1[Column2]), which would multiply the average value for the two columns. The same formula can be entered inside the table as =AVERAGE([Column1])*AVERAGE([Column2]).

Table 6-2 provides some examples of how structured references can be used.

Table 6-2. Examples of Structured References

Structured Reference	Refers To
=Table1[[#All],[Column1]]	All the cells in Column1
=Table1[[#Headers],[Column1]]	The header of Column1
=Table1[[#Totals],[Column1]]	The total of Column1 (returns null if there is no Totals row)
=Table1[[#All],[Column1]:[Column3]]	All the cells in Column1, Column2, and Column3
=Table1[[#Data],[Column1]:[Column3]]	All the data in Column1, Column2, and Column3
=Table1[[#All],[Column1]],Table1[[#All],[Column3]]	All the cells in Column1 and all the cells in Column3
=Table1[[#Headers],[#Data],[Column1]]	The header and data of Column1
=Table1[[#This Row],[Column1]]	The cell at the intersection of the current row and Column1

Structured Reference Syntax Rules

You should be aware of the following syntax rules when creating structured references:

- All table, column and special item specifiers must be enclosed in square brackets. If a specifier contains other specifiers, they should be enclosed in an outer set of brackets.

- Column headers are text strings but do not require quotation marks when being used in a structured reference. As column headers are text strings, you cannot use expressions within the brackets.

- If a column header contains one of the following special characters, the entire column header must be enclosed in square brackets: space, tab, line feed, carriage return, comma (,), colon (:), period (.), left bracket ([), right bracket (]), hash sign (#), single quotation mark ('), double quotation mark ("), left brace ({), right brace (}), dollar sign ($), caret (^), ampersand (&), asterisk (*), plus sign (+), equals sign (=), minus sign (-), greater than symbol (>), less than symbol (<), and division sign (/). The only exception to this is if the only special character used is a space.

- Some special characters have a specific meaning and require the use of a single quotation mark (') as an escape character. These are left bracket ([), right bracket (]), hash sign (#) and single quotation mark (')—for example, ['#Units].

- A structured reference cannot include both #Headers and #Totals specifiers—you must use #All if you want to refer to the entire table.

- You can insert a space after a left bracket and before a right bracket or after a comma to make structured references easier to read—for example, =Table1[[#Totals], [Column1]].

Removing an Excel Table

There are two ways that you can remove an Excel table from a worksheet: you can convert it back to a range so that you can retain the data, or you can delete it entirely. If you want to, you can restore a table to a range of data—for example, if you want to use the Subtotal or Outline function on the data instead. To convert a table to a range of data, select any cell in the table to display Table Tools, select the Design tab, and click Convert to Range in the Tools group. A box will appear asking if you want to convert the table to a normal range; click Yes. You can also convert a table to a range by right-clicking the table and pointing to Table in the context menu and selecting Convert to Range.

When you change a table back to a range, the Filter icons in the header row will disappear, although the data and most formatting should remain intact. Any formulas that included structured references for the table will now contain the cell references instead.

To remove a table and its data from a worksheet completely, you must delete it. To do this, select the entire table, including the header and total rows, by clicking twice in the top-left corner of the table (or by selecting a cell in the table and pressing Ctrl+A twice). Then, click Delete in the Cells group of the Home tab (or press Delete on the keyboard). All the table data, the header row, and any formatting will be removed.

CHAPTER 7

Creating PivotTables and PivotCharts

Pivot Tables are a well-respected feature of Excel and are used in a myriad of ways for dynamically exploring and analyzing large datasets in order to summarize data and make informed decisions. Once you create your initial PivotTable, you can quickly rearrange (or pivot) it in order to view your data in various ways. PivotCharts are interactive charts that can be used to visualize PivotTable reports to convey information about patterns and trends within the data. PivotTables and PivotCharts can take their source data from within Excel or from external sources like databases, Online Analytical Processing (OLAP) cubes, and text files. One of the big advantages of using PivotTables and PivotCharts is that they create new elements within the workbook that can be updated and formatted, leaving the original data source unaltered.

Excel 2007 has introduced some new features to PivotTables and PivotCharts as well as amending existing features. Improvements to PivotTables include new ways to select and rearrange fields, a more compact layout incorporating expand and collapse indicators, and easy formatting using PivotTable styles. PivotCharts also benefit from many of the adjustments to PivotTables and now can be formatted in much the same way as conventional charts. This chapter will examine how you can use PivotTables and PivotCharts to summarize and query data to create flexible and information-rich reports that will help you in your management and decision-making tasks.

Pivoting

PivotTables derive their name from the way they can be used to easily pivot data—that is, to interchange rows and columns. This ability to change the way you view the data can help you to spot important trends or to summarize the data using the most appropriate and informative layout. The easiest way to illustrate this is with a basic example. Figure 7-1 shows part of a table of data listing the number of students for various courses in a college.

	A	B	C	D	E	F	G
1	Subject	Faculty	Mode	Level	Students	Male	Female
2	Art	Humanities	Full-time	Undergraduate	80	39	41
3	Art	Humanities	Part-time	Undergraduate	85	24	61
4	Art	Humanities	Full-time	Postgraduate	23	9	14
5	Art	Humanities	Part-time	Postgraduate	62	12	50
6	Biology	Science	Full-time	Undergraduate	85	62	23
7	Biology	Science	Part-time	Undergraduate	88	50	38
8	Biology	Science	Full-time	Postgraduate	63	51	12
9	Biology	Science	Part-time	Postgraduate	53	25	28
10	Chemistry	Science	Full-time	Undergraduate	108	58	50
11	Chemistry	Science	Part-time	Undergraduate	123	58	65
12	Chemistry	Science	Full-time	Postgraduate	50	28	22
13	Chemistry	Science	Part-time	Postgraduate	59	24	35
14	Dentistry	Science	Full-time	Undergraduate	103	51	52
15	Dentistry	Science	Part-time	Undergraduate	125	66	59
16	Dentistry	Science	Full-time	Postgraduate	45	23	22
17	Dentistry	Science	Part-time	Postgraduate	29	14	15
18	Economics	Business	Full-time	Undergraduate	130	70	60
19	Economics	Business	Part-time	Undergraduate	115	41	74
20	Economics	Business	Full-time	Postgraduate	46	21	25

Figure 7-1. Source data

Figure 7-2 shows the same data summarized to show the number of postgraduate and undergraduate full-time and part-time students for each faculty. From the summary we can clearly see which faculty has the most full-time or part-time students as well as the total postgraduate and undergraduate students for each faculty.

	A	B	C	D
1				
2				
3	Sum of Students	Column Labels		
4	Row Labels	Full-time	Part-time	Grand Total
5	Business	803	893	1696
6	Postgraduate	257	382	639
7	Undergraduate	546	511	1057
8	Humanities	518	819	1337
9	Postgraduate	161	306	467
10	Undergraduate	357	513	870
11	Science	865	660	1525
12	Postgraduate	321	220	541
13	Undergraduate	544	440	984
14	Grand Total	2186	2372	4558
15				

Figure 7-2. This basic PivotTable summarizes the number of postgraduate and undergraduate students for each faculty.

In Figure 7-3, the data has been orientated in a different way. This time the faculties are being used as the column labels instead of the row labels. The emphasis in this summary is on how the numbers of postgraduate and undergraduate students are divided between the faculties.

	A	B	C	D	E
1					
2					
3	Sum of Students	Column Labels			
4	Row Labels	Business	Humanities	Science	Grand Total
5	⊟Postgraduate	639	467	541	1647
6	Full-time	257	161	321	739
7	Part-time	382	306	220	908
8	⊟Undergraduate	1057	870	984	2911
9	Full-time	546	357	544	1447
10	Part-time	511	513	440	1464
11	Grand Total	1696	1337	1525	4558

Figure 7-3. In this PivotTable, the division of postgraduate and undergraduate students between the faculties is clearly summarized.

Finally, the summary in Figure 7-4 uses the same data, but in this case, only the data for the full-time students is displayed. In this example, Mode (full-time or part-time) is a report filter field, which means that we can generate different reports to view a subset of the data for either full-time students or part-time students or view the data for all the students. From this summary, we can clearly see the total number of full-time students (and how they are split between postgraduate and undergraduate courses) for each of the three faculties.

	A	B	C	D	E
1	Mode	Full-time			
2					
3	Sum of Students	Column Labels			
4	Row Labels	Business	Humanities	Science	Grand Total
5	Postgraduate	257	161	321	739
6	Undergraduate	546	357	544	1447
7	Grand Total	803	518	865	2186
8					

Figure 7-4. This PivotTable displays the number of full-time students only for each faculty.

The three summary tables shown in Figures 7-2, 7-3, and 7-4 would take considerable time to produce manually from the raw data shown in Figure 7-1. With Excel's PivotTable tool we can produce all three (and many more summary reports) with just a few mouse clicks!

What Are PivotTables?

Basically, a PivotTable report is an interactive summary of the data in a database. The database can be a list or table within Excel, or it can originate from an external database or file. PivotTables provide us with a means of querying large amounts of data and enable us to quickly create summaries like cross-tabulations or frequency distributions. For example, a PivotTable could be used to summarize a sales database and provide information about the total sales per region or the number of orders placed by each customer. You can also create cross-tabulations to see which products sell best in different areas for each quarter. The uses for PivotTables are almost endless, but you don't have to write a single formula!

Once you have created a PivotTable, you can rearrange the data in almost any way you want, add and remove categories, and view as much or as little detail as you require. Data can be assigned to one of four areas in a PivotTable: the row labels area, the column labels area, the values area, or the report filter area. You can then move fields from one area to another to change the way the data is summarized, and you can create subtotals and grand totals using various summary functions like Sum or Average. In addition to producing subtotals by summing values, counting items, or calculating averages, you can create custom calculations in the form of calculated fields or calculated items. You can also group related fields together, expand or hide the detail, or sort and filter the data in a field.

What Type of Data Can Be Summarized in PivotTables?

PivotTables are designed to work with data stored in a tabular form, like a database, made up of rows (or records) of data. Each column is known as a field and will either consist of values (like the number of students in the previous examples) or categories (like the faculties in the previous examples). Even if the database does not consist of any values, you can still use a PivotTable to create tallies of items or to cross-tabulate fields. Some examples of the kind of questions that can be answered by PivotTables for different types of data are

- *Customer details*: What area do most customers come from?
- *Employee details*: Which department or branch employs the most staff?
- *Sales*: How does one product or sales rep compare with another?
- *Applicant details*: What level of education do most job applicants have?
- *Expenses*: How much was spent on corporate entertaining by each branch last year?

Of course, you could use other Excel tools to answer
other tool in Excel allows you as much flexibility and dat;
PivotTables do. This chapter will guide you through the
create a PivotTable using Excel 2007 and, with it, almost a
you will require.

Creating a PivotTable Report

If you have data laid out in an Excel table or in tabular form in a range where each
column has a heading, you can easily create a PivotTable report from it to interac-
tively summarize your data and produce cross-tabulations. Each column (or field) in
your source data will become a PivotTable field that you can use to analyze multiple
rows of data. With a few clicks, you can create complex groupings and summaries
incorporating thousands of items and using a variety of formulas in a format that
would take significantly longer to set up manually.

PivotTables are surprisingly easy to create and, with Excel 2007, using them has
just gotten easier. To create a PivotTable report, use the following steps:

1. If you want to create a PivotTable using data within Excel, select a cell in the
   range or table that you want to create a PivotTable from.

2. Select the Insert tab on the Ribbon and, in the Tables group, click PivotTable to
   open the Create PivotTable dialog box (see Figure 7-5). (If your data range is an
   Excel table, you can also select Summarize with Pivot from the Tools group on
   the Design tab under Table Tools.)

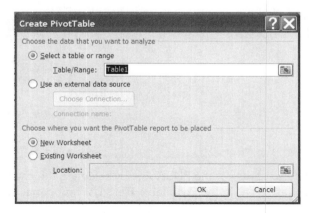

Figure 7-5. Choose the data that you want to use
for your PivotTable and the worksheet that you want
the PivotTable to appear on.

3. Enter the range for your data in the Table/Range field; if your source data is a table, the table name will already be entered here. If you want to use an external data source, select the "Use an external data source" option and click the Choose Connection button to open the Existing Connections dialog box, where you can select the connection you wish to use. You can enter a structured reference in the Table/Range field to refer to a table or part of a table—for example, Expenses[[Jan]:[Jun]] would refer to the range from the Jan column to the Jun column of the Expenses table. If the range is in a different worksheet in the same workbook or in a different workbook, enter the workbook and worksheet name in the following way: **[workbookname]sheetname!range**.

4. Select whether you want to place the PivotTable on a new or the existing worksheet. If you select Existing Worksheet, enter the first cell of the destination range in the Location box.

5. Click OK. An empty PivotTable will appear on the grid with a Field List task pane detailing the fields that can be included in the PivotTable (see Figure 7-6). PivotTable Tools will be added to the Ribbon, incorporating an Options tab and a Design tab.

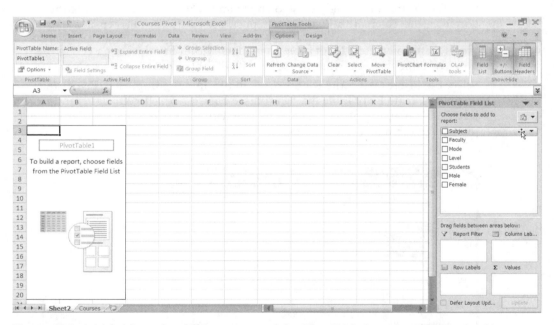

Figure 7-6. Add fields to the different areas of the PivotTable by selecting the checkboxes or by dragging them to the appropriate areas in the PivotTable Field List task pane.

Adding (and removing) fields to the different areas of the PivotTable is really simple in Excel 2007. You can use the checkboxes or the new area drop zones within the PivotTable Field List task pane to distribute fields on the PivotTable. For those of you who prefer to use the traditional method, you still have the option to drag and drop onto the PivotTable area by selecting the Classic PivotTable layout option on the Display tab of the PivotTable Options dialog box (select the Options tab under Pivot-Table Tools and, in the PivotTable group, click Options to open the PivotTable Options dialog box).

To populate the PivotTable, you can select the fields you want to include by using the checkboxes provided in the Field List task pane. As you select each field, Excel will automatically add the field to the PivotTable using the following rules:

- If the field has a numeric data type, it will be added to the Values area along with a summary function of Sum (provided it does not contain any blank cells).
- If the field has a non-numeric data type, it will be added to the Row Labels area.
- OLAP date and time hierarchies are added to the Column Labels area.
- As more non-numeric fields are added, they will be placed on the inside of the fields already in the PivotTable, therefore building a hierarchical structure.

TIP Use the down arrow beside the Close button on the PivotTable Field List task pane to reveal a menu that allows you to move, resize, or close the task pane.

Each of the four areas in the PivotTable is represented by an area in the Pivot-Table Field List task pane. The Report Filter area holds fields that the entire PivotTable is filtered by (previously known as page fields), allowing you to focus on a subset of data. The Row Labels area is where you place fields that you want to use as labels for the values and to appear to the left of the values. The Column Labels area can also be used to hold fields that will act as labels for the values and will appear above the values. Finally, the fields that are summarized by the PivotTable will go in the Values area. If the fields are numeric (and do not contain blank cells), the Sum function is applied by default; if the fields are non-numeric, the Count function will be applied.

As you select the fields for your PivotTable you will notice that, in addition to being added to the PivotTable report, the name of each field will appear in the appropriate area in the areas section at the bottom of the PivotTable Field List task pane. The areas make it easier for you to identify which part of the PivotTable a field is currently placed in. You can add fields to specific areas of the PivotTable by dragging them to the appropriate box in the areas section and you can also drag fields between areas to pivot or change the location of the fields on the PivotTable. Another way that you can change the layout of the PivotTable is by clicking on a field in the areas section of the PivotTable Field List task pane and selecting where you want it to go from the menu that appears.

> **TIP** You can select how the fields and areas are displayed by clicking the View button near the top of the PivotTable Field List task pane and selecting your preferred option. You can choose between Fields Section and Areas Section Stacked, Fields Section and Areas Section Side by Side, Fields Section Only, Areas Section Only (2x2), or Areas Section Only (1x4). To hide the Field List completely, click the Options tab on the Ribbon and, in the Show/Hide group, click Field List, or right-click any field in the PivotTable and select Hide Field List.

Adding and Removing Fields

In order to cross-tabulate and summarize your data, you need to lay out your Pivot-Table report by selecting the fields you want to appear in each area of your PivotTable as follows:

1. Add the fields you want to be included in your PivotTable by selecting their checkboxes in the Field List task pane or by dragging them to the correct area of the list. You can add a field more than once in order to summarize it in different ways. If you cannot see a field that you require in the list, refresh the PivotTable report by right-clicking the PivotTable and selecting Refresh. This will update the PivotTable Field List task pane with any new fields, calculated fields, measures, calculated measures, or dimensions that you have added since creating the PivotTable.

2. To change the location of a field, drag it to another area or click on it in its current area of the PivotTable Field List task pane and, from the menu that appears, select Move to Report Filter, Move to Row Labels, Move to Column Labels, or Move to Values.

3. To change the position of a field within an area in relation to other fields in the same area, click on it in the area of the PivotTable Field List task pane and select Move Up, Move Down, Move to Beginning, or Move to End from the menu as appropriate.

4. To remove a field from the PivotTable, deselect the checkbox in the PivotTable Field List task pane and all instances of the field will be removed from the report. Alternatively, click the field in the areas section of the list and select Remove Field, or right-click the field in the PivotTable and select Remove "field name".

Switching Between Automatic and Manual Updating

By default, adding or removing fields will result in the PivotTable report being auto-matically updated to display the new layout; however, if you are working with a large external data source, this can become quite inefficient. To avoid this problem, you can switch to manual updating while you add, move, or remove fields and then switch back to automatic updating to view the results. To switch to manual updating, select the Defer Layout Update checkbox at the bottom of the PivotTable Field List task pane and then click the Update button when you are ready to update the Pivot-Table report.

If you switch to manual updating, you cannot use the PivotTable report again until you switch back to automatic updating. To return to automatic updating, de-select the Defer Layout Update checkbox.

> **CAUTION** If you close the PivotTable Field List task pane, change to Fields Only view or exit Excel while manual updating is enabled; any changes that you have made to the layout of the PivotTable report will be discarded without confirmation.

Selecting Data in a PivotTable

As PivotTables contain different types of data including labels, data and totals, there are a number of ways to select data. To select the entire PivotTable, click in any cell in the PivotTable, choose the Options tab, and in the Actions group, click Select and then Entire Table (see Figure 7-7). Alternatively, you can use the keyboard shortcut, Ctrl+A. To select all the items in a field, point to the top edge of the field until the mouse pointer becomes a down arrow and then click. If you want to select all the instances of a single item, point to the top edge of a column field item or the left edge of a row field item until the mouse becomes an arrow and then click. When you have selected the items in a field, you can then select only the labels for the items, only the data for the items, or both the labels and data for the items by clicking the Select command in the Actions group and choosing the appropriate option. Appendix B lists some of the other ways that you can select data in a PivotTable.

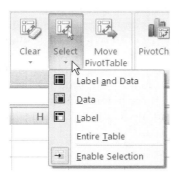

Figure 7-7. The Select menu in the Actions group

Grouping and Ungrouping Fields

You can outline the data in a PivotTable report by creating groups of related items, which can then be expanded or collapsed to show or hide the detail as necessary. You can also insert or remove subtotals for the grouped data in the same way as for standard fields. You can group items by selecting them manually or, for numeric data or dates, you can specify upper and lower limits and Excel will form the groups. You can only group items that belong to the same item in the next level—for example, if you have field levels for Country and City, you cannot group cities that are in different countries.

If you want to group text items or to create custom groupings, you need to manually select the items that are to be grouped together. To manually group items, select the items that you want to group together and click the Options tab under PivotTable Tools. In the Group group, click the Group Selection command. A new field will be created, which will be assigned a default name derived from the name of the field that the grouped data belongs to. Excel will also apply a default name to the new group, such as Group1. Continue creating groups until you have the outline you require. If your PivotTable is in Compact Form, the new field may not be obvious because the field names will not be displayed (see the section "Changing the Layout and Cell Display" later in this chapter).

If you want to group numeric items or date and time data at regular intervals, you can use the Group Field command. To do this, select the numeric or date/time field in the PivotTable that you want to group and click the Options tab under PivotTable Tools. In the Group group, click the Group Field command to open the Grouping dialog box. Enter the first value, date, or time you want to group in the Starting at box and enter the last value, date, or time to group in the Ending at box. Finally, in the By box enter the interval for each group or, for date or time data, select one or more time periods for the groups (if you select Days, choose a value in the Number of days box) and click OK. To group dates by weeks, select only Days in the By box and 7 in the "Number of days" box. You can then add additional time periods such as Month to group by if required. If your data spans more than one year and you do not want months from different years to be combined, make sure you select Years as well as Months.

If you no longer want items to appear in groups, you can remove the groupings to restore the items to their original state. To ungroup items again, select the items that you want to ungroup and click the Options tab under PivotTable Tools. In the Group group, click the Ungroup command. If the grouped items were grouped by manual selection, only the selected items will be ungrouped; if the items were grouped as part of a numeric or date and time field, all groups within the field will be ungrouped.

Expanding and Collapsing Fields

You can expand and collapse the items within the fields of a PivotTable in a similar way to ordinary outlined data. This allows you to control how much detail is shown for the items in your PivotTable. To expand or collapse a single item in a field, use the expand (+) and collapse (-) buttons beside the label for the item in the PivotTable. Or you can right-click the item in the PivotTable, point to Expand/Collapse on the context menu, and select either Expand or Collapse.

To expand or collapse all items in a field, click the Expand Entire Field or Collapse Entire Field command in the Active Field group of the Options tab. Or you can right-click the field in the PivotTable, point to Expand/Collapse on the context menu, and select either Expand Entire Field or Collapse Entire Field.

The Expand/Collapse context menu will display all the fields on an axis, allowing you to expand or collapse to a particular field. To expand or collapse to a given field, right-click on the field in the PivotTable, point to Expand/Collapse on the context menu, and select either Expand to "name of field" or Collapse to "name of field".

Another useful feature of PivotTables is the ability to expand a value cell to display (on a new worksheet) the rows from the source data that were included when calculating the aggregate value. To view the details for a cell, right-click the value cell in the PivotTable that you want to expand to detail and select Show Details. A new worksheet will be created that lists the rows used in the calculation.

> **TIP** To hide (or show if they are already hidden) the Expand and Collapse buttons on the field labels, select the Options tab and, in the Show/Hide group, click +/- buttons.

Formatting a PivotTable

Once you have created your PivotTable report, you can improve its appearance and readability in a variety of ways. You can manually format it using the Font group on the Home tab or by applying cell styles, or you can use one of the predefined PivotTable styles to apply automatic formatting to the entire PivotTable report. You can also choose among a compact, tabular, or outline layout, and you can decide whether to include subtotals or grand totals.

PivotTable Styles

Like Excel tables, PivotTables can now benefit from a new gallery of styles to allow quick and consistent formatting of PivotTable reports. To apply a PivotTable style, do the following:

1. Select the Design tab under PivotTable Tools (see Figure 7-8).

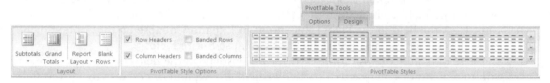

Figure 7-8. Select the Design tab under PivotTable Tools to apply a PivotTable style.

2. Click the up and down arrows to the right of the PivotTable Styles group to scroll through the PivotTable Styles gallery. Click the More arrow at the bottom-right corner of the PivotTable Styles group to open the PivotTable Styles gallery.

3. As you move the mouse pointer over a PivotTable style, the formatting will be applied to your PivotTable, allowing you to preview the style with your actual data. The name of the style will also appear beside the style as a ToolTip. Click the style that you want to apply. If you have already applied any manual formatting, you can right-click the PivotTable style and select either Apply and Clear Formatting or Apply (and Maintain Formatting). If you want to set the style as the default style for all your PivotTables, right-click it and select Set As Default.

4. Select or deselect the Row Headers, Column Headers, Banded Rows, and Banded Columns checkboxes in the PivotTable Style Options group on the Design tab as required (see Figure 7-8).

To remove a PivotTable style, click the More arrow at the bottom-right corner of the PivotTable Styles group and click Clear, or select None (usually the first style) in the PivotTable Style gallery. The PivotTable style formatting will be removed, but any manual formatting will remain intact.

Creating a Custom PivotTable Style

As with regular table styles, you can create your own custom PivotTable styles to accommodate corporate requirements or your personal preferences. To create a custom PivotTable style, do the following:

1. On the Design tab, click the More arrow in the bottom-right corner of the PivotTable Styles group. (Alternatively, on the Home tab, in the Styles group, click Format as Table.)

2. Select New PivotTable Style to open the New PivotTable Quick Style dialog box (see Figure 7-9).

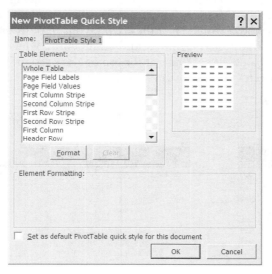

Figure 7-9. Clicking New PivotTable Style opens the New PivotTable Quick Style dialog box.

3. Enter a name for your new PivotTable style in the Name box.

4. Select an element of your style that you want to format from the Table Element list and click the Format button.

5. Use the Font, Border, and Fill tabs of the Format Cells dialog box to specify the font settings for that element of your new style. Click OK when you have finished choosing settings for that element.

6. Continue selecting Font, Border, and Fill settings for each table element that you wish to format.

7. If you want to make your new PivotTable style the default style for any new PivotTables you insert in the current document, select the "Set as default PivotTable quick style for this document" checkbox in the New PivotTable Quick Style dialog box.

8. Click OK when you have finished.

Changing the Layout and Cell Display

Excel 2007 has a new default layout for displaying items in the Row Labels area in order to make PivotTables more compact and easier to read. Instead of each field in the Row Labels area occupying a separate column as in previous versions, all the items from the different fields are displayed in the same column, with indentation used to distinguish between items from different fields, therefore reducing the overall amount of white space. This new Compact Form, as it is called, is one of three row layout options that you can choose from. The other two layout options are Tabular Form, which is similar to the traditional layout, and Outline Form, which resembles Tabular Form except that you can have subtotals at the top of every group. Figure 7-10 illustrates the difference between Compact Form and Outline Form.

	A	B	C	D	E	F	G	H	I
1	Compact Form				Outline Form				
2									
3	Sum of Students	Column Labels			Sum of Students			Mode	
4	Row Labels	Full-time	Part-time		Faculty	Level	Subject	Full-time	Part-time
5	⊟Business	803	893		⊟Business			803	893
6	⊟Postgraduate	257	382			⊟Postgraduate		257	382
7	Economics	46	58				Economics	46	58
8	HRM	92	85				HRM	92	85
9	Management	53	149				Management	53	149
10	Marketing	66	90				Marketing	66	90
11	⊟Undergraduate	546	511			⊟Undergraduate		546	511
12	Economics	130	115				Economics	130	115
13	HRM	161	120				HRM	161	120
14	Management	122	152				Management	122	152
15	Marketing	133	124				Marketing	133	124
16	⊟Humanities	518	819		⊟Humanities			518	819
17	⊟Postgraduate	161	306			⊟Postgraduate		161	306
18	Art	23	62				Art	23	62
19	English	44	50				English	44	50
20	French	40	64				French	40	64

Figure 7-10. The Compact Form and Outline Form layouts for PivotTable reports

To change the layout of a PivotTable report, select the Design tab in PivotTable Tools and, in the Layout group, click Report Layout. Select Show in Compact Form, Show in Outline Form, or Show in Tabular Form as required and use the Blank Rows dropdown to insert or remove blank rows after each item.

You can choose to merge cells for outer row and column items so that the items are centered horizontally and vertically. To merge and center cells containing labels, select the Options tab under PivotTable Tools and, in the PivotTable group, click Options to open the PivotTable Options dialog box. Select the Layout & Format tab (see Figure 7-11) and, in the Layout section, select or deselect the "Merge and center cells with labels" checkbox and click OK. You can also change the width of the indent for row labels in Compact Form here.

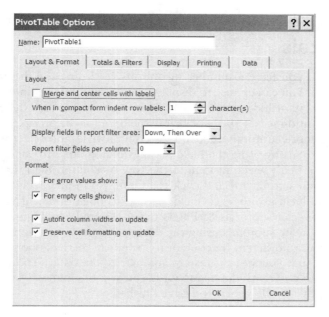

Figure 7-11. The Layout & Format tab of the
PivotTable Options dialog box

Often in a PivotTable, there will be empty cells where no data is available, or error messages will appear in cells when calculations cannot be completed. You can control what is displayed in such cells to remove error messages entirely or to display a more appropriate label such as NA or 0 for missing data or erroneous calculations. To specify the text displayed for errors or in empty cells, open the PivotTable Options dialog box and select the Layout & Format tab. In the Format section, select either (or both) the "For error values show" and the "For empty cells show" checkboxes. Enter the required text in the appropriate box, or leave the box empty to display blank cells. To display zeros in empty cells, deselect the "For empty cells show" checkbox. Click OK when you have finished.

If the data for your PivotTable has come from an OLAP data source, you can decide whether to display or hide row or column items that have no values. To specify whether to include items with no data in the PivotTable, first open the PivotTable Options dialog box and select the Display tab. Select or deselect the "Show items with no data on rows" and "Show items with no data on columns" checkboxes as required and click OK.

If your PivotTable was created in a version of Excel prior to Office 2007, you can choose to display or hide item labels where no fields are in the Values area. Select the Display tab in the PivotTable Options dialog box and select or deselect the "Display item labels when no fields are in the values area" checkbox as required and click OK.

Adding and Removing Subtotals and Grand Totals

With a PivotTable report, you have a number of options regarding the display of subtotals and grand totals. You can choose to display or hide subtotals for individual row or column fields, display or hide grand totals for rows or columns for the entire report, and whether to position totals above or below the data for the group.

You can add one or more subtotals to a row or column field and select which function(s) to use for subtotals by using the Field Settings dialog box. To change the settings for subtotals for a field, select an item in the row or column field that you want to change the subtotal settings for and click the Options tab under PivotTable Tools. Then, in the Active Field group, click Field Settings to open the Field Settings dialog box. Make sure that the Subtotals & Filters tab is selected (see Figure 7-12) and choose Automatic to create subtotals using the default summary function. Alternatively, select Custom to use a different function or to include more than one subtotal and select the function(s) that you want to use to summarize the data. (You cannot use a custom function with an OLAP data source.) If you want to remove subtotals for that field, select None. Click OK when you have finished.

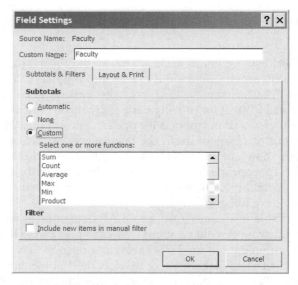

Figure 7-12. You can select the function to be used in subtotals using the Field Settings dialog box.

> **TIP** To quickly insert (or remove) subtotals for a field, right-click the field to reveal the context menu and click Subtotal "field name".

When working with a PivotTable, it may not be appropriate to display subtotals or grand totals because the way the data is summarized will render these values meaningless or misleading. If you do decide to display subtotals, you can choose whether they should appear at the top or the bottom of the group. You can select to show or hide subtotals in fields in your PivotTable report, and where to position them if they are shown, by selecting the Design tab under PivotTable Tools and, in the Layout group, clicking Subtotals. Select Show all Subtotals at Bottom of Group, Show all Subtotals at Top of Group, or Do Not Show Subtotals as required. Note that in Tabular Form, you cannot show subtotals at the top of a group but only at the bottom.

You can also hide or display grand totals for rows and columns by using the Design tab. To change the settings for grand totals, click Grand Totals in the Layout group and select Off for Rows and Columns, On for Rows and Columns, On for Rows Only, or On for Columns Only as required.

Creating a PivotChart Report

To display the data in your PivotTable report in a visual manner, you can create a PivotChart. PivotCharts basically look like regular charts, but in addition to the usual features you expect to find in a chart, PivotCharts have special elements that correspond to the PivotTable report, such as Report Filter, Values, Legend Fields (the series), and Axis Fields (the categories). Also, unlike with standard charts, you can interact with a PivotChart to display the data in a variety of ways by altering the layout or the fields that are displayed. Figure 7-13 shows the data from the summary report in Figure 7-2 displayed as a PivotChart. You can pivot the data in the PivotChart report in the same way as for a PivotTable report, by selecting, deselecting, or moving fields in the PivotTable Field List task pane.

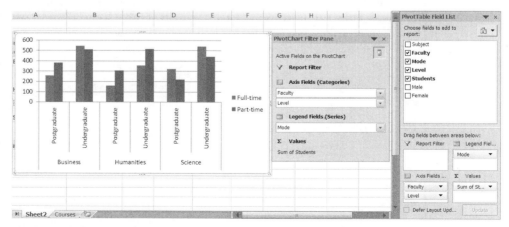

Figure 7-13. You can use the PivotChart Filter Pane to filter the data that is summarized in a PivotChart.

PivotCharts can be created directly from the source data, without creating a PivotTable report first, although a PivotTable report will be created automatically when you create the PivotChart. To create a PivotChart report from a range or table, follow these steps:

1. Select a cell in the range or table that you want to create a PivotChart from.

2. Select the Insert tab on the Ribbon and, in the Tables group, click the down arrow below PivotTable and select PivotChart to open the Create PivotTable with PivotChart dialog box.

3. Enter the range for your data in the Table/Range field (if your source data is a table, the table name will already be entered here). You can enter a structured reference in the Table/Range field to refer to a table or part of a table, such as Expenses[[Jan]:[Jun]]. If the range is in a different worksheet in the same workbook or in a different workbook, enter the workbook and worksheet name in the following way: **[workbookname]sheetname!range**. If you want to use an external data source, select the "Use an external data connection" option and click the Choose Connection button to open the Existing Connections box, where you can select the connection you wish to use.

4. Select where you want to place the PivotChart by clicking New worksheet or Existing worksheet. (If you select Existing worksheet, enter the first cell of the destination range in the Location box.)

5. Click OK. An empty PivotTable and PivotChart area will appear on the grid with a PivotTable Field List and a PivotChart Filter Pane (see Figure 7-14). PivotChart Tools will be added to the Ribbon, incorporating Design, Layout, Format, and Analyze tabs. Excel will assign a default name to the PivotChart—for example, Chart 1. To rename the PivotChart, select the Layout tab under PivotChart Tools and, in the Properties group, enter a new name in the Chart Name box.

6. Add the fields you want to be included in your PivotChart by selecting their checkboxes or by dragging them to the correct area in the PivotTable Field List task pane. See the earlier section "Creating a PivotTable Report" for more information on using the PivotTable Field List task pane.

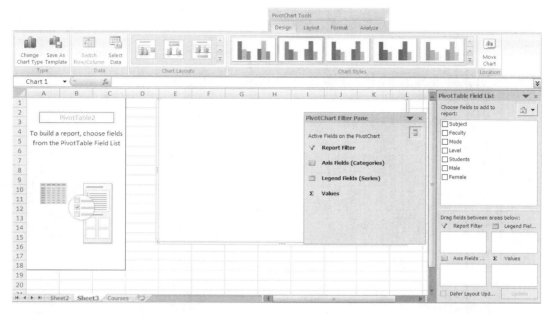

Figure 7-14. Add fields to the different areas of your PivotChart by selecting the checkboxes or dragging them to appropriate areas of the PivotTable Field List task pane.

If you have already created a PivotTable report, the process is different. To create a PivotChart report from an existing PivotTable report, follow these steps:

1. Select a cell in the PivotTable that you want to create a PivotChart from.

2. Select the Options tab on the Ribbon and, in the Tools group, click PivotChart to open the Insert Chart dialog box (see Figure 7-15).

3. Select the chart category and chart type that you want for your PivotChart (or use an existing template) and click OK. A PivotChart will be created from your PivotTable and will appear on the same sheet along with the PivotChart Filter Pane.

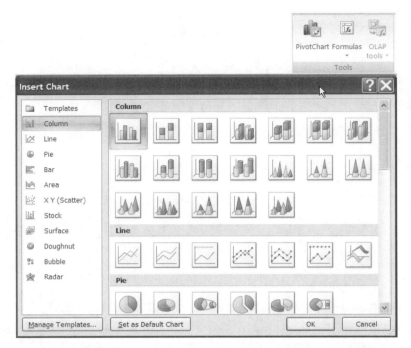

Figure 7-15. Select a category and chart type for your PivotChart from the Insert Chart dialog box.

> **NOTE** You cannot use a Scatter (XY), Bubble, or Stock chart type for a PivotChart report.

If you create a PivotChart report from a PivotTable report, the initial position of the fields on the PivotChart will be determined by the layout of the PivotTable. If you create a PivotChart first, you can determine the layout of the fields and a corresponding PivotTable report will be created automatically. You can adjust the layout of your PivotChart by rearranging the fields in the PivotTable Field List task pane: either drag a field to the new area or click the field and select the correct option from the menu that appears. Any changes that you make to the layout of a PivotChart will be reflected in the associated PivotTable, and vice versa. To show or hide details for a category in a PivotChart report, right-click the category label (or the pie or doughnut slice in a pie or doughnut chart), point to Expand/Collapse on the context menu, and make a selection from the fly-out menu that appears.

Excel 2007 has augmented many of the layout and formatting options for PivotCharts to make them behave more like regular charts and to improve consistency. PivotCharts can adopt the same styles and formatting as ordinary charts, and you can now ensure that most of the formatting you apply to a PivotChart will remain intact after it has been refreshed.

You can format a PivotChart in the same way as you would format an ordinary chart, using the Design, Layout, and Format tabs on the Ribbon. Use the Design tab to change the chart type, save it as a template, change the data source, alter the chart layout, select a chart style, or move the chart to a different location. The Layout tab allows you to adjust specific sections of the chart, such as the chart and axis titles, legend, and data labels. You can also use the Layout tab to format the axes and the background for the chart, and to add features like Trendlines, Drop Lines, High-Low Lines, or Up/Down Bars. The Format tab can be used to choose Shape and WordArt styles, align objects, and resize the chart. The formatting of charts is discussed in detail in Chapter 11.

> **TIP** To convert a PivotChart to an ordinary static chart that cannot be changed, simply delete the associated PivotTable report. To create a static chart from a PivotTable report, copy the data from the PivotTable and, using Paste Special, paste the values onto a range outside of the PivotTable report. Create a chart from the pasted values as normal.

Creating and formatting a PivotTable or PivotChart report is only the beginning. In Chapter 8 you will see how you can manipulate the data within your PivotTable or PivotChart using familiar Excel tools like Sorting and Filtering. I will also introduce you to some features specific to PivotTables and PivotCharts, such as calculated fields and calculated items.

Editing PivotTables and PivotCharts

Once you have created the basic layout of your PivotTable or PivotChart report, you have laid the groundwork for creating a vast range of summary reports and charts. In this chapter, you will learn how you can edit your PivotTable or PivotChart report so that it displays *your* information *your* way. As with lists and tables, you can sort and filter the data within your PivotTable to control which items are shown and the order in which they are displayed. You can also change the settings for a field to alter the function used to summarize data or to amend the layout of the data within the field, or if you want to perform any custom calculations on a Pivot-Table, you can insert a calculated field or a calculated item. The location of the PivotTable or PivotChart and the source of the data can also be updated, and you can quickly remove any filters or clear a PivotTable entirely so that you can begin constructing it again. By the end of this chapter, you could find that PivotTables are the only data analysis tool you'll ever need.

Sorting a PivotTable or PivotChart Field

In a PivotTable, you can display the data in the same order as the data source or you can change the order of items in a field. There are three main ways that you can sort the items in a PivotTable field in the Row Labels or Column Labels area to control the order that they appear in. You can simply sort the items in ascending or descending order based on item names, you can sort them in ascending or descending order based on the values in another field, or you can manually rearrange them to appear in the order that you require.

To perform a basic sort in ascending or descending order, select the row or column label in the PivotTable. Then, select the Options tab under PivotTable Tools and, in the Sort group (see Figure 8-1) click the appropriate sort icon: Sort A to Z or Sort Z to A for text, Sort Oldest to Newest or Sort Newest to Oldest for dates, or Sort Smallest to Largest or Sort Largest to Smallest for numeric data. To open the Sort (field name) dialog box (see Figure 8-1) to view the other sort options, click Sort.

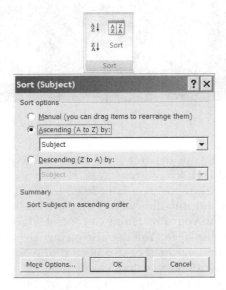

Figure 8-1. Use the icon buttons in the Sort group to quickly sort a field in ascending or descending order, or click Sort to open the Sort dialog box.

In the Sort (field name) dialog box, select Manual if you want to rearrange items by dragging them to new positions in the field. Alternatively, you can sort the field by the values in another field by selecting Ascending or Descending and the field whose values you want to sort the items by. A description of your sort choices will be displayed in the Summary section at the bottom of the dialog box. To reveal further sort options, click the More Options button, and the More Sort Options dialog box will open (see Figure 8-2).

Figure 8-2. The More Sort Options
dialog box

If you want the sort operation to be carried out each time the PivotTable report is
updated, select the "Sort automatically every time the report is updated" checkbox. If
you deselect this checkbox, you can change the "First key sort order" setting to sort
using a custom list instead of normal alphabetical, numerical, or chronological order
(see Chapter 3 for more on custom lists).

> **NOTE** Use the checkbox in the Totals & Filters tab of the PivotTable Options
> dialog box to enable or disable sorting by custom lists. (To open the Pivot-
> Table Options dialog box, right-click the PivotTable and select PivotTable
> Options.) Disabling this option may improve performance if you are sorting a
> large amount of data.

If appropriate, you can also sort by the grand total or by the values in a selected
row or column (you will need to enter a reference for a cell in the row or column containing the values you want to sort by). Click OK to close the More Sort Options
dialog box and click OK again to close the Sort dialog box when you have finished.

You can also rearrange the order of row or column labels or items in a label by
right-clicking the item or label, pointing to Move in the menu that appears, and
selecting one of the commands in the Move menu, as shown in Figure 8-3.

Figure 8-3. You can use the Move context menu to manually arrange the fields in a PivotTable.

The options available when sorting a field in the Values area are slightly different. If you select a field in the Values area and click Sort in the Sort group of the Options tab, the Sort By Value dialog box will open, providing you with two choices: Sort options and Sort direction (see Figure 8-4). Sort options allows you to select Smallest to Largest or Largest to Smallest; Sort direction provides you with the option to sort the values in the selected column from Top to Bottom or to sort the values in the selected row from Left to Right.

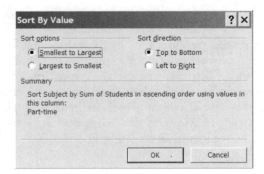

Figure 8-4. The Sort By Value dialog box

Filtering Data in a PivotTable or PivotChart

PivotTables are designed to work well with large datasets, but you may find that you do not want to include all the data in your summary. Filtering allows you to specify criteria and then only display the data that meet the criteria. PivotTable data can be filtered in much the same way as data stored in a regular Excel table, although you cannot filter PivotTable data by cell or font color or cell icon. You can filter labels or items in a PivotTable or PivotChart using one of the common or dynamic filters or by manually selecting the items to include in the filtered data. Filters are automatically reapplied every time you refresh the PivotTable data. To filter labels, do the following:

1. Click the filter arrow beside the name of a field in the column or row area of a PivotTable (or right-click a PivotChart field and select Sort and Filter) to reveal the filter options and the list of values (see Figure 8-5). If necessary, you can change the field by selecting a different field in the Select field box at the top.

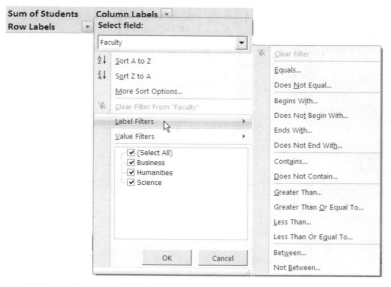

Figure 8-5. Label filters for a PivotTable field

2. To manually filter a field to display only selected items, deselect the (Select All) option and select the checkboxes of the items that you want to include. If you want to resize the Filter menu, click and drag the handle at the bottom-right corner.

3. To apply a common or dynamic filter, select Label Filters (or Date Filters if the field contains dates) or Value Filters to choose from a list of filters like Begins With or Ends With for Labels (see Figure 8-5), Before or After for Dates, or Greater Than or Less Than for Values, and so forth. You can then enter criteria in the Label Filter, Date Filter, or Value Filter dialog box to compare the items in the field with and consequently select which items to display. Date filters include dynamic filters like This Week, Next Month, Last Quarter, and so on; you do not need to enter further criteria for these filters because they are reevaluated automatically based on the current date. See Chapter 5 for more information on filtering data.

4. Click OK when you have finished to apply the filter(s). If you have applied more than one type of filter, they will be evaluated in the order of manual, label or date, and then value.

To filter an item within a label, right-click an item in the field and point to Filter to reveal the filter options for items (see Figure 8-6). You can then click Label Filters to open the Label Filter dialog box or Value Filters to open the Value Filters dialog box. An alternative way to manually filter a field is by using filter by selection—that is, the filter will be based on the contents of the selected cell. To do this, select the items that you want to either hide or display and right-click them. Then, point to Filter in the context menu that appears and select either Keep Only Selected Items or Hide Selected Items. You can also display the top or bottom number, percent, or sum for a field by right-clicking an item, pointing to Filter, and selecting Top 10.

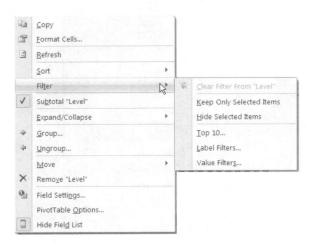

Figure 8-6. You can use the Filter context menu to filter by selection.

In some situations, particularly if you are working with a very large dataset, you may find it more efficient to filter a field before adding it to the PivotTable. You can do this by clicking the dropdown arrow beside the name of the field in the Fields Section of the PivotTable Field List task pane to reveal the filter options and the list of values. You can then manually filter the field by selecting the items you want to display or use one of the label, date, or value filters. When you have finished creating the filter, you can add the field to the PivotTable as normal. Once the field has been added to the PivotTable, you can continue to use the dropdown menu in the field list to apply, edit, or remove a filter, and the Sort options will also become available.

> **TIP** Use the checkboxes in the Display tab in the PivotTable Options dialog box to control whether to display field captions and filter dropdowns and whether to allow multiple filters per field.

To remove the filter from a field, click the Filter icon beside the name of the field in the PivotTable or PivotChart Filter Pane. If necessary, change the field by selecting a different field in the Select Field box at the top, then select Clear Filter from "field name". To remove all filters from the PivotTable, select the Options tab and, in the Actions group, click Clear and select Clear Filters.

Using the Report Filter Area

PivotTable report filters are particularly useful if you want to quickly view different subsets of your data without having to create individual PivotTable or PivotChart reports. If you add a field to the Report Filter area (previously known as the Page Field area) of a PivotTable or PivotChart, you can use it to display a subset of your data by selecting one or more items from the field. The overall structure of the Pivot-Table or PivotChart report will remain unaffected, but only the data for the selected items will be displayed. For example, you can use the Report Filter area to display the data for individual years or for selected departments. The result is like having separate "virtual pages" for each item or combination of items in the Report Filter field.

You can view only the data for a particular item or items within a field by adding the field to the Report Filter area of a PivotTable or PivotChart report and then selecting the items whose data you want to display. To filter the PivotTable data using the Report Filter area, do the following:

1. Add the field that you want to filter the entire PivotTable or PivotChart report by to the Report Filter area by dragging it to the Report Filter area of the PivotTable Field List task pane.

2. Click the filter arrow beside the name of the field in the PivotTable or the PivotChart Filter Pane to reveal the filter menu for the Report Filter field (see Figure 8-7).

Figure 8-7. Select the item or items that you want to filter the entire PivotTable or PivotChart report by.

3. Select the item whose data you want to display from the filter list. To select more than one item check the Select Multiple Items checkbox and deselect All before selecting the items. When you click OK only the data for the selected field items will be displayed on the PivotTable or PivotChart.

Excel can automatically create separate worksheets within the workbook to display each Report Filter page. To display a worksheet for each item in a Report Filter field, make sure that you have at least one field in the Report Filter area of the Pivot-Table. Select the Options tab on the Ribbon and, in the PivotTable group, click the down arrow beside Options and select Show Report Filter Pages. In the Show Report Filter Pages dialog box, select the field that you want to show all the Report Filter pages for and click OK.

If you have more than one field in the Report Filter area of a PivotTable or PivotChart report, you can use the PivotTable Options dialog box to control how the different fields are displayed. To arrange the fields in the Report Filter area, use the following steps:

1. Click the PivotTable report (or the PivotTable associated with a PivotChart) and select the Options tab on the Ribbon.

2. In the PivotTable group, click Options to open the PivotTable Options dialog box.

3. In the "Display fields in report filter area" box, select Down, Then Over from the dropdown list to display fields from top to bottom in the Report Filter area before starting a new column, or select Over, Then Down to display fields in the Report Filter area from left to right before starting a new row.

4. In the "Report filter fields per column" or "Report filter fields per row" box, enter the number of fields to display before starting a new column or row depending on your selection in the "Display fields in report filter area" box. Click OK to close the PivotTable Options dialog box.

Changing Field Settings

Excel will normally apply default settings to a field when you add it to a PivotTable or PivotChart report but often these will not be appropriate to your needs. Through the Field Settings dialog box you can update the settings for a field in various ways, including changing the layout of the data within the individual field or by applying filters or a different summary function. If the field is in the Values area of the Pivot-Table, you can use the Value Field Settings dialog box to change the function or how values are displayed; for example, you can show the value as a percentage of the total or as a running total. To open the Field Settings or Value Field Settings dialog box for a field, do one of the following:

- Click the field name in the areas section of the PivotTable Field List and select Field Settings.
- Right-click the field in the PivotTable and select Field Settings or Value Field Settings.
- Select the field in the PivotTable and choose the Options tab on the Ribbon. In the Active Field group, click Field Settings.

In the Field Settings dialog box, you can amend various settings as follows:

- To change the name of the field, enter the new name in the Custom Name box.
- To change the function used to summarize the field data, select the Subtotals & Filters tab and select the Custom option. Choose the new function(s) from the list provided.
- To remove the summary function used to summarize the field data, select the Subtotals & Filters tab and select None.
- To include any new data in filters applied to the field, in the Subtotals & Filters tab, select the "Include new items in manual filter" checkbox.
- If the field holds numeric data, you can click the Number Format button to select a number format (for example, currency or percentage) or to create a custom number format for the data.

- To change the layout of the data for that field, click the Layout & Print tab and select "Show items in outline form" or "Show items in tabular form". If you select outline form, you can also select the options "Display items from the next field in the same column (compact form)" and "Display subtotals at the top of each group".

- In the Layout & Print tab, you can also select or deselect the "Insert blank line after each item label" and "Show items with no data" options.

- To print each item on a new page, select the "Insert page break after each item" checkbox.

In the Value Field Settings dialog box, you can alter the following settings:

- To change the name of the field, enter the new name in the Custom Name box.

- To change the function used to summarize the field data, select the Summarize by tab. Choose the new function from the list provided.

- To create a custom calculation, click the "Show values as" tab and select the desired option from the "Show values as" list. Your choices include Difference From, % Of, % Difference From, Running Total in, % of Row, % of Column, % of Total, or Index. Select the appropriate field from the Base field list and, if necessary, select an item from the Base item list. The Base field should not be the selected field.

- To change the number format, click the Number Format button to select a number format (for example, currency or percentage) or to create a custom number format for the data. You can also change the function used to summarize the data in a Values field by right-clicking the field in the PivotTable and pointing to Summarize Data By. You can then select a function from the list displayed or click More options to open the Value Field Settings dialog box.

TIP To quickly change the Custom Name of the selected field or item without opening the Field Settings or Value Field Settings dialog box, select the Options tab (or the Analyze tab if the field or item is in a PivotChart report) and, in the Active Field group, enter the new name in the Active Field text box. The name of the field or item in the data source will not be affected.

Refreshing a PivotTable Report or PivotChart Report

If changes have been made to the data that your PivotTable (or PivotChart) is derived from, you need to refresh your report to reflect any alterations to the source data. To refresh a PivotTable or PivotChart report, select a cell in the PivotTable and click the Options tab under PivotTable Tools. Then, in the Data group, click the Refresh command to update the PivotTable data. Alternatively, you can right-click the Pivot-Table and select Refresh from the context menu (or right-click the chart area of a PivotChart and select Refresh Data).

If your PivotTable obtains its data from an external query, you should refresh the query each time you open the workbook to make sure that you are using the most recent version of the data. You can have Excel do this automatically by selecting the Options tab on the Ribbon and, in the PivotTable group, clicking the Options command. In the PivotTable Options dialog box, choose the Data tab and select the "Refresh data when opening the file" checkbox.

You can choose to automatically adjust column widths when you refresh the data in a PivotTable or to retain the current widths regardless of any changes in the data. You can also protect any formatting you have applied to cells. To change any of these formatting settings for a PivotTable, select the Options tab in PivotTable Tools and in the PivotTable group, click Options to open the PivotTable Options dialog box. Select the Layout & Format tab and, in the Format section, select or deselect the "Autofit column widths on update" and/or the "Preserve cell formatting on update" check-boxes as required and click OK. Selecting the "Preserve cell formatting on update" checkbox will also protect PivotChart formatting, although trendlines, data labels, error bars, and other changes to data series will not be preserved.

Changing the Data Source for a PivotTable

Occasionally you may need to change the range, or the external data connection, for the data that your PivotTable is based on. To do this, you can use the Change Data Source command on the Options tab as follows:

1. Select a cell in the PivotTable and click the Options tab under PivotTable Tools.
2. In the Data group, click the Change Data Source command to open the Change PivotTable Data Source dialog box.
3. Enter the new range for the data source in the Table/Range box or click the Choose Connection button to open the Existing Connections dialog box and amend the connection for a PivotTable based on external data.
4. Click OK to close the Change PivotTable Data Source dialog box.

nging the Location of a PivotTable ᴏ. ꝑivotChart

To move the current PivotTable to a different location, either to a new worksheet or to a specified position in an existing worksheet, you can use the Move PivotTable button on the Options tab as described in these steps:

1. Select the Options tab under PivotTable Tools.
2. In the Actions group, click the Move PivotTable button to open the Move PivotTable dialog box.
3. To move the PivotTable to a new worksheet, select New Worksheet and a new worksheet will be created with the PivotTable located there. To move the PivotTable to a new location in an existing worksheet, select Existing Worksheet and enter the sheet and/or cell reference where you want the PivotTable to be positioned in the Location box.
4. Click OK to close the Move PivotTable dialog box.

To move the current PivotChart to a different location, either to a new worksheet or to an existing worksheet, you can use the Move Chart command on the Design tab as follows:

1. Select the Design tab under PivotChart Tools.
2. In the Location group, click Move Chart to open the Move Chart dialog box.
3. To move the PivotChart to a new worksheet, select New sheet and enter a name for the new worksheet in the box. To move the PivotChart to an existing worksheet, select Object in and select the sheet from the dropdown list.
4. Click OK to close the Move Chart dialog box and move the PivotChart.

Creating Formulas Using Calculated Fields or Calculated Items

As the nature of a PivotTable prohibits the insertion of rows or columns, you cannot add formulas to carry out calculations on the data within a PivotTable in the same way as you can for a regular table or data range. When analyzing data using a Pivot-Table, you may find that you want to include additional calculations to the summary functions, subtotals, and grand totals available. To perform a custom calculation on any of the data in a PivotTable or PivotChart report that is not based on an OLAP data source, you need to insert a calculated field or a calculated item. You can then build a formula that accepts data from specified fields or items and display the result in a separate field or as a separate item within a field.

For example, if your PivotTable summarizes the sales for each sales rep for this year, you could use a calculated field to display the target sales for all the sales reps for next year. This would insert an additional field, which would use the same formula to calculate the target sales for each rep. If you want to use data from one or more specific items within a field, you can use a calculated item—to work out the commission for each sales rep using different rates, for instance. You could create a separate item within the field for each sales rep's commission, using a different formula for each item.

You can use operators, expressions, and constants in formulas for calculated fields or calculated items, but you cannot use cell references or defined names. In addition, you cannot use array functions or functions that require cell references or defined names as arguments. Calculations resulting from calculated fields or calculated items in a PivotTable report will be reflected in any associated PivotChart report.

Inserting a Calculated Field

A calculated field is basically a calculation that takes data from other fields, allowing you to display new information in your PivotTable. It will be inserted in the Values area and cannot be moved to the Report Filter, Row Labels, or Column Labels area. For example, if sales for January are expected to increase by 10% next year, you could insert a calculated field to display the result of multiplying January's sales by 1.1. To insert a calculated field, follow these steps:

1. Select the Options tab under PivotTable Tools and, in the Tools group, select Formulas.

2. Click Calculated Field to open the Insert Calculated Field dialog box (see Figure 8-8).

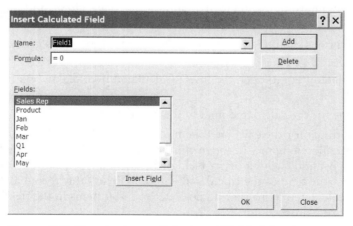

Figure 8-8. Use the Insert Calculated Field dialog box to create a field based on a formula.

3. Enter a name for the calculated field in the Name box.

4. Enter the formula for the calculated field in the Formula box (for example, =Jan*1.1). You can insert field names in the formula by selecting the field from the Fields list and clicking Insert Field or by double-clicking the field. You can also create calculated fields that do not refer to other fields by simply entering a formula or a value.

5. When you have finished constructing your formula, click Add.

6. Continue adding calculated fields or click OK to return to the PivotTable report. The new calculated field will be added to the end of the fields in the Values area.

To change the formula for a calculated field, select Calculated Field from the Formulas dropdown menu to open the Insert Calculated Field dialog box, and select the field from the dropdown list in the Name box. Edit the formula in the Formula box and click Modify. To permanently remove a calculated field, select it from the dropdown list in the Name box and click Delete. If you want to hide a calculated field without removing it permanently, deselect it in the PivotTable Field List task pane.

Inserting a Calculated Item

A calculated item refers to other items within a single field and must appear in the Report Filter, Row Labels, or Column Labels area of a PivotTable. You can use a calculated item to create a formula using data from one or more specific items in a field. The calculated item will then be inserted as an additional item within the field. For example, if you want to use a different formula to calculate the commission for each sales rep, you can create a calculated item for each rep and include these values in the subtotals and total. To insert a calculated item use this procedure:

1. Select a cell in the field in the Report Filter, Row Labels, or Column Labels area, where you want the calculated item to appear. To add a calculated item to a grouped field, ungroup the items first, add the calculated item, and then regroup the items.

2. Select the Options tab under PivotTable Tools and, in the Tools group, select Formulas.

3. Click Calculated Item to open the Insert Calculated Item dialog box (see Figure 8-9).

4. Enter a name for the calculated item in the Name box.

5. Enter the formula for the calculated item in the Formula box. You can insert field names and item names in the formula by selecting them from the Fields list or the Items list and clicking Insert Field or Insert Item. You can only refer to items in the same field as the calculated item in a PivotTable formula. You can also create calculated items that do not refer to other items in the field by simply entering a formula or value.

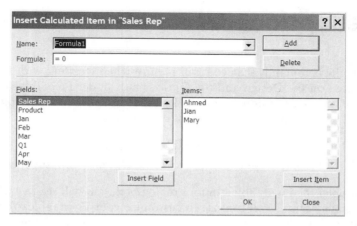

Figure 8-9. Use the Insert Calculated Item dialog box to create an item based on a formula.

6. When you have finished constructing your formula, click Add.

7. Continue adding calculated items or click OK to return to the PivotTable report. The new calculated item will be added to the end of the list of items in the field.

To change the formula for a calculated item, select Calculated Item from the Formulas dropdown list to open the Insert Calculated Item dialog box. Select the item from the dropdown list in the Name box, edit the formula in the Formula box, and click Modify. To permanently remove the calculated item, select it from the dropdown list in the Name box and click Delete. If you want to hide a calculated item without removing it permanently, right-click the item, point to Filter, and select Hide Selected Items.

You can enter different formulas cell by cell for calculated items. For example, if the commission for a sales rep is different for December, you can change the formula in the cell for December by selecting the cell and adjusting the formula in the formula bar. You should take care when inserting calculated items; they may render any totals incorrect because items may be included twice in the total. If this is the case, you can hide grand totals using the Grand Totals command in the Layout group on the Options tab.

If a value in a PivotTable cell is affected by more than one calculated item, its value is determined by the last formula in the solve order. To rearrange the solve order for calculated items, select the Options tab and, in the Tools group, click Formulas and select Solve Order. In the Calculated Items Solve Order dialog box, select a calculated item and change its position in the solve order using the Move Up or Move Down button. To remove the calculated item, click Delete. To display a list of the PivotTable formulas, click Formulas in the Tools group of the Options tab and select the List Formulas command. A new worksheet will be created, displaying the calculated fields and calculated items for the PivotTable.

PivotTable Options

Whilst most of the commands that you will require when working with PivotTables are visibly located on the Design and the Options tabs under PivotTable Tools, you can access more advanced options using the PivotTable Options dialog box. To open the PivotTable Options dialog box, do one of the following:

- Select the Options tab and, in the PivotTable group, click Options.
- Right-click the PivotTable and select PivotTable Options from the menu.

When you open the PivotTable Options dialog box, you will see five tabs, which contain the various options you can use to customize your PivotTable. You can also change the name of the PivotTable by amending the entry in the Name box. Here is an outline of the PivotTable features you can define using each of the tabs in the PivotTable Options dialog box:

- *Layout & Format tab*: Use this tab to merge and center cells with labels, set the indentation for row labels in compact form, specify how fields in the Report Filter area are displayed and the number of report filter fields per column, control what is displayed in empty cells and for error values, and indicate whether to autofit column widths and preserve cell formatting when updating the PivotTable.
- *Totals & Filters tab*: Use this tab to activate grand totals for rows and columns or subtotals for filtered page items, to specify whether to allow multiple filters per field, and to specify whether custom lists can be used when sorting.
- *Display tab*: Use this tab to show or hide the following: expand/collapse buttons, contextual tooltips (row, column, and value information), properties on tooltips (for PivotTables based on OLAP data sources), field captions and filter dropdowns arrows, Classic PivotTable layout (to enable the dragging and dropping of fields onto the grid), items with no data on rows and items with no data on columns (for PivotTables based on OLAP data sources), or item labels when no fields are in the Values area. You can also decide whether to sort the Field List in alphabetical order or in the order the fields appear in the data source.
- *Printing tab*: Use this tab to indicate if you want to print the expand/collapse buttons, repeat row labels on each printed page, and set print titles.

NOTE To print labels you need to select the Page Layout tab on the Ribbon and, in the Page Setup group, click Print Titles. On the Sheet tab of the Page Setup dialog box, enter the appropriate values in the "Rows to repeat at top" and "Columns to repeat at left" boxes.

- *Data tab*: Use this tab to specify if you want to save the source data with the file, enable show details, or refresh data when opening the file for non-OLAP data sources. You can also change the number of items per field deleted from the data source to retain (i.e., the number of items that the PivotTable will "remember" after they have been removed from the data source so that if they are included again, the PivotTable will treat them in the same way as before they were deleted) from the default to none or the maximum.

Deleting a PivotTable or a PivotChart Report

In Excel 2007 you can quickly remove all the fields and formatting from a PivotTable to restore it to its initial state before you first added any fields, allowing you to begin constructing the PivotTable again. To do this, select the Options tab under PivotTable Tools and, in the Actions group, click the Clear command to display the dropdown menu; to remove all the fields from the PivotTable, select Clear All. You can also find the Clear command in the Data group of the Analyze tab under PivotChart Tools.

> **CAUTION** If there is a PivotChart linked to the PivotTable, selecting Clear All will remove any fields and formatting from the PivotChart and the PivotTable. If you are using a shared data connection or sharing data between two or more PivotTables, selecting Clear All may remove any groupings or calculated fields or items in the other PivotTable reports.

If you no longer want a PivotTable or PivotChart in a workbook, you can delete it entirely. To delete a PivotTable or a PivotChart report, select the entire PivotTable or the PivotChart and press the Delete key. Deleting a PivotTable will convert any associated PivotCharts to ordinary charts; however, deleting a PivotChart will not generally affect the associated PivotTable report.

CHAPTER 9

What-If Analysis

What-if analysis basically involves asking questions of the type "What if a value changes?" and is used every day by those involved in data analysis and decision making. "What will our profit be if our sales increase?" or "What will the future value of an investment be if we increase the annual deposit?" are common examples of what-if type questions. The flexible nature of spreadsheets makes them ideal for carrying out what-if analyses, and Excel provides a number of tools to simplify the process of creating dynamic models, such as data tables, the Scenario Manager, Goal Seek, and Solver. These tools will allow you to explore various outcomes or solve complex problems without having to enter multiple versions of formulas.

A one-variable data table can be used to carry out multitudinous calculations for one or more formulas using different values for one input variable. Alternatively, you can create a two-variable data table to accept different values for two input variables and display the varying results for a single formula. Data tables avoid the need to enter the same formula or function repeatedly for each different input value or combination of input values, and enable you to see the effect of changing the input values by displaying the different results in a convenient table layout. Excel's Scenario Manager can be used when you want to vary more than two input cells, allowing you to store each set of values as an individual scenario. You can then display a selected scenario on the worksheet or create a summary of all your scenarios on a separate worksheet using either an outline or a PivotTable format.

Goal Seek looks at what-if analysis in reverse and provides you with a way to discover the input value required to produce a given result to a calculation. Solver is an add-in that operates in a similar way to Goal Seek but with the functionality to work out values for multiple input cells and to impose constraints on the values that these cells can have. As a result, Solver can be used to find solutions to complex problems that would take a long time to solve otherwise.

In this chapter we will look at each of these tools in turn and how they can be used to answer what-if type questions, solve problems, and aid decision making.

Data Tables

Excel data tables allow you to view how changing certain values in your formulas will affect the results of the formulas. In one operation you can produce multiple versions of your calculations and have the results laid out in a tabular form in your worksheet, enabling you to easily view and compare the various results. In Excel you can create either a one-variable data table or a two-variable data table depending on whether you want to test the effect of altering one or two variables. A one-variable data table can be used with numerous formulas, but a two-variable data table can have only one formula.

Creating a One-Variable Data Table

A one-variable data table can be used to view the effect of adjusting one variable on the outcome of one or more formulas. For example, you could use a one-variable data table to calculate the effect of different interest rates on the repayments for a loan. When designing a one-variable data table, you must have your input values listed down one column (column-oriented) or across one row (row-oriented). Formulas in a one-variable data table must refer to an input cell in which each input value in the data table is substituted. You can create a one-variable data table using the following procedure:

1. Type the list of values that you want to be substituted in the input cell down one column (leaving a blank row at the start) or across one row (leaving a blank column at the start).

2. If your values are in a column, type the formula that you want to use in your data table in the *row above the first value* and *one cell to the right of the column*. Enter any additional formulas in the cells to the right of the first formula. If your values are in a row, type the formula in the *column to the left of the values* and *one cell below the row*. Enter any additional formulas in the cells below the first formula.

3. Select the range of cells containing the formulas and substitute values (do not include any headings).

4. Select the Data tab on the Ribbon and, in the Data Tools group, click the down arrow beside What-If Analysis (see Figure 9-1). From the dropdown list, select Data Table to open the Data Table dialog box.

5. If your input values are listed across a row, enter the cell reference of the input cell in the "Row input cell" box. If your input values are listed down a column, enter the cell reference of the input cell in the "Column input cell" box.

6. Click OK. Excel will compute the results for the formula or formulas, using the different values for the input variable, and display each outcome in the data table. You can then format the data table as normal.

Figure 9-1. Select Data Table from the
What-If Analysis menu to open the
Data Table dialog box.

Figure 9-2 illustrates an example of a one-variable data table incorporating three formulas. At the top of the worksheet is a Profit Analysis model and below this is a column-oriented, one-variable data table. The window on the left shows the values displayed on the worksheet after the data table has been generated, and the window on the right shows the formulas used for each calculation. (Note that the data table itself is generated using a special function called the TABLE function.) The input cell is cell B4 (Units Sold) and the different values we want to use as the input variable in the formulas are listed in the range B12:B19.

	A	B	C	D	E
1		One-Variable Data Table			
2	Calculating how the number of Units Sold will affect the Profit				
3					
4	Units Sold	10000	Fixed Costs	$ 400,000	
5	Selling Price per Unit	$ 100	Variable Cost per Unit	$ 50	
6	Total Revenue	$1,000,000	Total Costs	$ 900,000	
7					
8	Profit	$ 100,000			
9					
10		Units Sold	Total Revenue	Total Costs	Profit
11			$ 1,000,000	$ 900,000	$100,000
12	This is the	9000	900000	850000	50000
13	list of	9500	950000	875000	75000
14	values that	10000	1000000	900000	100000
15	will be	10500	1050000	925000	125000
16	substituted	11000	1100000	950000	150000
17	in the input	11500	1150000	975000	175000
18	cell	12000	1200000	1000000	200000
19		12500	1250000	1025000	225000

	A	B	C	D	E
1		One-Variable Data Table			
2	Calculating how the number of Units Sold will affect the Profit				
3					
4	Units Sold	10000	Fixed Costs	400000	
5	Selling Price per Unit	100	Variable Cost per Unit	50	
6	Total Revenue	=B4*B5	Total Costs	=D4+(B4*D5)	
7					
8	Profit	=B6-D6			
9					
10		Units Sold	Total Revenue	Total Costs	Profit
11			=B4*B5	=D4+(B4*D5)	=B6-D6
12		9000	=TABLE(,B4)	=TABLE(,B4)	=TABLE(,B4)
13	This is the	9500	=TABLE(,B4)	=TABLE(,B4)	=TABLE(,B4)
14	list of values	10000	=TABLE(,B4)	=TABLE(,B4)	=TABLE(,B4)
15	that will be	10500	=TABLE(,B4)	=TABLE(,B4)	=TABLE(,B4)
16	substituted	11000	=TABLE(,B4)	=TABLE(,B4)	=TABLE(,B4)
17	in the input	11500	=TABLE(,B4)	=TABLE(,B4)	=TABLE(,B4)
18	cell	12000	=TABLE(,B4)	=TABLE(,B4)	=TABLE(,B4)
19		12500	=TABLE(,B4)	=TABLE(,B4)	=TABLE(,B4)

Figure 9-2. Use a one-variable data table to see how changing one variable will affect one or more formulas. The window on the right shows the formulas used.

The formulas to be evaluated in the data table are arranged in the cell range C11:E11 and calculate the Total Revenue, Total Costs, and Profit using the variable Units Sold (B4) and the constant values for Selling Price per Unit (B5), Fixed Costs (D4), and Variable Cost per unit (D5). As the three formulas also appear in cells B6 (Total Revenue), D6 (Total Costs), and B8 (Profit) in the Profit Analysis, you could use references to these cells in cells C11:E11 rather than retyping the formulas.

To create the data table in this example, you would have selected cells B11:E19 and entered B4 in the "Column input cell" box in the Data Table dialog box (Excel will make the input cell reference absolute). The resulting data table indicates the changes to the Total Revenue, Total Costs, and Profit for each of the different numbers of Units Sold listed. As you can imagine, this is much quicker and easier to compare than entering each of the values for the input variable in cell B4 in turn and viewing the changes to cells B6, D6, and B8.

If you change any of the input values in the data table, the data table will recalculate each formula automatically. If you extend the list of data values or add more formulas, you will need to select the new range and execute the data table again.

As Excel uses an array formula (the TABLE function) to create a data table, you cannot delete any of the results cells in a data table or change a results cell's value. If you try to edit an individual element of a data table, an error message will appear. To change the results, you must select the entire data table and execute the Data Table command again from the What-If Analysis dropdown menu. If you want to delete the results, you must select and delete the entire results array by pressing the Delete key. To remove the entire data table select all formulas, input values, and resulting values and press Delete.

Creating a Two-Variable Data Table

A two-variable data table will allow you to view the effect of changing two input variables on the result of a single formula. For example, you could use a two-variable data table to calculate the effect of different interest rates and number of repayments on the repayment amount for a loan. A two-variable data table can only use one formula, which must refer to two input cells. Use the following procedure to set up a data table to accept two input variables:

1. Enter the formula that refers to both input cells in a cell.

2. In the column below the formula, enter one of the sets of values that you want to use in your data table and, in the row to the right of the formula, enter the other set of values.

3. Select the range of cells containing the formula and both sets of values (do not include any headings).

4. Select the Data tab on the Ribbon and, in the Data Tools group, click the down arrow beside What-If Analysis. From the dropdown list, select Data Table to open the Data Table dialog box.

5. Enter the cell reference of the input cell that corresponds to the values in the row in the "Row input cell" box. Enter the cell reference of the input cell that corresponds to the values in the column in the "Column input cell" box.

6. Click OK. Excel will calculate the formula repeatedly using each combination of the different values for the input variables in turn and display the outcome for each calculation in the data table. You can then format the data table as normal.

Figure 9-3 shows an example of a two-variable data table indicating the Profit for different values of Units Sold and Selling Price per Unit. The formula for the data table (=B6-E6) has been entered in cell B11. Alternatively, we could enter a reference to cell B8 here to display the Profit. The various values we want to substitute for the Units Sold (column) input cell are entered in cells B12:B19 and the different values for the Selling Price per Unit (row) input cell are in cells C11:F11.

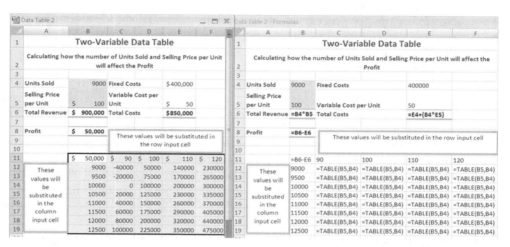

Figure 9-3. Use a two-variable data table to see how changing two variables will affect the outcome of a formula. The window on the right shows the formulas used.

To generate the data table shown in Figure 9-3, you would select cells B11:F19 and enter **B5** in the "Row input cell" box and **B4** in the "Column input cell" box in the Data Table dialog box. The completed data table shows the Profit for each combination of Units Sold and Selling Price per Unit using a TABLE function, which accepts the row input cell reference and column input cell reference as its arguments.

If your data table is particularly large, it can take quite a long time to recalculate each time you update any of the input variables. To switch off automatic updating for data tables, select the Formulas tab and, in the Calculation group, click the down arrow beside Calculation Options. You can then select either Automatic Except for Data Tables (to recalculate other elements of the worksheet automatically except for data tables) or Manual (to switch off automatic calculation altogether). To recalculate your data table at any time, click the Calculate Now icon in the Calculation group (or press F9 on the keyboard) to calculate your entire workbook, or click the Calculate Sheet icon in the Calculation group (or press Shift+F9) to calculate the current worksheet only. To switch back to automatic updating, select Automatic in the Calculation Options menu.

Scenarios

Scenarios are another of Excel's what-if analysis tools, which, like data tables, can be used to examine how varying input values affect results. However, unlike data tables, scenarios can accept more than two input variables. Each set of values that you insert in a worksheet model can be stored as a separate scenario, and the Scenario Manager can automate the process of creating, editing, and displaying scenarios for you. You can create a report that summarizes all of your scenarios on one worksheet, allowing you to compare them and helping you to make informed decisions, or you can create a PivotTable report to analyze your scenarios that way.

Scenarios are basically like different versions of the same worksheet model, with each version using a different set of input values. Before creating a scenario, you need to construct your model on the worksheet and decide which cells will be the input cells (changing cells) and which cells will be the results cells. To make it easier to create your scenarios and to make the resulting summary reports more comprehensible, you should label and define names for all the changing and results cells. Figure 9-4 illustrates a worksheet model that can be used to create scenarios to display the Total Revenue, Total Costs, and Profit for different values of Units Sold, Selling Price per Unit, Variable Cost per Unit, and Fixed Costs.

> **NOTE** A scenario can only have up to 32 changing cells. If you attempt to specify more than that, Excel will display an error message.

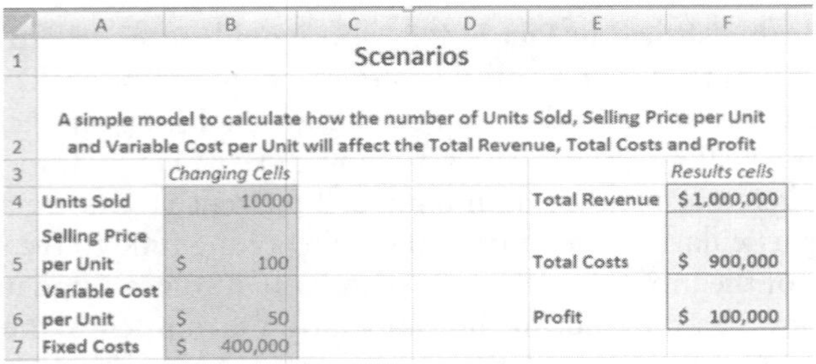

	A	B	C	D	E	F
1				Scenarios		
2		A simple model to calculate how the number of Units Sold, Selling Price per Unit and Variable Cost per Unit will affect the Total Revenue, Total Costs and Profit				
3		*Changing Cells*				*Results cells*
4	Units Sold	10000			Total Revenue	$ 1,000,000
5	Selling Price per Unit	$ 100			Total Costs	$ 900,000
6	Variable Cost per Unit	$ 50			Profit	$ 100,000
7	Fixed Costs	$ 400,000				

Figure 9-4. Before creating scenarios, construct a model, including changing cells and results cells.

In this example, the input or changing cells are B4:B7 and the results cells are F4:F6. All the changing cells and results cells can be named using the labels on their left to make the scenarios more meaningful. To create scenarios for a model like this, follow these steps:

1. Define names for the changing cells and results cells by selecting the cells and their corresponding labels. Select the Formulas tab and, in the Defined Names group, click the Create from Selection command.

2. In the Create Names from Selection dialog box, select the Left column checkbox (or the appropriate checkbox for the location of your labels) and click OK. Excel will name each cell according to its label, inserting underscore characters (_) to replace any spaces in the label. (See Chapter 3 for more information on defining names.)

3. Select the Data tab and, in the Data Tools group, click the down arrow beside What-If Analysis and select Scenario Manager. The Scenario Manager dialog box will open.

4. In the Scenario Manager dialog box, click the Add button to create your first scenario. The Add Scenario dialog box will appear (see Figure 9-5).

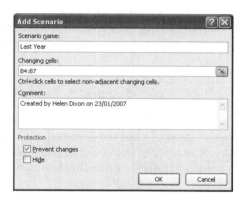

Figure 9-5. Enter the details for the scenario in the Add Scenario dialog box.

5. In the Add Scenario dialog box, type a name for your scenario in the Scenario name box. In the Changing cells box, enter the cell references for the cells whose values you want to change (B4:B7 in the example in Figure 9-4), using commas to separate noncontiguous cells. If you want to, edit or delete the text in the Comment box. Select any options you want under Protection; the Prevent changes and Hide options under Protection apply only when you protect the worksheet (by clicking Protect Sheet in the Changes group of the Review tab) and deselect the Edit scenarios checkbox in the Protect Sheet dialog box. Finally, click OK to go to the Scenario Values dialog box (see Figure 9-6).

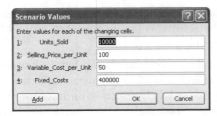

Figure 9-6. Enter the values for the changing cells in the Scenario Values dialog box.

6. In the Scenario Values dialog box, the current values for the cells (if any) will already be entered in the respective box for each changing cell. (If you have defined names for the changing cells, Excel will use these names to identify each cell; otherwise, it will use the cell reference.) If you do not want to keep the current values, enter the appropriate values for this scenario instead. Click the Add button to return to the Add Scenario dialog box to create another scenario (this time the reference for the changing cells will already be in the Changing cells box).

7. Continue creating scenarios by changing one or more values for the changing cells. When you have created your last scenario, click the OK button instead of the Add button to return to the Scenario Manager dialog box.

Once you have defined your scenarios, you can use the Scenario Manager to add new scenarios or to display, edit, or delete existing scenarios. You can also merge scenarios from another workbook or create a report or PivotTable to summarize the scenarios.

Displaying a Scenario and Creating a Summary Report

You can view individual defined scenarios at any time on the worksheet by using the Scenario Manager, or you can create a summary report or PivotTable to create a new worksheet outlining all the scenarios. Generally a Scenario Summary is best for viewing scenarios, although a PivotTable report may be beneficial if you have a large number of scenarios with multiple results cells (see Chapters 7 and 8 for more information on PivotTable reports).

To display scenarios using the Scenario Manager, do the following:

1. In the Data Tools group, click the down arrow beside What-If Analysis and select Scenario Manager. The Scenario Manager dialog box will open.

2. To display a particular scenario, select it in the Scenarios list and click the Show button. The worksheet will display the values for that scenario.

3. Alternatively, to create a summary of all the scenarios, click the Summary button.

4. In the Scenario Summary dialog box, select either Scenario summary or Scenario PivotTable report.

5. In the Results cells box, enter the references for the results cells in your worksheet (F4:F6 in the example in Figure 9-4) and click OK. You must have at least one results cell to generate a Scenario PivotTable report but you do not need results cells to create a Scenario Summary report. The Scenario Summary or Scenario PivotTable report will be displayed on a new worksheet. Figure 9-7 shows both the Scenario Summary and Scenario PivotTable worksheets for the model in Figure 9-4.

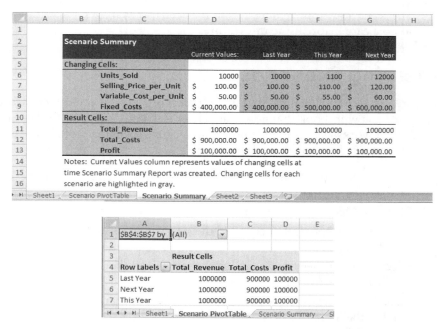

Figure 9-7. To display multiple scenario results, you can use either a Scenario Summary or a Scenario PivotTable report.

TIP Use the PivotTable's Report Filter field to view scenarios created by other users who have access to the workbook.

Editing and Deleting a Scenario

If you no longer require a scenario or if you want to change its name, comment, values, or protection settings, you can use the Scenario Manager to remove or modify it. To update your scenarios, do the following:

1. Open the Scenario Manager dialog box by selecting Scenario Manager from the What-If Analysis list.

2. To modify a scenario, select it in the Scenarios box and click the Edit button to open the Edit Scenario dialog box, which is similar to the Add Scenario dialog box. Change the name, cells, comment, or protection for the scenario as required.

3. Click OK to open the Scenario Values dialog box and alter the values for the changing cells if necessary. Click OK to return to the Scenario Manager dialog box.

4. To delete a scenario, select it in the Scenarios box and click the Delete button. The scenario will be removed from the Scenario Manager, but without warning, so take care before using this feature.

Merging Scenarios

If there are scenarios defined within another worksheet of the current workbook or another open workbook that uses a similar model, you can merge these scenarios into the current worksheet. This will allow you to create a summary of all the scenarios. To merge scenarios from other worksheets into the active worksheet, do the following:

1. Open the Scenario Manager by selecting Scenario Manager from the What-If Analysis list.

2. Click the Merge button to open the Merge Scenarios dialog box.

3. Select the workbook that contains the scenario worksheet from the Book dropdown list.

4. Select the worksheet that contains the scenario(s) that you want to merge from the Sheet dropdown list.

5. Click OK to return to the Scenario Manager. The merged scenario(s) will be listed in the Scenarios box.

6. Create a summary report or PivotTable report, edit or delete the merged scenarios as normal.

Goal Seek

If you already know the result you require and want to determine the value that will achieve this result, you can use Excel's Goal Seek feature. In the examples for data tables and scenarios, we supplied various input cell values and used Excel to calculate the profit. Goal Seek uses the opposite approach; it will allow us to specify the profit we require and which variable to change, and will return the solution. For example, if our Selling Price per Unit, Fixed Costs, and Variable Cost per Unit are constant, we can use Goal Seek to discover the number of units we need to sell to return a certain profit.

When setting up a worksheet to use Goal Seek, you need to have a formula in one cell and a variable for the formula, whose value you want to find, in another cell. You can have other variables in your formula, but Goal Seek can manipulate only one variable at a time so the others will remain constant. Goal Seek will find the solution (if there is one) by using an iterative method. Here are the steps required to use Goal Seek:

1. Select the Data tab and, in the Data Tools group, click the down arrow beside What-If Analysis and select Goal Seek.

2. In the Set cell box in the Goal Seek dialog box (see Figure 9-8), enter the reference for the Goal cell (the cell that contains the formula).

3. In the To value box, enter the desired value you want in the Goal cell.

4. In the "By changing cell" box, enter the reference to the Changing cell (the cell that contains the variable you want to find the value for).

5. Click OK. Excel will begin the iteration and display the Goal Seek Status dialog box, which will indicate if Goal Seek has found a solution. Click OK to accept the solution or Cancel to reject it.

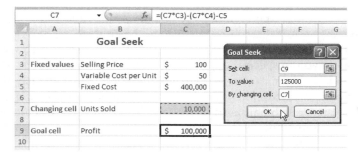

Figure 9-8. Use Goal Seek to find the input value required to generate a specified result to a formula.

Figure 9-8 illustrates Goal Seek being used to find the number of units that must be sold to achieve a profit of $125,000. The formula used here for the Profit is =(C7*C3)-(C7*C4)-C5—that is, the Total Revenue (Selling Price multiplied by Units Sold) minus the Total Variable Cost (Variable Cost per Unit multiplied by Units Sold) minus the Fixed Cost. In the Goal Seek dialog box, the reference for the Profit cell (C9) is entered into the Set cell box, the target value (125000) is entered into the To value box, and the Units Sold cell (C7) is entered into the "By changing cell" box. When you run the Goal Seek command, Excel repeatedly tries different values in cell C7 until it finds a value that returns 125000 in cell C9.

The example in Figure 9-8 is fairly simple and Goal Seek quickly finds an exact solution. For many calculations, it may be more difficult to obtain an exact solution and so you can set limits on iterative processes to prevent Excel searching for too long for an answer. To change the settings for iterative calculation, follow these steps:

1. Click the Microsoft Office button and click Excel Options.

2. Select the Formulas category and select the "Enable iterative calculation" checkbox under Calculation options.

3. To change the maximum number of times Excel will recalculate, enter the new value in the Maximum Iterations box.

4. To change the accuracy of the result that you will accept, enter the new value in the Maximum Change box.

5. Click OK to close Excel Options.

> **TIP** If a Goal Seek calculation is taking a long time, you can click the Pause button in the Goal Seek Status dialog box to stop the calculation or click the Step button to see the values that are being tried.

Solver

For multivariable formulas and equations, you can use the Solver Add-In, which is typically located on the Add-Ins tab on the Ribbon when installed and operates like an extension to the Goal Seek feature. As well as allowing you to include several variables, Solver enables you to specify conditions or constraints that must be met for the solution to be valid. You can also use Solver to search for a value for each of the variables that will produce a maximum or minimum result value for the formula. As there may be several possible combinations of values that will return the specified result for a formula, you can store models in Solver to retrieve later.

Solver can be used to find solutions to a wide variety of management and optimization problems from inventory to logistics. For example, you could use Solver to calculate the maximum number of different products you can manufacture given various inventory levels of shared components, or you could work out the minimum number of shipments required to transfer stock from factories to warehouses.

Generally Solver is not installed by default when you first set up Excel, but you can easily add it by clicking the Microsoft Office Button and clicking Excel Options. Select the Add-Ins category and, in the Manage dropdown list at the bottom of the dialog box, make sure that Excel Add-ins is selected and click Go. In the Add-Ins dialog box, select the Solver Add-in checkbox and click OK. An Add-Ins tab will now be displayed on the Ribbon (if it was not already there) with a Menu Commands group containing the Solver add-in. This process has to be carried out only once.

Solver is a much more complicated and powerful tool than Goal Seek and can be used to solve complex problems and equations. When designing a model to use with Solver, you need to have one or more changing (input) cells whose values you want to find. You also need a target cell that you want to set to a specified value or find a maximum or minimum value for. The target cell must depend on the changing or input cells. You also need to decide what constraints any solution must adhere to—for example, a correct solution may require that certain cells are greater than or less than a particular value or that a changing cell's value must be an integer (whole number).

Figure 9-9 shows Solver being used to work out the maximum number of three different items that can be produced using the available quantities of three components and with a minimum number of ten of each item being produced. The model in the worksheet shows the number of each component (A, B, and C) required to produce one unit of each of the three items X, Y, and Z. Cells C8:E8 contain formulas to calculate the total number of each component required to produce the numbers of each item specified in cells B5:B7. For example, cell C8 contains the formula =(B5*C5)+(B6*C6)+(B7*C7). The current inventory levels for each of the three components are also indicated in cells C11:E11.

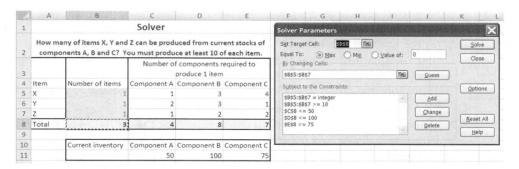

Figure 9-9. Use the Solver add-in to adjust the values in the input cells to produce the required result in the target cell, subject to specified constraints.

To utilize Solver to find a solution for the problem illustrated in Figure 9-9, you would use the following steps:

1. Select the Add-Ins tab on the Ribbon and, in the Menu Commands group, click Solver.

2. In the Set Target Cell box in the Solver Parameters dialog box, enter the reference for the cell whose value you want to specify, maximize, or minimize (B8). This cell must contain a formula. Select the appropriate option beside Equal To to indicate what you want Solver to return—that is, select Max to maximize the value in the Target Cell, select Min to minimize the value, or select Value of and enter a value in the box to find a specific value. In this example you would select Max because you want to maximize the number of items.

3. In the By Changing Cells box, enter the reference(s) to the cells or range whose values you want Solver to find (B5:B7), using commas to separate noncontiguous cells. Alternatively, you can click the Guess button to have Excel guess the cells or range based on the target cell.

4. To add the constraints to the problem, click the Add button to open the Add Constraint dialog box. The first constraint you are going to set is that the values in cells B5:B7 should be integers as you cannot produce a fraction of an item. To set this constraint, enter the reference of the cells that you want the constraint to apply to in the Cell Reference box (B5:B7), then select the option for integer (int) from the middle box, which will automatically enter Integer in the Constraint box. If the cells B5:B7 have been formatted to contain numbers with no decimal places, you will not need to set the constraint that these cells contain integers. Also, int and bin relationships can only be applied in constraints on adjustable cells. Click the Add button to add the next constraint.

5. Your second condition is that you must produce at least ten of each item. To set this constraint, enter the reference of the cells that you want the constraint to apply to (B5:B7) in the Cell Reference box, select the greater than or equal to operator (>=) in the middle box, and enter **10** in the Constraint box. Click Add to add the next constraint.

6. Next you need to set the limits for the number of each component in stock. To set the limit for Component A, enter **C8** in the Cell Reference box, select the less than or equal to (<=) operator in the middle box, and enter **50** in the Constraint box (or you could enter the cell reference C11). For nonlinear problems, each adjustable cell can have up to 100 constraints. Click Add and repeat this step for Component B and Component C.

7. When you have entered the final constraint, click OK to return to the Solver Parameters dialog box. All your conditions will be listed in the Subject to the Constraints box. To edit or delete a constraint, select the constraint in the Subject to the Constraints box and click Change to open the Change Constraint dialog box or Delete to remove the constraint.

8. To begin the solution process, click the Solve button (you can interrupt the solution process at any time by pressing the Esc key). When Solver has found a solution, the Solver Results dialog box will appear. If the maximum time or iterations is reached before Solver finds a solution, or if you have selected the Show Iteration Results option, the Show Trial Solution dialog box will appear. Use the Continue or Stop button to continue searching for a solution or to stop the process, or you can save the current solution as a scenario by clicking Save Scenario. At this stage you can do any of the following:

   - If you want to replace the values on the worksheet with the values that Solver has suggested, make sure that the Keep Solver Solution option is selected and click OK.

   - To retain the original values in the cell, select Restore Original Values and click OK.

   - To save the solution as a scenario that can be used in the Scenario Manager, click Save Scenario and enter a name for the scenario in the Scenario Name box in the Save Scenario dialog box.

   - To create an Answer, Sensitivity and/or a Limits report to view how Solver reached the solution, select one or more of the reports from the list and click OK. If Solver does not find a solution, this will not be available.

If you choose to create one or more reports, Excel will display each report on a new worksheet. Sensitivity and Limits reports will not be meaningful for problems with integer constraints; therefore, Excel will not produce them in this example.

> **NOTE** In the Constraints section of an Answers report, you will see either Binding or Not Binding under the Status for each constraint. Binding means that a constraint was satisfied at its limit and with no slack. If the constraint is not binding, the Status column will indicate how far the result is from the constraint.

You can set various options for Solver to maximize its likelihood of finding a solution, to speed up the solution process, or to control how it operates. For example, you can specify the maximum time or number of iterations that Solver will use in trying to find a solution or you can instruct Solver to assume that adjustable cells are non-negative—that is, they contain positive values. If Solver fails to find a solution to your problem it may be worthwhile adjusting one or more of the Solver options and running Solver again. To open the Solver Options dialog box, click the Options button in the Solver Parameters dialog box. Table 9-1 outlines the purpose of the various Solver Options.

Table 9-1. Solver Options

Solver Option	What It Does
Max Time	Sets the maximum time in seconds that Solver will spend on a problem, although the default of 100 is generally sufficient.
Iterations	Sets the maximum number of attempts (iterations) that Solver will make in trying to find a solution, although the default of 100 is usually adequate.
Precision	Specify the accuracy required to satisfy a constraint by entering a value between 0 and 1—the smaller the number (more decimal places), the higher the precision. Specifying less precision may reduce the time taken by Solver to find a solution; however, the result may be less accurate.
Tolerance	Sets the maximum percentage of error permitted for integer solutions. A higher tolerance may speed up the solution process.
Convergence	When the relative change in the target cell is less than this value for the last five iterations, Solver will stop. This should be a value between 0 and 1, and the smaller the number, the less relative change allowed (only relevant for nonlinear problems).
Assume Linear Model	Selecting this option may solve the problem more quickly, but it can only be used if all the relationships in the model are linear; in other words, it cannot be used if changing cells are multiplied or divided or if the problem uses exponents. If this option is selected, there is no restriction on the number of constraints.

Continued

Table 9-1. *Continued*

Solver Option	What It Does
Assume Non-Negative	Using this option will assume a lower limit of 0 for any adjustable cells that do not have a lower-limit constraint.
Use Automatic Scaling	Select this option when there are large differences in magnitude in your model.
Show Iteration Results	If this is selected, Solver will display the results after each iterative attempt.
Estimates	Specifies whether to use Tangent (linear) extrapolation or Quadratic extrapolation to obtain initial estimates of the basic variables in each one-dimensional search.
Derivatives	Specifies whether to use Forward or Central differencing to estimate partial derivatives of the objective and constraint functions. Use Forward for problems where constraint values change slowly and Central where constraint values change rapidly.
Search group	Specifies the algorithm used at each iteration to determine the search direction. Newton requires more memory but fewer iterations than Conjugate.
Load Model	Displays the Load Model dialog box, where you can specify a range containing a set of parameters that you want to load into Solver (enter the entire range that contains the problem model).
Save Model	Displays the Save Model dialog box, where you can specify a range where the model parameters should be saved to (enter the reference for the first cell of a vertical range of empty cells). Allows you to define more than one problem for a worksheet.

TIP For more information about Solver and the additional products that are available, check out www.solver.com.

CHAPTER 10

Formulas and Functions

I t is in formulas and functions that Excel's true power resides because it is through them that calculations and evaluations are processed and relationships between items of data are created. Formulas can range from simple addition or subtraction calculations to formulas that handle nonnumerical data and more sophisticated three-dimensional or array formulas. Functions are basically predefined formulas built into Excel to facilitate complex or cumbersome calculations and to enable you to carry out a wide variety of analytical tasks. Most of Excel's analytical tools, like the Pivot-Tables or data tables discussed in previous chapters, are simply user-friendly facades for the multiple complex formulas and functions required to produce particular analyses and reports.

Excel has over 300 built-in functions divided into various function categories, including

- Financial
- Logical
- Text
- Date & Time
- Lookup & Reference
- Math & Trig
- Information
- Database

Several additions to the list of built-in functions have been made with Excel 2007, although some of these are not completely new as it was possible to access them in earlier versions by installing the Analysis TookPak add-in. Consequently, there are now three new categories of functions:

- Statistical
- Engineering
- Cube

Of course, it would be impractical to try to cover all of the different types of formulas and functions that can be constructed in Excel in this chapter. However, we will take a look at the essentials of writing formulas and some of the more commonly used functions.

Constructing Formulas

Formulas in Excel can be of varying length and complexity, but they all follow a similar basic format and will start with an equals sign (=) followed by one or more operands, separated by one or more operators. Operands can be values, text, cell references, ranges, defined names, or function names. Operators are symbols used to represent the various arithmetic and comparison operations you can perform on the operands. Arithmetic operators are the mathematical operators required to perform calculations like addition and multiplication. Comparison operators such as *equals to* and *greater than* compare two values or cells and return a logical value of TRUE or FALSE. Table 10-1 lists the arithmetic and comparison operators that can be used in formulas and illustrates how they can be utilized.

Table 10-1. Formula Operators

Operator	Name	Example	Result
+	Addition	=5+6	11
-	Subtraction	=7-2	5
*	Multiplication	=8*3	24
/	Division	=9/3	3
-	Negation	= -5 =--5	-5 5
^	Exponentiation (raise a number to a power)	=4^3	64
%	Percentage	=5%	0.05
&	Concatenation (join two text items)	="Room "&"10a"	Room 10a
=	Equal to	=11=12	FALSE
>	Greater than	=11>12	FALSE

Operator	Name	Example	Result
<	Less than	=11<12	TRUE
>=	Greater than or equal to	=11>=12	FALSE
<=	Less than or equal to	=11<=12	TRUE
<>	Not equal to	=11<>12	TRUE

TIP Excel 2007 can work with bigger formulas than ever before and can now deal with 8,192 characters and 64 levels of nesting compared to 1,024 characters and 7 levels of nesting in Excel 2003. To accommodate larger formulas, you can increase the size of the formula bar by dragging down its bottom edge. This will allow you to view the entire formula without overlapping onto the grid.

In addition to the operators used when working with numbers and text, you can include reference operators to combine cell references or ranges. Table 10-2 outlines the reference operators that can be used in Excel formulas.

Table 10-2. Reference Operators

Operator	Name	Refers To	Example
: (colon)	Range	All the cells between the two cell references	A1:E6 i.e., all the cells between A1 and E6
(space)	Intersection	The intersection of two ranges (overlapping cells)	A1:E6 C3:G8 i.e., all the cells between C3 and E6
, (comma)	Union	The union of two ranges (all cells in both ranges)	A1:E6,C3:G8 i.e., all the cells between A1 and E6 and all the cells between C3 and G8 (overlapping cells will be counted twice)

As formulas often consist of several parts and can contain numerous operands, Excel utilizes certain rules when deciding the order in which each section is processed. It is important to take these rules into consideration when constructing formulas to make sure that the completed formula returns the correct result. Table 10-3 outlines the order of precedence for operators in formulas.

Table 10-3. Order of Precedence for Operators

Operation	Symbol	Order of Precedence
Range	: (colon)	1
Intersection	(space)	2
Union	, (comma)	3
Negation	–	4
Percentage	%	5
Exponentiation	^	6
Multiplication Division	* /	7
Addition Subtraction	+ –	8
Concatenation	&	9
Comparison	= < > <= >= <>	10

NOTE Where operators have the same order of precedence, Excel will evaluate them in order from left to right.

You can exert some control over the order of precedence to ensure your formula returns the correct result by using parentheses because Excel will evaluate any expressions contained within parentheses first before processing the remainder of the formula. For example, Excel will calculate the formula =4+3*5-2 as 17 (as multiplication has a higher precedence than addition or subtraction) but will return a result of 21 if the formula is entered as =(4+3)*(5-2). Parentheses can also be used to raise a number by a fractional power; for example, =5^(1/3) will return the cube root of 5 (raise 5 by the power of one third). Parentheses can be nested within other parentheses if necessary to gain even further control, but check that you have closed all parenthetical terms by making sure that you have equal numbers of left parentheses and right parentheses.

Generally, you should refer to cells in formulas rather than use the actual values of the cells. This ensures that if the value of a cell changes, the result of the formula will update accordingly. You can type cell references into a formula directly, or you can click the cell and Excel will insert the correct reference for you.

To view the formula in a cell at any time, you can select the cell and the formula will be displayed in the formula bar. To view all the formulas in a worksheet, select the Formulas tab on the Ribbon and, in the Formula Auditing group, click Show Formulas or press Ctrl+` (the backquote) to toggle between showing formulas and showing values.

Error Values in Formulas

If, when you enter a formula, you get a value beginning with #, you have entered the formula incorrectly and Excel is unable to return a result. To remove this error value, you will need to correct the mistake or adjust the value in the cell that is producing the error. Cells that contain errors will produce a ripple effect, resulting in other cells that depend on the cell also displaying an error value. Table 10-4 outlines the error values that can appear when Excel is unable to calculate a formula. Chapter 13 discusses how to find and correct errors in formulas in more detail.

Table 10-4. Error Values

Error Value	What Is Wrong
#DIV/0	The formula is attempting to divide a value or cell by zero or by an empty cell.
#N/A	The formula directly or indirectly refers to a cell that uses the NA function to indicate that data is not available. Functions like VLOOKUP and HLOOKUP may return #N/A.
#NAME?	The formula uses a name that Excel is not able to recognize or that has been deleted. It can also occur if you fail to match quotation marks when entering text.
#NULL!	The formula refers to an intersection between two ranges that do not intersect.
#NUM!	Occurs when there is a problem with a number; e.g., the formula may refer to a cell that contains a negative number when it should contain a positive number.
#REF!	The formula includes an invalid cell reference.
#VALUE!	One of the operands or arguments in the formula is the wrong type.

TIP If Excel returns a value of ###### where a number is expected, it does not mean that there is an error; rather, it indicates that the column is not wide enough to display the number. Widen the column or change the number format to display the number in full.

Another common error in formulas is a circular reference, where a formula refers (directly or indirectly) to itself. This is known as a circular reference because the calculation could go on indefinitely as each time the formula is calculated the value in the cell changes and the formula must be recalculated. For example, if you enter the formula =A1+B2*C3 in cell C3, Excel will display a message warning you that cell references in the formula refer to the formula's result. If you click OK, Excel will display the Help topic for circular references; if you click Cancel, Excel allows the formula to remain as is and will display Circular Reference: C3 in the Status bar to remind you that a circular reference exists.

If you have changed the settings to enable iterative calculation, Excel will not highlight circular references but will perform the calculation until the maximum iterations or maximum change limit has been reached. If you want to intentionally create a circular reference, you must have iterative calculation enabled. To enable iterative calculations, click the Microsoft Office Button and click Excel Options. Select the Formulas category and select the Enable Iterative Calculations checkbox. If you want to, change the default values in the Maximum iterations field or the Maximum change field to control when Excel should stop performing iterations.

Formula AutoComplete

Excel 2007 has attempted to make formula construction quicker and simpler by introducing Formula AutoComplete. This feature can help to prevent spelling or syntax errors by providing a dropdown list of function names (including user-defined functions), range names, enumerated arguments (like the *function_num* argument in the SUBTOTAL function), and structured references for tables that match the characters that you type into your formula. All the items appear in alphabetical order, and the data type of each item is identified by a symbol. The item at the top of the list is selected automatically with a ScreenTip providing a description for it; you can use the arrow keys to navigate to the required item on the list. To insert the selected item from the list into your formula, press the Tab key or double-click the item. If you do not wish to insert the item, you can continue typing; Excel will update the options in the list as you type more characters into the formula.

If you select a function, Excel will insert the function name and the opening parenthesis. The ScreenTip will change to display the syntax for the function and, where appropriate, Formula AutoComplete will suggest function arguments. By displaying syntax and descriptions for functions, you can easily select a function and enter the correct arguments without having to memorize a function's format or refer to the Help feature or other guides. Figure 10-1 shows an example of Formula Auto-Complete being used to insert the SUBTOTAL function and demonstrates how the options displayed update as more characters are entered.

As Figure 10-1 shows, once you enter the characters =s, Formula AutoComplete will display a list of the functions and named ranges beginning with S. As more letters are entered, the list is narrowed down to the SUBTOTAL function and a descriptive ScreenTip appears to help you to decide if this is the function you are looking for. Once the function is inserted, Formula AutoComplete provides you with possible arguments—in this case, a list of enumerated functions that can be used to subtotal the data. You can select an enumerated function from this list (4 is entered for the MAX function in this example) and then, as you start to enter the next argument, Formula AutoComplete will again list suggestions. In Figure 10-1, it is the named range George that we want to find the maximum value in. The ScreenTip that is displayed to describe the defined name is the comment that was entered when it was created. Once the named range has been inserted into the formula, all that remains to be done is to close the parentheses and press the Enter key.

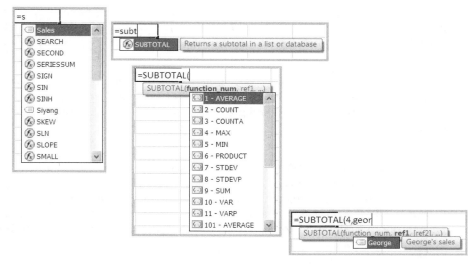

Figure 10-1. As you start typing a formula, Excel will display a list of options that matches what you type.

If you do not want to use Formula AutoComplete to select items, you can still continue to enter a formula by typing it directly. If you want to turn the feature off altogether, simply click the Microsoft Office Button and click the Excel Options button. Select the Formulas category, and under "Working with formulas" deselect the Formula AutoComplete option.

Using Relative and Absolute Referencing

When constructing a worksheet, you can save time by copying a formula into other cells rather than retyping it. Formulas can be copied by using the Copy and Paste commands or by using the Fill Handle, and Excel is generally able to adjust the cell references in the formula automatically to suit each new location. For example, if cell B4 contains the formula =B2*B3 and this is copied to cell C4, the formula in cell C4 will be =C2*C3. This is known as *relative referencing* because Excel looks at the relative position of the cell references rather than the actual location of the cells. In other words, Excel will interpret the formula in cell B4 as instructing it to multiply the contents of the cell two rows above this cell with the contents of the cell one row above this cell.

In some situations, you may want one or all of the cell references in a formula to remain constant when the formula is copied. To stop Excel from adjusting a cell reference when a formula is copied to another cell, you need to use *absolute referencing*. You can make a cell reference absolute by inserting a dollar sign ($) before the references for the column and the row—for example, $B$7. You can also use mixed referencing where you make either the reference for the column or the reference for the row absolute. For example, if you enter the reference into the formula as $B7, when the formula is copied to another cell the row will update (if appropriate) but the column will not; or if you enter the reference as B$7 and copy the formula, the column will adjust (if appropriate) but the row will not.

> **TIP** You can use the F4 key to change a cell reference to a mixed or an absolute reference by clicking to the left of the cell reference (or between the column and row references) and pressing F4 repeatedly until you get the format you require.

In the worksheet in Figure 10-2, the Discount is calculated using a formula that includes both a relative reference and an absolute reference. The cell reference for the Discount rate is entered into the formula in B5 as an absolute reference and is not adjusted in cells C5 and D5. The cell reference for the Total is entered as a relative reference in the formula in B5 to enable the formula to update when it is copied to C5 and D5.

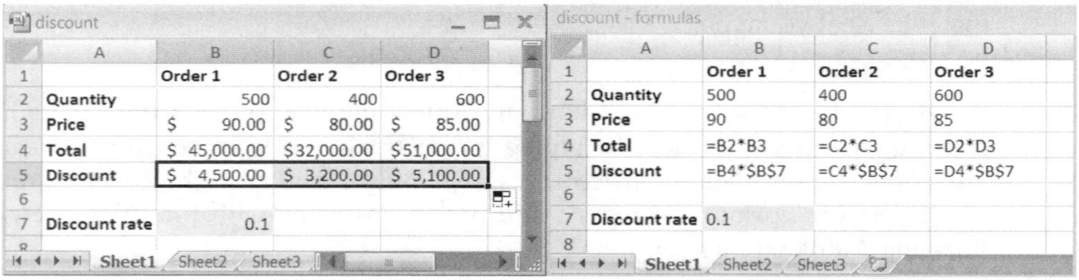

Figure 10-2. For the formula in B1 to be copied correctly, the reference to the Discount rate cell (B7) should be absolute.

When you move or cut and paste a cell containing a formula, the cell references will not change and the formula will continue to refer to the original cells. If you want to copy a formula (or part of a formula) containing relative cell references without the relative references adjusting, select the cell containing the formula that you wish to copy, select the entire formula in the formula bar and copy it, press Esc to deactivate the formula bar, select the cell that you want to copy the formula to, and paste it there.

> **TIP** If a cell contains a formula whose value will not change, you can convert the formula to the value by double-clicking the cell, pressing F9, and then pressing Enter. If you want to convert multiple formulas to their respective values, you can use Paste Special (see Chapter 3).

Formulas and Defined Names

Defined names can be used in place of cell references when referring to cells or ranges in formulas. As defined names generally refer to absolute cell references, when you copy a formula that uses a defined name the range will not change. Using defined names will ensure that the formula will always refer to the same cells. To insert a defined name into a formula, select the Formulas tab on the Ribbon and, in the Defined Names group, click Use in Formula. A list of all your defined names will appear and you can click the required name to insert it. Alternatively, you can select the name in Formula AutoComplete, or if you can remember it, type it in directly.

You can take defined names even further when creating formulas by naming the formula as well as the cells and ranges referred to in it. This can be particularly useful where a formula is used repeatedly. To assign a name to a formula, do the following:

1. Select the Formulas tab on the Ribbon and, in the Defined Names group, click Define Name. The New Name dialog box will open.
2. In the Name box, enter a name for the formula.
3. In the Scope box, select the worksheet that you want the formula name to apply to or select Workbook to use the formula name in any sheet in the current workbook.
4. If you want, add a description for the formula in the Comment box.
5. Remove any entry already in the Refers to box and type an equals sign (=) followed by the formula there. Click OK when you have finished.

Once you have assigned a name to the formula, each time you want to enter the formula into a cell all you have to do is type an equals sign followed by the formula name and press Enter, and the result of the formula will be displayed. The formula name will even appear in Formula AutoComplete to make using it even simpler.

Referring to Cells in Other Worksheets and Workbooks

When constructing formulas, you may wish to refer to a cell in a different worksheet or even another workbook. To reference a cell in another worksheet, you need to enter the sheet name followed by an exclamation mark (!) and then the cell reference. For example, to add cell A1 in Sheet2 to cell B2 in the current worksheet use a format similar to the following:

=Sheet2!A1+B2

If the sheet name contains spaces, you will need to enclose it in single quotations marks; for example, for a sheet named Jan Sales the formula would be as follows:

='Jan Sales'!A1+B2

TIP You can quickly insert references to cells in other open worksheets by clicking the sheet tab and then the cell. Excel will automatically insert these references as absolute references.

If the cells you want to reference in your formula are in separate workbooks, you will need to precede the reference with the name of the workbook enclosed in square brackets. For example, to add cell A1 of Sheet2 in a workbook named January to cell B2 in the current worksheet you would use the following format:

=[January]Sheet2!A1+B2

If the name of the workbook contains spaces, it must be enclosed in single quotation marks, along with the sheet name as follows:

='[January 2006]Sheet2'!A1+B2

If the other workbook is not open, you will need to enter the full path to the reference:

='C:\My Documents\[January 2006]Sheet2'!A1+B2

If you have several worksheets containing similar data, it is also quite likely that you will want to create formulas that take values from the different worksheets—for example, to summarize the data across the worksheets. You can use a 3D reference to refer to a cell or range on multiple worksheets. A 3D reference will take a format similar to **Sheet1:Sheet3!A1**. For example, if you store sales data for each month on separate worksheets and cell J25 in each worksheet contains the monthly total, you can create a summary worksheet of totals for the year and use the following 3D formula to sum the totals for all the months:

=SUM(Sheet1:Sheet12!J25)

To enter a 3D SUM function, you can type in the 3D reference directly or you can select the sheets and cells with the mouse.

1. Select the cell where you want the result of the formula to appear.
2. Type =**SUM(** in the cell.
3. Click the tab for the first worksheet. Hold down the Shift key and click the tab for the last worksheet.
4. Select the cell containing the value that you want to sum.
5. Type) to close the parentheses and press Enter to finish the formula.

TIP Define names for 3D cell references to simplify the process of entering 3D formulas. You will need to enter the 3D reference in the Refers to box in the New Name dialog box (see Chapter 3 for information on how to define names). You can then use the defined name in your 3D formula instead of selecting the worksheets and cells.

Not all functions can be used as a 3D formula. Here is a list of functions that can be used in 3D formulas:

AVERAGE	AVERAGEA
COUNT	COUNTA
MAX	MAXA
MEDIAN	MIN
MINA	OR
PERCENTILE	PRODUCT
QUARTILE	RANK
SKEW	SMALL
STDEV	STDEVA
STDEVP	STDEVPA
SUM	VAR
VARA	VARP
VARPA	

Array Formulas

An array formula acts on two or more sets of arguments, performing multiple calculations, and can return either a single result or multiple results. Each array argument must have the same number of rows and columns. Array formulas are created in a similar way to ordinary formulas except that instead of pressing the Enter key when you have finished typing the formula, you press Ctrl+Shift+Enter to enter an array formula. Excel will automatically insert the formula between {} (curly braces) to indicate that it is an array formula.

Using an Array to Produce a Single Result

By using an array formula that produces a single result, you can enter a single formula to perform a calculation that otherwise would require multiple formulas. For example, the array formula shown in cell B5 in Figure 10-3 calculates the total hours required to produce an array of products without the need to calculate the total for each product first. The array formula is created by entering the formula into B5 as follows:

=SUM(B2:D3*B3:D3)

You then press Ctrl+Shift+Enter. Excel calculates the total by multiplying the number of units and hours per unit for each product and adding each total together. As you can see from the formula bar, Excel automatically encloses the formula in braces.

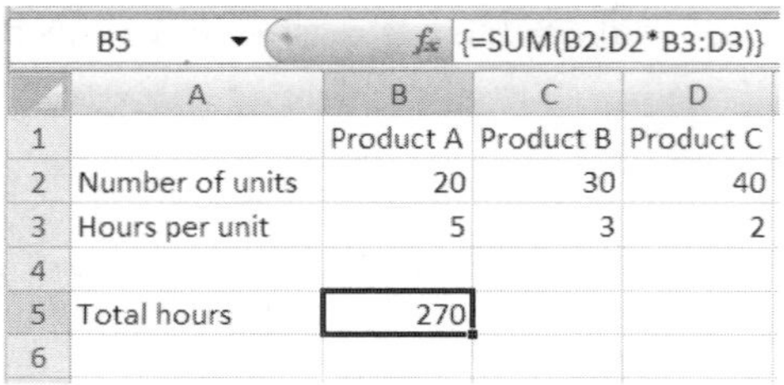

Figure 10-3. To use an array formula to produce a single result, type the formula and press Ctrl+Shift+Enter.

Using an Array to Produce Multiple Results

In some situations you may use an array within a formula, or a function will require an array of values as an argument. It is also possible to construct a formula that will return an array as its result. If you want an array formula to return multiple results, you must enter it into a range that contains the same number of rows and columns as the array arguments. Figure 10-4 shows a simple example of an array formula being used to produce multiple results. In this example, the array formula is used to calculate the total labor cost to produce the given number of units for each of the three products. The window on the right shows the formulas used.

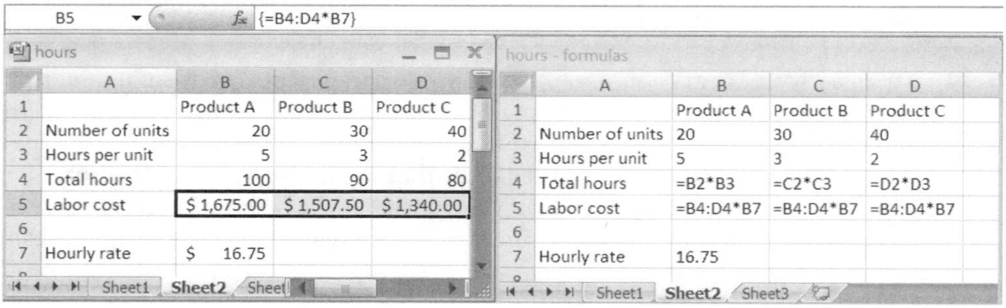

Figure 10-4. To use an array formula to produce multiple results, make sure that you select a range that contains the same number of rows and columns as the array arguments.

To enter the array formula in Figure 10-4, you would select the range that you want to use for the array formula (cells B5:D5 in Figure 10-4) and enter the formula using the range reference for the cells that correspond to the results cells. In this example, the labor cost is calculated by multiplying the Total hours for each product (B4:D4) by the Hourly rate (cell B7) so the formula will be =B4:D4*B7. *Do not press Enter*—to enter the formula as an array, you must press Ctrl+Shift+Enter. Excel will insert the same formula in each cell; however, it will calculate the result for each cell by using the input value in the corresponding cell.

When working with an array, you must select all the array cells. If you try to edit or delete part of an array, Excel will display an error message. As Excel treats all cells in an array as a single unit, you must select the entire array before making any changes to it. You can quickly select all the cells in an array by clicking one of the cells and pressing Ctrl+/. To edit an array formula, you must select all the array cells, make the necessary changes, and press Ctrl+Shift+Enter to enter the amended array formula. To change the size of an array, select all the cells, activate the formula bar, and press Ctrl+Enter to make the array formula an ordinary formula. You can then change the cell range and press Ctrl+Shift+Enter to reenter the formula as an array. Finally, to delete an array you must select all the cells and press Delete.

Using Array Constants

If you do not want to refer to worksheet cells in an array, you can enter the values directly into the array as arguments. To use an array constant in a formula, use the following guidelines:

- Enclose all the values in braces ({})
- To enter values as a column, separate each value with a semicolon (;); for example, {2;4;6;8} would represent the following:

  2

  4

  6

  8

- To enter values as a row, separate each value with a comma (,); for example, {3,5,7,9} would represent the following:

  3 5 7 9

- Use both commas and semicolons to structure the values in a matrix; for example, {2,3,4,5;6,7,8,9} will enter the values in a range of two rows and four columns as follows:

  2 3 4 5

  6 7 8 9

Controlling When Formulas Are Calculated

By default, Excel will recalculate any formulas in a worksheet as soon as any of their input data changes. If your worksheet is particularly large or contains multiple complex formulas, it can take a few seconds, or longer, to recalculate each time a change is made. It may, therefore, be beneficial to switch to manual calculation if you are editing a large worksheet so that you can control when Excel recalculates. You can turn off automatic calculation and switch to manual calculation by selecting the Formulas tab on the Ribbon and, in the Calculation group, clicking the down arrow beside Calculation Options and selecting Manual from the dropdown menu. When you are ready to recalculate, click Calculate Now in the Calculation group (or press F9) to recalculate all open worksheets or Calculate Sheet in the Calculation group (or press Shift+F9) to recalculate the active worksheet only.

> **TIP** When using manual calculation, the word *Calculate* will appear in the Status bar any time the data in your worksheet changes to indicate that you need to recalculate.

Using Functions

Excel functions can be used on their own, as part of a formula or even as the arguments for other functions. Although functions are used to perform a diverse range of calculations each function has a similar format:

NAME(*argument1*, *argument2*, ...)

Function names are often displayed in uppercase letters (although they do not have to be entered in uppercase). Function arguments (if required) are always enclosed in parentheses and separated by commas. Even if a function does not have any arguments, the parentheses are still included; for example, you enter the TODAY function, which is used to return the current date, as **=TODAY**(). Arguments are the input data used to process the function and can be optional or required. Text, numbers, expressions, cell references, ranges, defined names, arrays, and the outcome of other functions can all be used as function arguments. In this section we will look at some of the more useful functions available in Excel 2007.

To input a function into a cell or a formula, you can simply type it in directly or you can select it in Formula AutoComplete. If you are not sure which function you require, you can select the Formulas tab on the Ribbon and browse through the various categories in the Function Library group (see Figure 10-5) to help you identify the correct function.

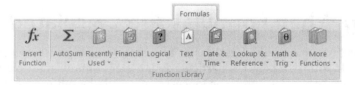

Figure 10-5. Select a category in the Function Library to view all the functions in that category or use the Insert Function command to open the Insert Function dialog box.

As Figure 10-5 shows, the Financial, Logical, Text, Date & Time, Lookup & Reference, and Math & Trig categories are clearly displayed in the Function Library group. The Statistical, Engineering, Cube, and Information categories can be accessed by clicking More Functions. For convenience, a Recently Used category is also available, or you can click the down arrow below the AutoSum icon to access the popular Sum, Average, Count Numbers, Max, or Min functions. If you prefer to search for a function using the traditional Insert Function dialog box, you can click Insert Function in the Function Library group.

If you select a function from the Function Library or the Insert Function dialog box, the Function Arguments dialog box will appear. The Function Arguments dialog box helps you to enter a function correctly by listing the arguments that can be included in the function along with fields where you can enter the values or cell or range references for each argument. It also provides a brief description of the formula and the selected argument as well as an indication of the result given the current entries. Figure 10-6 shows an example of the Insert Function dialog box for the FV function used to calculate the future value of an investment.

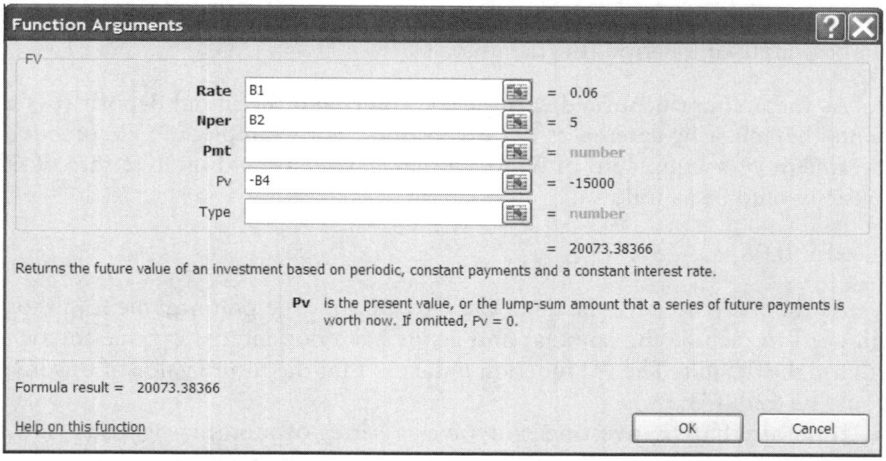

Figure 10-6. You can insert the arguments into a function by entering values or cell references into the field for each argument.

The remainder of the chapter will examine some of the more popular functions from the Financial, Logical, Text, Date & Time, Lookup & Reference, Math & Trig, Statistical, Information, and Database categories.

Financial Functions

Excel is often used to perform calculations involving money, from basic home budgets to complex financial decision making. Consequently, Excel's function library contains over 50 financial functions that can be used to calculate everything from loan repayments to the future value of an investment.

The FV Function

In financial models the future value of an investment is equal to the present value plus interest or the combined value of all the deposits over the term of the investment plus any interest. The FV function will return the future value of an investment based on periodic, constant payments and a constant interest rate. You use the syntax

FV(*rate, nper, pmt, pv, type*)

where

- *rate* is interest rate per period; if payments are monthly this will be divided by 12.
- *nper* is the total number of payments.
- *pmt* is the fixed amount deposited each period (assumed to be zero).
- *pv* is the initial deposit or present value (assumed to be zero).
- *type* is 0 if payment is due at the end of a period or 1 if payment is due at the beginning of a period (the default is 0).

As the amount deposited each period (pmt) and the initial deposit (pv) are payments they must be entered as negative values. For example, the FV function for an investment of a lump sum of $15,000 that has an annual interest rate of 6% over 5 years would be as follows:

=FV(0.06, 5,, -15000)

As there are no periodic deposits, we can omit the pmt argument (although you still need to include the comma) and as we have not entered a value for *type*, Excel will use the default. The FV function indicates that the future value of this investment would be $20,073.38.

If an alternative investment involves a series of monthly deposits of $250 per month over a 5-year period with no initial deposit, the function arguments would be as follows:

=FV(0.06/12,5*12,-250)

In this example, as the deposits are made monthly, the interest rate is divided by 12 and the number of periods is multiplied by 12. The future value of this investment is calculated at $17,442.51.

> **NOTE** The units for *rate* and *nper* should always be consistent; for example, if the payment periods are monthly the years the payments are made should be multiplied by 12 and the annual interest rate should be divided by 12 to calculate the monthly equivalent.

The PV Function

The PV function returns the present value of an investment—that is, the total amount that a series of future payments is worth now or the original loan amount for loan repayments. With the PV function, the monthly payments will be constant. The syntax of the PV function is

PV(*rate, nper, pmt, fv, type*)

where

- *rate* is the interest rate (if payments are monthly this must be divided by 12).
- *nper* is the total number of payments (multiply years by 12 for monthly payments).
- *pmt* is the amount of the periodic payments.
- *fv* is the future value of the investment (for a loan this will be 0).
- *type* is 0 if payments are made at the end of the period or 1 if they are made at the beginning of the period.

The following function shows how you can use the PV function to calculate the original loan amount for a 36-month loan where the monthly payments are $396.24 and the annual interest rate is 4.5%:

=PV(0.045/12, 36, -396.24)

The function returns a value of $6999.99 as the original loan amount.

The NPV and XNPV Functions

The NPV function will return the net present value of an investment based on a discount rate and a series of future payments (negative values) and income (positive values). Unlike PV, the payments (or income values) do not have to be fixed. Its syntax is

NPV(*rate, value1, value2, ...*)

where

- *rate* is the discount rate (e.g., rate of inflation or cost of capital) over one period.
- *value1, value2*, etc., are 1–254 arguments that represent payments (negative) and income (positive).

The values must be spaced equally in time—for example, yearly.

NPV is based on future cash flows. If the initial investment is made at the beginning of the first period, it must be added to the NPV result and not included with the other values (arguments). If the investment is made at the end of the first period, it is included with the arguments.

For example, you can use the NPV function to calculate the net present value of an investment where $15,000 must be paid a year from now and annual incomes of $4,800, $4,700, $5,500 and $4,900 are expected for the four years after that; the discount rate is 12%. As the initial investment is made at the end of the first period, it will be included with the other values; therefore, the function should be entered as follows:

=NPV(0.12, -15000, 4800, 4700, 5500, 5800)

The function will return a net present value of $545.47.

If the investment is made at the beginning of the first period, it will be added to the NPV instead of included with the values. The formula will be

=NPV(0.12, 4800, 4700, 5500, 5800)+-15000

This time the net present value will be $633.32.

The XNPV function (which was previously available in the Analysis TookPak add-in) allows you to calculate the net present value where the cash flows are not spaced equally in time. Its syntax is

XNPV(*rate, values, dates*)

where

- *rate* is the discount rate (e.g., rate of inflation or cost of capital) over one period.
- *values* is the series of cash flows that corresponds to the schedule of dates and must contain at least one positive and one negative value. The initial payment at the beginning of the investment can be included with the other values.
- *dates* is the schedule of dates that corresponds to the cash flows. The first date must be the initial cash flow and all other dates must be later than this, although they can be in any order.

For example, if the cash flows are in cells B3:B8 and the dates that the cash flows occur are in cells C3:C8, you could use the following formula to calculate the net present value given a discount rate of 12%:

=XNPV(0.12, B3:B8, C3:C8)

The PMT Function

The PMT function calculates the payments required for a loan based on constant payments and a constant interest rate (e.g., a fixed-rate mortgage). Its syntax is

PMT(*rate, nper, pv, fv, type*)

where

- *rate* is the interest rate (if payments are monthly, divide it by 12).
- *nper* is the total number of payments (monthly repayments over 5 years will equal 60).
- *pv* is the present value (this will be negative for a loan).
- *fv* is the future value.
- *type* is 0 if payment is made at the end of the period or 1 if payment is made at the beginning of the period.

For example, you can use the PMT function to calculate the monthly payments required for a $150,000 loan, paid back over 25 years at an interest rate of 4.75%, by entering the following formula:

=PMT(0.0475/12, 25*12, -150000)

The monthly payments are calculated at $855.18.

The RATE Function

The RATE function is used to return the interest rate of an annuity or loan. Its syntax is

RATE(*nper, pmt, pv, fv, type, guess*)

where

- *nper* is the number of payments.
- *pmt* is the fixed payment amount (this will be negative for a loan payment).
- *pv* is the present value.
- *fv* is the future value.
- *type* is 0 if the payment is at the end of the period or 1 if the payment is at the beginning of the period.
- *guess* is assumed to be 10% if no other value is entered.

To use the RATE function to calculate the interest rate that is being charged for a loan where $9,000 is being paid back at $600 per month over 24 months, you would enter the arguments as follows:

=RATE(24, -600, 9000)

The interest rate is calculated at 4%, or 4.16% when displayed to two decimal places.

Logical Functions

Excel's Function Library includes seven logical functions: AND, OR, NOT, TRUE, FALSE, IF, and IFERROR. Logical functions return a value of TRUE or FALSE and are often used in combination with other functions or as part of a formula.

The AND Function

The AND function will return the value TRUE if *all* of its arguments are TRUE and the value FALSE if *any* of its arguments are FALSE. The arguments for the AND function must evaluate to logical values such as TRUE or FALSE or must be arrays or references that contain logical values. Its syntax is

AND(*logical1*, *logical2*, ...)

where *logical1*, *logical2*, etc., are up to 255 conditions that will be evaluated to either TRUE or FALSE.

For example, if cell A1 contains the value 25, the function

=AND(A1>20, A1<30)

will return TRUE because A1 is greater than 20 AND A1 is less than 30. If cell A1 contains the value 30, the function will return FALSE because 30 is greater than 20 but is not less than 30; therefore, both conditions are not TRUE.

The OR Function

The OR function is similar to the AND function except that it will return a value of TRUE if any of its arguments are TRUE, and it will return FALSE if all of its arguments are FALSE. The arguments for the OR function must evaluate to logical values, such as TRUE or FALSE, or must be arrays or references that contain logical values. Its syntax is

OR(*logical1*, *logical2*, ...)

where *logical1*, *logical2*, etc., are up to 255 conditions that will be evaluated to either TRUE or FALSE.

For example, if cell A1 contains the value 25 and cell A2 contains the value 35, the formula

=OR(A1>30, A2>40)

will return FALSE as neither argument is TRUE. If cell A1 contains the value 31 and cell A2 contains the value 35, the function will return TRUE because one of the conditions is now TRUE.

The NOT Function

The NOT function reverses the value of its argument and is generally used to ensure a value is not equal to a particular value. Its syntax is

NOT(*logical*)

where *logical* is a value or expression that can be evaluated to TRUE or FALSE. If *logical* is FALSE, the NOT function will return TRUE; if *logical* is TRUE, the NOT function will return FALSE. For example, if cell A1 contains the value 5, the formula

=NOT(A1=5)

will return FALSE.

The TRUE and FALSE Functions

The TRUE function will return the logical value TRUE and its syntax is TRUE (). Similarly, the FALSE function will return the logical value FALSE using the syntax FALSE(). Of course, you can simply enter the value TRUE or FALSE into a cell; however, the functions are provided to facilitate compatibility with other spreadsheet applications.

The IF Function

The IF function will return one value if the result of a logical test is TRUE and another value if the result of the logical test is FALSE. Its syntax is

IF(*logical_test*, *value_if_true*, *value_if_false*)

where

- *logical_test* is a value or expression that can be evaluated to either TRUE or FALSE.
- *value_if_true* is the value that is returned if *logical_test* is TRUE.
- *value_if_false* is the value that is returned if *logical_test* is FALSE.

The following example illustrates an IF function being used to determine if a student's examination result (in cell D2) is a Pass or a Fail, where the pass mark is 50:

=IF(D2>=50, "Pass", "Fail")

The function will display the text *Pass* if the value in D2 is greater than or equal to 50; otherwise, it will display *Fail*.

IF functions are commonly nested within each other to return a variety of results depending on the value of a cell. For example, we can use nested IF functions to display the student's grade from A to D depending on their examination result. A score of 85 or over will equal an A grade, 70–84 will equal a B, 55–69 will be a C, and 40–54 will be a D. A result of less than 40 will be Ungraded. When creating nested functions, it is often useful to write the function out in words first:

IF(Mark>=85, "A",

IF(Mark>=70, "B",

IF(Mark>=55, "C",

IF(Mark>=40, "D", else "Ungraded"))))

We can then nest our four IF statements into one formula, as follows:

=IF(D2>=85, "A", IF(D2>=70, "B", IF(D2>=55, "C", IF(D2>=40, "D", "Ungraded"))))

When nesting IF statements, check the formula to make sure that the number of left and right parentheses balance. Excel will usually alert you and suggest a correction if they don't.

The IFERROR Function

The IFERROR function will return a value that you specify if a formula results in an error value (i.e., #NA, #Value!, #Ref!, #Div/0!, #Num!, #Name?, or #Null). Otherwise, it will return the result of the formula. Its syntax is

IFERROR(*value*, *value_if_error*)

where

- *value* is the argument to be evaluated.
- *value_if_error* is the value to return if the formula produces an error.

The IFERROR function can be used to identify and handle errors in a formula; for example, the formula

=IFERROR(C3, "Incorrect calculation")

will display the text *Incorrect calculation* if the formula in C3 evaluates to an error value.

If the value argument is an array formula, IFERROR will return an array of results corresponding to each cell in the range specified in value. For example, you could use IFERROR to trap errors when the values in cells A1:A5 are divided by the values in cells B1:B5 by selecting cells C1:C5, entering the formula

=IFERROR(A1:A5/B1:B5, "Incorrect calculation")

and pressing Ctrl+Shift+Enter to enter an array formula. Each cell in the range C1:C5 will contain the result of the corresponding division calculation; otherwise, the text *Incorrect calculation* will appear where there is a blank cell in B1:B5.

Text Functions

While functions are most commonly associated with numerical data, E
vide a suite of text functions that can be used with text strings or cells c...........
strings. In this section, we will discuss functions that can be used to change the case of
text, concatenate (join) text strings, and even replace portions of text strings with
substitute text.

The CONCATENATE Function

The CONCATENATE function is used to join two text strings together to make a
single text string. Its syntax is

    CONCATENATE(*text1*, *text 2*, ...)

where *text1*, *text2*, etc., are text strings, numbers, or individual cell references.

   For example, if cell B2 contains the text *Monday* and cell C2 contains the time
5.00PM, the formula

    =CONCATENATE(B2, " at ", C2)

will return the string "Monday at 5.00PM". You can concatenate up to 255 text
items using the CONCATENATE function. You can also concatenate text items using
the ampersand (&) calculation operator. Note that strings will be concatenated without an intervening space character; therefore, you need to include this in the
concatenation—for example, =CONCATENATE(A1, " ", B1) or =A1& " " &B1.

The LOWER, UPPER, and PROPER Functions

The LOWER, UPPER, and PROPER functions all operate in a similar manner in that
they change the case of text. Consequently, their syntax is similar:

    LOWER(*text*), UPPER(*text*) and PROPER(*text*)

where *text* is a text string or reference for a cell containing text.

   The LOWER function will convert uppercase letters to lowercase, the UPPER
function will convert lowercase letters to uppercase, and the PROPER function will
capitalize the first letter of each text string and any letter that occurs after a character
other than a letter. For example, if cell C4 contains the string "Room GF-2b", the
three functions will return the string as follows:

    =LOWER(C4)

will return "room gf-2b";

    =UPPER(C4)

will return "ROOM GF-2B"; and

=PROPER(C4)

will return "Room Gf-2B".

The EXACT Function

The EXACT function is used to compare two text strings and will return TRUE if they are identical and FALSE if they are not. The EXACT function is case-sensitive but will ignore differences in formatting and is often used to check data being entered into a worksheet. Its syntax is

EXACT(*text1*, *text2*)

where *text1* and *text2* are the two text strings that you want to compare.

If cell A1 contains the text *Sales* and cell B1 contains the text *sales*, the function

=EXACT(A1,B1)

will return FALSE. You can also use the double equals (==) comparison operator to test if two strings are identical.

The TRIM and CLEAN Functions

The TRIM function will remove spaces from text except for single spaces between individual words and is commonly used to "tidy up" imported data that has inconsistent spacing. Its syntax is

TRIM(*text*)

where *text* is the text that you want to remove additional spaces from.

The CLEAN function, which has a similar syntax,

CLEAN(*text*)

operates in the same manner but will remove all nonprinting characters (i.e., 7-bit ASCII code values 0–31). The TRIM function will not remove nonbreaking space characters.

The LEN Function

If you want to count the characters in a string, you can use the LEN function. The LEN function is often used as part of a formula or with other functions like the IF function and its syntax is

LEN(*text*)

where *text* is the string whose characters you want to count. The LEN function includes any spaces in the string in the result; therefore, the formula

=LEN("Ninth Street, Berkeley CA")

will return 25.

The SUBSTITUTE and REPLACE Functions

At times you may want to use a function to replace part of a text string with other text. Excel provides two functions for this purpose: the SUBSTITUTE function and the REPLACE function. The SUBSTITUTE function can be used when you know the current characters that you want to replace even if you do not know their position in the string. Its syntax is

SUBSTITUTE(*text*, *old_text*, *new_text*, *instance_num*)

where

- *text* is the text, or the reference of the cell containing the text, whose characters you want to substitute.
- *old_text* is the current text you want to replace.
- *new_text* is the text that you want to replace *old_text* with.
- *instance_num* specifies which occurrence of *old_text* you want to replace. If it is omitted, all occurrences of *old_text* will be replaced.

  For example, the formula

  =SUBSTITUTE("November 11, 2011", "1", "2", 4)

will only substitute the fourth instance of 1 and will return November 11, 2012, whereas

=SUBSTITUTE("November 11, 2011", "1", "2")

will substitute all occurrences of 1 and will return November 22, 2022.

The REPLACE function can be used if you do not know the exact text to be replaced but you do know its position within the string. Its syntax is

REPLACE(*old_text*, *start_num*, *num_chars*, *new_text*)

where

- *old_text* is the text, or the reference of the cell containing the text, that contains characters you want to replace.
- *start_num* is the position of the first character in *old_text* that you want to replace.
- *num_chars* is the number of characters in *old_text* that you want to replace with *new_text*.
- *new_text* is the text that will replace the characters in *old_text*.

For example, if cell A1 contains 1234-5678, the formula

=REPLACE(A1, 5, 1, "*")

will return 1234*5678, whereas the formula

=REPLACE(A1, 5, 4, "*")

will return 1234*8.

The CODE and CHAR Functions

The CODE function can be used to return the numeric code for a character depending on the character set used by the computer (i.e., ANSI for Windows or Macintosh character set for a Macintosh). Its syntax is

CODE(*text*)

where *text* is the text that you want to find the code for. If *text* is a string, the code for the first character will be returned. For example,

=CODE("a")

will return 97, as will

=CODE("apple")

The CHAR function will perform the opposite of the CODE function and will return the character represented by a numeric code. Its syntax is

CHAR(*number*)

where *number* is a number between 1 and 255. For example,

=CHAR(65)

will return the uppercase letter A.

Date and Time Functions

The Excel Function Library contains several functions related to the display and analysis of dates and times. These include functions to return the current date or date and time, or to convert dates into Excel's date-time code (the serial numbers that Excel uses to represent dates and times). Excel uses December 31, 1899, as its starting point for dates and stores all dates since then as the number of days after that date. Therefore, January 1, 1900, is 1 and January 1, 2007, is 39083. Times are represented as fractions of a day starting at midnight, so noon on January 2, 1900, would be 2.5 or 6.00 PM on January 2, 2007, would be 39084.75. By storing dates and times like this, Excel is able to facilitate a variety of calculations on date and time values.

Problems may arise when the year is entered as two digits because different versions of Excel may treat them differently. Prior to Excel 97, a year entered as 00 to 19 is assumed to be 2000 to 2019 and a year entered as 20 to 99 is interpreted as 1920 to 1999. However, in versions since Excel 97, a year entered as 00 to 29 is regarded as being 2000 to 2029 and a year entered as 30 to 99 is assumed to be 1930 to 1999. To avoid this problem, it is best to enter years as four digits. Alternatively, you can change how Windows (and Excel) interprets two-digit years by doing the following:

1. Open the Windows Control Panel from the Start button and double-click the icon for Regional and Language Options.
2. Make sure that the Regional Options tab is selected and click Customize to open the Customize Regional Options dialog box.
3. Select the Date tab and adjust the value for the maximum year under "When a two-digit year is entered, interpret it as a year between".
4. Click OK to close the Customize Regional Options dialog box and click OK again to close the Regional and Language Options dialog box.

The DATE Function

Excel's DATE function will return the serial number that represents a given date using the syntax

DATE(*year*, *month*, *day*)

and can be used to build dates out of components that have been generated separately. If the format of the cell was General before the function was entered, the result will be formatted as a date.

In the DATE function, the year argument can be entered as a one- to four-digit number; however, it is best to use four-digit values where possible to avoid inconsistencies. For example, Excel will interpret

=DATE(7,8,16)

as August 16, 1907, and not 2007.

The *month* argument can be entered as an integer from 1 to 12 representing the month. If a negative number is entered for the month, Excel will subtract that number of months plus one from the first month of the specified year. Therefore,

=DATE(2008, -2, 23)

will return October 23, 2007. If a value over 12 is entered as the *month* argument, Excel will adjust the year accordingly so that

=DATE(2007,14,14)

will be returned as February 14, 2008.

The DATEVALUE Function

The DATEVALUE function is similar to the DATE function except that it will return the serial number for a date entered as text. Its syntax is

DATEVALUE(*date_text*)

where *date_text* is text that represents a date from January 1, 1900 (January 1, 1904, if you are using a Macintosh) to December 31, 9999—for example "9-Dec-1973" or "12-09-1973". If no year component is included in *date_text*, the current year is used and any time information in *date_text* is ignored.

The TODAY and NOW Functions

The TODAY function will return the serial number of the current date and the NOW function will return the serial number of the current date and time. Neither function requires any arguments and their syntax is simply TODAY() and NOW(), respectively.

If the cell format was General prior to the function being entered, the result will be formatted as a date. The TODAY and NOW functions can be used to enter the date or date and time directly into a cell or as part of a formula, function, or expression. Both functions are dynamic and will update automatically when a worksheet is recalculated or reopened. You can also enter the current date into a cell by pressing Ctrl+; (semicolon), and you can enter the current time by pressing Ctrl+: (colon). However, these values will not update when the worksheet is recalculated.

The DAY, MONTH, and YEAR Functions

You can use the DAY, MONTH, and YEAR functions to return the component parts of a date as an integer. The DAY function will return the day of a date as a number between 1 and 31, the MONTH function will return the month as a number between 1 and 12, and the YEAR function will return a value between 1900 and 9999 to represent the year. The syntax for the three functions is as follows:

DAY(*serial_number*)

MONTH(*serial_number*)

YEAR(*serial_number*)

where *serial_number* is a date entered directly into a the function or into a cell using the DATE function or as the result of another formula or function.

For example, if cell C3 contains the date October 29, 2004, the functions will return the following results:

=DAY(C3)

will return 29;

=MONTH(C3)

will return 10; and

=YEAR(C3)

will return 2004.

> **NOTE** Dates should be entered using the DATE function or as the result of other formulas or functions.

The NETWORKDAYS Function

The NETWORKDAYS function can be used to calculate the number of working days between two dates, that is, the number of days excluding weekends and days identified as holidays. Its syntax is

NETWORKDAYS(*start_date*, *end_date*, *holidays*)

where

- *start_date* is a date representing the start date.
- *end_date* is a date representing the end date.
- *holidays* is optional and is entered as dates or a range of cells or an array constant of the dates that represent the holidays to be excluded.

All dates should be entered using the DATE function or as the result of other functions or formulas. For example, if cell A1 contains the date December 01, 2007; cell A2 contains January 31, 2008; cell A3 contains December 25, 2007; and cell A4 contains January 01, 2008, the formula

=NETWORKDAYS(A1, A2, A3:A4)

will return 42—the number of working days between December 01, 2007, and January 31, 2008, excluding the Christmas Day and New Year's Day holidays.

The WORKDAY Function

The WORKDAY function allows you to calculate the date that is a given number of days before or after a specified start date excluding any weekends or days identified as holidays. Its syntax is

WORKDAY(*start_date*, *days*, *holidays*)

where

- *start_date* is a date representing the start date.
- *days* is the number of days before or after the start date (excluding weekends and holidays) that you want to calculate the date for (a positive number will return a future date and a negative number will return a past date).
- *holidays* is optional and is entered as dates or a range of cells or an array constant of the dates that represent the holidays to be excluded.

...efore, if cell A1 contains the date December 01, 2007; cell A2 contains 28; ... contains December 25, 2007; and cell A4 contains January 01, 2008, the ...la

=WORKDAY(A1, A2, A3:A4)

will return January 11, 2008 (or serial number 39458).

The WEEKDAY Function

If you want to know which day of the week a date will fall on, you can use the WEEKDAY function. Its syntax is

WEEKDAY(*serial_number*, *return_type*)

where *serial_number* is the serial number of the date you want to know the day for and *return_type* specifies the type of return value.

By default, *return_type* is 1 and will return a number from 1 to 7, where 1 is Sunday and 7 is Saturday for a given date unless you specify a different return type. If you enter 2 for *return_type*, the numbers used will be 1 for Monday through 7 for Sunday. A *return_type* of 3 will display 0 for Monday through 6 for Sunday. For example, if cell A4 contains the date January 01, 2007, the formula

=WEEKDAY(A4)

will return 2. If the formula is entered as

=WEEKDAY(A4, 2)

the result will be 1.

> **NOTE** Dates should be entered using the DATE function or as the result of other formulas or functions.

Lookup and Reference Functions

As the name implies, Lookup and Reference functions are used to return values by looking up corresponding values in tables, vectors, references, arrays, and so forth. The GETPIVOTDATA function used to construct PivotTables is an example of a Lookup and Reference function. In this section we are going to look at three more examples: the HLOOKUP, VLOOKUP, and LOOKUP functions.

The HLOOKUP and VLOOKUP Functions

The HLOOKUP (horizontal) function will search for a value in the top row of a table or array of values and return the corresponding value from the same column in a row that you specify. The VLOOKUP (vertical) function will search for a value in the first column of a table or array and return a corresponding value in the same row and from a column that you specify. The syntax for each of the functions is

$$HLOOKUP(lookup\_value, table\_array, row\_index\_num, range\_lookup)$$
$$VLOOKUP(lookup\_value, table\_array, col\_index\_num, range\_lookup)$$

where

- *lookup_value* is the value to look for in the first row/column of the table. This is usually the cell reference where you will enter the value you wish to look up.
- *table_array* is usually the cell references (or defined name) for the table or array.
- *row_index_num*/*col_index_num* is the number of the row/column that contains the value you want to return.
- *range_lookup* is a logical value indicating if you want to return an exact match or an approximate match. If this is FALSE, the lookup function will only return an exact match; otherwise #N/A will be returned. If it is TRUE or omitted, an exact *or* approximate match is returned. If an exact match is not found, the function will return the next largest value that is less than *lookup_value*.

> **TIP** If *range_lookup* is TRUE, the first row of the HLOOKUP table or the first column of the VLOOKUP table must be sorted in ascending/alphabetical order; otherwise, the function may not return the correct result.

Figure 10-7 shows an example of a horizontal lookup table and a vertical lookup table.

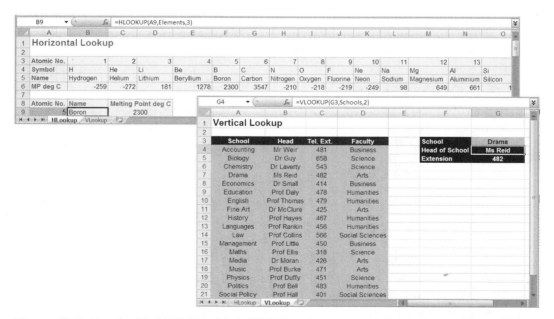

Figure 10-7. Use the HLOOKUP or VLOOKUP function to search for a given value and return the corresponding value in the specified row or column.

In the horizontal lookup table in Figure 10-7, the *lookup_value* is cell A9 and the *table_array* is the table (which has been given the defined name Elements) containing the atomic number, symbol, name, and melting point of the elements. Cells B9 and C9 use HLOOKUP functions to retrieve the name and melting point, respectively, from the Elements range for the element whose atomic number is entered in cell A9. To return the element's name (from row 3 of the Elements table) in cell B9 you would enter the following formula:

=HLOOKUP(A9, Elements, 3)

To return the melting point of the element (row 4 of the Elements table) in cell C9, you would enter this formula:

=HLOOKUP(A9, Elements, 4)

The vertical lookup table in Figure 10-7 uses cell G3 as the *lookup_value* cell and the *table_array* has been named Schools. Cell G4 uses the following VLOOKUP function to return the Head of School (column 2 of the Schools table) for the school entered in G3:

=VLOOKUP(G3, Schools, 2)

Similarly, cell G5 returns the telephone extension number for the school (column 3 of the Schools table) using the following function:

=VLOOKUP(G3, Schools, 3)

TIP If the *lookup_value* is a text string, you can use wildcard characters (* and ?) but make sure that *range_lookup* is set to FALSE.

The LOOKUP Function

If your data is not arranged in tabular form or if the value you want to look up is not in the first row or column, you can use the LOOKUP function instead of HLOOKUP or VLOOKUP. The LOOKUP function looks for a value in a one-row or one-column range and returns the corresponding value in the same position in a second one-row or one-column range. Its syntax is

LOOKUP(*lookup_value, lookup_vector, result_vector*)

where

- *lookup_value* is the value to be looked for in the *lookup_vector*.
- *lookup_vector* is the one-column or one-row range, sorted in ascending order, that contains the values to be looked up.
- *result_vector* is the one-column or one-row range, the same size as *lookup_vector*, that contains the values to be returned.

For example, Figure 10-8 shows how you could use the LOOKUP function to return a value in the first column of a table (Employee number) by looking up a value in the middle of the table (Last name).

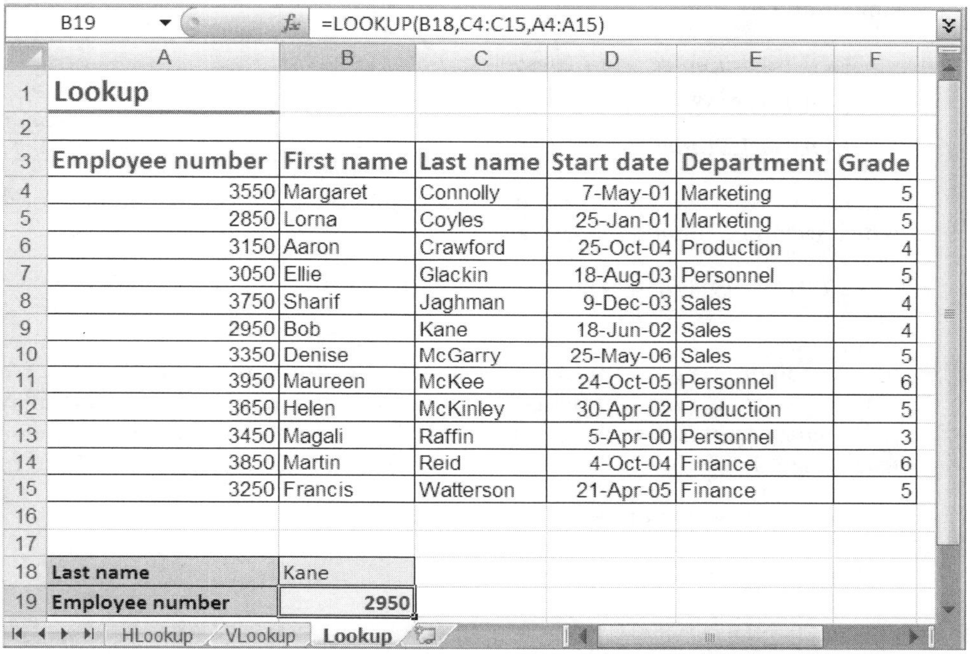

B19	▼		f_x	=LOOKUP(B18,C4:C15,A4:A15)		⊻

	A	B	C	D	E	F
1	**Lookup**					
2						
3	**Employee number**	**First name**	**Last name**	**Start date**	**Department**	**Grade**
4	3550	Margaret	Connolly	7-May-01	Marketing	5
5	2850	Lorna	Coyles	25-Jan-01	Marketing	5
6	3150	Aaron	Crawford	25-Oct-04	Production	4
7	3050	Ellie	Glackin	18-Aug-03	Personnel	5
8	3750	Sharif	Jaghman	9-Dec-03	Sales	4
9	2950	Bob	Kane	18-Jun-02	Sales	4
10	3350	Denise	McGarry	25-May-06	Sales	5
11	3950	Maureen	McKee	24-Oct-05	Personnel	6
12	3650	Helen	McKinley	30-Apr-02	Production	5
13	3450	Magali	Raffin	5-Apr-00	Personnel	3
14	3850	Martin	Reid	4-Oct-04	Finance	6
15	3250	Francis	Watterson	21-Apr-05	Finance	5
16						
17						
18	**Last name**	Kane				
19	**Employee number**	2950				

◄ ◄ ► ► HLookup VLookup **Lookup**

Figure 10-8. You can use the LOOKUP function to look up a value that is not in the first column of the table.

In Figure 10-8, the *lookup_value* is cell B18, the *lookup_vector* is the Last name column (C4:C15), and the *result_vector* is the Employee number column (A4:A15). The LOOKUP function to return the employee number for a given last name from the table in Figure 10-8 is as follows:

=LOOKUP(B18, C4:C15, A4:A15)

Math and Trigonometry Functions

While many of Excel's math and trigonometry functions are used for specific mathematical operations, some of them are also useful in a wider context. In particular, the SUM function is probably used by every Excel user at some stage. Functions like ROUND, SUMPRODUCT, SUMIF, and the newly added SUMIFS also have a broad range of applications within Excel worksheet models and are among the functions outlined in this section.

The ROUND, ROUNDDOWN, and ROUNDUP Functions

The ROUND, ROUNDDOWN, and ROUNDUP functions are used to round a number to a specified number of digits and can be useful if decimal places are insignificant or you want to approximate amounts. The syntax for each of the three functions is similar and is

ROUND(*number, num_digits*)

ROUNDDOWN(*number, num_digits*)

ROUNDUP(*number, num_digits*)

where *number* is a number or cell reference and *num_digits* is the number of digits to which it will be rounded. For example,

=ROUND(9.87654, 2)

will return 9.88.

Although this may appear to be the same as formatting a number to 2 decimal places, rounding a number actually changes its value, not just how it is displayed.

If *num_digits* is 0, *number* will be rounded to the nearest integer and if *num_digits* is less than 0, *number* will be rounded to the left of the decimal point. Therefore,

=ROUND(9.87654, 0)

will return 10 and

=ROUND(789.87, -1)

will return 790.

The ROUNDDOWN and ROUNDUP functions operate in a similar way to ROUND but can be used if you want to be specific about whether a number is rounded down toward 0 or up away from 0. Therefore, if cell A1 contains the value 789.499, the formula

=ROUNDDOWN(A1, 2)

will return 789.49 and the formula

=ROUNDUP(A1, 2)

will return 789.5.

The EVEN and ODD Functions

You can also use the EVEN or ODD functions to round numbers up to the nearest even or nearest odd number, respectively. The number, whether positive or negative, will always be rounded up away from 0. For example, if cell A2 contains 1.3,

=EVEN(A2)

will return 2 and

=ODD(A2)

will return 3. If cell A3 contains -1.3,

=EVEN(A3)

will return -2 and

=ODD(A3)

will return -3.

The SUMPRODUCT Function

Excel's SUMPRODUCT function can be used to multiply corresponding components in specified arrays and return the sum of those products. Its syntax is

SUMPRODUCT(*array1, array2, array3 ...*)

where *array1, array2, array3,* and so on are up to 255 arrays whose components you want to multiply and then add.

For example, the formula

=SUMPRODUCT(A1:B2, C1:C2)

will return the same result as the formula

=A1*C1 + B1*D1 + A2*C2 + B2*D2

The SUMIF and SUMIFS Functions

The SUMIF function allows you to specify criteria and then sum those cells in a range that meet the criteria. Its syntax is

SUMIF(*range, criteria, sum_range*)

where

- *range* is the range of cells that you want to evaluate using the *criteria*.
- *criteria* is a number, text, cell reference, or expression that defines which cells will be added.
- *sum_range* is the range of cells that will be added if their corresponding cells in *range* meet the *criteria*. *sum_range* is optional and, if it is omitted, the cells in *range* that meet the *criteria* will be added.

Figure 10-9 shows an example of SUMIF being used to total the expenses for each of three different projects. In the example, the *range* is cells B2:B12 (named Project) and the *sum_range* is cells C2:C12 (named Cost). The result in cell C14 is calculated using cell B14 as the *criteria* and the function is entered as

=SUMIF(Project, B14, Cost)

The totals in C15 and C16 are calculated in a similar manner, with the *criteria* argument being replaced by B15 and B16, respectively.

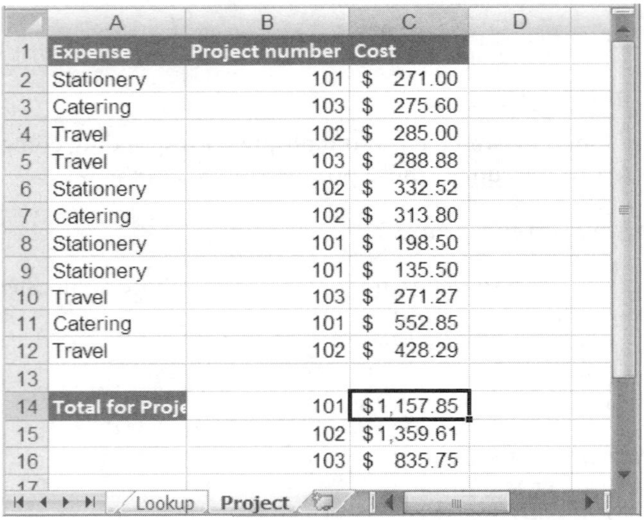

	A	B	C	D
1	**Expense**	**Project number**	**Cost**	
2	Stationery	101	$ 271.00	
3	Catering	103	$ 275.60	
4	Travel	102	$ 285.00	
5	Travel	103	$ 288.88	
6	Stationery	102	$ 332.52	
7	Catering	102	$ 313.80	
8	Stationery	101	$ 198.50	
9	Stationery	101	$ 135.50	
10	Travel	103	$ 271.27	
11	Catering	101	$ 552.85	
12	Travel	102	$ 428.29	
13				
14	**Total for Proje**	101	$1,157.85	
15		102	$1,359.61	
16		103	$ 835.75	
17				

H ◀ ▶ H / Lookup **Project**

Figure 10-9. The SUMIF function is used to sum those cells within a range whose contents match the specified criteria.

If you want to evaluate the cells in a range using multiple criteria, you can use the SUMIFS function. SUMIFS can accept up to 127 criteria in the form of numbers, text, cell references, or expressions. Its syntax is

=SUMIFS(*sum_range*, *criteria_range1*, *criteria1*, *criteria_range2*, *criteria2*, …)

where

- *sum_range* is the range of cells that you want to sum.
- *criteria_range1*, *criteria_range2*, etc., are the ranges in which the associated criteria are to be evaluated.
- *criteria1*, *criteria2*, etc., are the criteria that will define which cells in *sum_range* are to be added.

Using the worksheet in Figure 10-9, SUMIFS can be used to find the total spent on Travel for Project 101 by entering the following formula, assuming that cells A2:A12 have been named Expense:

=SUMIFS(Cost, Expense, "Travel", Project, "101")

Note that the order of the arguments is different for the SUMIFS function than for SUMIF and that *sum_range* is the first argument in SUMIFS but the third argument in SUMIF.

Statistical Functions

Excel is a popular tool for carrying out statistical analyses on data, and there are numerous functions within the Function Library that can be used for calculating statistical measures, such as the average, median, mode, and standard deviation. In addition, the functions that were previously available in the Analysis ToolPak add-in have now been incorporated into the main Function Library so that they are readily accessible. This section examines some of the more prevalent statistical functions that are available in Excel and illustrates how they are typically used.

> **TIP** To quickly find out the average, maximum, minimum, number of cells, or number of cells containing numbers in a range of cells, right-click the Status bar and select the Average, Maximum, Minimum, Count, or Numerical count options. When you select a range of cells, Excel displays the selected statistics in the Status bar.

The MAX, MIN, MAXA, and MINA Functions

The MAX and MIN functions allow you to quickly identify the largest and smallest values respectively in a range of values. Their syntax is

MAX(*number1, number2, ...*)

MIN(*number1, number2, ...*)

where *number1, number2*, and so on are up to 255 numbers from which you want to find the maximum or minimum value.

For example, we can use these functions to return the maximum and minimum value for the length of reaction time for the different samples in the experiment recorded in Figure 10-10.

	A	B	C	D	E
1	Sample	Time (mins)			
2	1	19		MAX	19
3	2	16		MIN	12
4	3	18		MINA	0
5	4	13			
6	5	12		AVERAGE	15.07692
7	6	17		MEDIAN	15
8	7	18		MODE	12
9	8	FALSE		AVERAGEA	13.06667
10	9	14			
11	10	15		AVERAGE(B1:B16)	15.07692
12	11	12		AVERAGEA(B1:B16)	12.25
13	12	12			
14	13	FALSE		COUNT	13
15	14	13		COUNTA	15
16	15	17		COUNTBLANK	0
17					

Experiment

Figure 10-10. Reaction times for different samples in an experiment

Using the data in Figure 10-10, the formula

MAX(B2:B16)

will return 19 and the formula

MIN(B2:B16)

will return 12.

If you want to include text representations of numbers or logical values, you can use the MAXA or MINA function to return the maximum or minimum value. A value of TRUE will evaluate to 1 and FALSE will evaluate to 0; therefore, for example,

=MAXA(0.1, TRUE, 0.8, 0.4)

will return 1 (the value for TRUE) as it is the largest value, and

=MINA(TRUE, 0.5, 0.4, FALSE)

will return 0 (the value for FALSE) as the minimum value. In the example in Figure 10-10,

=MINA(B2:B16)

returns 0 as the minimum value.

The AVERAGE, AVERAGEA, MEDIAN, and MODE Functions

Often, when working with numerical data, it is useful to compute measures of location like the mean (average), median, and mode. These measures help you to assess how close a value is to a typical value for the set. As their names imply, the AVERAGE, MEDIAN, and MODE functions will display the average (arithmetic mean), median (middle value), and mode (most frequently occurring value) for a range of values. Text, logical values, or empty cells in an array or reference argument will be ignored; however, logical values and text representations of numbers typed directly into the list of arguments will be included. Using the data in Figure 10-10,

=AVERAGE(B2:B16)

will return 15.07962 (196 divided by 13),

=MEDIAN(B2:B16)

will return 15, and

=MODE(B2:B16)

will return 12.

In some datasets there may be more than one mode. Excel will only return the first modal value and does not indicate if there is more than one mode. If there are no repeated values, the MODE function will return a #N/A error.

If you want to find the mean of a range of values that includes logical values or text representations of numbers, you can use the AVERAGEA function. Values of TRUE will evaluate to 1 and values of FALSE will evaluate to 0; arrays or references that contain text or empty text ("") will evaluate to 0, and if an argument is an array or reference, only values within that array or reference are used—text and empty cells are ignored. Therefore, the formula

=AVERAGEA(B2:B16)

in Figure 10-10 is calculated as 196 divided by 15 and will return a value of 13.06667 as the two cells containing the logical value FALSE are included in the calculation. If you typed the values in cells B2:B16 directly into the AVERAGE function, it would return the same result as the AVERAGEA function because logical values and text representations of numbers are included when typed directly into the list of arguments.

As AVERAGEA also includes arguments that contain text, if cell B1 is included in the calculation,

=AVERAGEA(B1:B16)

will return a value of 12.25 as the average is now calculated by dividing 196 by 16. Including cell B1 in a calculation using the AVERAGE function will not affect the result because cells containing text are ignored by the AVERAGE function.

The STDEV, STDEVA, STDEVP, and STDEVPA Functions

A popular measure of statistical dispersion is the standard deviation, which measures how the values in a dataset vary from the arithmetic mean. If all the values are close to the mean, the standard deviation will be near to 0; the larger the standard deviation, the more widely spread the values are. A standard deviation of 0 indicates that all the values are equal.

Excel provides us with four functions for calculating the standard deviation of a dataset, which operate in a similar manner to the AVERAGE function. The STDEV function will return the standard deviation based on a sample and the STDEVP function will calculate the standard deviation based on an entire population. Both these functions will ignore logical values and text. The STDEVA and STDEVPA functions are similar to the STDEV and STDEVP functions but will include text and logical values in the dataset, with text and values of FALSE evaluating to 0 and values of TRUE evaluating to 1. All the standard deviation functions can be entered using a similar format—for example, =STDEV(B2:B16).

The COUNT, COUNTA, COUNTBLANK, COUNTIF, and COUNTIFS Functions

The COUNT function can be used to count the number of cells that contain numbers or to count the numbers within a list of arguments. In the worksheet in Figure 10-10, the formula

=COUNT(B2:B16)

returns a value of 13 as only the cells containing numbers are counted. To count all the nonblank cells—that is, cells containing values, text, or error values—you can use the COUNTA function. COUNTA will also include cells containing empty text (" "). In Figure 10-10 the formula

=COUNTA(B2:B16)

returns 15 because this time the two logical values of FALSE are counted as well as the numbers. The COUNTBLANK function can be used to do the opposite of COUNTA and count the number of cells that are blank.

If you want to count only those cells that meet specified criteria, you can use the COUNTIF function. Its syntax is

COUNTIF(*range*, *criteria*)

where *range* is the range of cells you want to count and *criteria* is the number, text, reference, or expression that defines which cells are to be counted.

In the worksheet in Figure 10-10, the formula

COUNTIF(B2:B16, ">15")

would return the value 6 because six cells in the range B2:B16 contain values greater than 15.

The COUNTIFS function operates in a similar way to COUNTIF except that it allows you to specify more than one criterion. Its syntax is

COUNTIFS(*range1*, *criteria1*, *range2*, *criteria2*, …)

Again, using the worksheet in Figure 10-10, the formula

=COUNTIFS(B2:B16, ">15", B2:B16, "<18")

will return a value of 3 because three cells in the range B2:B16 contain values greater than 15 and less than 18.

Information Functions

Information functions are probably not as commonly utilized in Excel as the other types of function, but they may prove useful if information about cells, worksheets, formulas, or applications is required. This section will take a brief look at the INFO function and the different IS functions.

The INFO Function

The INFO function allows you to access information about the current operating environment. Its syntax is

INFO(*type_text*)

where *type_text* specifies the information that you want.

Table 10-5 lists the possible values for the *type_text* argument and what each returns.

Table 10-5. Values That Can Be Used for the type_text Argument in the INFO Function

type_text Value	What Is Returned
"directory"	The path of the current directory or folder
"numfile"	The number of active worksheets in open workbooks
"origin"	The absolute cell reference of the top and leftmost cell visible in the window preceded by $A—for example, *$A:$G$6*
"osversion"	The current operating system version, for example *Windows (32 bit) NT 5.01*
"recalc"	The current recalculation mode, i.e., *Automatic* or *Manual*
"release"	The current version of Microsoft Excel—for example, *12.0*
"system"	The name of the operating environment, i.e., *mac* for Macintosh or *pcdos* for Windows

...rosoft Office Excel 2007 no longer supports the "memavail", "memused", ...mem" *type_text* values, which could be used in previous versions to return ...information. These *type_text* values will now return a #N/A error value.

The IS Functions

Excel has nine IS functions that will return a value of TRUE or FALSE depending on the value being evaluated. They all have a similar syntax, which takes the format ISBLANK(*value*), where *value* is a cell reference or function or formula result. Table 10-6 outlines when each will return a value of TRUE.

Table 10-6. IS Functions

Function	Returns TRUE If Value Refers To
ISBLANK	An empty cell
ISERR	Any error value except for #N/A
ISERROR	An error value (i.e., #N/A, #VALUE!, #REF!, #DIV/0!, #NUM!, #NAME?, or #NULL!)
ISLOGICAL	A logical value (i.e., TRUE or FALSE)
ISNA	The #N/A (value not available) error value
ISNONTEXT	Any item that is not text (including a blank cell)
ISNUMBER	A number
ISREF	A reference
ISTEXT	Text

NOTE There are also the ISODD and the ISEVEN functions, which accept a number as their argument and will return TRUE or FALSE depending on whether the number is odd or even.

Database Functions

If you are working with data that is set out in a list or database, you can use one of Excel's database functions to analyze the data based on criteria that you specify. Twelve database functions are available in Excel 2007, among them DAVERAGE, DCOUNT, DCOUNTA, DMAX, DMIN, and DSUM, which all operate in a similar manner to their regular counterparts except that you can apply conditions to control which records in the list are included in the function. The database functions all take the format of

DFUNCTION(*database*, *field*, *criteria*)

where

- *database* is the range of cells that you want to evaluate using the criteria.
- *field* is the name of the field or column that is to be used in the function. This can be entered using the column name, enclosed in double quotation marks, or by entering the number that refers to the column's position within the list.
- *criteria* is the range of cells that contain the conditions that will be used to determine which cells are included in the operation. The criteria range works in the same way as it does for advanced filtering and must include at least one column heading and one cell below the column heading containing the condition for the column. If all the criteria fields are blank, all the records in the list will be used in the operation. See the "Advanced Filtering" section in Chapter 5 for more information on creating criteria.

The database functions can by typed directly into a cell, or they can be accessed by selecting the Database category in the Insert Function dialog box. If you name the database and criteria ranges, you can use these names instead of the cell references in the function (see Chapter 3 for more information on naming ranges).

Figure 10-11 illustrates a simple example of database functions being used to analyze data about room bookings in a hotel. In this example, cells A6:H20 have been named *database* and cells A1:A2 have been named *criteria*. Cells D1, D2, and D3 contain the three database functions shown in the shaded section to return the maximum, minimum, and average number of nights booked for the room type specified in cell A2. The number 2 in the function arguments refers to the position of the Nights column in the list. If you prefer, you can enter the functions using the name of the column instead of its position—for example, **=DMAX(database, "Nights", criteria)**.

	A	B	C	D	E	F	G	H	I
1	Room		Maximum nights	7		=DMAX(database, 2, criteria)			
2	Family		Minimum nights	3		=DMIN(database, 2, criteria)			
3			Average nights	5.3333333		=DAVERAGE(database, 2, criteria)			
4									
5									
6	Booking ref	Nights	Accommodation	Room	Adults	Children	Rate per night	Total cost	
7	140107	2	Half board	Double	2		$ 180.00	$ 360.00	
8	140108	1	Room only	Twin	2		$ 120.00	$ 120.00	
9	140109	7	Bed and breakfast	Family	2	1	$ 200.00	$1,400.00	
10	140110	4	Half board	Double	2		$ 180.00	$ 720.00	
11	140111	3	Bed and breakfast	Twin	1	1	$ 140.00	$ 420.00	
12	140112	3	Half board	Family	2	2	$ 250.00	$ 750.00	
13	140113	4	Bed and breakfast	Double	2		$ 160.00	$ 640.00	
14	140114	5	Bed and breakfast	Double	2		$ 160.00	$ 800.00	
15	140115	4	Bed and breakfast	Twin	2		$ 160.00	$ 640.00	
16	140116	6	Half board	Family	2	2	$ 250.00	$1,500.00	
17	140117	8	Bed and breakfast	Single	1		$ 80.00	$ 640.00	
18	140118	3	Room only	Double	2		$ 120.00	$ 360.00	
19	140119	4	Half board	Double	2		$ 180.00	$ 720.00	
20	140120	7	Bed and breakfast	Twin	2		$ 140.00	$ 980.00	

Figure 10-11. Use database functions to analyze records in a list or database that match conditions that you specify.

CHAPTER 11

Charts

Office 2007 introduces a variety of changes to Excel's charting element, the most obvious being the new formatting features and special effects that are available. Creating eye-catching charts has never been easier, and in Excel 2007 you can choose to manually format or change individual elements of your chart or to quickly apply a predefined chart layout and chart style. The implementation of document themes in the latest version of Office also stretches to Excel charts, and the added ability to store chart formats and layouts as a template will help ensure the consistency of charts within your overall workbook or document portfolio.

Behind the scenes, a major reform has occurred in that the chart engine for Excel will also now be used for Word 2007 and PowerPoint 2007, rendering Microsoft Graph obsolete (unless you are working in Compatibility mode in Word). Because the Excel worksheet is the default chart datasheet for Word and PowerPoint as well, charts created in these applications can take advantage of Excel's key attributes, thus enabling them to incorporate formulas, filtering, sorting, and the ability to link the chart to external data sources like SQL Server Analysis Services.

In this chapter we look at the different types of charts that can be created in Excel and the features that can be included to contribute to the analysis of the data. We also investigate some of the enhancements that have been made to the general appearance of charts in Excel and how charts can be modified once they have been created.

Creating Charts

Charts are used within Excel for numerous purposes, from column charts depicting a company's sales of different products to more intricate scientific charts recording the results of an experiment as a scatter graph. Excel provides you with an assortment of chart types and subtypes, most of which can be customized to fit your exact graphing needs, furnishing you with the ability to graphically display data in an almost infinite number of ways. As a chart series is linked to the worksheet data that it plots, any changes to the worksheet will normally be reflected automatically in the chart. This dynamic trait of charts, along with the ease with which they can be modified, make them a very flexible medium with which we can communicate the key points emerging from our worksheet data.

Chart Types in Excel

Before starting to create a chart in Excel, it is useful to have some idea of the type of chart that would be most suitable for displaying the data in your worksheet in a manner that is going to be comprehensible to anyone referring to the chart. Excel provides you with 11 main chart types, each of which contains a range of subtypes. You will probably find that you only use a few of these chart types, and some of the more unusual chart types have limited applicability to most types of data analysis. If you only use one particular chart type or there is a chart type that you use most frequently, you can set this as the default chart type. Table 11-1 lists some of the different chart types and subtypes available in Excel 2007 and provides an indication of when they might be used.

Table 11-1. Excel Chart Types and Subtypes

Type	Subtypes	Descriptions
Column	Clustered Column 3-D Clustered Column	Compare values (displayed vertically) across categories or time (arranged horizontally). Different series are displayed side by side to highlight variations between series within each category.
	Stacked Column Stacked Column in 3-D	Values for each series are stacked across categories, showing the contribution of each to the total for each category. Useful when you have multiple data series and want to emphasize the total for each category.
	100% Stacked Column 100% Stacked Column in 3-D	Similar to stacked column but compare the percentage each value contributes to the total for each category. Use a 100% stacked column chart where you want to emphasize the contribution of each value to the whole, especially if the total for each category is the same.

Type	Subtypes	Descriptions
Column (continued)	3-D Column	Uses three axes (horizontal, vertical, and depth) and compares data points along the horizontal and depth axes. Data series are displayed in rows along the x-axis in a 3-dimensional arrangement. Use a 3-D column chart to compare data across the categories and across the series equally.
Bar	Clustered Bar Clustered Bar in 3-D	Compare values (displayed horizontally) across categories (arranged vertically). Different series are displayed side by side within each category. Avoid using a time-based scale as the category as this can be confusing. Bar charts can be useful if your category labels are lengthy.
	Stacked Bar Stacked Bar in 3-D	Values for each series are stacked to show the contribution of each to the total for each category.
	100% Stacked Bar 100% Stacked Bar in 3-D	Similar to stacked bar except compare the percentage each value contributes to the total for each category. Useful alternative to multiple pie charts.
Line	Line Line with Markers 3-D Line	Display changes in a series over time or categories. Useful for showing trends over time or ordered categories with markers being used to indicate individual values. A line chart without markers is best if there are numerous categories or if the values are approximate.
	Stacked Line Stacked Line with Markers	Display the trend of the contribution of each value to the total over time or ordered categories. Do not use markers if there are numerous categories or the values are approximate.
	100% Stacked Line 100% Stacked Line with Markers	Display the trend of the percentage each value contributes to the total over time or ordered categories. Use a 100% stacked line without markers if there are several categories or if approximate values are used.

Continued

Table 11-1. *Continued*

Type	Subtypes	Descriptions
Pie	Pie Pie in 3-D	Display the contribution of each value to the total. Can only show one data series and values must be positive (negative values will be converted to positive) but are useful for emphasizing a significant element in the data. Categories represent parts of the pie and data points are displayed as a percentage of the whole pie. Pie charts are most useful where there are no more than seven categories, none of the values are negative and almost none of the values are zero values.
	Exploded Pie Exploded Pie in 3-D	Display the contribution of each value to a total while emphasizing individual values.
	Pie of Pie Bar of Pie	A pie chart with user-defined values extracted and combined into a second pie or stacked bar chart. For example, smaller items can be grouped together in the main pie chart and then broken down again in a smaller pie or bar chart beside the main chart. Useful for making small slices in a pie chart easier to see.
X Y (Scatter)	Scatter with only Markers Scatter with Smooth Lines and Markers Scatter with Smooth Lines Scatter with Straight Lines and Markers Scatter with Straight Lines	Compare pairs of values and are often used for scientific, statistical or engineering data. A scatter graph has two value axes and combines pairs of values into single data points. Scatter graphs can be used when values are not in x-axis order or where they represent separate measurements. Data points can be connected using smoothed or straight lines to emphasize a trend.
Area	Area 3-D Area	Display the trend of values over time or categories. Useful for emphasizing the differences between sets of data over time.

Type	Subtypes	Descriptions
Area (continued)	Stacked Area Stacked Area in 3-D	Display the trend of the contribution of each value to the total over time or categories. Useful for highlighting the total.
	100% Stacked Area 100% Stacked Area in 3-D	Display the trend of the percentage each value contributes to the total over time or categories.
Doughnut	Doughnut Exploded Doughnut	Similar to a pie chart but can contain multiple data series. Display data as a "ring" with different rings representing different data series.
Radar	Radar Radar with Markers Filled Radar	Compare the aggregate values of multiple data series. Display changes in values compared to a center point.
Surface	3-D Surface Wireframe 3-D Surface Contour Wireframe Contour	Show trends in values across two dimensions in a continuous curve. Colors and patterns indicate areas that are in the same range of values. A contour chart is a 3-D surface chart viewed from above. A wireframe 3-D surface or wireframe contour chart is a 3-D surface or contour chart without color.
Bubble	Bubble Bubble with a 3-D effect	Similar to a scatter graph except that they compare sets of three values with the third value displayed as the size of the bubble marker.
Stock	High-Low-Close Open-High-Low-Close Volume-High-Low-Close Volume-Open-High-Low-Close	Usually used for stock market data, though sometimes used for scientific data. Data must be organized in the correct order to create stock charts.

NOTE Column and bar charts can also be created using cylinders, cones, or pyramids as the data markers instead of columns or bars. You can also create a combination chart by using more than one chart type in your chart, although not all chart types can be combined.

Creating a Chart from Data in a Worksheet

Once you have entered the data you want to display as a chart into a worksheet and decided which type of chart you require, you can create it with just a few mouse clicks. You can check out the Help facility in Excel for advice on how to best structure the data on your worksheet for different chart types. Use the following procedure to quickly create a chart on the current worksheet:

1. Select the cells on your worksheet containing the data that you want to display as a chart. (You can select cells that are not adjacent using the Ctrl key, but make sure that the selected ranges form a rectangle.)

2. Select the Insert tab and, in the Charts group, click the chart type you require. A gallery of thumbnail images for the related chart subtypes will appear. To see the name and a brief description of any subtype, hover the mouse pointer over the thumbnail image. Click the required chart subtype to create the chart, or click All Chart Types to open the Insert Chart dialog box and choose from all available chart types. Alternatively, click the Dialog Box Launcher in the bottom-right corner of the Charts group to open the Insert Chart dialog box and see all the available chart types (see Figure 11-1). You can also change the default chart type in the Insert Chart dialog box by selecting a chart type and clicking the Set as Default Chart button.

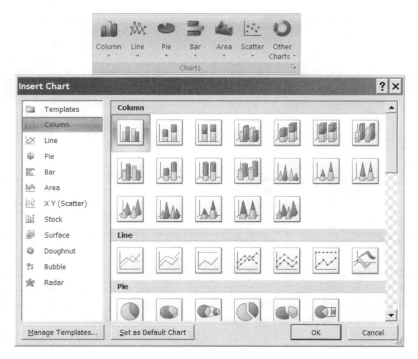

Figure 11-1. Select a chart type from the Charts group or click the Dialog Box Launcher to open the Insert Chart dialog box.

3. When you have selected a subtype, a chart will be created as an object in the worksheet and Chart Tools will appear on the Ribbon incorporating Design, Layout, and Format tabs. Excel will give the chart a default name, such as Chart 1, but you can rename it in the Properties group of the Layout tab under Chart Tools.

> **TIP** To quickly create a chart of the selected data (based on the default chart type) as an object in the current worksheet, press Alt+F1. To create a chart of the selected data as a new sheet, press F11; Excel will insert a new chart sheet into the workbook with a default name like Chart1.

To move an embedded chart to another location in the worksheet, click and drag it with the mouse to the new location. To resize a chart, click and drag one of the sizing handles around its border or change the entries in the Shape Height and Shape Width boxes in the Size group of the Format tab under Chart Tools.

Charting Data from a Different Worksheet

It is possible to display a chart on one worksheet using data from a different worksheet. The source data can even come from a separate open workbook. To create a chart using data from a different worksheet, do the following:

1. Click a blank cell in the worksheet that you want the chart to be displayed in.

2. Select the Insert tab on the Ribbon and choose a chart type and subtype from the Charts group.

3. Select the Design tab under Chart Tools on the Ribbon and click Select Data in the Data group. The Select Data Source dialog box will open (see Figure 11-2).

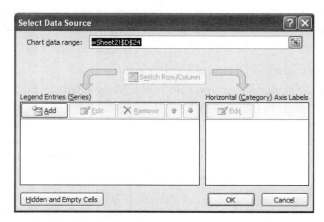

Figure 11-2. Use the Select Data Source dialog box to specify or edit the data range for a chart.

4. Enter the data range that you want to use for the chart in the "Chart data range" box by clicking the Collapse Dialog icon to the right of the "Chart data range" box and selecting the workbook and/or worksheet and then the cell range that you want to use for the data source. Click the Expand Dialog icon to the right of the Select Data Source dialog box when you have finished. Alternatively you can type the data range into the "Chart data range" box in the format **Sheet2!$A$10:$D$15** if you are charting the data in cells A10 to D15 in Sheet2 of the current workbook. If you want to use data from a sheet (Sheet1) in a different workbook (Workbook2), the format would be **[Workbook2]Sheet1!$A$10:$D$15**. If the name of either the worksheet or workbook contains spaces, enclose the workbook and worksheet name in single quotes—for example, **'[Sales2007]Jan Sales!'$A$10:$D$15**.

5. Click OK to close the Select Data Source dialog box.

Editing Charts

Once you have created your basic chart in Excel 2007, you can use the Design, Format, and Layout tabs to modify it in a variety of ways, allowing you to customize it to accurately convey the desired message or just to add your own personal touches to the finished display. You can easily change the type or location of the chart; edit features like axes, gridlines, and the legend; or add components such as error bars or trendlines.

Changing the Location of a Chart

Charts are generally embedded as objects in the current worksheet or created on a new chart sheet; however, they can be relocated either to an existing worksheet or to a new sheet. You can use the Design tab to quickly change the location of an existing chart in the current workbook using the following steps:

1. Select the chart that you wish to move by clicking it.

2. Select the Design tab under Chart Tools and click Move Chart in the Location group. The Move Chart dialog box will open.

3. To move the chart to a new sheet, select the New sheet option and enter a name for the new sheet in the box. To move the chart to an existing sheet, select the Object in option and choose an existing sheet from the dropdown list.

4. Click OK to close the Move Chart dialog box.

> **TIP** You can also use Cut (or Copy) and Paste to move a chart to another location or another document.

Changing the Type of a Chart or Data Series

For most charts you can change the type or subtype for the entire chart to display the data in a different way. You can also change the type for an individual data series, thereby creating a combination chart. To change the type of a chart or data series, do the following:

1. To change the type of an entire chart, click the chart area or plot area to select the chart and display the Chart Tools. To change the type of an individual data series, click the data series to select it.

2. Select the Design tab and, in the Type group, click Change Chart Type. The Change Chart Type dialog box will open (which is similar to the Insert Chart dialog box).

3. Select the new type and/or subtype for the chart or data series, or click Templates to select a type that has been saved as a template.

4. Click OK when you have finished to close the Change Chart Type dialog box.

You can change only one data series at a time. To change more data series, repeat steps 1–4 for each data series.

Changing the Data Source for a Chart

After creating a chart, you may wish to alter the range entered as the data source or switch between using the data in the rows or the data in the columns as the series. You can use the Select Data Source dialog box to change the range of cells whose data is to be plotted and to specify how this data is presented in a chart.

Changing the Chart Data Range

It is possible to vary the source data for a chart without having to re-create the chart. To adjust the range identified as the source data for a chart, use the following steps:

1. Click within the chart to display the Chart Tools and select the Design tab.

2. In the Data group, click Select Data to open the Select Data Source dialog box (see Figure 11-2).

3. Enter the new data range that you want to use for the chart in the "Chart data range" box by clicking the Collapse Dialog icon to the right of the "Chart data range" box and selecting the cell range that you want to use for the data source. (If you want to use data in a different worksheet, select the worksheet first and then the cells.) Click the Expand Dialog icon to the right of the Select Data Source dialog box when you have finished.

4. Click OK to close the Select Data Source dialog box.

> **TIP** A quick way to change the data range for an embedded chart is to drag the range outline that appears around the source data when you select a chart or data series. Simply click one of the corner sizing handles and drag the range outline to extend or contract the data range.

Changing How Rows and Columns Are Plotted

When you create a chart, Excel will guess which range of cells should be the data series; however, sometimes it misinterprets the orientation of the data. With Excel 2007 it is much easier to change how the rows and columns on your worksheet are plotted, thus allowing you to quickly specify which should be used as the data series. Users can now click Switch Row/Column in the Data group of the Design tab under Chart Tools to toggle between using rows or columns as the data series (in earlier versions, this option was embedded in the Chart Wizard). Alternatively, you can click the Switch Rows/Columns button in the Select Data Source dialog box.

Changing the Legend Entries (Series)

You can use the Select Data Source dialog box to add, edit, delete, and rearrange the data series for your chart without impacting the actual worksheet. The following steps outline how you can adjust the legend entries for an existing chart:

1. Click within the chart to display the Chart Tools and select the Design tab.
2. In the Data group click on Select Data to open the Select Data Source dialog box.
3. Change the legend entries by doing one or more of the following:
   - To add a data series, click the Add button. The Edit Series dialog box will open. In the Series name box, enter a name for the series by typing it in or by clicking a cell containing the name in the worksheet. In the Series values box, enter the array of values for the data series or select a range of cells on the worksheet. Click OK to return to the Select Data Source dialog box.
   - To edit a data series, select it in the Legend Entries (Series) area and click Edit. The Edit Series dialog box will open. To change the name for the series, type the new name in the Series name box or click a cell containing the name in the worksheet. To change the values for the series, change the entry in the Series values box by typing the new values in or by selecting the relevant cell range on the worksheet. Click OK to return to the Select Data Source dialog box.
   - To remove a series from the chart, select the data series in the Legend Entries (Series) area and click Delete. The series will be removed from the Legend Entries (Series) area.
   - To rearrange the order of the data series on the chart, select the series that you want to move and click the up or down arrow the required number of times to position the data series in the desired order.
4. Click OK to close the Select Data Source dialog box and implement your changes.

Changing the Horizontal (Category) Axis Labels

You can also use the Select Data Source dialog box to edit the labels used for the horizontal or category axis in your chart. To modify the labels for the horizontal axis, do the following:

1. Click within the chart to display the Chart Tools and select the Design tab.
2. In the Data group, click Select Data to open the Select Data Source dialog box.
3. Click the Edit button in the Horizontal (Category) Axis Labels section of the dialog box; the Axis Labels dialog box will open.
4. Change the labels by selecting the new range of cells on the worksheet. Click OK to return to the Select Data Source dialog box.
5. Click OK to close the Select Data Source dialog box.

> **TIP** Often Excel will not identify numerical values—for example, years—as category labels but will plot them as a data series instead. If this happens, delete the series from the Legend Entries (Series) list and click Edit beside Horizontal (Category) Axis Labels to select the cells containing the category labels.

Changing How Hidden or Empty Cells Are Displayed

In some situations you may have hidden or empty cells within your chart data range. By default, hidden data will not be included in a chart and empty cells will be displayed as zeros. You can indicate that you want hidden cells to be plotted in an existing chart or that you want empty cells to be displayed as gaps or bridged by a line by doing the following:

1. Click within the chart to display the Chart Tools and select the Design tab.
2. In the Data group, click Select Data to open the Select Data Source dialog box.
3. Click the Hidden and Empty Cells button; the Hidden and Empty Cells Settings dialog box will open.
4. If your data range contains empty cells, you can choose the appropriate option from Gaps, Zeros, and "Connect data points with line" depending on your data and chart type. If you want hidden data to be plotted in the chart, select the "Show data in hidden rows and columns" option. Click OK to return to the Select Data Source dialog box.
5. Click OK to close the Select Data Source dialog box.

> **TIP** Hiding rows or columns can be a handy way of controlling what data is plotted on the chart. If your data is filtered or outlined, the hidden data will not appear on your chart.

Adding a Secondary Axis

If your data contains mixed data types or widely varying values, you can add a secondary vertical axis and plot one or more data series on it. This will allow smaller values in a series to be displayed clearly and can help to show the relationship between series. For example, you could use separate axes to plot how different levels of advertising affect sales. You can then also add a secondary horizontal axis, which may be beneficial if your chart is a scatter chart or a bubble chart. To plot a data series on a secondary vertical axis, follow these steps:

1. Click the data series to select it (or click the chart and select the data series from the dropdown list in the Current Selection group on the Format tab under Chart Tools).

2. On the Format tab, in the Current Selection group, click Format Selection to open the Format Data Series dialog box (see Figure 11-3). Note that the Format Data Series dialog box will appear differently for different chart types.

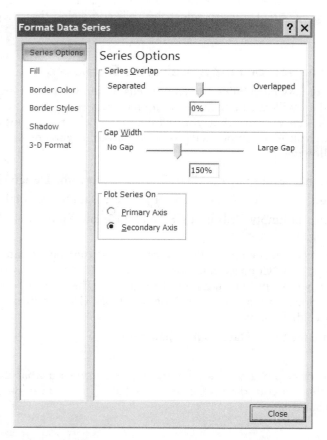

Figure 11-3. Use Series Options in the Format Data Series dialog box to plot a data series on a secondary axis.

3. Make sure that Series Options is selected and, in the Plot Series On area, select Secondary Axis. You can use the Format Data Series dialog box to change formatting settings for a data series like the fill and border color for a column or bar chart or the line style and color for a line chart.

4. Click Close to close the Format Data Series dialog box. The selected data series will now be plotted using a secondary vertical axis.

You may want to change the chart type for the series plotted on the secondary axis to emphasize it. See the section "Changing the Type of a Chart or Data Series" earlier in this chapter for instructions on how to do this. Once you have added a secondary vertical axis, you can add a secondary horizontal axis if required by clicking the chart containing the secondary vertical axis and selecting the Layout tab under Chart Tools. In the Axes group, click Axes and point to Secondary Horizontal Axis. Select the appropriate option from the menu that appears. To remove a secondary axis, select the Layout tab and, in the Axes group, click Axes; point to Secondary Horizontal Axis or Secondary Vertical Axis and select None. Figure 11-4 shows an example of a combination chart containing a secondary vertical axis and a secondary horizontal axis. The column chart plotted on the primary vertical axis represents the number of advertisements for a product. The line chart plotted on the secondary vertical axis represents the sales of the product.

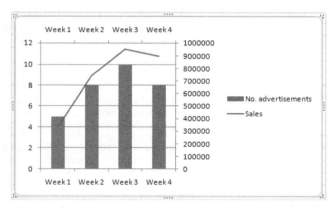

Figure 11-4. A combination chart with primary and secondary horizontal axes and primary and secondary vertical axes

Analysis Features for Charts

There are a range of features that you can add to a data series in a chart to assist in analyzing the data represented by the chart, such as trendlines, series lines, drop lines, high-low lines, up/down bars, and error bars. These features are used to emphasize trends, ranges, or errors within the data and can make reading the chart much easier while making the data more meaningful. You can incorporate these features within your chart by using the Analysis group on the Design tab of Chart Tools (see Figure 11-5).

Figure 11-5. You can use the Analysis group to add special features to your chart, like a Trendline or Error Bars.

Table 11-2 outlines the elements that can be added to a data series using the Analysis group, although the exact features available will depend on the type of the chart or data series.

Table 11-2. Analysis Features for Chart Data Series

Feature	Options	Description
Trendline	None	Removes the selected trendline or all trendlines if none is selected.
	Linear Trendline	Adds a linear trendline (straight line of best fit) for the selected series to highlight any general trend in the data. Used to show if something is increasing or decreasing at a steady rate.
	Exponential Trendline	Adds an exponential trendline (curved line) for the selected series. Used when data values increase or decrease at increasingly higher rates. Cannot be used if there are zero or negative values.
	Linear Forecast Trendline	Adds a linear trendline with a two-period forecast for the selected series. Used to predict future values based on the trendline.
	Two Period Moving Average	Adds a two-period moving average trendline for the selected series. Used to smooth out fluctuations in the data in order to display a pattern or trend more clearly. The number of periods can be changed by selecting More Trendline Options.
	More Trendline Options	Provides further options including Logarithmic, Polynomial and Power Trendlines, Trendline Name, Forecast, Set Intercept, "Display Equation on chart", "Display R-squared value on chart", and various formatting options.

Feature	Options	Description
Lines	None	Removes any drop lines, high-low lines, or series lines.
	Series Lines	Displays series lines connecting a data series on a 2-D stacked column or bar chart, a pie of pie chart, or a bar of pie chart.
	Drop Lines	Shows drop lines on an area or line chart running from each data point to the category (x) axis. Used to identify the position of data points on the category axis of a line chart more clearly or to clarify where one data marker ends and another begins on an area chart.
	High-Low Lines	Shows high-low lines running from the highest value to the lowest value for each category on a 2-D line chart.
Up/Down Bars	None	Removes up/down bars.
	Up/Down Bars	Shows up/down bars on a line chart with multiple data series to indicate the difference between the data points in the first and last series.
	More Up/Down Bar Options	Provides formatting options for up/down bars.
Error Bars	None	Removes error bars for the selected series or all error bars if no series is selected.
	Error Bars with Standard Error	Displays error bars for the selected series using standard error. Used to illustrate the possible error amounts for each data point in a 2D area, bar, column, line, XY (scatter), or bubble chart. XY (scatter) or bubble charts can display error bars for both the X and the Y values.
	Error Bars with Percentage	Displays error bars for the selected series with 5% value. The percentage value can be changed by clicking More Error Bars Options.
	Error Bars with Standard Deviation	Displays error bars for the selected series with one standard deviation. The number of standard deviations can be changed by clicking More Error Bars Options.
	More Error Bars Options	Provides more options for error bars including Direction, End Style, and the ability to change the error amount as well as various formatting options.

Formatting Charts

Excel 2007 has streamlined the formatting of charts with the introduction of predefined chart styles and chart layouts that allow you to instantly modify the look of your chart without having to format individual elements of it. These quick styles and quick layouts, as they are known, can be applied as they are, or they can be customized to accommodate your own preferences or color schemes and saved as a chart template so that you can use them again. You can format almost every aspect of a chart, including titles, axes, legends, data series, gridlines, the plot area, and the overall chart area. Some examples of alterations you may want to make to a chart include changing the scale of an axis or changing how numbers are displayed on the axis, formatting titles and labels, changing the color of a data series or a data point, and adding special effects to a chart element. This section will look at how you can customize your charts in Excel 2007.

Selecting a Chart Layout and Style

Each chart type in Excel has a range of associated predefined layouts that change the overall layout of a chart by specifying various settings for features like titles, gridlines, data tables, and legends. To apply a chart layout to a chart, select the chart and click the Design tab under Chart Tools. Select a layout from the Chart Layouts group (see Figure 11-6) or use the up and down arrows to the right of the group to scroll through the chart layouts. Alternatively, click the More icon in the bottom right of the group to view all available layouts for the selected chart type. (If you have reduced the size of the Excel window, click Quick Layout in the Chart Layouts group to view the chart layouts.) Click the chart layout that you want to use to apply it to your chart.

Figure 11-6. The Chart Layouts and Chart Styles groups for a line chart

To ensure that the formatting for your chart complements your overall document style, you can apply one of the predefined chart styles that are available for your chart type. As these are based on the selected document theme, they will coordinate with other elements of your workbook and other Office documents using the same theme. To apply a chart style to a chart, select the chart and click the Design tab under Chart Tools. Select a style from the Chart Styles group (see Figure 11-6) or use the up and down arrows to the right of the group to scroll through the chart styles. Alternatively, click the More icon in the bottom right of the group to view all available styles.

(If you have reduced the size of the Excel window, click Quick Styles in the Chart Styles group to view the chart styles.) Click the chart style that you want to use to apply it to your chart.

Manually Changing a Chart's Layout

There are numerous ways you can customize the layout of a chart. For example, you can add or remove items like the legend, the data table, titles, data labels, and gridlines. You can alter the layout of a chart or an individual element of a chart by using the Layout tab under Chart Tools. To do this, select the chart or the element of the chart that you want to modify by clicking it. Alternatively, select the Layout tab under Chart Tools and in the Current Selection group, click the down arrow in the Chart Elements box to reveal a list of chart elements that you can select from.

As you move your mouse over a chart element, a ScreenTip will appear displaying the name of the element. Elements like data labels and data series are made up of individual elements that can be selected after you have selected the group. For example, click a data point once to select the series and click again to select the individual data point. With the Layout tab selected, choose options from the Labels, Axes, and Background groups as desired (see Figure 11-7). Note that the exact range of available options will depend on the type of your chart and further options are available for each feature by selecting the appropriate command, for example More Title Options or More Legend Options.

Figure 11-7. You can manually change the layout of your chart by making selections from the Labels, Axes, and Background groups on the Layout tab.

In the Labels group, you will find commands for the Chart Title, Axis Titles, Legend, Data Labels, and the Data Table. Within each command are the various options that you can choose from to determine how that element is displayed. For example, you can decide to show the legend at the top, bottom, left, or right, or you can display data labels inside the end or inside the base of data points. If you have selected a data point or data series and apply data labels, the data labels will only be applied to the selected data point or data series. If you have selected the chart, the data labels will be applied to all the data series.

The Axes command in the Axes group allows you to specify how you want the Primary Horizontal Axis or Primary Vertical Axis displayed. For example, you can decide whether to display labels or tick marks, or you can choose to represent numbers in thousands or millions. If you have a secondary axis, options will be available for the Secondary Horizontal Axis or Secondary Vertical Axis as appropriate. The Gridlines command in the Axes group houses the various options for Primary Horizontal Gridlines and Primary Vertical Gridlines. You can choose to display gridlines for major units, minor units, or both major units and minor units. If appropriate, options will also be available for Secondary Horizontal Gridlines, Secondary Vertical Gridlines, and Depth Gridlines.

The Background group allows you to switch between showing the Plot Area using the default fill color or clearing the Plot Area. If you have chosen a 3-D chart type, you can also choose to show the Chart Wall or Chart Floor using the default fill color or to clear the Chart Wall or Chart Floor fill. To change the options for the formatting of 3-D rotation, you can use the 3-D Rotation command.

Manually Changing a Chart Element's Style

You can change the style of an individual element of a chart by using the Format tab under Chart Tools. To change an element of a chart, select the element of the chart that you want to modify by clicking it. Alternatively, select the Format tab under Chart Tools and in the Current Selection group, click the down arrow in the Chart Elements box (in Figure 11-8 the series "Apples" is selected in the Chart Elements box) to reveal a list of chart elements that you can select from.

Figure 11-8. To manually change the style of a chart element, use the Current Selection, Shape Styles, and WordArt Styles groups on the Format tab.

In the Current Selection group, click Format Selection and choose the formatting options that you want. Or, with the Format tab selected, apply a quick style from the Shape Styles group or click Shape Fill, Shape Outline, or Shape Effects in the Shapes Styles group and choose formatting options as desired.

To format the text in a chart element, select it or right-click it and select formatting options from the Mini toolbar that appears, or use the options in the Font group of the Home tab on the Ribbon. To format the text using WordArt, select a style from the WordArt Styles group or use the Text Fill, Text Outline, or Text Effects icon buttons in the WordArt Styles group. To remove any custom formatting from a chart element so that it matches the overall theme of the document again, click Reset to Match Style in the Current Selection group.

Saving a Chart As a Template

Once you have formatted your chart to your satisfaction, you can save it as a template so that you can use the same formatting and layout again with charts you create in the future. To do this, select the chart that you want to save as a template by clicking it. Select the Design tab under Chart Tools and, in the Type group, click Save As Template to open the Save Chart Template dialog box. Make sure that the Charts folder is selected in the Save in box, type a name for the template in the File name box, and click Save.

To apply a chart template to an existing chart or to create a new chart using a template, select the data that you want to plot using a chart template or select the chart that you want to apply a template to. Select the Insert tab and click the Dialog Box Launcher in the bottom-right corner of the Charts group to open the Insert Chart dialog box/Change Chart Type dialog box. Click the Templates folder to view thumbnail icons of your chart templates. To view the name of a template as a ScreenTip, hover your mouse over it (see Figure 11-9).

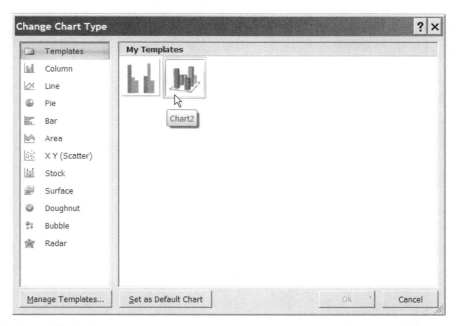

Figure 11-9. Select a chart template from the Templates folder to apply it to the selected chart or to plot the selected data using the template.

If you have stored a chart template in a folder other than the Charts folder, click Manage Templates, locate the template, and copy or move it to the Charts folder within the Templates folder. Click a chart template and click OK to apply it to the selected chart or to plot the selected data using it.

Deleting a Chart or a Chart Element

To delete a chart or an element of a chart like the legend or title, select the chart or the element and press the Delete key, or right-click a chart element and click Delete in the menu that appears. If you select a data point, the entire data series will be deleted.

CHAPTER 12

Adding Graphics to a Worksheet

Excel allows you to insert a variety of graphics into a worksheet, including pictures, clip art, WordArt, and shapes. These graphics are often integral to the usability of a spreadsheet, such as product images included in a spreadsheet used as an order form or a diagram used to explain a process. Or they can be purely aesthetic, like shapes used to emphasize text or arrows added to draw attention to particular results or forecasts. Either way, many Excel users will probably use some type of graphics within their workbooks at some stage.

As well as the familiar AutoShapes and clip art images, Office 2007 introduces us to a new family of graphics in the form of SmartArt, a collection of graphics that can be used to create high-impact lists or diagrams. Like many of the other formatting features discussed in earlier chapters, SmartArt is linked to the document theme and accessible via other Office 2007 applications, allowing you to create your most professional-looking documents ever.

Inserting and formatting pictures in a worksheet is easier than ever before in Excel 2007. The Insert tab on the Ribbon has an Illustrations group where users can quickly select the type of image they want to insert. In this section we will look at some of the different types of graphics that can be used in Excel, including stored images, clip art, shapes, and the new SmartArt range of graphics. We will also look at two features used to add text to a document: text boxes and WordArt.

Inserting Pictures and Clip Art

Graphics are included in worksheets for a wider range of reasons than many users may initially realize. More obvious uses are pictures inserted to decorate an otherwise bland-looking data display or corporate logos that have to be added to authenticate official documents. However, often worksheet designers incorporate graphics for more original purposes, such as illustrating inventory items, to add meaning to charts or to increase the visibility of noteworthy results.

The simplest way to add pictures to a worksheet or chart is to insert one of the built-in clip art images or to use a picture that is stored as a file on your computer, network, or other storage device. You can use the Illustrations group on the Insert tab to insert a picture, clip art, a shape, or SmartArt (see Figure 12-1). Pictures can be inserted on a worksheet in a variety of forms, including as the background or in headers and footers. You can also use an image as the fill for a data series or a shape.

Figure 12-1. Use the Illustrations group on the Insert tab to insert a picture, clip art, a shape, or SmartArt.

Inserting a Picture from a File

The most common way to use a picture in a worksheet is to embed it as an object. To insert a picture from a file as an object in a worksheet, select the Insert tab on the Ribbon and, in the Illustrations group, click Picture. The Insert Picture dialog box will open. Select the picture that you want to insert and click the Insert button. The picture will be added to your worksheet and Picture Tools will appear on the Ribbon. To reposition the picture, click it and drag it to the desired location. If you want to change a picture, right-click it and select Change Picture from the menu that appears to reopen the Insert Picture dialog box.

You can also use an image as the background for your worksheet, although this generally serves no greater purpose than embellishing the display. If you are applying a sheet background, your choice of image is very important as it may make your worksheet more difficult to read and will greatly increase the file size. A sheet background will only appear on the screen and will not be printed. To use an image as the background, select the Page Layout tab and, in the Page Setup group, click Background. In the Sheet Background dialog box, select the image that you want to apply as the background and click Insert. You will probably find that removing the gridlines and using a solid color shading for cells that contain data will improve the overall readability of the sheet.

Inserting Clip Art

The term *clip art* is probably an understatement for the media that can be inserted by this method as it now incorporates photographs, movies (animations), and sound files as well as the traditional artwork files. In addition to the selection of files that are available with Office 2007, you can access a wider range of clip art through Office Online, or you can download collections from other third-party sources. To insert a clip art file, follow these steps:

1. Select the Insert tab and, in the Illustrations group, click Clip Art. The Clip Art task pane (see Figure 12-2) will appear on the right of the screen.

Figure 12-2. Enter a keyword to search through the Clip Art collections on your computer and the files available through Office Online.

2. In the "Search for" box, enter a keyword or phrase to describe the file that you want to search for in Clip Art.

3. Click the down arrow in the "Search in" box to choose which collections you want to search (e.g., My Collections, Office Collections, and Web Collections). To search all collections, select Everywhere.

4. Click the down arrow in the "Results should be" box to refine your search by selecting the type of file you want to retrieve (e.g., Clip Art, Photographs, Movies, and Sounds). To return any type of file, select All Media Types.

TIP Click the plus sign to the left of a collection or media type to see more items that you can select or deselect to narrow your search even further.

5. When you have finished making selections, click the Go button to run the search. Thumbnails of the images and pictures retrieved (if any) will be displayed in the task pane; movie and sound files will be represented by an icon. If there is no match for your search in the selected collections, (No results found) will be displayed.

6. Click a thumbnail or icon to insert that file in your worksheet and drag it to the required location (or use the arrow keys to move it one pixel at a time for more precision). If you have selected an image file, Picture Tools will appear on the Ribbon.

> **TIP** To view details like the file name and the size and type of the file, hover your mouse over the thumbnail or icon. Also, you can click the down arrow that appears to the right of a clip art file when you move your mouse over it in the task pane and select Preview/Properties from the context menu to open the Preview/Properties dialog box. Here you can view additional details about the file, view any animations, add a caption, or edit the keywords for the file.

You can use the Clip Organizer to view and manage media files by clicking the Organize Clips hyperlink at the bottom of the Clip Art task pane. If you have graphics that you regularly insert into your worksheet, such as a company logo, you can add them to the Clip Organizer. To do this, follow these steps:

1. Select the Insert tab and, in the Illustrations group, click Clip Art to open the Clip Art task pane.

2. Click Organize Clips at the bottom of the task pane to open the Clip Organizer.

3. Click the File menu, point to Add Clips to Organizer, and select On My Own. This will open the Add Clips to Organizer dialog box, where you can locate and select the file.

4. Click the Add To button to open the Import to Collection dialog box and select a collection, or click New to create a new collection, enter a name for the new collection, and click OK.

5. Click OK to close the Import to Collection dialog box and click Add to close the Add Clips to Organizer dialog box.

6. Click the Close button (X) button at the top of the Clip Organizer when you have finished.

Formatting Pictures

Once you have inserted a picture or clip art image into your document, you can use the Format tab under Picture Tools to customize it (see Figure 12-3). It is easy to tweak the picture by making adjustments to features like the brightness, contrast, or color. You can also use one of the predefined picture styles, or you can create your own style for the shape and border or to apply special effects like a frame, shadow, or beveling.

Figure 12-3. Use the Format tab under Picture Tools to alter features of an image.

Adjusting Pictures

You can use the Adjust group on the Format tab under Picture Tools to adjust various aspects of a picture. To change the brightness or contrast for a picture, click Brightness or Contrast in the Adjust group. You can then select a positive percentage to increase the brightness or contrast, or a negative percentage to decrease it (see Figure 12-4). If the required percentage is not listed, select Picture Corrections Options to open the Format Picture dialog box at the Picture options and change the value for Brightness or Contrast by using the slider or changing the value in the box (see Figure 12-4).

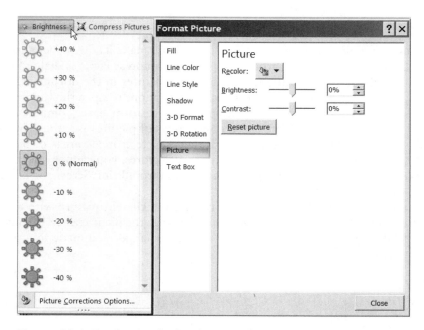

Figure 12-4. To change the brightness of a picture, select a percentage from the options available or click Picture Corrections Options to open the Format Picture dialog box.

To quickly change the color for a picture, click Recolor in the Adjust group and select a color mode or variation from the options available (see Figure 12-5). If none of the variations shown are suitable, point to More Variations to select the required color. To make a color in the image transparent, click Recolor in the Adjust group and select Set Transparent Color. Click a color in the image to make it transparent.

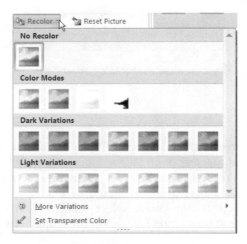

Figure 12-5. Select Recolor in the Adjust group to vary the color of a picture or make a color in the picture transparent.

To compress a picture (reduce its color format) and make its file size smaller, click Compress Pictures in the Adjust group to open the Compress Pictures dialog box. To compress only the selected picture (and not all the pictures in the document), select the "Apply to selected pictures only" option. Click Options to open the Compression Settings dialog box and select the "Automatically perform basic compression on save" option. If you want to delete any cropped areas of pictures (see the "Cropping Pictures" section later in this chapter), select the "Delete cropped areas of pictures" option. Note that if you delete the cropped areas of pictures, you cannot reset the picture to its original state. Select the appropriate option from Print, Screen, or E-mail in the Target output area and click OK.

You can also use the Adjust group to replace the current picture with another image. To open the Insert Picture dialog box and change the picture, click Change Picture in the Adjust group. To discard any formatting changes you made to a picture, click Reset Picture in the Adjust group.

Changing the Style of Pictures

You can quickly add a professional touch to your pictures by applying one of the predefined pictures styles. Each style uses a different combination of decorative effects, such as adding a frame; applying effects like beveling, shadows, or rotation; or changing the shape of a picture. You can apply a style to the selected image by clicking one of the thumbnails in the Picture Styles group of the Format tab. Use the up and down arrows to scroll through the available styles, or click the More arrow below the down arrow to view all the styles.

You can also change the visual style of a picture manually by choosing your own shape, border, and effects. Select the picture that you want to format and select the Format tab under Picture Tools. Customize the picture by doing any or all of the following:

- In the Picture Styles group, click Picture Shape to choose a different outline shape for the picture.
- Click Picture Border in the Picture Styles group to specify settings for the color, weight, and dashes of the border. As you move your mouse over the range of options for border color, weight, and dashes, your image will update, thus allowing you to preview the possible settings.
- Click Picture Effects to view the various effects that can be applied to the picture, such as Shadow, Reflection, and Glow. Point to an effect and choose an option from the fly-out menu to apply any effect. You can see the result of any effect on your picture just by moving your mouse over it.
- Click Reset Picture in the Adjust group to remove any formatting you have applied to the picture.

Inserting Shapes

Microsoft Office provides you with an assortment of customizable shapes (formerly known as AutoShapes) that you can use individually to display text or draw attention to sections of a document or that you can combine to create diagrams or flow charts. The various categories of shapes available include Lines, Rectangles, Basic Shapes, Block Arrows, Equation Shapes, Flowchart, Stars and Banners, and Callouts. To insert a shape in Excel, use the following procedure:

1. Select the Insert tab and, in the Illustrations group, click Shapes. The Shapes gallery will appear illustrating the various shapes, subdivided into categories (see Figure 12-6).

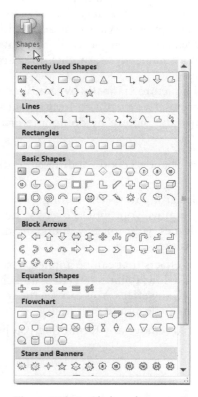

Figure 12-6. Click a shape to insert it into your document.

| **TIP** Click and drag the sizing handle in the bottom-right corner of the Shapes gallery to resize it. To view the name of any shape, hover your mouse over it.

2. Click a shape to select it, then click in the document and drag the shape to the required size. (To draw a perfect square or circle, or to create other shapes in proportion, hold down the Shift key as you drag the shape to the required size.) If you have selected Freeform, you can click repeatedly to draw straight lines and then click near the first point to close the shape. (If you have selected a shape other than Freeform, you can double-click in your document to insert it using the default dimensions.) Drawing Tools will appear and a Format tab will be added to the Ribbon.

3. If the shape you have selected is suitable, you can type text into it directly.

4. To reposition the shape, click it and drag it to the required location.

If you want to create multiple occurrences of the same shape, select Shapes in the Illustrations group, right-click the shape in the gallery, and select Lock Drawing Mode. Click and drag the shape as many times as you require, then press Esc when you have finished to unlock drawing mode. You can also insert duplicate shapes by using Copy and Paste.

Once you have inserted a shape, you can change it to another shape or convert it to freeform and edit its points individually. To change a shape, select the shape you want to edit and, in the Insert Shapes group on the Format tab (see Figure 12-7), click Edit Shape. To change the shape to another shape, point to Change Shape in the menu that appears and select a different shape from the gallery. To change a shape to a freeform shape, click Convert to Freeform. Click Edit Shape again and select Edit Points. Adjust the shape by dragging any of the vertexes (indicated by a black dot) that outline the shape.

Figure 12-7. Use the Insert Shapes group to insert a new shape or change an existing shape.

While you have the Format tab under Drawing Tools selected, you can also use the Insert Shapes group to quickly add more shapes without having to switch to the Insert tab. Use the up and down arrows to scroll through the shapes, or click the More arrow below the down arrow to view all the shapes.

TIP For some shapes, when you select the shape you will see a small yellow dot, which you can click and drag to change the outline of the shape. The effect will vary for each shape, so experiment and see the results.

If you need to insert comments, descriptions, explanations, and so forth in a worksheet, you may find that using text boxes will give you more flexibility over the appearance and flow of the text. To insert a text box into a worksheet, select the Insert tab and, in the Text group, click Text Box. Alternatively, click Text Box (or the Text Box icon) in the Insert Shapes group of the Format tab under Drawing Tools. Click and drag the text box to the required size, or simply click on the location on your worksheet where you want the text box to appear and type the text to make the text box resize to accommodate the text.

You can use the Format tab under Drawing Tools to change the style and size of the text box in the same way as for a shape (see the next section, "Formatting Shapes"). To select a text box, press the Ctrl key as you click it. You can then move it by dragging the border or by using the arrow keys. You can delete a text box by selecting it and pressing Delete.

Formatting Shapes

Once you have inserted a shape in your document, you can modify it in numerous ways. For example, you can reposition it, format it, add text to it, and even link it to a worksheet cell so that it displays the contents of the cell. In this section we will look at various ways that you can customize shapes in Excel 2007.

Changing the Style of Shapes

If you want to quickly format a shape or shapes that you have added to your document, you can apply one of the predefined shape styles that are linked to the selected document theme. Each style uses a different combination of settings for the fill, outline, and visual effects options to offer you a variety of coordinated looks for your shapes. You can apply a style to the selected shape or shapes by clicking one of the styles in the Shape Styles group of the Format tab (see Figure 12-8).

Figure 12-8. Select a predefined shape style or choose your own settings for the shape fill, outline, and effects from the Shape Styles group.

Use the up and down arrows to scroll through the available styles, or click the More arrow below the down arrow to view all the styles. As you move your mouse over a style, it will be applied to the selected shape(s), allowing you to preview it. A ScreenTip will appear indicating the name of the style.

If none of the shape styles in the gallery are suitable, click Other Theme Fills at the bottom of the gallery to see further suggestions. Alternatively, you can change the visual style of a shape manually by choosing from the wide range of fill, outline, and effects options. The following steps describe how you can do this:

1. Select the shape that you want to format. To format multiple shapes together, select them using the Ctrl key. Select the Format tab under Drawing Tools.

2. Customize the shape by doing any or all of the following:
   - In the Shape Styles group, click Shape Fill to choose a different fill color for the shape. Point to Gradient or Texture to view other options for special fills, or click Picture to select a picture file to use to fill the shape. The selected shape will update as you move your mouse over the different options.

- Click Shape Outline in the Shape Styles group to specify settings for the color, weight, and dashes of the border. As you move your mouse over the range of options for border color, weight, and dashes, your shape will update, allowing you to preview the possible settings.
- Click Shape Effects to view the various effects that can be applied to the shape. Point to an effect and choose an option from the fly-out menu to apply that effect. You can see the result of any effect on your shape just by moving your mouse over it.

You can also format a shape by clicking the Dialog Box Launcher in the bottom-right corner of the Shapes Styles group and choosing options from the Format Shape dialog box.

TIP If you are using multiple objects like pictures, shapes, text boxes, or WordArt, you can group them together so that they can be manipulated as one object. This technique is particularly useful if you are using multiple shapes to create a diagram. To select multiple objects, select the first object and hold down the Shift or the Ctrl key as you click the other objects. To cancel the selection of one of the objects, hold down the Shift or Ctrl key as you click the object that you want to deselect. To group the selected objects together, click Group in the Arrange group and select Group. You will then be able to move, resize, or format the objects together. You can still modify an individual object in a group by selecting the group and then clicking the object and editing it as normal. To ungroup the objects again, click Group in the Arrange group and select Ungroup.

Displaying Text or Cell Contents in Shapes

You can use the majority of shapes (excluding lines, of course) to display text or the contents of a cell. As soon as you have finished dragging out the shape, you can type the text you want it to display in directly. To change the text displayed in a shape, simply click the shape to select it and delete or edit the text as required. To format the text in a shape, select it and use the Mini toolbar that appears or the commands in the Font and Alignment groups on the Home tab.

Although you cannot type formulas into shapes, you can use a shape to display the contents of a cell that contains data or a formula. This ensures that the value displayed in the shape will always reflect the current value in the linked cell. To link a shape you have inserted to the contents of a cell, follow these steps:

1. Enter the data or formula into the appropriate worksheet cell.
2. Select the shape that you want to use to display the contents of a cell.

3. Click in the formula bar and type an equals sign (=) followed by the reference of the cell whose contents you want to display in the shape, for example, =B4 (or click the cell to enter the reference).

4. Press the Enter key; the contents of the cell will be displayed in the shape. If the contents of the cell change, the value displayed in the shape will update accordingly.

> **NOTE** Only the current value of the cell will be displayed in the shape; it will not reflect the formatting of the linked cell.

Resizing Pictures and Shapes

There are various ways that you can change the size of an image or shape that you have inserted. To resize a picture or shape manually, you can simply click it and drag one of the sizing handles around the edge of the picture to the desired height and/or width. To maintain the position of the center of the image or shape as you resize it, hold down the Ctrl key as you drag one of the sizing handles. To keep the height and width of the image or shape in proportion as you resize, hold down the Shift key as you drag a corner sizing handle. To maintain both the center position and the proportions of the image, press Ctrl+Shift as you drag a corner sizing handle.

To set an image or shape to a specific height and/or width, right-click the image or shape and select Size and Properties from the menu that appears to open the "Size and Properties" dialog box. Make sure that the Size tab is selected, and change the values in the Height and/or Width boxes in the "Size and rotate" area or in the "Scale" area (see Figure 12-9).

Figure 12-9. The Size tab of the Size and Properties dialog box

Alternatively, you can quickly specify the size by selecting the image or shape and choosing the Format tab under Picture Tools or Drawing Tools. In the Size group, adjust the entry in the Height box and/or Width box (see Figure 12-10).

Figure 12-10. You can resize a picture or shape by changing the values in the height and width boxes in the Size group. Note that the Crop command is not available in the Size group under Drawing Tools.

To change the height and width independent of each other when using the Size and Properties dialog box or the Size group, you will need to deselect the "Lock aspect ratio" option on the Size tab of the Size and Properties dialog box. You can open the Size and Properties dialog box from the Size group by clicking the Dialog Box Launcher in the bottom-right corner of the Size group.

You can change the size of multiple images or shapes together by selecting the first object and holding down the Ctrl key as you select the others; then resize all the objects by dragging one of the sizing handles on one of the pictures or shapes. To set all the selected objects to a specific height and/or width, change the height and/or width in the boxes in the Size group.

If you change your mind about resizing an image, you can revert to its default dimensions. To restore an image to its original height and width, click Reset Picture in the Adjust group or click the Reset button on the Size tab of the Size and Properties dialog box. You cannot reset a shape, although you can use the Undo command on the Quick Access Toolbar to undo any size changes.

Objects like embedded charts, pictures, and shapes are placed on the drawing layer of a worksheet, allowing them to be moved, resized, copied, and deleted without affecting the underlying cells on the worksheet. Using the Properties tab of the Size and Properties dialog box, you can adjust how an object moves or sizes with the underlying cells by selecting one of the following three options:

- Select "Move and size with cells" to move the object if rows or columns are inserted or deleted and resize the object if the height of the rows or width of the columns changes.

- Select "Move but don't size with cells" to move the object if rows or columns are inserted or deleted but not resize the object if the height of the rows or width of the columns changes.

- Select "Don't move or size with cells" to ensure the position and size of the object is unaffected by changes to the underlying cells.

You can also use the Properties tab to specify whether or not to print the object and to lock the object and its text if appropriate. If you are intending to place a worksheet containing an image or shape on the Web, you may want to specify alternative text to display if the graphic does not load properly. To do this, select the Alt Text tab in the Size and Properties dialog box and enter the text in the Alternative text box.

> **TIP** You can also attach an object to a cell by clicking the Microsoft Office Button, clicking Excel Options, and selecting the Advanced category. In the Cut, Copy and Paste section, select the "Cut, copy and sort inserted objects with their parent cells" option.

Cropping Pictures

If you only want to display a portion of any image (excluding animated GIFs), you can use the cropping tool to trim off the superfluous edges. To activate the cropping tool and manually trim an image, follow these steps:

1. Select the image to display the Format tab under Picture Tools and, in the Size group, click Crop (see Figure 12-10). The cropping handles will be displayed on the image and the mouse pointer will change to a cropping pointer.

2. Crop the image by doing any of the following:
   - To crop one side, drag the center cropping handle for the side inward.
   - To crop both the width and height from any corner, drag the corner cropping handle inward.
   - To crop opposite sides together equally, hold down the Ctrl key and drag either center cropping handle inward.
   - To crop all four sides together equally, hold down the Ctrl key and drag one of the corner cropping handles inward.

3. Click outside of the image when you have finished, deactivating the cropping tool.

If you want to crop your image to exact proportions, you can use the Size and Properties dialog box to specify how much you want to trim from each side. Right-click the image and select Size and Properties from the menu that appears to open the Size and Properties dialog box. Make sure that the Size tab is selected and change the values in the Left, Right, Top, and Bottom boxes in the Crop from area (see Figure 12-9). If you change your mind about cropping an image, you can restore it to its original settings by clicking the Reset button to return the image to its original form.

> **TIP** To add a margin around a picture, you can *outcrop* by dragging the cropping handles outward (use the Ctrl key and drag a corner handle to add a margin to all sides equally) or by entering negative values in the boxes in the Crop from area of the Size and Properties dialog box.

Rotating or Flipping Pictures or Shapes

It is easy to rotate a picture or shape to alter the orientation of it; to rotate an object manually just click the rotation handle (indicated by a green dot above the picture) and drag it in the required direction. If you want to restrict the rotation to 15-degree angles, hold down the Shift key as you drag the rotation handle.

If you want to specify a particular rotation for an object, select it to display Picture Tools or Drawing Tools. On the Format tab, in the Arrange group, click Rotate. To rotate the object by 90 degrees to the left or right, click Rotate Right 90° or Rotate Left 90°. To select a different rotation value, click More Rotation Options to open the Size and Properties dialog box. On the Size tab, adjust the value in the Rotation box under "Size and rotate" and click OK.

If you want to reverse a picture or create a mirror image of it, you can flip it by 90°. To do this, select the picture to display Picture Tools and in the Arrange group, click Rotate. Select either Flip Horizontal or Flip Vertical as required. To create a mirror image of a picture, create a copy of it, flip the copy, and drag it to a position where it will mirror the original.

Filling a Shape or Chart Element with a Picture

You can use a picture to fill a chart area, plot area, or a data series in some chart types, such as column, bar, or pie charts. For example, you could use an image of a house to represent house sales in a column chart. You can also use a picture to fill a shape that you have inserted (see the "Formatting Shapes" section earlier in this chapter). You can do this by following these steps:

1. Right-click the chart area, plot area, or data series of a chart, or the shape that you want to fill using a picture and select Format Chart Area, Format Plot Area, Format Data Series, or Format Shape as appropriate.

2. In the Format Chart Area, Format Plot Area, Format Data Series, or Format Shape dialog box, select Fill and choose the "Picture or texture fill" option. (If you are formatting a shape, the dialog box will change to a Format Picture dialog box.)

3. Do one of the following:
   - Click the File button to open the Insert Picture dialog box, choose the picture you want to use, and click Insert.
   - Click the Clipboard button to use an image you have copied to the Clipboard.
   - Click the Clip Art button to select a clip art image.

4. Select any other options as necessary in the dialog box before clicking Close. Figure 12-11 shows how you can use an image of a house to depict house sales.

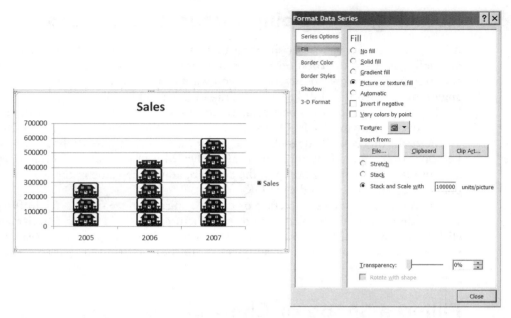

Figure 12-11. You can use an image to fill a data series of a chart.

> **TIP** If you want the image to be repeated to represent units in a column or bar chart (as in Figure 12-11), select the Stack option in the Format Data Series dialog box. If your values are large, select the "Stack and Scale with" option and enter how many units each picture should represent.

Creating and Editing SmartArt

If you use spreadsheets as a means of communicating information as well as analyzing data, you will probably find the new SmartArt collection a welcome addition to the Office suite of applications. By using this built-in range of graphics to create diagrams or illustrate processes and lists, you can produce designer-quality documents without the need for specialized graphics or publishing software. SmartArt is a significant improvement to the Diagram Gallery used by previous versions of Microsoft Office and has 70 graphics subdivided into the following categories: List, Process, Cycle, Hierarchy, Relationship, Matrix, and Pyramid. This allows you to create a wide range of diagrams, such as organization charts, flowcharts, decision trees, and Venn diagrams.

To use SmartArt in your document, just follow these steps:

1. Select the Insert tab and, in the Illustrations group, click SmartArt. The Choose a SmartArt Graphic dialog box will appear, illustrating the various lists and diagrams that can be inserted (see Figure 12-12).

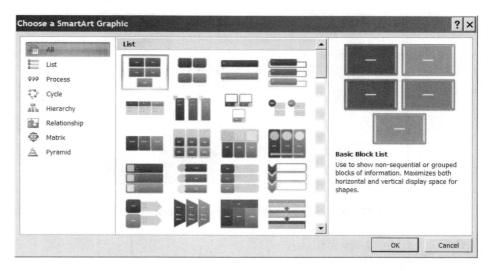

Figure 12-12. Select a type and layout for your SmartArt from those available.

2. Select a type to view the layouts for that type or select All to view all the available SmartArt layouts.

3. Click a SmartArt graphic to view an example and a description of it in the area to the right.

4. When you have chosen which SmartArt graphic you want to use, click it to select it and click OK. The SmartArt will appear on your worksheet along with a Text pane. A Design tab and a Format tab will be added to the Ribbon under SmartArt Tools (see Figure 12-13).

5. Use the Text pane beside the SmartArt graphic to add text to each component of your list or diagram. Press the down arrow key to move to the next component and press the Enter key to insert a new component. If you want to create a sublevel bullet point, press the Tab key.

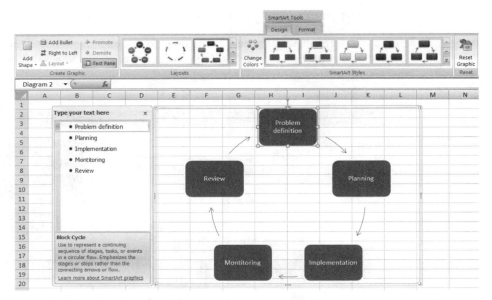

Figure 12-13. Add text to the various components of the SmartArt using the Text pane.

> **NOTE** Some SmartArt layouts contain a picture placeholder that allows you to insert a picture into the SmartArt graphic. Just click the picture icon to open the Insert Picture dialog box.

6. When you have finished entering text, click the Close button (X) in the top-right corner of the Text pane to close it. To display the Text pane again, click the arrows to the left of the SmartArt graphic or select the Design tab under SmartArt Tools and, in the Create Graphic group, click Text Pane or the Text Pane icon (see Figure 12-13).

Changing the Structure and Layout of SmartArt

You can make alterations to the structure of your SmartArt after you have created it using the Design and Format tabs under SmartArt Tools. You can edit the actual layout of the list or diagram, add bullet points, and even change the direction. Use the following points as a guide:

- To add another component to the SmartArt, click an existing component and, in the Create Graphic group, click the down arrow beside Add Shape. Select the appropriate option from the menu—for example, Add Shape Above or Add Shape Before.

- To add another bullet point to a component (where appropriate), click the component and, in the Create Graphic group, click Add Bullet.

- To reverse the order of the components or the flow of a SmartArt graphic, click it and in the Create Graphic group, click Right to Left.

- To promote or demote a bullet within a component, click the bullet either in the component or in the Text pane, and click Promote or Demote in the Create Graphic group.

- To delete a component, click it to select it and press the Delete key, or select the text for the component in the Text pane and press Delete twice.

You can also customize your SmartArt by changing the shape of individual components of a SmartArt graphic. Simply select the component(s) that you want to change, click the Format tab under SmartArt Tools, and in the Shapes group, click Change Shape. Choose a new shape from the gallery to apply it to the selected component(s). If your SmartArt has a 3-D style, you can click Edit in 2-D in the Shapes group to convert it to a 2-D style for editing. Click on Edit in 2-D again when you have finished to change it back to 3-D.

You can quickly change the layout of a SmartArt graphic to display your data in a different way. To change the layout of a SmartArt graphic, select the SmartArt graphic to display SmartArt Tools. Select the Design tab and click a different layout in the Layouts group to apply it. Use the up and down arrows to the right of the Layouts group to scroll through the options, or click the More arrow in the bottom-right corner of the Layouts group to view all the layouts.

If you want to change the actual type of the SmartArt, select the Design tab and click the More arrow in the bottom-right corner of the Layouts group. Select More Layouts to open the Choose a SmartArt Graphic dialog box. Choose the type and layout that you require and click OK.

> **TIP** You can also open the Choose a SmartArt Graphic dialog box by right-clicking the SmartArt and selecting Change Layout from the menu that appears.

Displaying Cell Contents in SmartArt

You cannot use a SmartArt graphic to link to a cell in the same way as you can with a shape. If you want to display the contents of a cell in your diagram or list, you will have to convert your SmartArt to individual shapes and then link one of the shapes to the cell. To convert SmartArt to ordinary shapes, follow these steps:

1. Click the SmartArt graphic and press Ctrl+A to select all the shapes within it.
2. Select the Home tab and, in the Clipboard group, click the Copy icon.
3. Click in a different area of your worksheet and click Paste in the Clipboard group. The SmartArt will be pasted as ordinary shapes.
4. Click in the shape that you want to use to display the contents of a cell to select it, click in the formula bar, and type an equals sign (=) followed by the reference of the cell, and press Enter.

Formatting SmartArt

There are numerous ways that you can modify a SmartArt graphic. Excel provides us with a range of predefined layouts and formatting styles along with the different shape styles that can be used for the individual components of the list or diagram. This section will look at the main ways that you can edit and format your SmartArt graphics.

Resizing SmartArt

You can resize a SmartArt in the same way as you resize a basic shape; however, with SmartArt you can resize the entire graphic or an individual component. To resize an individual SmartArt component (or multiple selected components together), do either of the following:

- Select the component(s) and drag one of the sizing handles to the desired height and/or width.
- Select the component(s), click the Format tab under SmartArt Tools and, in the Shapes group, click Larger or Smaller.

NOTE When you are resizing part of a SmartArt graphic, the unselected components may also resize to accommodate the changes to the selected component(s). The size of the entire graphic will remain unchanged.

To resize an entire SmartArt graphic manually, click it and drag one of the sizing handles around the edge the required direction. To maintain the position of the center of the graphic as you resize it, hold down the Ctrl key as you drag one of the sizing handles. To keep the height and width of the graphic in proportion as you resize, hold down the Shift key as you drag a corner sizing handle. To maintain the center position and the proportions of the graphic, press Ctrl+Shift as you drag a corner sizing handle.

You can also specify the exact height or width of a SmartArt graphic, but you cannot specify exact dimensions for a component. To set SmartArt to a specific height and/or width, do either of the following:

- Right-click the SmartArt graphic and select Size and Properties from the menu that appears to open the Size and Properties dialog box. Make sure that the Size tab is selected and change the values in the Height and/or Width boxes in the "Size and rotate area" or in the Scale area. Select "Lock aspect ratio" to keep the height and width in proportion to each other.
- Select the SmartArt graphic and choose the Format tab under SmartArt Tools. Click Size and adjust the entry in the Shape Height or Shape Width box.

Changing the Style of SmartArt

For each SmartArt layout, there are a variety of predefined 2-D and 3-D styles that you can apply to instantly format your graphic. You can also choose from a wide range of colors linked to your document theme, allowing you to coordinate your diagrams with the rest of your workbook. To change the formatting style of your SmartArt, select the SmartArt graphic to display SmartArt Tools. Select the Design tab and click a different style in the SmartArt Styles group to apply it. Use the up and down arrows to the right of the SmartArt Styles group to scroll through the options, or click the More arrow in the bottom-right corner of the SmartArt Styles group to view all the available styles. To change the color scheme for the SmartArt, click Change Colors in the SmartArt Styles group and choose one of the options from the gallery. You can restore your SmartArt to its default formatting by clicking Reset Graphic on the Design tab.

In addition to applying a style to an entire SmartArt graphic, you can format individual components using predefined styles or by changing the fill, outline, or effects options of the component in the same way as you can change the style of a basic shape. See "Changing the Style of Shapes" earlier in this chapter for instructions on how to customize the components of your SmartArt graphic.

Using WordArt

The WordArt gallery of text styles allows you to insert high impact text into a document using various special effects like beveling, shadows and even mirrored text. For example, you can use WordArt to create a heading for a worksheet. To insert WordArt, select the Insert tab on the Ribbon and, in the Text group, click on WordArt. Choose a WordArt style from the gallery that appears (see Figure 12-14) and type the text that you want to use for the WordArt. A Format tab under Drawing Tools will appear on the Ribbon.

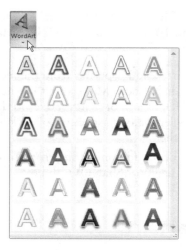

Figure 12-14. Click a WordArt style in the gallery to insert a WordArt graphic.

You can quickly change the appearance of your WordArt by changing the style of all or part of the text. Each style uses a different combination of settings for the fill, outline, and effects of the text, offering a choice of interesting looks for your WordArt. As you move your mouse over a style, it will be applied to the selected text, allowing you to preview it with your text. A ScreenTip will appear indicating the name of the style. You can change the style by selecting all or part of the text in the WordArt and clicking on the styles in the WordArt Styles group of the Format tab. Use the up and down arrows to scroll through the available styles, or click the More arrow below the down arrow to view all the styles. To remove the WordArt style (without deleting the text), select the WordArt, click the More arrow below the down arrow in the WordArt Styles group, and choose Clear WordArt.

TIP To select a WordArt, press the Ctrl key as you click it. To move a WordArt, select it and then drag the border to the new location or use the arrow keys to move it one pixel at a time.

If none of the WordArt styles in the gallery are suitable, you can create a custom style by choosing from the wide range of different fill, outline, and effects options for the text. The following steps describe how you can do this:

1. Select the WordArt text that you want to format. The Format tab will be displayed under Drawing Tools.

2. Customize the text by doing any or all of the following:

- In the WordArt Styles group, click the Text Fill icon to choose a fill color for the text. Point to Gradient or Texture to view other options for special fills or click Picture to select a picture file to use to fill the WordArt text. The selected text will update as you move your mouse over the different options.

- Click the Text Outline icon in the WordArt Styles group to specify settings for the color, weight, and dashes of the border. As you move your mouse over the range of options for border color, weight, and dashes, your text will update, allowing you to preview the possible settings.

- Click the Text Effects icon to view the various visual effects that can be applied to the text. Point to an effect and choose an option from the fly-out menu to apply this effect. You can see the result of any effect on your text just by moving your mouse over it.

You can change the style of WordArt text by clicking the Dialog Box Launcher in the bottom-right corner of the WordArt Styles group and choosing options from the Format Text Effects dialog box. For example, you can use this dialog box to change the alignment or direction of the text or to apply a shadow or 3-D format. You can also customize the shape surrounding the WordArt using the Shape Styles group on the Format tab. See "Changing the Style of Shapes" earlier in this chapter for more information on how to do this.

To change the text displayed in the WordArt, simply click the WordArt to select it and delete or edit the text as required. To format or change the font size of the text, select it and use the Mini toolbar that appears or the commands in the Font and Alignment groups on the Home tab. To delete a WordArt, hold down the Ctrl key as you click the WordArt to select it and press Delete.

Changing the Stacking Order of Objects

As you add objects like pictures, shapes, text boxes, or WordArt to a document, they automatically stack in individual layers. By default, new objects will be stacked on top of older objects and, if they overlap, the object on the top will cover part or all of the object below it. To select an object that is positioned below other objects, select the top object and press the Tab key to cycle forward, or press Shift+Tab to cycle backward until you reach the object you require.

You may want to change the stacking order of objects in order to achieve a certain effect. This can be done by moving each object back or forward until they are in the correct order. To change the stacking order of objects, use these steps:

1. Select the object that you want to move. This will display either Picture Tools or Drawing Tools.

2. Select the Format tab and, in the Arrange group, do any of the following (you can also right-click the object to bring up any of these options):

   • To move the selected object to the top, click Bring to Front.

   • To bring the selected object forward one place, click the down arrow beside Bring to Front and select Bring Forward.

   • To place the selected object at the bottom, click Send to Back.

   • To move the selected object back one place, click the down arrow beside Send to Back and click Send Backward.

3. Continue moving objects until you achieve the order that you require.

In Excel 2007 you can also use the Selection pane to reorder objects. The Selection pane will display a list of all the images, shapes, text boxes, WordArt, and SmartArt on a worksheet (see Figure 12-15). To open the Selection pane, click Selection Pane in the Arrange group of the Format tab. You can then use the arrows to change the stacking order of the objects. You can also hide objects by clicking the icon beside the object's name, or click the Show All or Hide All button to display or hide all the objects.

Figure 12-15. Use the Selection pane to rearrange the stacking order of objects.

Aligning and Distributing Objects

Rather than trying to drag objects to align them, you can select an option from the Align menu in the Arrange group to do it automatically. You have six options when aligning objects: Align Left, Align Center, Align Right, Align Top, Align Middle, or Align Bottom. The alignment options will align the selected objects based on the position of the objects on the extreme left, right, top, and bottom. You can also use the Align menu to distribute objects evenly on the page so that they are equally spaced either horizontally or vertically. To align or distribute objects, do the following:

1. Using the Ctrl key, select all the objects that you want to align. If any of your objects are hidden or behind text, select the Home tab and, in the Editing group, click Find & Select, choose Select Objects, and then click and drag a box over the objects you want to select.

2. Select the Format tab and, in the Arrange group, click Align.

3. Select the appropriate option from the menu that appears (see Figure 12-16).

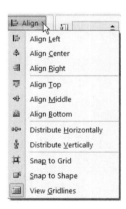

Figure 12-16. Choose an option from the Align menu
to align or distribute objects on a worksheet.

To align objects so that they line up with the cells on the grid, you need to turn on the Snap to Grid option in the Align menu. Once you have selected the Snap to Grid option, any objects that you create or resize will be aligned to the cells on the grid, and if you move an object its top-left corner will always be positioned at the corner of a cell. You can also select Snap to Shape to align objects you are moving with the edge of any surrounding shapes. To temporarily turn off Snap to Grid, hold down the Alt key as you move or resize an object. If you prefer to turn off the gridlines when working with objects, click the View Gridlines option in the Align menu; the feature will still work even without the lines being displayed.

CHAPTER 13

Preventing and Correcting Errors

Excel incorporates several tools to help you to prevent or correct errors in your spreadsheets. Starting with the actual data entry process, you can apply restrictions to the type of data that a cell can accept using data validation criteria. For example, you can specify that a cell can only contain a whole number or a date that falls within a particular timeframe. This can help avoid errors resulting from a cell containing the wrong type of data or a value outside the permitted range.

Often Excel will display an alert if you try to insert an incorrect formula or if your formulas contain inconsistencies. If Excel is unable to calculate a formula, it will return an error value, making it clear that something is wrong. However, sometimes formulas that are able to return results can still contain inconsistencies and it may be necessary to audit your formulas manually to ensure that your worksheet is error free. This can become quite difficult where formulas are nested or are constructed using references to other cells containing formulas.

To help with formula auditing, Excel allows you to easily identify or trace cells that contain formulas that refer to a selected cell (dependents) or cells that are referred to by the formula in the selected cell (precedents). By tracing precedent and dependent cells, you can easily confirm that the formula in the cell is taking data from and supplying data to the correct cells. You can also use the Evaluate Formula command to step through a formula and evaluate it at each stage to check how it arrives at its result. If you want to keep track of cells as you edit a worksheet, you can watch them in the Watch Window to see how changes to other parts of the worksheet affect the watched cells.

Data Validation

Prevention is always better than cure, and one way to help ensure the accuracy of your spreadsheet is to check the validity of the data as it is being entered. You can do this by applying data validation rules to cells to prevent users from entering data of the wrong type or value. For example, you can use data validation to restrict the values that can be entered to whole numbers within a specified range or to text of a particular length. To clarify the process for users, you can also display a message to advise users on what values they can enter, and you can customize the alert used to warn users that an entry is invalid.

Allowing Numbers in a Range

You can control the entry of numerical data in your worksheet by specifying that values should be either whole numbers or decimals, and by imposing a maximum and/or minimum value that can be entered. For example, a spreadsheet used to enter orders could have restrictions to ensure that values in the quantity column are whole numbers and that they are over a certain value if there is a minimum order quantity or under a certain value if there is a maximum order quantity. Use the following steps as a guideline to setting up data validation for the entry of numbers in a worksheet:

1. Select the cell or cells that you want to validate.

2. Select the Data tab and, in the Data Tools group, click the Data Validation icon (see Figure 13-1).

Figure 13-1. Click Data Validation in the Data Tools group to open the Data Validation dialog box.

3. In the Settings tab of the Data Validation dialog box, select either Whole number or Decimal from the Allow dropdown list (see Figure 13-2).

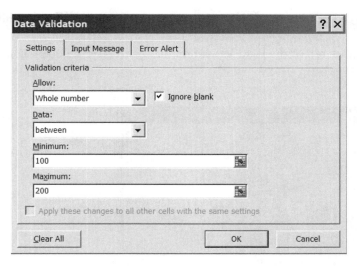

Figure 13-2. Enter validation criteria to control the data that can be entered into the selected cell.

4. To specify the range of values that can be entered, select an option from the Data dropdown list. You can choose from between, not between, equal to, not equal to, greater than, less than, greater than or equal to, and less than or equal to. Note that the fields in the Settings tab may change depending on your selection in the Data field.

5. Enter values, formulas, or cell references in the Value or the Minimum and/or Maximum boxes as appropriate. For example, if the validated cell should contain a value that is less than 20% of the value in cell B2, you would select less than in the Data box and enter the formula =B2*0.2 in the Maximum box.

6. Select or deselect the Ignore blank option to determine how you want blank or null values to be handled.

Allowing Values from a List

Often in a worksheet model there will be a range of cells that should contain one of a finite group of values, such as the name of a department or a project cost code. Using data validation you can restrict a user's entry to this group of values and you can even provide the options in the form of a dropdown list to facilitate the data entry. The following steps show you how to set up data validation to accept only values from a specified list:

1. Select the cell or cells that you want to validate and click the Data Validation button.

2. In the Settings tab of the Data Validation dialog box (see Figure 13-3), select List from the Allow dropdown list.

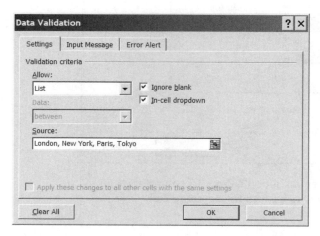

Figure 13-3. You can restrict the allowed values in a cell to options from a list.

3. Enter the options (separated by commas), or references for cells containing the options, that the users can choose from in the Source box.

> **TIP** If your options are listed in a range of cells, you may wish to sort the cells first in the order that you want the options to appear in the dropdown list. You may also find it more convenient to name the range so that you can simply type **=name** in the Source box, especially if the range of cells is in another worksheet.

4. Select or deselect the Ignore blank option to determine how you want blank or null values to be handled. Note that if you select Ignore blank and you have specified a named range containing a blank cell as your permitted values (or if any cell referenced by a validation formula is blank), any value can be entered into the validated cell.

5. If you want the options to be available as a dropdown list that the user can select from, make sure that the In-cell dropdown option is selected.

Allowing Dates or Times in a Range

In the same way as you can control the range of numbers that can be entered into a worksheet cell, you can also specify limits for dates or times. This allows you to ensure that users do not enter dates or times before a given start date or time, after a given end date or time, or outside a specified range. The following steps show you how to set up data validation to control the input of dates or times:

1. Select the cell or cells that you want to validate and click the Data Validation button.

2. In the Settings tab of the Data Validation dialog box (see Figure 13-4), select Date or Time from the Allow dropdown list.

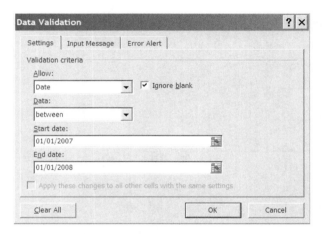

Figure 13-4. You can restrict the allowed values in a cell to dates within a particular timeframe.

3. To specify the range of dates or times that can be entered, select an option from the Data dropdown list. You can choose from between, not between, equal to, not equal to, greater than, less than, greater than or equal to, and less than or equal to. Note that the fields in the Settings tab may change depending on your selection in the Data field.

4. Enter dates or times, formulas, or cell references in the Date or Time box, the Start date and/or End date boxes, or the Start time and/or End time boxes, as appropriate. For example, if the validated cell should contain a date that is less than seven days after today's date, you would select less than in the Data box and enter the formula =**TODAY**()-7 in the End date box. Or if the validated cell should contain a time that is more than three hours after the time in cell C3, you would select greater than in the Data box and enter the formula =**C3+3** in the Start time box.

5. Select or deselect the Ignore blank option to determine how you want blank or null values to be handled.

Allowing Text of a Particular Length

If a cell is going to be used to enter text, you can use validation criteria to control the number of characters that will be accepted. Although this will not prevent incorrect text from being entered, it will go some way toward identifying data entry errors such as too few characters in a product code. The following steps show you how to set up data validation to control the length of text:

1. Select the cell or cells that you want to validate and click the Data Validation button.

2. In the Settings tab of the Data Validation dialog box (see Figure 13-5), select Text length from the Allow dropdown list.

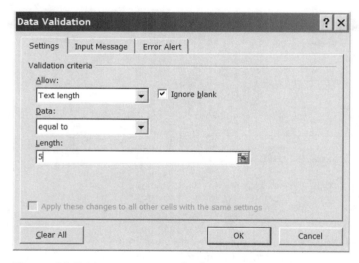

Figure 13-5. You can restrict the length of text that can be entered into a validated cell to an exact length or a range.

3. To specify the length of text strings that will be accepted, select an option from the Data dropdown list. Note that the fields in the Settings tab may change depending on your selection in the Data field.

4. Enter values, formulas, or cell references in the Length or the Maximum and/or Minimum boxes as appropriate. For example, if the validated cell should contain a string that contains the same number of characters as cell D4, you would select equal to in the Data box and enter the formula =**LEN(D4)** in the Length box.

5. Select or deselect the Ignore blank option to determine how you want blank or null values to be handled.

Creating Custom Validation Criteria

If none of the predefined validation criteria discussed earlier are suitable for your requirements, you can use a formula to create custom validation criteria by selecting Custom from the Allow dropdown list in the Data Validation dialog box. You can then use the Formula box to enter a formula whose result will determine what is allowed in the cell. Table 13-1 lists some examples of formulas that could be used for data validation.

Table 13-1. Examples of Formulas for Validating Data Entry

To Ensure That . . .	Enter This Formula
Cell A1 only contains text	=ISTEXT(A1)
Cell A1 can only be updated if cell B1 is greater than cell C1	=B1>C1
Cell A1 can only be updated if cell B1 is equal to 5 and cell C1 is less than 5	=AND(B1=5, C1<5)
All the cells in the range A1:A25 contain unique values	=COUNTIF($A$1:$A$25, A1)=1 (Enter the formula in the validation for the first cell and then fill down to the other cells so that the second argument in the COUNTIF function will update for the other cells.)
Cell A1 is always greater than the sum of cells B1 and C1	=IF(A1>B1+C1, TRUE, FALSE)
The contents of cell A1 must begin with BT	=LEFT(A1, 2)="BT"
The contents of cell A1 must begin with BT and have exactly 10 characters	=AND(LEFT(A1, 2)= "BT", LEN(A1)=10)

Of course, these are only a small sample of formulas that you can use as a basis for custom validation. Experiment with different variations and combinations of them to refine the range of values that will be allowed in the cell. The more restrictions you impose, the less room there will be for errors.

Displaying an Input Message and an Error Alert

If you have applied data validation to a cell, you may find it useful to create an input message, which will appear as a comment when the cell is selected, to guide users when entering data. Typically this will contain instructions for the user on what values can be entered into the cell. In the same way, you can also design a custom error alert to be displayed if a user attempts to enter a value outside of the permitted range or list. This can be used to inform the user why the entered value has not been accepted and remind the user of what should be entered. The following steps explain how to create an input message and an error alert for a cell that is subject to a validation rule:

1. Select the cell that you have applied a validation rule to.

2. Select the Data tab and, in the Data Tools group, click the down arrow beside Data Validation and select Data Validation from the menu that appears.

3. To display a message to instruct users on what they can enter into the cell, select the Input Message tab in the Data Validation dialog box (see Figure 13-6).

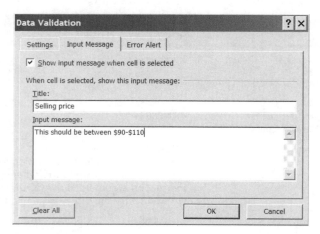

Figure 13-6. You can create your own input message to advise users on what values they should enter in the validated cell.

4. Make sure that the "Show input message when cell is selected" option is selected and enter a title for the message in the Title box if desired.

5. Enter any instructions that you want to provide for users in the Input message box. This will appear as a comment when the cell is selected, as shown in Figure 13-7.

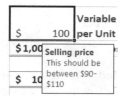

Figure 13-7. Your input message will appear as a comment when the cell is selected.

6. To display an alert if a user attempts to enter invalid data into the cell, select the Error Alert tab in the Data Validation dialog box (see Figure 13-8).

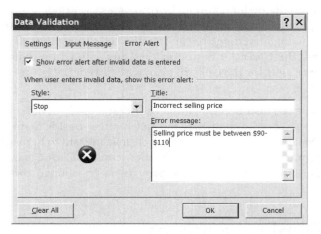

Figure 13-8. You can design a custom error alert to be displayed if a user enters invalid data.

7. Make sure that the "Show error alert after invalid data is entered" option is selected.

8. Choose Stop, Warning, or Information from the Style box; the icon displayed will change depending on your selection.

9. Enter a title for your error alert in the Title box if desired and type the text that you want displayed in the Error message box. This will appear if the user enters a value that is not allowed, as shown in Figure 13-9.

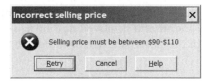

Figure 13-9. You can design a custom alert to be displayed if a user tries to enter a value that is not allowed.

10. Click OK when you have finished. When you have added validation to a cell, try entering correct and incorrect data to test that the validation criteria is working as expected and to check how the error alert will appear.

NOTE If you do not specify any text for the error alert, Excel will use a default alert if a user enters an incorrect value.

Changing or Removing Data Validation

To change the validation criteria, input message, or error alert for a cell, select it, open the Data Validation dialog box, and make the changes on each tab as necessary. Select the option "Apply these changes to all other cells with the same settings" to update other cells with similar settings to the selected cell. To remove the validation criteria for a cell, click the Clear All button in the Data Validation dialog box; the input message and error alert for the cell will also be removed.

> **TIP** Data validation can also be applied to cells that already contain data to check their contents. You can then click the down arrow beside Data Validation (or the Data Validation icon) and select Circle Invalid Data to highlight any cells whose content does not meet the validation criteria. Click Clear Validation Circles in the Data Validation dropdown menu to remove the circles again.

Removing Duplicate Values

The presence of duplicate values in a worksheet will often result in errors. A duplicate value occurs when all the values in a row match the values in another row. This can happen when a record is mistakenly entered more than once. As well as making your spreadsheet larger than necessary, this can erroneously inflate totals and formula results. In Excel 2007 you can quickly check your data for duplicated data and remove the repeated rows, leaving you with a list of unique values. As with any process that deletes data, this should be done with care to ensure that important data is not lost. Consequently, it is advisable to make a copy of the worksheet or table before removing duplicates.

To check your data for duplicates, select the range of cells that you want to check or, if your data is in an Excel table, select any cell in the table. Select the Data tab and, in the Data Tools group, click Remove Duplicates. Select the columns that you want to check for duplicate values and click OK. A message will appear informing you of how many duplicate values (if any) were found and removed and how many unique values remain. Click OK. Only cells within the selected range or table will be affected; other cells will not be removed.

Formula Auditing

A common source of errors in spreadsheets is the inaccurate construction of formulas, which, in turn, causes misleading results. If the result of an incorrect formula is later used in other formulas, cells, or documents, the error will be propagated throughout the worksheet or other documents. Formula auditing involves checking formulas for mistakes and inconsistencies. Identifying and correcting formula errors is an essential task in ensuring the validity of your results. Often Excel will not allow you to enter an invalid formula and will offer to correct the error automatically. However, in other cases you may need to check each formula in a spreadsheet manually to confirm that there are no inconsistencies. This section will explain how you can find and resolve errors in formulas in Excel 2007.

Identifying Errors in Formulas

When you enter a formula in a cell, Excel will employ various rules to check it for errors. Common mistakes that can occur when typing a formula include failing to match parentheses, not including the correct number of arguments in a function, inserting references to cells that contain the wrong data type, and failing to use single or double quotation marks where required. In some cases—say you omit a closing parenthesis or enter too many arguments—Excel will immediately identify that an error has occurred and suggest a correction. At other times a formula will return an error value and it is obvious that a mistake has been made. Table 13-2 lists the error values that can result when a mistake is made in a formula and suggests ways you can resolve them.

Table 13-2. Resolving Error Values in Formulas

Error	What to Do
#######	Widen the column or ensure that dates and times are not negative (i.e., prior to January 1, 1900).
#DIV/0	The formula is trying to divide by 0—check that you have entered the correct cell reference or that you have not deleted data by mistake.
#N/A	The formula is referring to a cell containing the NA function—check that you have entered the correct cell reference. If you are using a lookup function, check that there is a match for the lookup value and that you have sorted the table correctly. If you are using an array formula, make sure that any arguments have the same number of rows and columns as the range holding the array formula. If the formula is a custom formula, it may not be available or you may have omitted an argument.
#NAME?	Check your spelling—you may have spelled a function or defined name incorrectly or you may have forgotten to enclose text in double quotation marks. Also check that you have not omitted the colon in a range reference or the single quotation marks around a sheet name.
#NULL!	Make sure that you have entered references to cell ranges correctly—the formula may be referring to a nonexistent intersection between two ranges. Also check that you are using the correct range operator and that you have not entered a space instead of a comma.

Continued

Table 13-2. *Continued*

Error	What to Do
#NUM!	Check that the arguments in the function are numbers or cells containing numbers. If you are using an iteration function like IRR or RATE, Excel may not be able to find a result; you can try increasing the number of iterations in Excel Options. A #NUM! error will also appear if a number is too large or too small for Excel to calculate.
#REF!	Check the cell references—you may have deleted a cell or cut or copied the formula, rendering any references invalid. If you are using an OLE link, make sure that the program is running or you may be linking to a DDE topic that is not available.
#VALUE!	Check that the arguments in the function are the correct data type, that you have used the correct operands, or that you have entered an array formula properly.

To resolve an error, you may need to see where a formula is getting its data from. To view all the precedent arrows for a cell displaying an error value, select the cell, choose the Formulas tab, and in the Formula Auditing group (see Figure 13-10), click the down arrow beside Error Checking and click Trace Error.

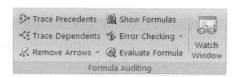

Figure 13-10. The Formula Auditing group contains various commands to help you check formulas.

Excel will also display an error indicator in the form of a triangle in the top-left corner of a cell containing a formula if it matches one of the following error-checking rules:

- The cell contains a formula that results in an error.
- There is an inconsistent calculated column formula in a table.
- The cell contains a year represented as two digits.
- A number has been formatted as text or preceded by an apostrophe.
- The cell's formula is inconsistent with other formulas in the region.
- The cell's formula omits cells in the same region.
- An unlocked cell contains a formula.
- The cell's formula refers to an empty cell.
- Data entered in a cell in a table is invalid.

Hover your mouse over a cell displaying an error indicator to see a ScreenTip explaining the cause of the error. You can select which rules Excel should use when performing background error checking, or you can turn off this feature altogether by clicking the Microsoft Office Button, clicking Excel Options, and selecting the Formulas category. Select or deselect the appropriate checkboxes under "Error checking rules" to control which rules are used, or deselect the "Enable background error checking" option under Error Checking to stop Excel from indicating cells that may contain inconsistencies.

Error Checking

When you select a cell displaying an error indicator, the Error Checking button will appear beside it. You can click this button to find out why the cell has been flagged with an error indicator and to access a number of options to enable you to deal with the error (see Figure 13-11).

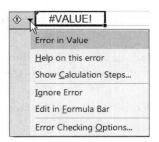

Figure 13-11. Click the Error Checking button and select an option from the context menu to deal with a formula flagged with an error indicator.

The options available when you click the Error Checking button will vary depending on the cause of the error, which is indicated by the first item on the list. If you select "Help on this error", the Excel Help facility will open; if you select Error Checking Options, Excel Options will open at the Formulas category. Selecting Show Calculation Steps will open the Evaluate dialog box, allowing you to step through each part of the formula.

If your worksheet is large, you may find it easier to use the Error Checking command in the Formula Auditing group to go through each error, one at a time, in a similar manner to a spelling checker. To check a worksheet for errors, do the following:

1. Select the worksheet that you want to check and, if you have turned off automatic calculation, press F9 to recalculate the worksheet.

2. Select the Formulas tab on the Ribbon and, in the Formula Auditing group, click Error Checking. The Error Checking dialog box will open (see Figure 13-12). Note that the options available in the Error Checking dialog box will vary depending on the type of error.

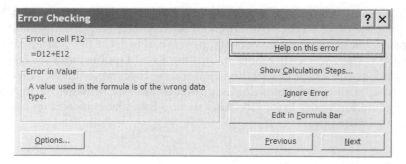

Figure 13-12. Use the Error Checking dialog box to help you deal with errors in your worksheet.

3. In the Error Checking dialog box, do one (or more) of the following:
   - Click the "Help on this error" button to open the Excel Help facility and find out more about formula errors.
   - Click the Show Calculation Steps button to open the Evaluate dialog box and step through each part of the formula.
   - Click the Copy Formula from Left or Copy Formula from Above button to insert the same formula that is used in adjacent cells (for Inconsistent Formula errors).
   - Click the Trace Error button to display the precedent arrows for the cell.
   - Click the Ignore Error button to mark the error to be ignored in any following error checks.
   - Click the Edit in Formula Bar button to go to the formula bar and change the formula.
   - Click the Options button to open Excel Options at the Formulas category so that you can change the settings for error checking.

4. When you have finished dealing with that error, click Previous or Next to move to another error. When you have checked all the errors, a message will appear saying that the error check is complete for the entire sheet.

Sometimes in Excel a formula may appear to calculate correctly but on closer examination you find that it has returned an incorrect result. Reasons why a formula may return an inaccurate result include

- An apparently empty cell actually contains a space character and, therefore, technically is not blank.
- Formula operators are not being evaluated in the correct order. You can rectify this by using parentheses.
- Excel stores numbers with a precision of 15 digits, which occasionally may result in a loss of accuracy. For example, Excel may return a number close to zero when zero is expected.

- The number of decimal places displayed means that the value displayed is not the actual value of the cell. Excel will calculate results based on the actual stored value of the cell, not the displayed value. To permanently change the value of a cell to equal the displayed value, click the Microsoft Office Button, select the Advanced category, and under "When calculating this workbook", check the "Set precision as displayed" checkbox.

TIP To check text and other data in your worksheet, you can use the Spelling, Research, Thesaurus, and Translate commands in the Proofing group on the Review tab.

Dealing with Circular References

A common type of error in formulas is a circular reference where a formula refers (directly or indirectly) to itself. For example, a circular reference will result if cell C1 contains the formula =A1+B1−C1 as the formula refers to the cell containing it. This can cause problems because the calculation could continue indefinitely; each time the formula is calculated, the value in the cell changes and the formula must be recalculated. Excel will not be able to automatically calculate all the open workbooks if one of them contains a circular reference.

If you enter a formula containing a circular reference, Excel will display a message warning you that cell references in the formula refer to the formula's result. If you click OK, Excel displays the Help topic for circular references; if you click Cancel, Excel allows the formula to remain as it is and displays "Circular Reference: *cell reference*" in the Status bar to remind you that a circular reference exists. If there is no cell reference beside Circular Reference in the Status bar, the circular reference is in another worksheet.

If you want to locate a circular reference when carrying out formula auditing, select the Formulas tab and, in the Formula Auditing group, click the down arrow beside Error Checking. Select Circular Reference and click the cell reference in the submenu. You can then edit the formula to correct the circular reference. When you have corrected all the circular references in a workbook, Circular Reference will no longer be displayed in the Status bar.

There are occasions when you may want to allow circular references—for example, you may wish to use a circular reference to calculate the depreciation on an asset or the value of an investment. Consequently, you can change the settings in Excel Options to allow iterative calculation. Once you do this, Excel will not highlight circular references but will perform the calculation until the maximum iterations (the number of times Excel will recalculate) or maximum change limit (the amount of change between calculations) has been reached. If you want to intentionally create a circular reference, you must have iterative calculation enabled. To do this, click the Microsoft Office Button and click Excel Options. Select the Formulas category and select the "Enable iterative calculation" checkbox. If you want to, change the default values in the Maximum Iterations field or the Maximum Change field to control when Excel should stop performing iterations.

Viewing and Hiding Formulas

When you enter a formula into a cell, Excel displays the result automatically within the cell. To view the actual formula so that you can check it, you can select the cell and look in the formula bar. To identify all the cells in the active sheet or selected range that contain formulas, follow these steps:

1. Select the Home tab and, in the Editing group, click Find & Select.

2. Select Go To Special from the menu and select Formulas in the Go To Special dialog box.

3. Select or deselect the Numbers, Text, Logicals, and Errors options to choose the type of formulas you want to highlight based on the formula result and click OK. Those cells containing the appropriate formulas will be highlighted and you can use the Tab key to select each cell in turn.

If you want to view all the formulas in a worksheet so that you can print them or audit them, you can select the Formulas tab on the Ribbon and, in the Formula Auditing group, click Show Formulas. Click Show Formulas again to hide the formulas and display the values once more. You can also press Ctrl+` (backquote) to toggle between showing and hiding formulas.

If others will have access to the worksheet, you may not want to reveal the formulas you have used or allow them to be altered. You can protect selected cells to prevent the formulas within them from being displayed in the formula bar and, consequently, from being edited. The following steps explain how this can be done:

1. Select the cells containing the formulas that you want to hide, using the Ctrl key to select noncontiguous cells or ranges.

2. Select the Home tab on the Ribbon and, in the Cells group, click Format and select Format Cells.

3. Click the Protection tab in the Format Cells dialog box, select the Hidden checkbox, and click OK to close the dialog box.

4. In the Cells group, click Format again and select Protect Sheet.

5. Make sure that the "Protect worksheet and contents of locked cells" option is selected, then enter a password in the "Password to unprotect sheet" box if desired and click OK. (If you have entered a password, you will be asked to confirm it.)

If a user selects a cell whose formula has been hidden, the formula bar will be blank and, if someone tries to edit a protected cell, a message will appear warning that the cell is protected. To unprotect cells again so that the formula will be displayed in the formula bar and the cells can be edited, follow these steps:

1. Click Format in the Cells group and select Unprotect Sheet. If necessary, enter the correct password and click OK.

2. Select the cells whose formulas you want to unhide.

3. Click Format in the Cells group of the Home tab and select Format Cells.

4. In the Protection tab in the Format Cells dialog box, deselect the Hidden checkbox and click OK to close the dialog box.

Viewing the Relationships Between Cells

In Excel, formulas will usually take values from cells in the worksheet, which in turn, may depend on other cells for their input values. Consequently, changing the value in one cell may influence the result of several different formulas. When auditing formulas or trying to resolve errors, you may find it helpful to view the relationships between cells and identify for a particular cell which cells are precedents (cells that supply data to the cell) and which cells are dependents (cells that take data from the cell). As each cell can refer to and be referred to by numerous other cells, tracing a cell's precedents and dependents may prove invaluable in finding the source of an error.

To display tracer arrows indicating a cell's precedents so that you can check where a formula is obtaining its inputs from, do the following:

1. Select the cell containing the formula that you want to view the precedents for.

2. Select the Formulas tab on the Ribbon and, in the Formula Auditing group, click Trace Precedents. Tracer arrows will be displayed indicating the cells that are referred to by the formula. Cells that contain no errors are represented by blue arrows; cells that cause errors are indicated by red arrows. If the formula contains a reference to a cell in another worksheet or workbook, a black arrow pointing to a worksheet icon will be displayed.

3. Double-click an arrow to go to the cell at the other end of it. If you double-click a black arrow, the Go To dialog box will open, listing the references to other sheets or workbooks. Select a reference in the Go to list and click OK to go to that cell. Note that if the reference is in another workbook, that workbook must be open before you can go to it.

4. To view the next level of precedent cells, click Trace Precedents again. Excel will beep when it cannot trace any further levels of precedents for the formula.

5. To remove all the tracer arrows, click Remove Arrows in the Formula Auditing group. To remove the precedent arrows one level at a time, click the down arrow beside Remove Arrows in the Formula Auditing group and select Remove Precedent Arrows for each level that you want to remove.

You may also want to check which cells use the selected cell as one of their input values and are, therefore, influenced by its contents. To display tracer arrows identifying a cell's dependents, do the following:

1. Select the cell that you want to view the dependents for.

2. Select the Formulas tab on the Ribbon and, in the Formula Auditing group, click Trace Dependents. Tracer arrows will be displayed indicating the cells that refer to the selected cell. Relationships that do not result in an error are represented by blue arrows; relationships that do result in an error are indicated by red arrows. If the cell is referred to by a formula in a cell in another worksheet or open workbook, a black arrow pointing to a worksheet icon will be displayed.

3. Double-click an arrow to go to the cell at the other end of it. If you double-click a black arrow, the Go To dialog box will open, listing the references to other sheets or workbooks. Select a reference in the Go to list and click OK to go to that cell. Note that formulas located in another workbook cannot be traced if that workbook is closed.

4. To view the next level of dependent cells, click Trace Dependents again. Excel will beep when it cannot trace any further levels of dependents for the formula.

5. To remove all the tracer arrows, click Remove Arrows in the Formula Auditing group. To remove the dependent arrows one level at a time, click the down arrow beside Remove Arrows in the Formula Auditing group and select Remove Dependent Arrows for each level that you want to remove. The tracer arrows will also disappear if you make any changes to the formula in the selected cell, insert or delete rows or columns. or move or delete cells in the worksheet.

Figure 13-13 shows an example of tracer arrows being used to identify the precedents and dependents for a cell (B7). In this example, you can see that B7 takes inputs from cells B1, B5, and B6 (its precedents) and that cell B1 in turn takes a value from a cell in another worksheet (indicated by a dashed black arrow). Cell B7 also has dependents and is used as an input in cell B10, although this relationship causes an error (indicated by a red arrow), and contributes its value to another worksheet (indicated by a dashed black arrow).

	A	B	C	D
1	Units Sold	10000		
2	Selling Price per Unit	$ 100		
3	Total Revenue	$1,000,000		
4				
5	Fixed Costs	$ 400,000		
6	Variable Cost per Unit	unknown		
7	Total Cost	#VALUE!		
8				
9				
10	Profit	#VALUE!		
11				

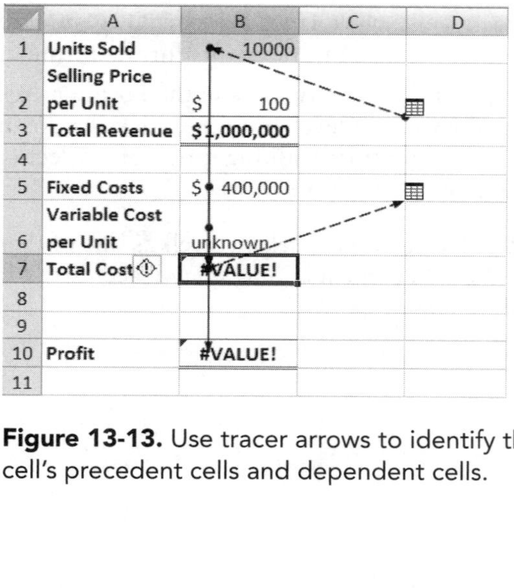

Figure 13-13. Use tracer arrows to identify the selected cell's precedent cells and dependent cells.

TIP To view all the tracer arrows for a worksheet, click in an empty cell and type **=**. Click the Select All icon in the top-left corner of the worksheet and press Enter. Select the cell and click Trace Precedents in the Formula Auditing group twice.

You can also check to see which cells supply the value for each argument in a formula. Just select the cell and press F2 to switch to editing mode and view the color-coded precedents for each of the arguments. Each cell or range reference in the formula will be displayed in a different color, and the corresponding cell or range on the worksheet will be surrounded by a border of the same color, allowing you to quickly identify the cells that are being referenced by the formula. You can then edit the formula directly in the cell if necessary.

Evaluating Formulas

If a formula consists of several calculations or logical tests, it can be difficult to ascertain how it actually reaches its final result. The Evaluate Formula dialog box simplifies the task of auditing nested formulas by allowing you to view how the formula is calculated and see the intermediate results for each part of the calculation. The following steps explain how to evaluate a formula:

1. Select the cell containing the formula that you want to evaluate.

2. Select the Formulas tab and, in the Formula Auditing group, click Evaluate Formula. The Evaluate Formula dialog box will open (see Figure 13-14).

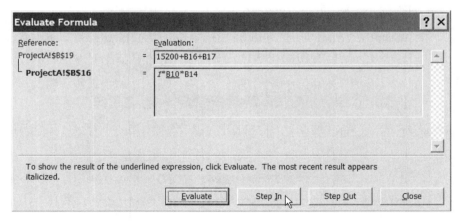

Figure 13-14. Use the Evaluate Formula dialog box to help you to debug a formula.

3. Click the Evaluate button to show the result of the underlined expression. The most recently evaluated expression will be displayed in italics. If the underlined expression is a reference to another formula, you can click the Step In button to view the other formula in the Evaluation box. Click the Step Out button to return to the previous cell and formula. Note that if the underlined reference has already appeared in the formula or if the formula references a cell in another workbook, the Step In button will not be available.

4. When you have finished evaluating each part of the formula, you can click the Restart button to begin the evaluation again or click the Close button to close the Evaluate Formula dialog box.

> **NOTE** Formula components that use the IF or CHOOSE function may not be evaluated in the Evaluate Formula dialog box, and functions that are recalculated each time the worksheet changes may display different results in the Evaluate Formula dialog box than in the cell.

Watching Formulas

When working with a large worksheet, you may find it helpful to use the Watch Window to keep track of certain cells so that you can continually audit the cells' formulas and results as you make changes to the worksheet. The Watch Window can be moved around the worksheet or docked to the top, bottom, left, or right of the worksheet and will display the workbook, sheet, name, cell, value, and formula for each entry. If you make a change to the worksheet that affects any of the cells being watched, the Watch Window will update automatically. To use the Watch Window to keep track of a cell's properties, follow these steps:

1. Select the Formulas tab and, in the Formula Auditing group, click Watch Window. The Watch Window will open (see Figure 13-15).

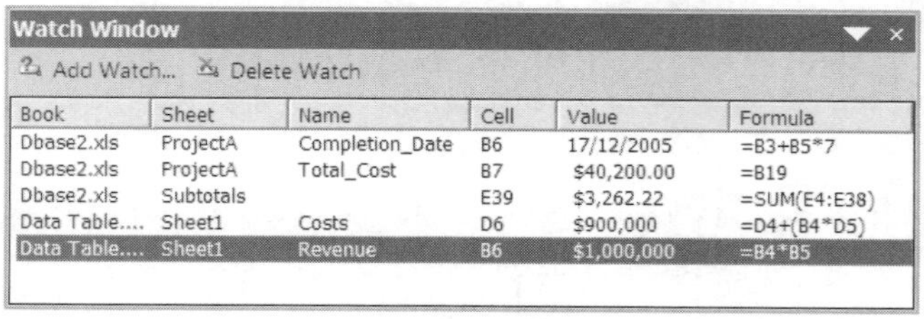

Figure 13-15. Click Add Watch to add cells to the Watch Window.

2. Click Add Watch in the Watch Window and type the reference for the cell or range that you want to keep track of into the field in the Add Watch dialog box (or select the cell or range in the worksheet). Click Add to add the cell or range to the Watch Window. If you have selected a range of cells, each cell will have a separate entry in the Watch Window.

3. Drag the title bar of the Watch Window to move it to the desired position. To resize the Watch Window, drag one of its edges or corners. You can also drag the boundary between the column headings to adjust the width of the columns. As you edit the worksheet, the cell properties will be updated in the Watch Window.

4. To go to a cell that you are watching, double-click its reference in the Watch Window.

5. If you no longer wish to track a cell, select its reference in the Watch Window and click Delete Watch.

6. Click the Close button in the top-right corner to close the Watch Window. The references to the watched cells will be stored in it until you reopen it again as long as the workbook remains open.

NOTE You can watch cells in different workbooks in the Watch Window, but when you close a workbook, references to cells within it will disappear from the Watch Window.

CHAPTER 14

Protection and Security

Spreadsheets are often used to store sensitive or confidential data, from client details to corporate finances. When a workbook is only intended to be viewed by the author or a limited group of users, it is advisable to apply some form of protection to it to prevent any unauthorized access. At other times, a number of people may require access to a spreadsheet, leaving it vulnerable to accidental or deliberate alteration. A spreadsheet designer will want to protect his or her work from tampering and may even want to keep elements of the workbook, such as formulas or particular sheets, hidden. If your spreadsheet is being used to record important data, you may wish to apply protection to reduce the risk of data being corrupted or being used by those it is not intended for.

To reassure users that a spreadsheet is authentic and to confirm the origin of the spreadsheet, you can add a digital signature to it. This can help to assure the integrity of the data and prove that the spreadsheet has not been edited since it was signed. Digital signatures can be visible or invisible, and Office 2007 even provides a signature line that can be used to display a visible representation of a signature.

Another new feature with Office 2007 is the Trust Center, which acts as a one-stop shop for all your security settings. You can use the Trust Center to specify trusted publishers and file locations and to change settings for external content, add-ins, macros, and ActiveX controls. You can also use the Document Inspector to help you track down and remove any hidden content or personal information that you do not want to be made available to others accessing the document. This chapter will look at all of these features, which could prove beneficial in helping to protect the confidentiality, safety, and integrity of your Excel documents.

Protecting Worksheets and Workbooks

Excel provides you with protection tools to help you to maintain the security of your worksheet data against deliberate or accidental misuse. For instance, if your worksheet contains data of a confidential nature, you may want to prevent unauthorized users from accessing a workbook. To do this, you can protect the workbook with a password when you are saving it, which users must enter to open the file. In other cases, you may want other users to be able to open the file but not be able to modify certain parts of the worksheet. To prevent users from making deliberate or accidental changes to the data, you can protect worksheet or workbook elements, either with or without a password. This section will show you how you can apply protection to your Excel files to control who can access or edit them.

> **CAUTION** Applying passwords to workbooks will provide some protection; however, these passwords are not infallible and can be removed by anyone using the correct software.

Protecting the Contents of a Workbook

There are two ways you can protect a workbook in Excel with a password: you can require users to enter a password to open and view the workbook, or you can specify a password that a user must enter to modify the workbook and save any changes. Obviously, restricting overall access to a workbook is the most secure method of protection, and this password will be encrypted to help protect your data from any unauthorized access. The password to modify the workbook will not be encrypted but can be used to assert some control over which users can then edit the file. Consequently, for optimum security you should apply *both* passwords to the workbook. You can also display a prompt recommending that users open the workbook as "read-only," which could prevent them from accidentally saving changes to it.

Setting a Password to Open or Modify a Workbook

You can assign a password to control which users can open a workbook, a password to control which users can modify a workbook, or both. The following steps describe how you can set a password for a workbook:

1. Click the Microsoft Office Button and click Save As. (To save the workbook in a different format, point to Save As, and select the format that you want to save the workbook in.)

2. Click the Tools button in the bottom-left corner of the Save As dialog box and select General Options from the menu that appears. Excel will display the General Options dialog box (see Figure 14-1).

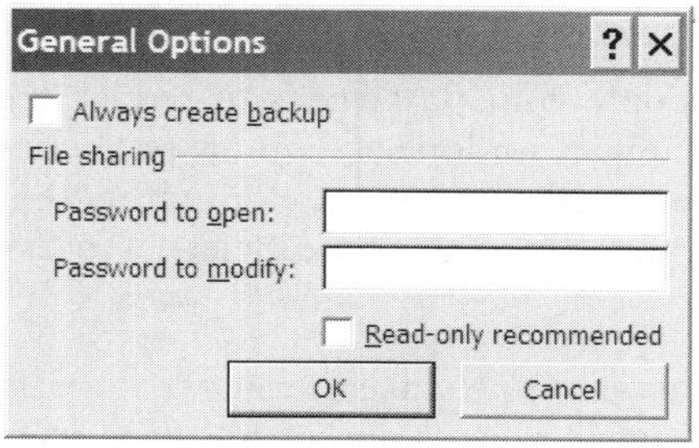

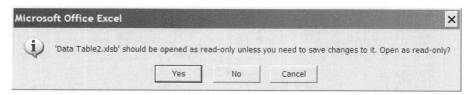

Figure 14-1. Enter a password to open and/or modify the file.

3. In the General Options dialog box, enter a password in the "Password to open" and/or in the "Password to modify" fields.

> **TIP** Choose a password that uses a combination of uppercase and lowercase letters, numbers, and symbols and will not be easy for unauthorized users to guess. If you are assigning passwords to open and to modify the workbook, use a different combination of characters for each password.

4. If you want to prompt users to open the file as read-only, select the Read-only recommended option. When a user opens the file, Excel will display a message asking if they want to open the file as read-only (see Figure 14-2).

Microsoft Office Excel

'Data Table2.xlsb' should be opened as read-only unless you need to save changes to it. Open as read-only?

Yes   No   Cancel

Figure 14-2. Excel can prompt users to open a file as read-only.

5. If you want to automatically generate a backup copy of the file, select the "Always create backup" option.
6. Click OK. You will be prompted to confirm your password(s). Enter the password(s) again and click OK.
7. Continue to save your file in the normal way.

> **CAUTION** Make sure that you keep a record of your passwords in a secure location as Microsoft cannot retrieve any passwords that have been forgotten.

Changing or Removing a Password

It is good practice to periodically update your passwords to reduce the chance of them being discovered. Also, if a document no longer requires protection, you may wish to remove the password(s) to enable all users to open or modify the workbook. The following steps describe how you can change or delete a password for a workbook:

1. Open the document for which you want to change or remove the password. You will be prompted to enter the password to open and/or for write access. Enter the correct passwords to open the file for write access. If you are prompted to open the file as read-only, click the No button.

2. Click the Microsoft Office Button and select Save As.

3. Click the Tools button in the bottom-left corner of the Save As dialog box and select General Options from the menu that appears.

4. In the General Options dialog box, do either of the following:
   - To change either password, enter a new password in the "Password to open" and/or in the "Password to modify" fields and click OK. Retype the new password to confirm it and click OK.
   - To remove either password, delete the password from the appropriate field and click OK.

5. Continue to save your file in the normal way.

Protecting the Contents of a Worksheet

If other users will be accessing your worksheet, you may want to prevent them from adjusting the contents of some cells while allowing them to enter data in other cells. When you protect a worksheet in Excel, by default all cells are locked. However, if you want users to be able to edit certain cells, you can unlock them before applying protection. You can also unlock any graphics that you want users to be able to edit, or hide formulas so that they cannot be viewed by other users. When you protect a worksheet, you can decide whether users are allowed to do each of the following:

- Select locked cells
- Select unlocked cells
- Format cells
- Format rows
- Format columns
- Insert columns
- Insert rows
- Insert hyperlinks
- Delete columns

- Delete rows
- Sort
- Use AutoFilter
- Use PivotTable reports
- Edit objects
- Edit scenarios

CAUTION Protecting worksheet elements can help to avoid accidental corruption of data or formulas but will only provide limited security against malicious intent. Excel passwords can easily be broken by determined users and may not provide sufficient protection for very sensitive data.

Allowing Users to Edit Selected Cells or Objects

When you apply protection to a worksheet, by default all cells will be locked. If you want to lock the entire worksheet except for a few selected cells or objects, you must select the cells that users will be allowed to edit and unlock them before protecting the worksheet. You can do this as follows:

1. Select the worksheet that you want to apply protection to.
2. If you want users to able to change certain cells, select the cells and go to the Home tab. In the Cells group, click Format and deselect Lock Cell. The selected cells will now be unlocked.
3. If you want to unlock any graphics, hold down the Ctrl key as you click the objects you want to unlock. Picture Tools or Drawing Tools will be displayed on the Ribbon. On the Format tab, click the Dialog Box Launcher in the bottom-right corner of the Size group. Select the Properties tab in the Size and Properties dialog box and deselect the Locked option (and the Lock text option if available). Click Close.
4. To protect the remainder of the worksheet, select the Review tab and, in the Changes group, click Protect Sheet (see Figure 14-3). (Alternatively, you can select the Home tab and, in the Cells group, click Format and then Protect Sheet.)

Figure 14-3. The Changes group contains commands for protecting sheets and workbooks.

5. In the Protect Sheet dialog box, select the appropriate checkboxes in the "Allow all users of this worksheet to" list to control what other users can and cannot do (see Figure 14-4).

Figure 14-4. Use the checkboxes to select what you want users to be allowed to do.

6. If you want to prevent other users from removing the protection that you have added, enter a password in the "Password to unprotect sheet" box. If you do not use a password, other users will be able to unprotect the worksheet and modify the protected elements.

7. Click OK. If you have applied a password you will be asked to confirm it. Retype the password and click OK.

Once a worksheet has been protected, the Protect Sheet command in the Changes group will become Unprotect Sheet. To remove protection from a worksheet so that it can be edited, click Unprotect Sheet in the Changes group and, if necessary, enter the correct password.

Preventing Users from Editing Selected Cells or Objects

If there are only a few cells or objects on your worksheet that you do not want users to edit, it is easier to unlock the entire worksheet and then lock the elements that you want to protect. To do this, follow these steps:

1. Select the worksheet that you want to apply protection to.

2. Click the Select All button in the top-left corner of the grid to select the entire worksheet and go to the Home tab. In the Cells group, click Format and deselect Lock Cell. All the cells will now be unlocked.

3. To lock particular cells, select the cells that you do not want to be edited and go to the Home tab. In the Cells group, click Format and select Lock Cell.

4. If you want to lock any graphics, hold down the Ctrl key as you click the objects you want to lock; Picture Tools or Drawing Tools will be displayed on the Ribbon. On the Format tab, click the Dialog Box Launcher in the bottom-right corner of the Size group. Select the Properties tab in the Size and Properties dialog box and select the Locked option and the Lock text option if available. Click Close.

5. If you want to hide any formulas, select the cells containing the formulas and go to the Home tab. In the Cells group, click Format and then Format Cells. In the Format Cells dialog box, select the Protection tab and select the Hidden option. Click OK.

6. To protect the worksheet, click Protect Sheet in the Changes group and in the Protect Sheet dialog box, select the appropriate checkboxes in the "Allow all users of this worksheet to" list to control what other users can and cannot do.

7. Enter a password in the "Password to unprotect sheet" box (if desired) and click OK. If you have applied a password, you will be asked to confirm it. Retype the password and click OK.

Specifying Which Ranges Can Be Edited by Which Users

If you need to apply different levels of access for users, you can specify which ranges each user can edit. The following steps explain how to do this:

1. Select the worksheet that you want to apply protection to.

2. Select the Review tab and, in the Changes group, click Allow Users to Edit Ranges.

3. To specify a new range that can be unlocked by a password when the worksheet is protected, click New. The New Range dialog box will open (see Figure 14-5).

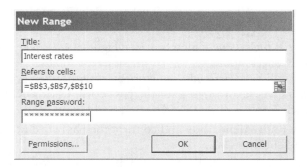

Figure 14-5. Enter the title, reference, and password for the range in the appropriate fields.

4. In the New Range dialog box, enter a name for the range in the Title box.

5. In the "Refers to cells" box, type an equals sign (=) and the reference for the range that you want to unlock.

6. In the Range password box, type the password that will allow users to unlock the range. If you do not specify a password, any user will be able to edit the cells.

7. Click the Permissions button to open the Permissions for *Range name* dialog box and click Add to specify the authorized users for the range. The Select Users or Groups dialog box will open (see Figure 14-6).

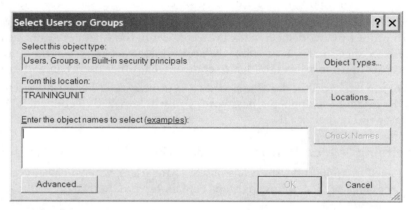

Figure 14-6. Enter the names of the users who are permitted to edit the range.

8. In the "Enter the object names to select" box, type the names of the users who will be allowed to edit the range. Click the examples link for guidance on how the names should be entered. Click Check Names to check that you have entered the name correctly. When you have finished, click OK to close the Select Users or Groups dialog box.

9. In the Permissions for *Range name* dialog box (see Figure 14-7), select either the Allow or the Deny checkbox to set the permissions for the user. If you select Allow, the user will be able to edit the worksheet without entering the password—other users will be prompted for the password. Click OK to close the dialog box or click Apply and then Add again to add another user.

10. Click OK in the New Range dialog box and confirm the password if necessary by typing it again and clicking OK.

11. In the Allow Users to Edit Ranges dialog box, click Protect Sheet (see Figure 14-8).

12. In the Protect Sheet dialog box, select any other elements that you want users to be able to change and in the "Password to unprotect sheet" box, type the password to be used. Type the password again to confirm it and click OK.

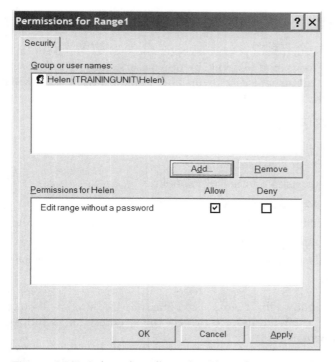

Figure 14-7. Select the Allow checkbox if you want the user to be able to edit the range without entering a password.

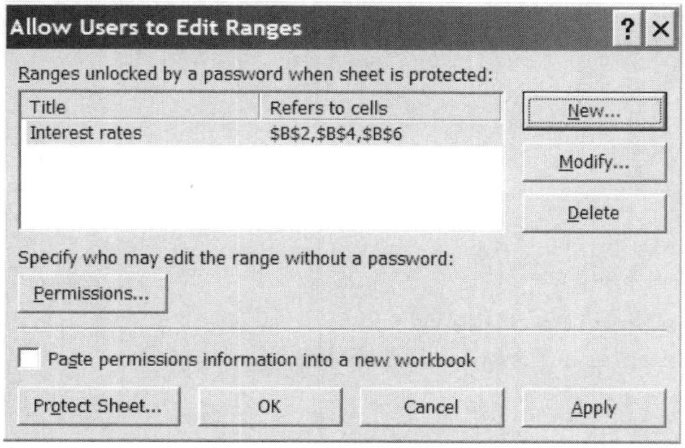

Figure 14-8. Click Protect Sheet to select which elements you want users to be able to edit.

NOTE If a cell belongs to several ranges, those users with permission to edit any of the ranges will be able to edit the cell.

Protecting the Structure of a Workbook

You can also protect the structure of your workbook and the size and position of windows for the workbook from modifications by other users, either with or without a password. If you protect the structure of a workbook, unauthorized users will not be permitted to do any of the following:

- Hide worksheets or view hidden worksheets.
- Move, delete, or rename worksheets.
- Insert new worksheets or chart sheets.
- Move or copy worksheets to another workbook.
- Display source data for a cell in the data area of a PivotTable report.
- Display report filter pages for a PivotTable report on separate worksheets.
- Create a scenario summary report.
- Use tools in the Analysis ToolPak that return results onto a new worksheet.
- Record new macros.

If you protect the windows for a workbook, unauthorized users will not be able to move, resize, or close the windows. To protect the structure and windows for a workbook, do the following:

1. Select the Review tab and, in the Changes group, click Protect Workbook. The Protect Structure and Windows dialog box will appear (see Figure 14-9).

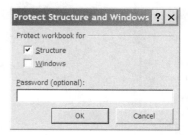

Figure 14-9. Select the Structure or the Windows checkbox, or both, and enter a password if desired.

2. In the Protect Structure and Windows dialog box, select or deselect the Structure and Windows options as appropriate.

3. If you want to prevent other users from removing the protection that you have added, enter a password in the box. If you do not use a password, other users will be able to unprotect the workbook and modify the previously protected elements.

4. Click OK. If you have applied a password, you will be asked to confirm it. Retype the password and click OK.

When a workbook has been protected, the Protect Workbook command in the Changes group will change to Unprotect Workbook. To unprotect the workbook again so that you can make changes to the structure or windows, click Unprotect Workbook in the Changes group. If you assigned a password to protect the workbook, the Unprotect Workbook dialog box will appear. Type the password in the box and click OK.

Protecting a Shared Workbook

If you are intending to make your workbook a shared workbook that can be accessed by multiple users simultaneously (as will be discussed in Chapter 16), you can protect the sharing of the workbook. This allows you to control what ranges each user has access to, to protect worksheets or workbook elements, set passwords for viewing and modifying the workbook, and turn on track changes. The following steps explain how to do this:

1. Make sure that all other users save and close the shared workbook and that the workbook is not already protected.

2. Before you can apply a password to protect the sharing, you must remove the workbook from shared use. Select the Review tab and, in the Changes group, click Share Workbook. The Share Workbook dialog box will open (see Figure 14-10).

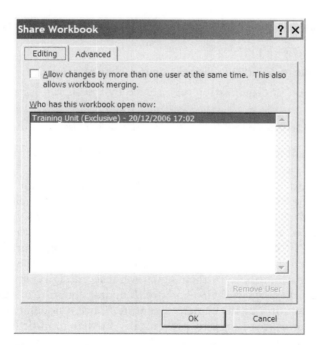

Figure 14-10. You can view a list of all the users who have the current workbook open on the Editing tab of the Share Workbook dialog box.

3. On the Editing tab of the Share Workbook dialog box, make sure that you are the only user listed in the "Who has this workbook open now" list.

4. Make sure that the checkbox beside "Allow changes by more than one user at the same time. This also allows workbook merging." is deselected. Click OK to close the Share Workbook dialog box. If an alert appears asking if you want to remove the workbook from shared use, click Yes.

5. Using the previous sections as a guide, protect workbooks or worksheet elements, or specify which users can edit certain ranges.

6. Select the Review tab on the Ribbon and, in the Changes group, click Protect and Share Workbook.

7. Select the checkbox next to "Sharing with track changes" in the Protect Shared Workbook dialog box.

8. Enter a password to prevent other users from turning off track changes or removing the workbook from shared use and click OK. Type the password again to confirm it and click OK.

Digital Signatures

Digital signatures are becoming a popular method of ensuring the authenticity and integrity of electronic documents and of proving the origin of the signed content. For a digital signature to make these assurances, it needs to satisfy the following criteria:

- The digital signature is valid.
- The certificate associated with the digital signature has not expired.
- The publisher (person or organization represented by the digital signature) is trusted.
- The certificate is issued to the publisher by a reputable certificate authority (CA).

Microsoft Office will alert you when you open a digitally signed document if there is a problem with any of these criteria.

Digital signatures can be visible or invisible. In Word and Excel, if the signature is to be visible, you can insert a signature line, which resembles a typical signature placeholder that would be used in a printed document. This enables you to enter details about the intended signer and instructions for the signer. When the document is sent electronically to the intended signer, he or she will see the signature line and a message that their signature is requested. To sign the document, the signer can double-click the signature line and type their signature, insert a digital image of their signature or, with a Tablet PC, write their signature. A digital signature is added along with the visible representation of the signer's signature. Once a document has been digitally signed, it becomes read-only to prevent any further modifications being made.

You can quickly determine if a document has been digitally signed by checking for the Signatures icon in the Status bar (see Figure 14-11). Clicking this icon will display or hide the Signatures task pane, which can be used to view digital signatures.

Figure 14-11. Signatures icon

Using a Signature Line

By adding a signature line to a document, you can specify where the signer should add their signature and provide any necessary instructions. If the document is going to be sent to more than one person for signing, you can add a signature line for each recipient. To add a signature line to a worksheet, follow these steps:

1. Select the worksheet, and click in the location where you want the signature line to appear.

2. Select the Insert tab and, in the Text group, click Signature Line and select Microsoft Office Signature Line. The Signature Setup dialog box will appear.

3. Enter the intended signer's details in the appropriate boxes and enter any instructions in the "Instructions to the signer" box.

4. If you want the signer to be able to add comments, select the "Allow the signer to add comments in the Sign dialog" option.

5. If you want to add the date to the signature line, select the "Show sign date in signature line" option.

6. Click OK. Repeat the process to add any further signature lines. Figure 14-12 shows an example of what a signature line looks like.

Figure 14-12. Double-click the Signature Line to add a visible representation of your signature.

If you have received a document for signing, you can add a visible representation of your signature to the signature line by typing a signature, by inserting a digital image of your signature, or by using a Tablet PC. When you add your signature to a document, a digital signature will be added simultaneously. To sign the signature line of a document, follow these steps:

1. Double-click the signature line where your signature is to appear (see Figure 14-12). The Sign dialog box will appear (see Figure 14-13).

Figure 14-13. Enter a visible representation of your signature in the box beside the X.

2. After checking the document for accuracy, do one of the following:
   - Type your name in the box beside the X.
   - Click Select Image and, in the Select Signature Image dialog box, find and select your signature image file and click Select.
   - Use the inking feature in a Tablet PC to sign your name in the box beside the X.
3. Click Sign. The document will now be read-only and cannot be modified unless the digital signature is removed.

In some cases a visible signature is not desired, but you may still want to provide an assurance as to the authenticity of a document. To do this you can add an invisible signature, which is not apparent in the actual contents of the document but can be viewed by the recipient if required. As with visible signatures, the document will become read-only when it has been digitally signed. To add an invisible signature to a document, click the Microsoft Office Button, point to Prepare, and select Add a Digital Signature. The Sign dialog box will appear. If desired, type the reason for signing the document in the Purpose for signing this document box and then click Sign.

Viewing a Digital Signature

If you have received a digitally signed document, you will probably want to view the details of the digital signature to check if it is trustworthy. To view the digital signature(s) for a document, click the Signatures icon in the Status bar at the bottom of the screen (or click the Microsoft Office Button, point to Prepare, and select View Signatures) to open the Signatures task pane (see Figure 14-14).

Figure 14-14. The Signatures task pane

In the Signatures task pane, select the signature that you want to view, click the down arrow to the right of the signature, and select Signature Details. You can then click the View button to view the certificate information or click the "See the additional signing information that was collected" link to view the additional information stored with the signature.

> **NOTE** If an X in a red circle is displayed beside the digital signature, there is a problem with the signature. This may be because the signature has expired, the certificate was not issued by a certificate authority, the publisher is not trusted, or the signature is invalid (for example, the document has been modified since the signature was added). If there is a problem with a digital signature, contact the source of the signed content or your IT administrator for advice.

If you want to edit a digitally signed document you will need to remove the digital signature. To remove a digital signature from a document, point to the signature in the Signatures task pane, click the down arrow to the right of the signature, and select Remove Signature. Click Yes when asked if you are sure that you want to permanently remove the signature and click OK to close the Signature Removed dialog box.

The Trust Center

Microsoft Office 2007 introduces a new component known as the Trust Center to help you view and control the security settings for all the programs in the suite. Previously, if you attempted to load a document that contained potentially harmful content, such as macros or ActiveX controls, an alert would be displayed asking if you wanted to enable or disable the content. In Excel 2007, potentially harmful content will be disabled by default and a Message bar will appear (similar to the pop-up blocker in Internet Explorer) indicating that content has been disabled. By clicking the Options button on the Trust Center Message bar, you can access a dialog box informing you why the content was blocked and providing you with the option to enable the content (see Figure 14-15).

Figure 14-15. Click the Options button on the Message bar to view the security options available. Note that the security warning and options will vary for different types of content.

To view the security settings in the Trust Center, click the Microsoft Office Button and click Excel Options. From the list of categories on the left, click Trust Center. A screen similar to Figure 14-16 will appear.

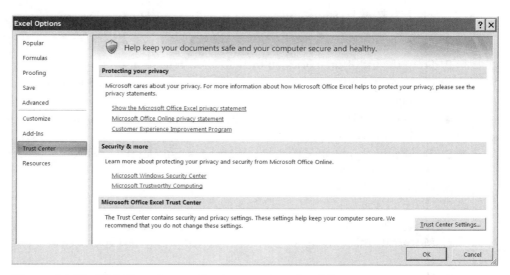

Figure 14-16. Click Trust Center Settings to view the different categories in the Trust Center.

Click the Trust Center Settings button and select any of the categories on the left to view or change the settings for that category. You can view and modify settings for Trusted Publishers, Trusted Locations, Add-ins, ActiveX Settings, Macro Settings, the Message Bar, External Content, and Privacy Options.

Adding, Viewing, and Removing Trusted Publishers

In the Trust Center you can see a list of publishers whose content is deemed to be reputable. A publisher is the developer of a macro, ActiveX control, add-in, or other application extension, and generally a trusted publisher should sign their code with a valid and current digital signature. If you try to run code from a potentially unsafe publisher, the Trust Center will disable the code and the Message bar will display a security warning. If you click the Options button in the Message bar, the Microsoft Office Security Options dialog box will appear, allowing you to leave the content disabled, to enable the content, or to trust all documents from the publisher. If you select "Trust all documents from this publisher" the publisher will be added to your list of trusted publishers; however, this option will only be available if the publisher's digital signature is valid.

> **CAUTION** You should never enable content or trust a publisher unless you are certain that the code is coming from a trustworthy source.

You can remove a publisher from your trusted publishers list or view a publisher's security certificate using the Trust Center as shown in the following steps:

1. Click the Microsoft Office Button and click Excel Options.
2. From the list of categories on the left, click Trust Center.
3. Click the Trust Center Settings button and select the Trusted Publishers category.
4. To view the certificate for a publisher, click the publisher's name in the Trusted Publishers list and click View.
5. To remove a publisher, click the publisher's name in the Trusted Publishers list and click Remove.
6. Click OK when you have finished.

> **NOTE** If you had trusted publishers that were used in earlier versions of Microsoft Office, these will be listed in the Prior Trusted Sources list.

Adding, Changing, and Removing Trusted Locations

A trusted location is basically a folder on your computer or network from which you want to be able to open files without them being checked by the Trust Center. For example, if you regularly use a file that contains a macro or other content that is disabled by the Trust Center and you are sure that the file does not have any unsafe content, you can move the file to a trusted location so that you can open it each time with the content enabled. This is much less risky than changing other security settings to a less safe option.

Some trusted locations will be created automatically when Microsoft Office 2007 is installed and will appear something like C:\Program Files\Microsoft Office\ Templates or C:\Program Files\Microsoft Office\Office12\XLSTART. If you are working as part of a large organization, your administrator may also have created trusted locations. To create further trusted locations, do the following:

1. Click the Microsoft Office Button and click Excel Options.
2. From the list of categories on the left, click Trust Center.
3. Click the Trust Center Settings button. Select the Trusted Locations category. A screen similar to Figure 14-17 will appear.

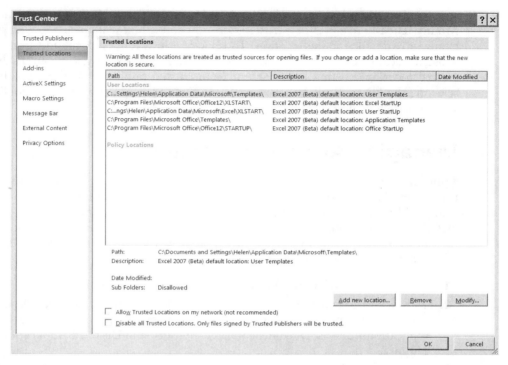

Figure 14-17. You can add, remove, modify, or disable Trusted Locations in the Trust Center.

4. If you want to add a new trusted location that is not on your computer, select the "Allow Trusted Locations on my network (not recommended)" checkbox.

5. Click the "Add new location" button.

6. In the Microsoft Office Trusted Location dialog box, enter the path of a secure location in the Path box (or click Browse to search for and select the location).

7. Select the "Subfolders of this location" checkbox if you want subfolders of the folder to also be considered trusted locations, and add a description for the location in the Description box.

8. Click OK when you have finished to close the Microsoft Office Trusted Location dialog box.

CAUTION Do not specify your entire My Documents folder or a public network drive as a trusted location as the security of these could easily be compromised, leaving you vulnerable to malicious code.

To edit a trusted location, click the location in the Trusted Locations list and click Modify. The Microsoft Office Trusted Location dialog box will open, allowing you to change the details for the location. To remove a location, click the location in the Trusted Locations list and click Remove. For additional security, you can disable all trusted locations so that only content from trusted publishers will be enabled by selecting the "Disable all Trusted Locations. Only files signed by Trusted Publishers will be trusted." checkbox.

Managing Application Add-ins

Application add-ins (for example, smart tags and global templates) provide additional functionality to a program or programs with extra commands or features. Many add-ins are installed with Microsoft Office 2007: examples of Excel add-ins include the Solver tool, used for solving equations, and the Analysis ToolPak, which provides various data analysis tools. You can view a list of the installed add-ins and add or remove add-ins as follows:

1. Click the Microsoft Office Button and click Excel Options.
2. From the list of categories on the left, click Add-Ins. All the installed add-ins will be listed under four categories: Active Application Add-ins, Inactive Application Add-ins, Document Related Add-ins, and Disabled Application Add-ins.
3. To make an add-in active or inactive, click the down arrow in the Manage field, select the type of add-in, and click Go.
4. Select the required options from the dialog box that appears. Click OK when you have finished.

Along with the many useful add-ins that can be installed, there are unsafe add-ins that are used to spread viruses or corrupt your system. You can change the security settings for add-ins using the Trust Center by selecting the Add-ins category and choosing from the following options:

- Select Require Application Add-ins to be Signed by Trusted Publisher if you want the Trust Center to check for a digital signature on the dynamic link library (DLL) file that contains the add-in. Only add-ins from trusted publishers will be loaded.
- Select "Disable notification for unsigned add-ins (code will remain disabled)" if you have selected the previous option and you want unsigned add-ins to be disabled without notification.
- Select "Disable all Application Add-ins (may impair functionality)" if you want all add-ins to be disabled without notification. The other options are not available while this option is selected.

I **NOTE** You will need to restart Excel for the new settings to take effect.

Changing Settings for ActiveX Controls

ActiveX controls are frequently used in web sites and applications and are basically OLE objects, or more specifically, COM (Component Object Model) objects. They can only be run from within host programs like Microsoft Office programs. ActiveX controls have full access to the Windows operating system and can change the Registry settings, making them a potential medium through which hackers can gain access to your system.

The Trust Center can help to protect you against malicious ActiveX controls by checking for the "kill bit," a feature that indicates that the control is known to be unsafe, and by checking if the control is marked as Safe for Initialization (SFI). If the document containing the ActiveX control also contains a VBA project, the Trust Center will apply more restrictions.

If the Trust Center judges a control to be potentially unsafe, it will be disabled and a security warning will be displayed in the Message bar. If you want to enable the control, click the Options button in the Message bar and select the "Enable this content" option. The ActiveX control will be enabled for that document for the current program session only.

> **CAUTION** You should only enable an ActiveX control if you are sure that it is safe.

You can change the security settings for ActiveX controls using the Trust Center by selecting the ActiveX Settings category and choosing from the following options:

- Select "Disable all controls without notification" if you want all ActiveX controls to be disabled without any notification. The Message bar will not be displayed.

- Select "Prompt me before enabling Unsafe for Initialization (UFI) controls with additional restrictions and Safe for Initialization (SFI) controls with minimum restrictions" if you want to disable all controls in documents with a VBA project and disable UFI controls but enable SFI controls in documents without a VBA project. (For disabled controls, if you choose to enable the control in the Message bar, UFI controls will be loaded with additional restrictions and SFI controls will be loaded with minimal restrictions.)

- Select "Prompt me before enabling all controls with minimal restrictions" if you want to disable all controls in documents with a VBA project and you want to disable UFI controls but enable SFI controls in documents without a VBA project. (For disabled controls, if you choose to enable a control in the Message bar in a document without a VBA project, UFI controls will be loaded with additional restrictions and SFI controls will be loaded with minimal restrictions. If you enable a control in a document with a VBA project, both SFI and UFI controls will be loaded with minimal restrictions.)

- Select "Enable all controls without restrictions and without prompting (not recommended; potentially dangerous controls can run)" option if you want to allow all ActiveX controls to run. This option should only be used temporarily and with caution as it will leave your computer susceptible to malicious code.
- Select "Safe Mode (helps limit the control's access to your computer)" option to only allow SFI ActiveX controls in Safe mode.

TIP If you want to load a document that contains safe ActiveX controls, move it to a trusted location so that it will not be subject to the settings in the Trust Center rather than choosing a less secure setting for all ActiveX controls. However, if a control has the "kill-bit" set, it will not be loaded, even from a trusted location.

Changing Settings for Macros

Macros can be used in a variety of ways within documents including Excel workbooks to automate processes that are carried out repeatedly. For example, a workbook may contain a macro that copies cells from different worksheets, pastes them to a new worksheet, and formats them in a specified manner. However, like add-ins and ActiveX controls, macros are sometimes used for harmful purposes. You can use the Trust Center to control how Excel deals with macros by choosing the Macro Settings category and selecting one of the following options:

- Select "Disable all macros without notification" if you want all macros to be disabled without notification. The Message bar will not be displayed.
- Select "Disable all macros with notification" if you want to disable all macros but you want a security alert to be displayed in the Message bar, allowing you to decide whether or not to enable macros for each document as it is opened.
- Select "Disable all macros except digitally signed macros" if you want to disable without notification all macros that are not digitally signed. If a macro is digitally signed by a publisher that you have not trusted, a security alert will be displayed in the Message bar. You can then click the Options button to enable the macro or to make the publisher a trusted publisher. Macros that have been digitally signed by a trusted publisher will be enabled automatically.
- Select "Enable all macros (not recommended; potentially dangerous code can run)" if you want to allow all macros to run. This setting should only be used temporarily and with caution as it leaves your computer susceptible to malicious code.

TIP If you want to load a document that contains safe macros, move it to a trusted location so that it will not be subject to the settings in the Trust Center rather than choosing a less secure setting for all macros.

Turning the Message Bar On and Off

If you do not want to see security alerts on the Message bar, you can disable it using the Trust Center. Select the Message Bar category and choose either of the following options:

- Select "Show the Message Bar in all applications when content has been blocked" if you want to view security alerts in the Message bar.
- Select "Never show information about blocked content" if you do not want to receive security alerts, regardless of the other settings in the Trust Center.

Changing Settings for External Content

External content is content that is linked to a workbook from the Internet or an intranet and can include items like data connections, hyperlinks, images, linked media, and templates. By default, Microsoft Office 2007 will block external content to protect you from web beacons and other dubious methods that hackers employ that may invade your privacy or cause you to unwittingly run malicious code. A security alert will be displayed in the Message bar informing you that data connections have been disabled. If you want to enable the content, you can click the Options button in the Message bar and select the "Enable this content" option.

You can change the security settings for external content for Excel using the Trust Center, as described here:

1. Select the External Content category in Trust Center Settings.
2. To change the settings for Data Connections, choose one of the following options:
   - Select "Enable all Data Connections (not recommended)" if you want to open all workbooks that contain external data connections and create connections to external data without security alerts being displayed. This option should only be used temporarily and if you are sure that you can trust the source of the external data connections.
   - Select "Prompt user about Data Connections" if you want the Message bar to display a security warning each time a workbook containing external data connections is opened or when an external data connection is created.
   - Select "Disable all Data Connections" if you want to disable all data connections in the current workbook and in any future workbooks that you open. This may restrict the functionality of some features.

3. To change the settings for Workbook Links, choose one of the following options:

   - Select "Enable automatic update for all Workbook Links (not recommended)" if you want to update links to other workbooks automatically without a security warning being displayed. This option should only be used temporarily and if you are sure that you can trust the workbooks that the data is linked to.

   - Select "Prompt user on automatic update for Workbook Links" if you want the Message bar to display a security warning each time you run automatic updates for links to data in another workbook.

   - Select "Disable automatic update of Workbook Links" if you want to disable automatic updating of links in the current workbook.

4. Click OK when you have finished.

> **TIP** If you want to load a document that contains safe external content, move it to a trusted location so that it will not be subject to the settings in the Trust Center rather than choosing a less secure setting for all external content.

Changing Privacy Options

The Privacy Options category in the Trust Center allows you to decide what information should be automatically downloaded from Microsoft; for example, you can choose to access online Help content or check for links to suspicious web sites. You can also access the Document Inspector in Privacy Options to check your workbook for hidden content like hidden worksheets, revision marks from track changes, and metadata, and to change the options for Translation and Research. You can access Privacy Options using the Trust Center, as described here:

1. Select the Privacy Options category in Trust Center Settings. A screen similar to Figure 14-18 will appear.

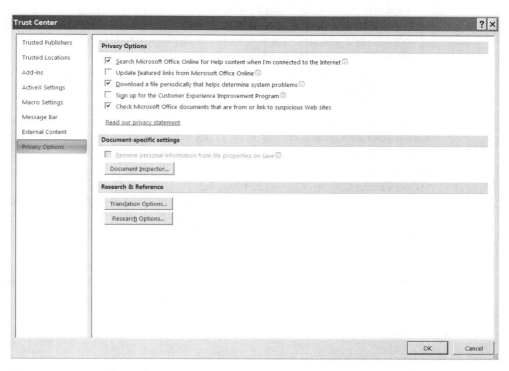

Figure 14-18. In the Privacy Options category, you can change the settings for Privacy Options, run the Document Inspector, or select Translation or Research options.

2. To change the settings for Privacy Options, select any of the following:
   - Select "Search Microsoft Office Online for Help content when I'm connected to the Internet" if you want Office to download Help content from Office Online.
   - Select "Update featured links from Microsoft Office Online" if you want to download up-to-date headlines and featured templates from Office Online.
   - Select "Download a file periodically that helps determine system problems" if you want to download a file to help track and solve crashes, hangs, and system failures.
   - Select "Sign up for the Customer Experience Improvement Program" if you want to allow Microsoft to collect data and statistics about problems, system configuration, and the features that you use most often.

- Select "Check Microsoft Office documents that are from or link to suspicious Web sites" if you want Office to display a security alert if you click a link in a document to a web site that may have a spoof domain name or if you open a file from a web site that may have a spoof domain name. This option is turned on by default and may protect you from phishing and homograph attacks, where fraudsters impersonate legitimate organizations or web sites in order to obtain personal or financial details.

3. To remove hidden and personal information from the file when you save it, check the "Remove personal information from file properties on save" option. This may be important if you are planning to share the document with others and want to avoid revealing editing or organizational data that may be stored as metadata or if you have used the Track Changes feature.

4. To check the document for hidden data, click the Document Inspector button. You can choose what content the Document Inspector will check for by selecting or deselecting the checkboxes before clicking Inspect. The inspection results will indicate if any hidden or personal contents have been found. If you want to delete any of the content, click the Remove All button for that content. See Chapter 16 for more information on inspecting a document before distributing it.

5. To change the options for Research and Translate commands (available in the Proofing group on the Review tab of the Ribbon), click the Research Options button or the Translate Options button and select or deselect options as required.

6. Click OK when you have finished.

CHAPTER 15

Getting Data from External Sources

Excel data can come from a variety of sources. If the data you want to analyze is available in another file or electronic format, you may be able to import it directly into Excel. For example, perhaps you want to view a subset of data from a large database in Excel, or you want to evaluate some of the enormous wealth of raw data that is available on the Web. Data sources that can be used with Excel include text files, Microsoft Access, Microsoft SQL Server Analysis Services (for OLAP databases), Microsoft Visual FoxPro, dBASE, Oracle, and Paradox. Excel 2007 has simplified the process of obtaining data from other sources and of managing the connections to these sources with most of the relevant commands available on the Data tab of the Ribbon. This chapter will show you how to import data from other sources like Access or the Web so that you can work with it in Excel.

Connecting to External Data Sources

Excel workbooks are often used to analyze or present data from sources outside of Excel. These sources can include web pages, other files such as text files or Microsoft Access files, or OLAP (Online Analytical Processing) cubes. In many cases, of course, you could just copy the data into Excel, but if you need to periodically import data, this could prove needlessly laborious and time-consuming. The alternative is to create a connection to the source so that you can refresh the data automatically or whenever you have to update your file.

To create a connection to an external source, you can use the Get External Data group on the Data tab, as shown in Figure 15-1. Here you will find commands allowing you to import data from Microsoft Access, from the Web, or from a text file. To import data from another source, like a SQL Server table, a SQL Server Analysis Services cube, or an XML file, you can use the From Other Sources command in the Get External Data group. If you want to access a data source that you have used previously, click the Existing Connections command.

Figure 15-1. The Get External Data group on the Data tab

> **NOTE** If connections to external data sources have been disabled on your computer, you will have to enable them using the Trust Center bar. If the data source is another file, you can put the file in a trusted location so that it can be opened without being checked by the Trust Center. Chapter 14 discusses the security issues around using external data sources in more detail.

Importing Data from an Existing Connection

If you want to import data from a source that you have previously used or defined, you can use the Existing Connections dialog box. This dialog box can be used to view all the connections in the current workbook, as well as any connection files on the computer and on the network. Connection files for some MSN MoneyCentral sites are installed by default.

1. To open the Existing Connections dialog box (see Figure 15-2), click Existing Connections in the Get External Data group on the Data tab.

2. By default, all connections are shown but you can choose a different option from the Show dropdown list. Options include viewing only the connections in the workbook, viewing the connection files on the network, or viewing the connection files on the computer. (If you cannot see the connection that you are looking for, click the Browse for More button to open the Select Data Source dialog box.)

Figure 15-2. The Existing Connections dialog box shows all connections.

3. To import data from a source, select the connection that you want and click Open. The Import Data dialog box will appear (see Figure 15-3). Note that the Import Data dialog box may vary for different types of data.

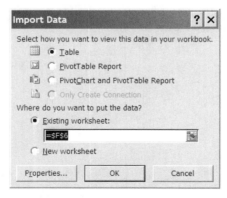

Figure 15-3. Select how you want the data to be imported in the Import Data dialog box.

4. In the Import Data dialog box, select how you want to view the imported data in your workbook by choosing from the Table, PivotTable Report, and PivotChart and PivotTable Report options. If you only want to create the connection so that it can be used later, select the Only Create Connection option. Note that these options are only available for certain types of data.

5. If you want to place the data in the current worksheet, select the Existing worksheet option and enter the cell reference of the first cell where you want the data to appear in the box. To create a new worksheet for the data, select the New worksheet option.

6. If you want to change the default settings for the refresh, formatting, or layout of the data, click the Properties button and choose the appropriate options.

7. Click OK to import the data to the selected location.

Importing Data from a Microsoft Access Database

If you have data stored in an Access database file, you can import the entire file directly into Excel, provided it does not exceed the number of rows and columns available. To import data from Access, click the Data tab and, in the Get External Data group, click From Access. In the Select Data Source dialog box, locate the Access file that you wish to import and click Open. The Import Data dialog box will appear, allowing you to select how you want to view the imported data in your workbook and where you want to place the data.

To retrieve only selected data from a database, you can create a query. For example, you could create a query so that you will only import the data for a particular product's sales in a specified region. If you do not require all the data in a database, you can use Microsoft Query to import a subset of the data. The following steps explain how you can do this:

1. Select the Data tab and, in the Get External Data group, click From Other Sources.

2. From the dropdown list that appears, select From Microsoft Query. The Choose Data Source dialog box will open (see Figure 15-4).

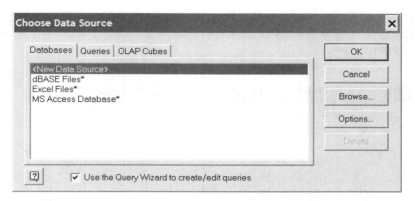

Figure 15-4. Selecting the From Microsoft Query option opens the Choose Data Source dialog box.

3. If you intend to use the data source again, you can create a new data source by selecting <New Data Source> and clicking OK. You then need to provide a name for the data source and select a driver for the database. Click Connect and provide any other information required. Excel will then list your new data source in the Choose Data Source dialog box. If you do not want to create a new data source, select MS Access Database and click OK. The Select Database dialog box will appear (see Figure 15-5).

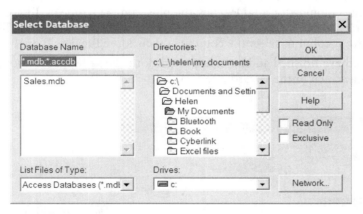

Figure 15-5. Use the Select Database dialog box to locate the database you want to query.

4. Locate and select the database that you want to query and click OK. The Query Wizard will open at the Choose Columns screen, which will be similar to Figure 15-6.

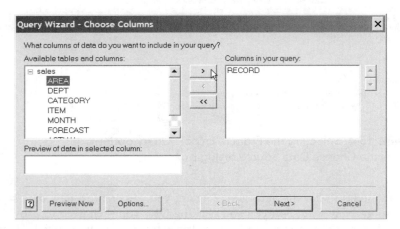

Figure 15-6. In the first step of the Query Wizard, choose the columns that you want to include in your query.

5. Choose the columns of data that you want to include in your query by selecting them from the available tables on the left and clicking the right arrow button. To view the columns for a table, click the plus sign (+) beside it. To add all the columns for a table, select the table and click the right arrow button. To preview the data for a column, select the column and click the Preview Now button.

6. When you have finished adding columns, click the Next button to move to the Filter Data screen of the wizard (see Figure 15-7).

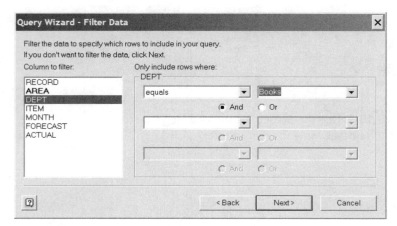

Figure 15-7. In the second step of the Query Wizard, filter the data to specify which rows you want to include in the query.

7. If you want to filter the data, select the column that you want to filter by from the "Column to filter" list. In the "Only include rows where" section, select an option from the first dropdown list—for example, equals or is greater than— and then choose an option from the second list that Excel will use to compare the records with. Add further criteria by selecting either And or Or and choosing more options. Columns that have a filter applied to them will appear in bold in the "Column to filter" list.

8. When you have finished adding filter criteria, click the Next button to proceed to the Sort Order screen (see Figure 15-8).

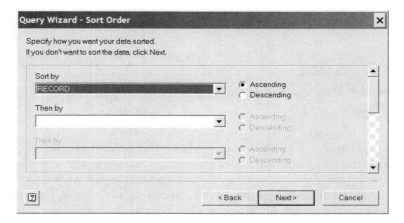

Figure 15-8. In the third step of the Query Wizard, you specify how you want the data to be sorted.

9. If you want to sort the data, select the column that you want to sort by from the dropdown list and choose either Ascending or Descending. You can sort the data by as many columns as you like.

10. When you have finished adding filter criteria, click Next to go to the Finish screen (see Figure 15-9).

11. If you want to save the query so that you can use it again, click the Save Query button and give the query a filename.

TIP By default, queries are saved to the Queries folder with a .dqy file extension. To open a saved query again, select the Queries tab in the Choose Data Source dialog box.

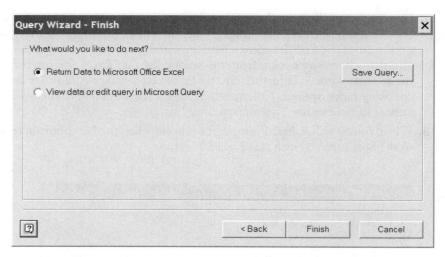

Figure 15-9. Click the Save Query button in the last step of the Query Wizard.

12. Select the Return Data to Microsoft Office Excel option and click Finish. The Import Data dialog box will appear, allowing you to select how you want to view the imported data in your workbook and where you want to place the data. If you want to change the default settings for the refresh, formatting, or layout of the data, click the Properties button and choose the appropriate options.

13. Click OK. The results of your query will be imported into the specified worksheet.

Importing Data from the Web

If you want to use data from the Web in your worksheet, you can create a web query. Web queries utilize web tables, which are commonly used by designers to organize and display web content, to capture data in a format that can be recognized by Excel. When you have found a web page containing the data that you require, use a web query to import that data into Excel as follows:

1. Select the Data tab and, in the Get External Data group, click From Web.

2. Using the special browser that opens, go to the web page that contains the data you want to use.

3. To select a table (or tables) to import, click on the yellow box containing a black arrow beside the table. (As you hover your mouse over the yellow box, it will change to green and a border will appear around the data.) When you click an arrow to select a table, it will change to a check mark (see Figure 15-10).

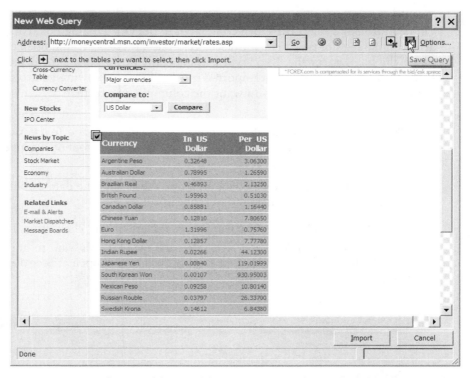

Figure 15-10. Select a table or tables to import in the New Web Query window.

4. When you have finished selecting tables, you can save the query by clicking the Save Query icon at the top of the browser window. Click Options to view or change the formatting and import settings.

5. To import the data, click the Import button at the bottom of the window.

6. In the Import Data dialog box that appears, select where you want the data to be placed. If you want to change the default settings for the refresh, formatting, or layout of the data, click the Properties button and choose the appropriate options.

7. Click OK. After a short delay, Excel will display the data you selected in the specified location.

Importing a Text File

If you want to import data saved as a text file into Excel, you can simply open the file in Excel or you can connect to the file as an external data range. Text files are generally either delimited text files (.txt), where a tab character is normally used to separate each field, or comma-separated values text files (.csv), where a comma is used to separate each field.

To convert a text file to a workbook by opening it into Excel, click the Microsoft Office Button and select the Open command. In the Open dialog box, click the down arrow in the Files of type field and select Text Files, then locate and open the required file. If the file is a .csv file, Excel will automatically open it using the default settings. If the file is a .txt file, the Text Import Wizard will start, allowing you to choose how the file is delimited and how you want the columns to be formatted.

> **TIP** If you want to change the settings for a .csv file using the Text Import Wizard, save it as a .txt file before opening it or import it by creating a connection.

If you want to create a connection to a text file so that the data can be refreshed, you can import the data as an external range as follows:

1. Select the Data tab and, in the Get External Data group, click From Text.
2. In the Import Text File dialog box, select the file that you want to import and click the Import button. The Text Import Wizard will open at Step 1 of 3 (see Figure 15-11).

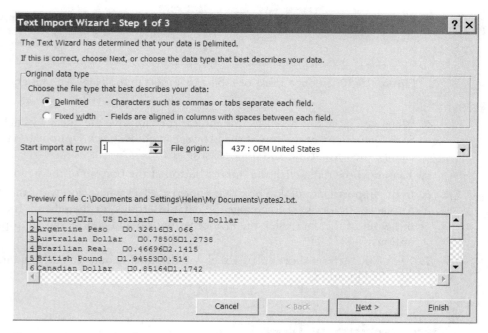

Figure 15-11. In the first step of the Text Import Wizard, select the data type that best describes your data.

3. In Step 1 of the Text Import Wizard, select whether your data is Delimited or Fixed width. If you want to start importing data from a row other than the first row, enter the appropriate number in the "Start import at row" field. Click Next to go to Step 2 of the wizard (see Figure 15-12).

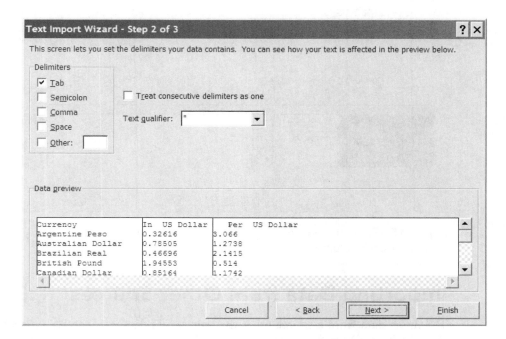

Figure 15-12. In Step 2 of the Text Import Wizard, choose how your data is delimited.

4. In the Delimiters section, select the character(s) that are used to delimit your data. The Data preview section will provide you with an indication of how your data will be imported. Click Next to go to the last step of the Text Import Wizard (see Figure 15-13).

5. To set the data format for a column, select the column and choose one of the options in the "Column data format" section. To omit a column, select it and choose the "Do not import column (skip)" option. Click Finish to close the Text Import Wizard.

6. In the Import Data dialog box that appears, select where you want the data to be placed. If you want to change the default settings for the refresh, formatting, or layout of the data, click the Properties button and choose the appropriate options.

7. Click OK to import the data to the specified location.

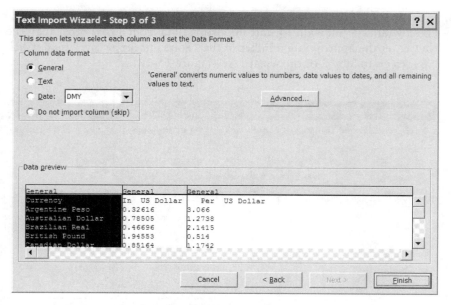

Figure 15-13. In Step 3 of the Text Import Wizard, you can set the data format for each column.

Importing Data from Other Sources

To import data from a source other than an Access database, the Web, or a text file, click the From Other Sources command in the Get External Data group and select the appropriate option from the menu that appears (see Figure 15-14). If you select From SQL Server or From Analysis Services, the Data Connection Wizard will launch and guide you through the process of connecting to a database server. To connect to a database server, you will need to know the name of the server and the password if necessary.

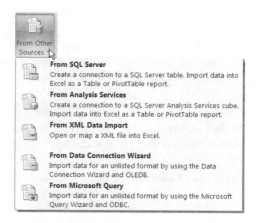

Figure 15-14. The From Other Sources menu

Managing Data Connections

Excel 2007 has made updating your external data and editing your connections much easier by providing a central location for browsing and managing all the connections in a workbook. Using the Connections group on the Data tab you can refresh your data, add or remove a connection, see where a connection is used, change the properties for a connection, or specify format and layout settings for an external data range. This section will look at how you can manage your data connections in Excel 2007.

Refreshing External Data

Once you have connected a PivotTable, table, or range of cells to an external data source, you can refresh it any time you want to display the most up-to-date data. This can be done either manually as required or automatically at specified intervals or each time the workbook is opened.

To manually refresh the data at any time, just click the arrow next to Refresh All in the Connections group (see Figure 15-15) and select Refresh (or Refresh All if you have more than one external data range in the workbook). If you have multiple workbooks open, you will need to click Refresh All in each workbook to update all the external data ranges. You can check the status of a refresh at any time by clicking Refresh Status in the Refresh All dropdown menu, and you can cancel a refresh by selecting Cancel Refresh.

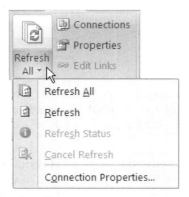

Figure 15-15. Select either Refresh All or Refresh to update external data.

> **TIP** If you are refreshing an imported text file, the Import Text File dialog box will appear, prompting you to select the file. You can prevent this from happening by deselecting the "Prompt for file name on refresh" option on the Usage tab of the Connection Properties dialog box (see Figure 15-16).

To avoid having to remember to refresh your data, you can set a workbook to refresh the external data automatically, either at regular time intervals or each time the workbook is opened. To do this, click the down arrow beside Refresh All in the Connections group, select Connection Properties to open the Connection Properties dialog box, and make sure that the Usage tab is selected (see Figure 15-16).

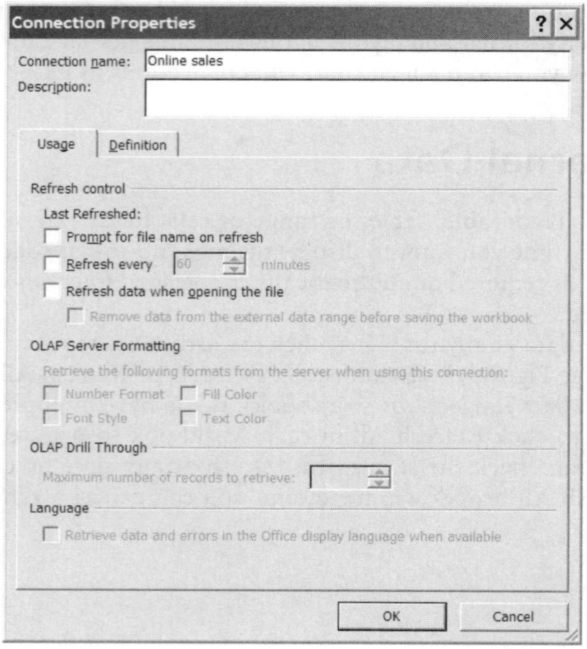

Figure 15-16. The Connection Properties dialog box

> **NOTE** The Connection Properties dialog box may differ for different types of connections. If the connection involves a query, the "Prompt for file name on refresh" option will be replaced by the "Enable background refresh" option.

To refresh the data at a regular time interval, select the Refresh every option and specify the interval in minutes that you want between each refresh. To make sure that an external data range is refreshed each time the workbook is opened, select the "Refresh data when opening the file" option. If you select this option, you can opt to save the query definition without the data by selecting the "Remove data from the external data range before saving the workbook" option.

If a connection involves a query (excluding OLAP queries), you can select the "Enable background refresh" option to allow you to continue working with Excel while the data is being refreshed. You can stop a background refresh by double-clicking the Background Refresh icon (which resembles a globe) in the Status bar to open the External Data Refresh Status dialog box and selecting Stop Refresh. To cancel a query when "Enable background refresh" is deselected, press Esc.

Editing Workbook Connections

You can view, edit, delete, or refresh connections in a workbook using the Workbook Connections dialog box (see Figure 15-17). To open the Workbook Connections dialog box so that you can manage one or more connections in the current workbook, click Connections in the Connections group.

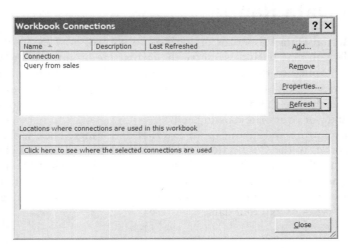

Figure 15-17. The Workbook Connections dialog box

To add a connection to the current workbook, click the Add button. The Existing Connections dialog box will open, allowing you to select a connection from those that have been previously used. If you cannot see the connection that you are looking for, click the Browse for More button to open the Select Data Source dialog box and choose a data source from there.

If you no longer want to be able to refresh a data range, you can delete the connection by selecting it and clicking Remove. This will only delete the connection, not the actual data. Removing a data connection may affect formula results or cause other features to function incorrectly, and if the workbook or data range is protected, this option will not be available.

If you want to edit a connection, click Properties to open the Connection Properties dialog box. You can then use the Usage tab to change features like the refresh settings or which OLAP server formats are to be retrieved with the data. Use the Definition tab in the Connection Properties dialog box to change the authentication settings, edit the query, or export the connection file.

To refresh a connection from the Workbook Connections dialog box, select it and click the Refresh button. To refresh all the connections in the workbook, click the down arrow on the Refresh button and select Refresh All. You can also check the status of a refresh or cancel it using the dropdown menu on the Refresh button.

If you want to view the locations in the workbook where a connection is used, select it and click the "Click here to see where the selected connections are used" link. This will display the sheet name, query name, location, value, and formula as appropriate for the selected connection.

Changing the Format and Layout of an External Data Range

You can use the External Data Properties dialog box to control how external data appears. For example, you may wish to preserve the formatting or any sort orders or filters that have been applied to the data when it is imported. You can also use the External Data Properties dialog box to control how changes in the numbers of rows should be dealt with each time the data is refreshed—for instance, whether to insert entire rows for new data or overwrite existing cells.

To change the formatting and layout of an external data range, click within the range and click Properties in the Connections group on the Data tab. This will open the External Data Range Properties dialog box (see Figure 15-18). Select the appropriate options to define how you want the data to be displayed and new data to be incorporated and click OK. Note that the External Data Range Properties dialog box may vary for different types of external data.

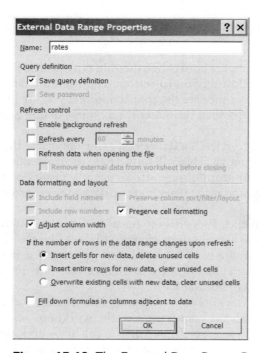

Figure 15-18. The External Data Range Properties dialog box can be used to change the formatting and layout settings for an external data range.

Sharing, Reviewing, and Distributing Data

In many organizations spreadsheets are often not the work of a sole author but include input from various users, such as the members of a project team. If several people need to be able to edit the contents of a workbook simultaneously, you can create a shared workbook and store it on a network location. You can then control which users should have access to the workbook and resolve any conflicting changes. When collaborating with colleagues on a workbook, it is usually important to keep a record of who edited what and any comments that reviewers have made. In this chapter I will discuss the reviewing features that are available in Excel and how you can track the changes that are made to a document.

When you have finished constructing your workbook, chances are you will want others to see it. In Excel 2007 you can distribute your data using one of several options. The methods that probably spring to mind first are to email it or fax it to the people you want to view it, or to print it and send them a hard copy. If you need to make a workbook available to different users, you can save it to a document management server, or if you have access to Excel Services through Microsoft Office SharePoint Server 2007, you can save it (or specific elements of it) to the server so that others can interact with it using a browser.

The medium that you use to distribute Excel data will depend on several factors. When choosing how to share data with others, questions you should ask include: "How much data do I want others to be able to view?" "Should they be able to interact with it or edit it?" "Will they have access to Excel and if so, which version?" This chapter will look at how you can share data by printing, emailing, and faxing it. Chapter 17 will discuss how you can use SharePoint and Excel Services to allow others to access workbook items.

Sharing and Reviewing Workbooks

If you need to collaborate with colleagues on a project or task, you can create a shared workbook that you can all use and store it in a shared network folder. This way, you can allow multiple users to access the workbook and edit the contents simultaneously. For example, a sales team could use a shared workbook for each rep to record his or her daily sales data.

Creating a Shared Workbook

You can share a new workbook or an existing workbook to make it available to other users. To create a shared workbook, do the following:

1. Open or create the workbook that you want to make available to multiple users. Note that the following features cannot be added to a workbook after it is shared so make sure you include them at this stage if required: merged cells, conditional formats, tables, pictures, objects (including drawing objects), charts, hyperlinks, data validation, data tables, scenarios, outlines, subtotals, PivotTable reports, workbook and worksheet protection, and macros.

2. Select the Review tab and, in the Changes group, click Share Workbook (see Figure 16-1).

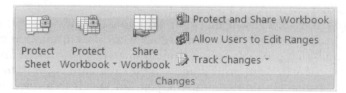

Figure 16-1. The Changes group on the Review tab

3. In the Share Workbook dialog box, make sure that the Editing tab is displayed and select the "Allow changes by more than one user at the same time. This also allows workbook merging." option.

4. Select the Advanced tab and choose the options that you want to use when tracking and updating changes and when conflicting changes occur (see Figure 16-2). You can also select whether to include print settings and filter settings in the personal view. When you have finished selecting settings, click OK.

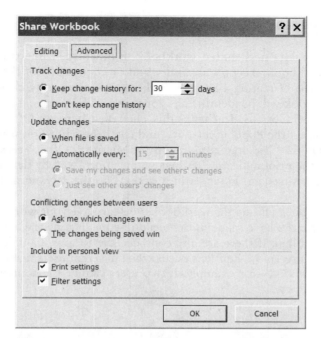

Figure 16-2. Use the Advanced tab of the Share Workbook
dialog box to specify settings for the shared workbook.

5. If you are creating a shared workbook from a new workbook, the Save As
   dialog box will open. If it is an existing workbook, click OK when prompted to
   save the workbook, then click the Microsoft Office Button and select Save As to
   open the Save As dialog box.

6. In the Save in box, select a folder on the network that can be accessed by all the
   users who will be sharing the workbook, change the entry in the File name box
   if desired, and click Save. (If the workbook contains links to other documents,
   you will need to verify the links and update any that are broken using the Edit
   Links command in the Connections group of the Data tab. Click the Save
   button on the Quick Access toolbar to save the file again when you have
   finished.) [Shared] will be displayed beside the name of the workbook in the
   Title bar to indicate that it is a shared workbook.

NOTE Any user who has access to the network folder will be able to view and
edit the shared workbook unless you restrict access by locking cells and protecting the worksheet. See Chapter 14 for more information on protecting a
shared workbook.

Editing a Shared Workbook

You can enter and edit data in a shared workbook in much the same way as you would in a regular workbook except you cannot add or change any of the features already mentioned in the "Creating a Shared Workbook" section. Any changes that you make to the workbook will be identified as yours and will use the name specified as the User name in Excel Options. To change this, click the Microsoft Office Button, click Excel Options, select the Popular category, and enter the name you want to use in the User name box in the "Personalize your copy of Microsoft Office" section. Any changes you make to the print and filter settings will also be saved by default unless you deselect the Print settings and Filter settings options on the Advanced tab of the Share Workbook dialog box.

When you have finished editing the workbook, you can save your work and view the changes that other users have made in the meantime by clicking the Save button on the Quick Access toolbar. If there are any conflicts, the Resolve Conflicts dialog box will appear (see Figure 16-3). Conflicts occur when different users make conflicting changes to the workbook—for example, if two users change the contents of the same cell to different values.

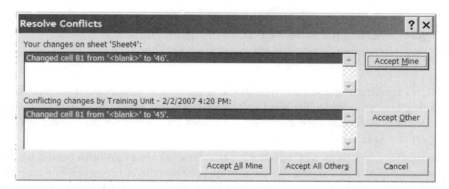

Figure 16-3. The Resolve Conflicts dialog box will appear if two users are editing the same workbook and attempt to save changes that affect the same cell.

To resolve conflicts in a shared workbook one at a time, compare your change with the conflicting change and click either Accept Mine or Accept Other in the Resolve Conflicts dialog box. To keep all of your changes or all of the other user's changes, click either Accept All Mine or Accept All Others. If you want, you can ensure that your changes always have preference over other changes without displaying the Resolve Conflicts dialog box each time. To do this, select the Review tab and, in the Changes group, click Share Workbook. Select the Advanced tab of the Share Workbook dialog box and, under "Conflicting changes between users" select the "The changes being saved win" option (see Figure 16-2).

If you want to stop sharing a workbook so that it cannot be edited by multiple users simultaneously, do the following:

1. Open the workbook and select the Review tab.

2. In the Changes group, click Share Workbook to open the Share Workbook dialog box.

3. Make sure that you are the only person listed in the "Who has this workbook open now" list on the Edit tab. If other users are connected, you will have to disconnect them but first, but make sure that they have saved any work they have carried out because any unsaved work will be lost. To remove a user, select their name and click Remove user.

4. To stop sharing the workbook, deselect the "Allow changes by more than one user at the same time. This also allows workbook merging." option. If this option is not available, you may need to unprotect the workbook (see Chapter 14 for information on removing protection from a workbook).

Tracking Changes

When a workbook is being edited by more than one user, it is useful to know who has made what changes. The Track Changes facility allows you to keep a record of the changes each user has made so that you can review them before deciding whether to accept or reject them. When using Track Changes, cells that have been edited will display an indicator in the form of a blue triangle in the top-left corner of the cell. When the mouse pointer is moved over the cell, Excel displays a comment text box indicating what change was made to the cell, by whom, and the date and time that it was made. To create a log of the changes to a document, use these steps:

1. Go to the Review tab and, in the Changes group, click Track Changes. Select Highlight Changes to display the Highlight Changes dialog box (see Figure 16-4).

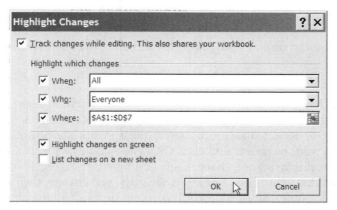

Figure 16-4. Select which changes to highlight and how to display them in the Highlight Changes dialog box.

2. In the Highlight Changes dialog box, select the "Track changes while editing. This also shares your workbook." option.

3. Next choose which changes you want to be highlighted using the options available:

- To highlight changes based on when they were made, select the When checkbox and choose from "Since I last saved," All, "Not yet reviewed," or Since date (and then enter a date in the box) in the dropdown list.

- To highlight changes based on whom they were made by, select the Who checkbox and choose from Everyone, Everyone but Me, or a particular user in the dropdown list.

- To highlight changes for a specific cell or range, select the Where option and enter the cell or range reference in the box.

4. Select the "Highlight changes on screen" option and/or the "List changes on a new sheet" option as desired and click OK. If you select the "List changes on a new sheet" option, a new sheet will be inserted in the workbook with the default name History. Figure 16-5 shows how edited cells are displayed on screen (top) and on the History sheet (bottom).

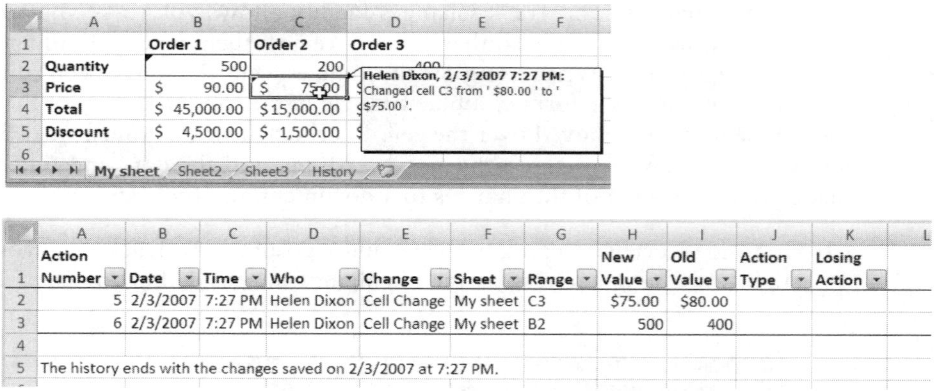

Figure 16-5. You can display changes on the screen or list them in a new History sheet.

To review the changes to a workbook so that you can accept or reject them, click Track Changes in the Changes group and select Accept/Reject Changes. In the Select Changes to Accept or Reject dialog box, select the appropriate options to choose which changes you want to review and click OK. The Accept or Reject Changes dialog box will appear, displaying the changes one at a time (see Figure 16-6). Click the Accept or the Reject button to accept or reject the displayed change, then move to the next change or click Accept All or Reject All to accept or reject all the changes.

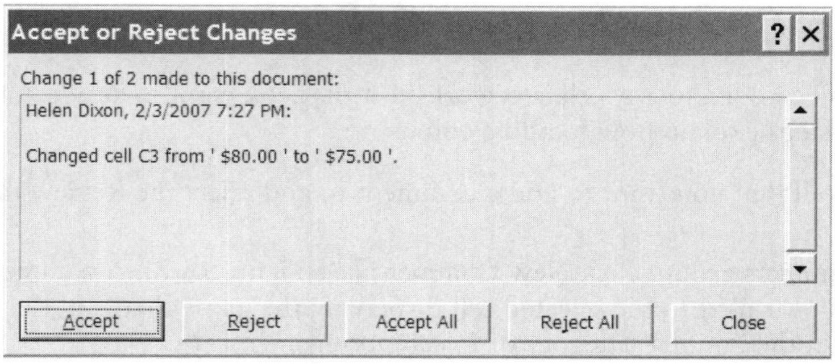

Accept or Reject Changes ? ✕

Change 1 of 2 made to this document:

Helen Dixon, 2/3/2007 7:27 PM:

Changed cell C3 from ' $80.00 ' to ' $75.00 '.

| Accept | Reject | Accept All | Reject All | Close |

Figure 16-6. Use the Accept or Reject Changes dialog box to review the changes to a workbook.

To stop highlighting changes to a workbook, click Track Changes in the Changes group and select Highlight Changes. In the Highlight Changes dialog box, deselect the "Track changes while editing. This also shares your workbook." option. A message will appear warning you that the workbook will be removed from shared use, that the change history will be erased, and that other users will not be able to save their changes. Click Yes to proceed.

Using Comments

When sharing a spreadsheet, you may find it useful to attach a note or comment to a cell to provide information about the contents of the cell or instructions for other users. Typical reasons for adding a comment to a cell include to clarify where a value has come from or to explain the purpose of a formula. Comments are particularly beneficial when creating a spreadsheet to be accessed or edited by other users.

Usually comments will be hidden but cells that have a comment attached will display an indicator in the form of a red triangle in the top-right corner of the cell (see Figure 16-7). Users can view the comment attached to a cell by hovering the mouse pointer over the cell that displays an indicator or using the commands in the Comments group on the Review tab. Comments are displayed in text boxes and are linked to the cell by an arrow.

Figure 16-7. Hover the mouse pointer over a cell containing a comment indicator to view the comment.

Adding a Comment to a Cell

Comments can be added to any cell in a worksheet that you want to attach a note to. The following steps explain how to add a comment:

1. Select the cell that you want to add a comment to and select the Review tab on the Ribbon.

2. In the Comments group, click New Comment (see Figure 16-8). A comment text box will appear next to the selected cell displaying the name that is in the User name box in the Popular category of Excel Options.

Figure 16-8. Click New Comment in the Comments group to attach a comment to a cell.

3. Type your comment text in the comment text box. If you want to remove the name, you can delete it.

4. To format the text in the comment, use the Font and Alignment groups on the Home tab. To change the color of the comment text, select the text, right-click the comment, and select Format Comment. Click the dropdown arrow in the Color box and choose a different color.

5. When you have finished creating the comment, click outside the comment text box. A comment indicator will be displayed in the top-right corner of the cell.

> **NOTE** If you sort your data, the comments will be sorted along with the data. However, in PivotTables, comments will not move with cells if you change the layout of the PivotTable report.

Viewing Comments

To view the comment attached to a cell at any time, just hover the mouse pointer over the cell; as you move the mouse pointer away from the cell, the comment will disappear. If you want to keep the comment for the selected cell displayed you can select the Review tab and, in the Comments group, click Show/Hide Comment. To hide a comment that you have displayed, click Show/Hide Comment again. To move between comments, simply click Previous or Next in the Comments group. To view or hide all the comments on a worksheet, click Show All Comments in the Comments group.

You can change the settings for displaying comments by clicking the Microsoft Office Button, clicking Excel Options, and selecting the Advanced category. In the

Display section, under "For cells with comments show" choose from the "No comments or indicators," "Indicators only, and comments on hover," or "Comments and indicators" options.

If a comment is overlapping another comment or hiding important data, you can reposition the comment text box by clicking it and dragging its border. You can also resize the comment text box by clicking and dragging any of the sizing handles on the sides or corners of the box until it is the required size.

Printing Comments

When you print a worksheet, the comments will not normally be included. If you want to include the comments in a printout of the worksheet, you have two choices: you can print them as they appear on the worksheet (next to the appropriate cell) or, so as not to obscure any worksheet data, you can print them at the end on a separate page. To print the comments along with the worksheet data, do the following:

1. Select the worksheet that you want to print the comments for.
2. Select the Page Layout tab on the Ribbon and click the Dialog Box Launcher in the bottom-right corner of the Page Setup group.
3. In the Page Setup dialog box, select the Sheet tab.
4. In the Print section, click the down arrow in the field beside Comments and choose either "At end of sheet" or "As displayed on sheet."
5. Click the Print Preview button in the Page Setup dialog box to check to see how your comments will appear when printed.
6. In Print Preview, click Print to continue with printing the document or click Close Print Preview to return to the worksheet.

Editing and Deleting Comments

You can use the commands in the Comments group on the Review tab to edit worksheet comments or to delete comments that are no longer required. Select the cell to which the comment that you want to edit is attached and, in the Comments group, click Edit Comment (the New Comment command is replaced by the Edit Comment command when you select a cell that already has a comment attached to it). Alternatively, if the comment is already displayed you can click on the text in the comment text box to edit it.

To format the text in a comment by changing the font or font size or to make the text bold, underlined, or italicized, you can use the Font group on the Home tab. If you want to change the alignment or orientation of the text in a comment, use the Alignment group on the Home tab. To change the color of the comment text, select the text, right-click the comment, and select Format Comment to open the Format Comment dialog box. Click the dropdown arrow in the Color box and choose a different color. You can also change the font, font size, and font style in the Format Comment dialog box.

If you want, you can customize the actual comment text box to change features like the fill color, line color, margins, or size. To do this, right-click the border of the comment text box and select Format Comment. A Format Comment dialog box will appear that contains several tabs. Format the comment as required using the following points as a guide:

- Use the Font tab to change the font, font size, font style, color, underline, or effects of the comment text.
- Use the Alignment tab to change the text alignment, orientation, and direction.
- Use the Colors and Lines tab to format the fill color and transparency and the line color, style, dash, and weight of the comment text box.
- Use the Size tab to alter the size or scale of the comment text box.
- Use the Protection tab to lock the comment so that it cannot be altered (this feature is not available in a shared workbook).
- Use the Properties tab to control whether the comment should be moved or sized with the cell.
- Use the Margins tab to set the margins for the comment text box.
- Use the Web tab to specify alternative text to be used in a web browser.

When you have finished formatting the comment, click OK to close the Format Comment dialog box.

To delete a comment from the worksheet, click the cell that the comment is attached to and, in the Comments group, click Delete Comment. The text box and the comment will be removed without confirmation, although you can click Undo in the Quick Access toolbar if you change your mind. If you delete the cell to which a comment is attached, the comment will be deleted also.

Preparing a Worksheet for Printing

If you are intending to create a hard copy of your data, you will probably want to change some features to make it more suitable for printing. Excel 2007 features the addition of a Page Layout view (in the Workbook Views group in the View tab) to accompany the existing Normal and Page Break Preview views. This allows you to view a worksheet as it will appear when it is printed so that you can identify where pages begin and end and to add a header or footer. It also includes horizontal and vertical rulers to help you see the exact width of cells or to position items like charts correctly on the page.

Before printing a hard copy of your spreadsheet, you may want to alter some of the page settings such as the width of the margins, or you may need to add a header or footer to display information such as the date. This section will look at how you can add these finishing touches to your document.

Using Headers and Footers

If you have information that you want to be printed on every page—for example, author details, file location, page numbers, or the date—you can insert it into the header or footer of the sheet. Any text that you want to appear at the top of every printed page will go into the header and any text that you want to print at the bottom of every page will go into the footer. You can also insert pictures, such as a company logo, into the header and footer. The new Page Layout view in Excel 2007 makes adding text or images to the header or footer area of a worksheet much simpler, as outlined in the following steps:

1. Select the worksheet that you want the header or footer to apply to and select the View tab.

2. In the Workbook Views group, click Page Layout (or Page Layout View). The worksheet will be displayed in Page Layout view (see Figure 16-9).

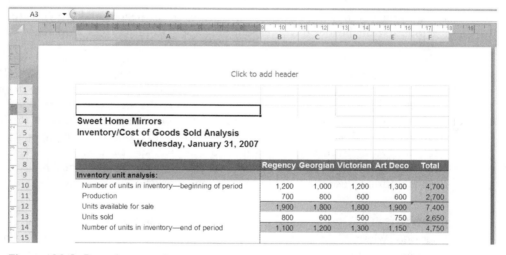

Figure 16-9. Page Layout view

3. To add a header, click on the "Click to add header" text at the top of the page above the grid (see Figure 16-9). To add a footer, scroll to the bottom of the page and click on the "Click to add footer" text. A Design tab under Header & Footer Tools will be added to the Ribbon (see Figure 16-10). A header area and a footer area, each with a left, center, and right text box, will be displayed on the sheet. (You can also add a header or footer by selecting the Insert tab and, in the Text group, clicking Header & Footer.)

Figure 16-10. The Design tab under Header & Footer Tools

4. Click in the left, center, or right header or footer text box at the top or bottom of the page and type the text that you want to appear on any printouts. Alternatively, you can click the Header or the Footer command in the Header & Footer group of the Design tab and select one of the predefined headers or footers, or you can use the commands in the Header & Footer Elements group to add elements such as the number of pages, date, or file name. You can use the Go to Header and Go to Footer commands in the Navigation group to quickly move between the header and footer.

5. Continue adding text, elements, or pictures to the header and footer as required. Note that the header or footer will only apply to the current worksheet.

If you want the header and footer on the first page to differ from the rest of the document, select the Different First Page option in the Options group on the Design tab. You can then add a different header or footer for the remainder of the document to the second page (or leave the header and footer on the second page blank if you only want to display the header and footer on the first page). If you want the header and footer for odd pages to differ from the header and footer on even pages, select the Different Odd & Even Pages option. You can also select the Scale with Document option to use the same font size and scaling as the worksheet and the Align with Page Margins option to use the same margins as the worksheet.

> **NOTE** For chart sheets and embedded charts, the Page Setup dialog box will appear when you click Header & Footer. Click Custom Header or Custom Footer and use the buttons to insert elements into the header or footer.

Changing the Layout for Printing

To print your worksheet using the most appropriate layout or with minimal paper waste, you can adjust the setup of the page by changing the margins or orientation. If you do not wish to print the entire worksheet, you can select a specific area to print; alternatively, you can resize the data so that it will span the width or height of a set number of pages when printed. You can also opt to print gridlines or headings or to repeat the rows and columns containing the titles on each page that is printed. The Page Setup, Scale to Fit, and Sheet Options groups on the Page Layout tab contain most of the commands you will need to prepare your worksheet for printing (see Figure 16-11).

Figure 16-11. Use the Page Setup, Scale to Fit, and Sheet Options group to prepare your worksheet for printing.

In Excel 2007 you can quickly change the settings for the margins to one of the handy predefined settings (see Figure 16-12). Click Margins in the Page Setup group and choose from Last Custom Setting (if available), Normal, Wide, or Narrow or click Custom Margins to open the Page Setup dialog box at the Margins tab, where you can enter your own margin settings.

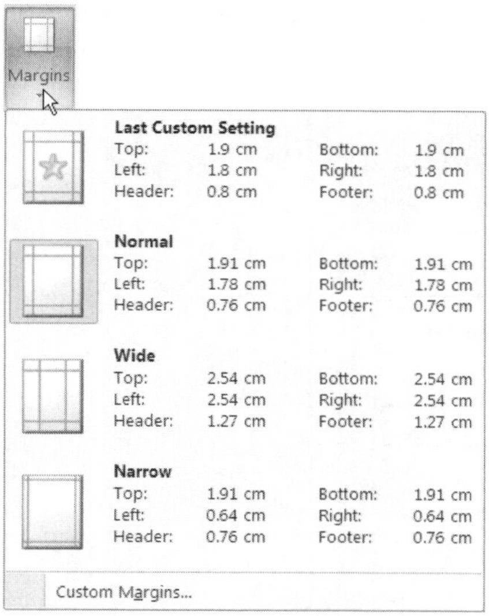

Figure 16-12. Choose a predefined setting for the margins or click Custom Margins to open the Page Setup dialog box at the Margins tab.

You can click the Orientation command in the Page Setup group to toggle between Portrait or Landscape orientation, and use the Size command to change the size of the page—for example, to Letter or A5. If you do not want to print the entire worksheet, you can specify the print area by selecting the cells that you want to print, clicking Print Area, and then clicking Set Print Area. Once you have set a print area, only that section of the worksheet will be printed (if you have selected noncontiguous ranges, they will be printed on separate pages). You can add more cells to the print area by selecting them and choosing Add to Print Area from the Print Area menu. To clear the print area so that the entire worksheet will be printed, choose Clear Print Area from the Print Area menu.

To control the position of page breaks in the worksheet, click Breaks in the Page Setup group and select the appropriate option. Alternatively, you can use Page Break Preview, which is available in the Workbook Views group on the View tab. This allows you to adjust page breaks by dragging them to the correct position. Automatic page breaks inserted by Excel are indicated by dashed blue lines; manual page breaks are displayed as solid blue lines.

If your workbook spans more than one page, you can repeat any rows or columns containing titles on each page. To do this, click Print Titles in the Page Setup group to open the Page Setup dialog box at the Sheet tab (see Figure 16-13). To repeat the row(s) containing your column labels, under Print titles, enter the reference for the rows you want to print at the top of each page in the Rows to repeat at top field (e.g., $1:$8 will repeat rows 1 to 8), or click in the field and select the rows on the worksheet. To repeat the column(s) containing your row labels, enter the reference for the columns that you want to print at the left of each page in the Columns to repeat at left field (e.g., $A:$A will repeat column A). You can also use this tab to control how cells containing errors are printed—for example, you can print them as they are displayed in the worksheet, as blank cells or using dashes (--) or #N/A.

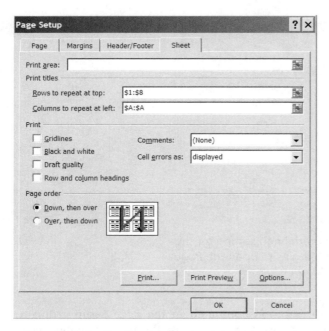

Figure 16-13. Use the Sheet tab of the Page Setup dialog box to specify rows or columns to use as print titles.

Excel can automatically reduce the width and/or height of your printed worksheet so that it will fit on the exact number of pages that you specify. For example, you can use this to make sure that the entire worksheet prints on a single page. In the Scale to Fit group, select the number of pages that you want to scale the worksheet to from the dropdown lists in the Width and Height boxes. Alternatively, you can shrink or stretch the printed output to a given percentage of its actual size by changing the value in the Scale box—to do this, Automatic must be selected in the Width and Height boxes. Finally, you can include the gridlines and the row and column headings in your printout by selecting the appropriate options in the Sheet Options group.

Using Print Preview

You should always check a document in Print Preview before sending it to be printed to ensure that it will print exactly as expected. Print Preview is now located in the Microsoft Office Button—point to Print and click Print Preview in the fly-out menu. The current worksheet will be displayed in Print Preview and the standard tabs on the Ribbon will be replaced by a Print Preview tab. Figure 16-14 shows how a worksheet will appear in Print Preview in Excel 2007.

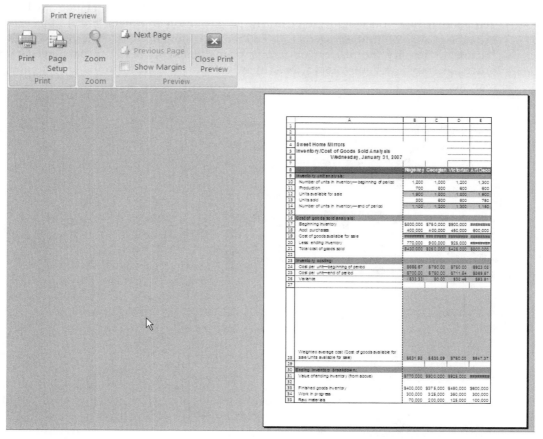

Figure 16-14. Use Print Preview to check how your data will print.

Use the Zoom command to zoom in and out (or you can click on the page) and click Next Page or Previous Page to move between pages (if appropriate). To open the Page Setup dialog box so that you can change the settings, click Page Setup. If you want to check your margin settings, click Show Margins to display dashed lines around the edges of the page indicating the position of the margins. When you have finished checking your document, click Print to open the Print dialog box or click Close Print Preview to return to the worksheet without printing.

Preparing a Document for Distribution

Excel 2007 includes various features to allow you to check the suitability of a document before making it available to others. For example, you may wish to check that your workbook does not contain any elements that will not be compatible with earlier versions of Excel, or you may want to ensure that it does not include any hidden content that you would prefer not to be passed on to others. Excel 2007 has brought a range of utilities together in the Prepare command in the Microsoft Office Button to simplify the process of getting your documents ready to be viewed by others, as shown in Figure 16-15. Note that the options available on your computer may vary.

Figure 16-15. Excel 2007 includes a range of features to help you prepare a document for distribution.

When you have finished inspecting and protecting your document, you can click the Microsoft Office Button and select Print (to print the data), Send (to email the workbook or fax it using an Internet fax service), or Publish (to view your other distribution options). Chapter 17 will look at how you can publish a workbook to Excel Services.

Changing the Document Properties

A document's properties (or metadata) are various details about the file, including such information as the author's name, the title of the document, and keywords in the content. By entering information into the document properties fields, you can make it easier to organize or search for documents. To view or change the document properties in Excel 2007, click the Microsoft Office Button, point to Prepare, and click Properties. A Document Information panel will appear above your worksheet, just below the Ribbon (see Figure 16-16). You can then type any information that you want to add into the appropriate field. If you want to view more properties or to add custom properties such as Checked by or Document number, click Document Properties at the top of the panel and select Advanced Properties (see Figure 16-16). If your document is saved to a document library or your organization has customized the Document Information panel, there may be other types of properties available in the Document Properties dropdown list.

Figure 16-16. Use the Document Information panel to add details to the document properties.

Inspecting a Document

Before distributing an Excel document, particularly to people outside your organization, you may want to check it for hidden or personal data stored either in the workbook or in the metadata that you do not want to be made available to others viewing the document. This includes data that is automatically included in your document when you collaborate on it or items that you deliberately designate as hidden. Although this data may not be immediately visible, other people may be able to access it. For example, you may not want to reveal how a document has been edited, the names of all those who contributed to the document, or other such data that can be retrieved via the Track Changes facility.

The Document Inspector will check your document to identify and remove hidden data or personal details so that you will not unwittingly disseminate information you would rather not divulge. Data that the Document Inspector can find and remove includes comments, annotations, document properties, headers, footers, watermarks, hidden rows, columns and worksheets, custom XML data, and objects that have been formatted as invisible. As it may not always be possible to undo any changes that the Document Inspector makes, it is advisable to create a copy of your document and use the Document Inspector on it so that the original remains intact. To check your document for hidden or personal data, click the Microsoft Office Button, point to Prepare, and click Inspect Document. The Document Inspector dialog box will open (see Figure 16-17).

Figure 16-17. Use the Document Inspector to check your data for hidden or personal information.

Use the checkboxes in the Document Inspector to select the type of content that you want to check the document for and click Inspect. The Document Inspector will check your document for the selected content and identify what has been found (see Figure 16-18). To remove any content from the document, click the Remove All button.

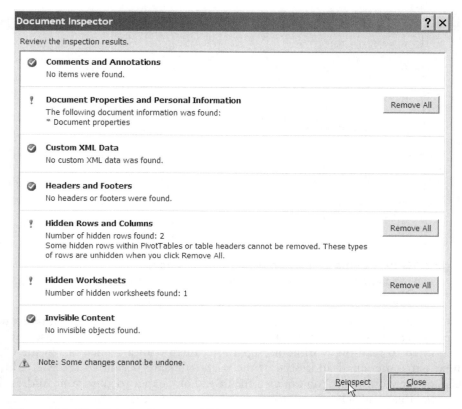

Figure 16-18. Click the Remove All button to remove any hidden or personal data before distributing a document.

Protecting and Finalizing a Document

To control access to your document, you can encrypt it using a password by selecting Encrypt from the Prepare fly-out menu and entering a password, although this will only provide limited protection against malicious intent. If you have the Windows Rights Management client installed, you can restrict access using Information Rights Management (IRM), which is available in Microsoft Office 2007. IRM allows you to control access permissions to documents to help prevent the unauthorized printing, forwarding, or copying of sensitive data. This can help to protect files that are being emailed as attachments in particular, as the usage restrictions are stored in the document file and therefore will remain with it. To use IRM to restrict access, select Restrict Permission in the Prepare fly-out menu to open the Permission dialog box (see Figure 16-19).

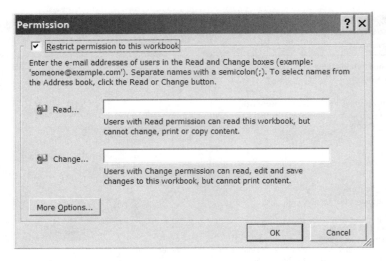

Figure 16-19. Use the Permission dialog box to specify who can read and who can change the workbook.

To specify who can read or change the file, select the "Restrict permission to this workbook" option. In the Read box, enter the email addresses of the users who are permitted to read the workbook, separating them with a semicolon. In the Change box, enter the email addresses of the users who are permitted to read, edit, and change the workbook. You can also click Read or Change to go to your Address book (if available) and select users from there. To view further options—for example, to allow users to copy or print content or to set an expiry date—click the More Options button.

When you have finished editing a document, you can mark it as final by selecting Mark as Final in the Prepare menu. This will enter Final in the Status field of the document properties and will prevent others from changing the document by making it read-only. Note that Mark as Final is not a security measure and users can edit a document if they remove the Mark as Final status from the document simply by clicking Mark as Final in the Prepare menu. It may, however, prevent users from accidentally changing a document and allows you to indicate to users that they are viewing the final version of the document.

If you want to authenticate the content of your document, you should use a digital signature. This will assure recipients of the document that it is valid and that it has not been tampered with. To add a digital signature to your document, select the Add a Digital Signature command in the Prepare menu. See Chapter 14 for more information on digital signatures, protection, and security or check out the Help facility to find out more about IRM.

Compatibility Issues and Saving in Other Formats

If you are planning to distribute a workbook to users who may be using an earlier version of Excel, you can run the Compatibility Checker to identify any features that you have included that may not be supported fully by earlier releases of Excel. Compatibility issues may cause a significant loss of functionality, such as functions that are not supported in other versions, or a minor loss of fidelity, such as changes to formatting. To check your document for unsupported features, click the Microsoft Office Button, point to Prepare, and select Run Compatibility Checker. The Compatibility Checker will check the workbook and display a summary of the Compatibility issues that may be lost or degraded if you save the file in an earlier file format. If you want to run the Compatibility Checker each time you save the workbook, select the "Check compatibility when saving the workbook" option. To create a report of the issues that the Compatibility Checker has found, click the Copy to New Sheet button. A sheet will be added to your workbook, with the default name Compatibility Report, detailing the compatibility issues for the workbook.

To save your workbook in another file format, such as an Excel Macro-Enabled Workbook, Excel Binary Workbook, or Excel 97–2003 Workbook, click the Microsoft Office Button, point to Save As, and select an option from those available, or select Other Formats to open the Save As dialog box. You can then select a format from the "Save as type" box. If you choose to save the workbook in an Excel 97–2003 Workbook format, the Compatibility Checker will run automatically. If you intend your document to be only viewed or printed, you can save it in a PDF (Portable Document Format) or XPS (XML Paper Specification) format, although you will need to install the Microsoft Save As PDF or XPS add-in first. These formats ensure that the file will retain the original layout and format when it is viewed or printed. For more information on installing and using the Microsoft Save As PDF or XPS add-in, click "Find add-ins for other file formats" in the Save As fly-out menu or check out the Help facility.

SharePoint and Excel Services

If your organization is using SharePoint 2007, or Microsoft Office SharePoint Server (MOSS) 2007 to give it its official title, you can expand the functionality of Excel to facilitate interactive access to workbook elements using a browser. In MOSS 2007 Microsoft has produced a versatile platform for building web pages for both internal and external users. Excel Services is a new component of SharePoint that allows you to host spreadsheets on a browser and offload calculations onto a separate server while retaining control centrally.

Along with its web-authoring capabilities, MOSS 2007 includes document-management solutions facilitating workflows for creating, editing, and approving documents. This allows for better Microsoft Office integration and improved document storage and control. It also enables organizations to centralize their data while providing efficient access to anyone who needs it. Excel Services will give you unprecedented flexibility in providing interactive access to real-time spreadsheet data to dispersed users without the need for specialist software on the client machines. What's more, most of this can be done without any programming knowledge, allowing managers and office administrators to update the data available at any time.

This chapter will provide you with a brief overview of some of the functionality that is now available through MOSS 2007 and Excel Services to allow you to distribute business information stored in spreadsheets throughout your organization and beyond. For those of you who are unfamiliar with SharePoint, I will begin with a quick introduction to what it is about. I will then describe how you can make an Excel 2007 workbook available to other users by publishing it to Excel Services. Unfortunately, it is not feasible to cover everything that you can do with SharePoint and Excel Services in this chapter, but hopefully it will give you an idea of what is possible.

Microsoft Office SharePoint Server 2007

The development of Microsoft Office SharePoint Server 2007 reflects the growing emphasis on business processes and collaboration in most organizations and the need for information to be made available to multiple users while remaining centrally managed. MOSS 2007 integrates various server capabilities to enable organizations to facilitate information-sharing and search facilities throughout the enterprise and to assemble intranet, extranet, and web application on one common platform. Some of the main features of SharePoint include

- The ability to house all your organization's documents and content in a centralized location (document library) where it can be retrieved and accessed by multiple users.

- A Business Data Catalog that can be used to search a SharePoint site and retrieve data from back-end systems. This provides a link between the portal site and other databases and line-of-business applications. There is also Enterprise Search, which assembles business data, documents, and web pages along with information about people to provide up-to-date, comprehensive results.

- A personal interface known as My Site, where users can access and contribute to the organization's intranet via the portal site. Users can store work or share it with others, or find and connect with colleagues and access their work. Within My Site is a public view or Profile page that contains the information you want to share with others as well as lists of colleagues and memberships. There is also a Personal site containing information specific to you where you can manage your documents, email, calendar, and so forth, and Personalization sites providing personalized views of portal sites.

- Workflows that can be used to attach custom business processes to documents or list items to control the life cycle of the document or item. By integrating these with other Microsoft Office applications, activities like document approval or version tracking can be simplified.

- A document policy management system to help manage documents and content in accordance with established business processes. This allows you to define customized document-management policies so that you can exercise control over how long a document is available and who can access it.

- The functionality to design and publish dynamic, customized web content without having to write custom code. Master pages and page layouts are the two main templates used when publishing content in MOSS 2007 and help to ensure a consistent appearance for the site.

- The ability to construct interactive business intelligence (BI) portals to retrieve and display information from various sources, using features such as dashboards, Web Parts (like the Excel Web Access Web Part), and key performance indicators (KPIs).

The feature of SharePoint on which this chapter focuses is Excel Services, which facilitates the loading, calculation, and display of Excel workbooks on MOSS 2007. It enables you to save workbooks to a SharePoint site so that other users can access them, or elements of them, via a browser. This allows you to share data with other users while maintaining control over what is displayed and the current version being used. It also allows the development of applications that call Excel Web Services to set, calculate, and retrieve values from worksheets or refresh external connections.

> **NOTE** For more information on MOSS 2007, check out the Help facility. You may also be interested in reading *Microsoft SharePoint: Building Office 2007 Solutions in C# 2005* or *Microsoft SharePoint: Building Office 2007 Solutions in VB 2005*, both by Scot Hillier and published by Apress.

Excel Services

Excel Services is new server technology, available with Excel 2007, which is built on the technology of SharePoint. It provides authors of spreadsheets with a means of sharing data with other users while being able to protect key elements of their spreadsheets and ensure that everyone is looking at "one version of the truth." This eliminates the common problem of version control for organizations that use numerous spreadsheets. You can also use document approval within Windows SharePoint Services to set up the document library so that any new workbooks that are saved to the library are not available to other users until they are approved.

Using Excel 2007, spreadsheet authors who have access to SharePoint can save their spreadsheets to a SharePoint document library and allow other users web-based access to a server-calculated version of that spreadsheet. For example, Excel Services could be used to share current marketing or inventory data across different offices, or members of a project team could use it to access information on the progress and deadlines for the project. The workbook is published to the browser using the Excel Web Access Web Part, and as calculations occur on the server, the business models used can remain hidden. This union of Excel Services and SharePoint provides Excel users with enhanced capabilities to facilitate processes such as auditing, requesting approval for a document, and controlling the version that is available. The spreadsheet author can also update the spreadsheet at any time without any assistance from IT personnel or having to translate the spreadsheet model into a programming language suitable for web applications.

> **NOTE** You cannot create spreadsheets in the browser—you must use Excel 2007.

With Excel Services, users can view a spreadsheet from portal sites even if they do not have Excel 2007 installed. When a user accesses the spreadsheet, Excel Services will load the spreadsheet, refreshing the external data and recalculating it if necessary, therefore ensuring that users are always interacting with the latest version of the data. Spreadsheet authors can protect their work by preventing users from opening the workbook using Excel or by restricting access to certain sheets or ranges within a sheet. Also, usage of the spreadsheet can be logged, helping to maintain security of the data.

Although Excel Services allows multiple users to access a spreadsheet, users will not be interacting with the original file, but rather each will have their own "session" with the file being opened as read-only. Even though several people may be using the file at any one time, each person's manipulation of the data is not seen by other users and is not saved to the original file. If users require Excel's full functionality to analyze a workbook, print data, or work offline, they can open it in Excel 2007 (provided they have the correct permissions).

These assurances of consistency and control make Excel Services an ideal medium for devolving access to spreadsheets to others without jeopardizing the original data. For example, if a finance company with several branches has a spreadsheet model that it uses to calculate interest payments for different bonds or investments, employees within each branch can access the model using Excel Services. Individual users can then input values and generate results independently of each other but without being able to modify the spreadsheet or even access the formulas used. The original spreadsheet can be controlled and updated centrally, as investment terms and interest rates change.

Excel Services Architecture

Excel Services consists of three core components that interact with one another to allow you to use workbooks as interactive reports throughout the organization, namely Excel Web Access, Excel Web Services, and Excel Calculation Services. These can be divided into two main groups: the components on the web front-end (Excel Web Access and Excel Web Services) and the component on the back-end server (Excel Calculation Services).

Excel Web Access is the visible Excel Services component that facilitates interaction with the Excel workbook using Dynamic Hypertext Markup Language (DHTML) and JavaScript, allowing users to view and interact with the data using a browser. Excel Web Access has a similar look and feel to Excel 2007 but can be used like any other Web Part in MOSS 2007 and does not require anything to be installed in the user's client computer.

Excel Web Services is the component that provides programmatic access and can be called by applications to set, calculate, and extract values from worksheets and to refresh external data sources. It allows developers to build custom programs based on the Excel workbook.

Excel Calculation Services is responsible for loading and calculating workbooks and refreshing external data. It maintains a session for the duration of interactions with the same workbook by a user, caching the opened workbooks, calculation states, and external data query results to improve performance.

As well as providing a browser-based interface to the server, Excel Services also provides you with a web server–based interface. In other words, the same spreadsheet that is viewed by users can also be accessed programmatically by any application that can interpret web services. With the right permissions, the application can even change values and recalculate the spreadsheet. This means that developers can use Excel Calculation Services without having to interact with Excel Web Access.

Publishing a Workbook to a Server

If you have access to a server running Microsoft Office SharePoint Services 2007, you can publish a workbook to that server to enable other users to access all or parts of it. You can also define parameters (named cells within the workbook) to allow users to change the values of specified cells and view the results. Although the entire workbook is published to the server, the author can define which parts of it users can view, such as named ranges, sheets, tables, PivotTables, or charts, and set permissions to protect the workbook from unauthorized access. The following steps explain how to publish a workbook to Excel Services and specify what sections will be viewable and which cells will be editable:

1. In Excel 2007, create or open the workbook that you want to publish to Excel Services. Using the Defined Names group on the Formulas tab, name any individual cells (that do not contain a formula) that you want to be editable by other users.

> **TIP** You may want to include a cell containing the NOW() function on the worksheet so that users can quickly see when the workbook was last calculated by the server.

2. Click the Microsoft Office Button, point to Publish, and select Excel Services (see Figure 17-1). The Save As dialog box will open.

Figure 17-1. You can use the Publish menu to save a document for Excel Services.

3. In the File name box, enter the path to the server (or locate the server in the Save in box) and enter a name for the file.

NOTE Workbooks can only be published to the server in Excel 2007 XML-based format (.xlsx) or Excel 2007 Binary file format (.xlsb). You cannot publish an Excel 2003 workbook or use Excel 2003 to publish a workbook to a document library on the server.

4. Click the Excel Services Options button in the Save As dialog box to open the Excel Services Options dialog box (see Figure 17-2).
5. On the Show tab, select Entire Workbook, Sheets, or Items in the Workbook from the dropdown list. If you select Sheets, choose which sheets you want to show by checking the appropriate checkboxes. If you select Items in the Workbook, choose the items that you want to show (for example, ranges, charts, tables, PivotTables, or PivotCharts). This will not affect how the workbook appears in Excel 2007, but only what is viewed on the server.

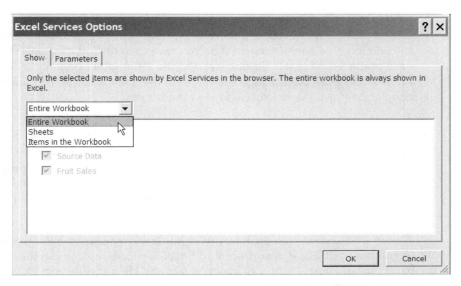

Figure 17-2. Use the Excel Services Options dialog box to select the items that will be shown by Excel Services in the browser.

6. If you want to specify cells that can be edited by users viewing the workbook through Excel Services, select the Parameters tab and click Add to open the Add Parameters dialog box (see Figure 17-3). Only single cells that have been named, that do not contain formulas, and that are not part of a PivotTable or table can be added as parameters. Each workbook can have up to 255 parameters.

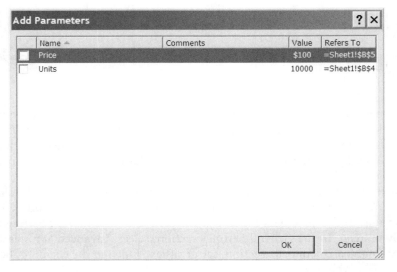

Figure 17-3. Use the Add Parameters dialog box to select the cells that will be editable by users.

NOTE Even if a cell specified as a parameter is not part of the sheets or items selected on the Show tab, and therefore is not visible by the user, the user can still edit its value on the server. When you save to Excel Services, cells that you have made editable will be displayed in the Parameters pane in Excel Web Access. Users can then change the values of the parameters in the Parameters pane and refresh the workbook to view the results.

7. In the Add Parameters dialog box, select the named ranges that you want to be editable by users and click OK. Click OK to close the Excel Services Options dialog box and return to the Save As dialog box. Save the file to appropriate document library on the server. The Open in Excel Services checkbox in the Save As dialog box is selected by default, allowing you to view the workbook in the browser and check that it loads and appears as it should.

Figure 17-4 shows how an Excel workbook will appear in a document library. When you have published a workbook to Excel Services, you can use the permissions in SharePoint to control who can access it (see the Help facility for MOSS 2007 for more information).

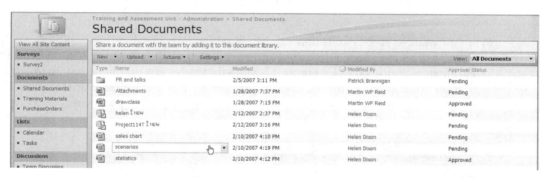

Figure 17-4. To make a workbook available through Excel Services, you need to add it to a document library.

To open the workbook in web browser view to check it, you can point to the workbook in the document library, click the arrow beside it, and select View in Web Browser from the menu that appears (see Figure 17-5). You can also use this menu to perform other tasks such as managing permissions for the workbook or to approve or reject a workbook.

Clicking a document in the document library will either open it in the client application or display it in the browser. To specify how documents should be displayed, click Settings in the document library and select Document Library Settings from the dropdown menu. In the General Settings section, select Advanced Settings and in the Browser-Enabled Documents section, select either "Open in the client application" or "Display as a Web page."

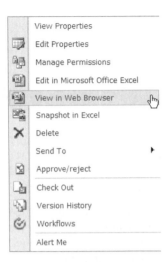

Figure 17-5. Select View in Web Browser
to open a document in a web browser.

Displaying an Excel Workbook in Excel Services

Once an Excel workbook has been saved to the document library, it can be viewed by other users using a browser. The Excel Web Access Web Part can be displayed on its own on a Web Part Page or it can be used with other Web Parts as part of a dashboard or Web Part Page. There are two main ways to load an Excel workbook in Excel Services so that other users can view and interact with it:

- Enter the URL or UNC path in the Excel Web Access Web Part "Workbook to display" property.
- Connect a List View Web Part of a document library to an Excel Web Access Web Part, and then pass the URL of the workbook stored in the document library to display it in Excel Web Access.

To display a workbook in Excel Services by entering the URL or UNC path, follow these steps:

1. Make sure that the workbook has been saved to a Microsoft Windows SharePoint Services document library or network folder.
2. Create a Web Part Page by clicking Site Actions and selecting Create (see Figure 17-6).

Figure 17-6. Select Create from the Site Actions menu to add a new Web Part Page.

3. Under Web Pages, select Web Part Page. Enter a name for the page in the Name box, select a layout from the Choose a Layout Template list, and select a document library from the Document Library dropdown list on the New Web Part Page screen (see Figure 17-7). Click Create when you have finished.

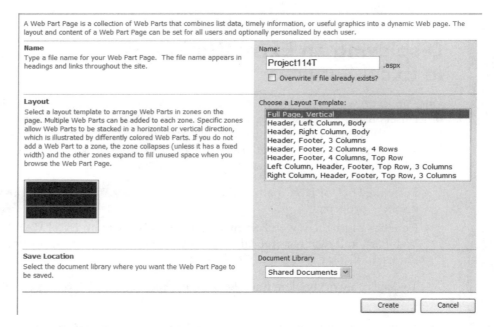

Figure 17-7. Use the New Web Part Page screen to specify the name, layout, and location of the new page.

4. Click Add a Web Part and scroll down the list until you find Excel Web Access. Select the checkbox for Excel Web Access and click Add.

5. Click the "Click here to open the tool pane" link to open the tool pane and enter the URL or UNC of the workbook in the Workbook box, or click the button beside the box to select a link (see Figure 17-8). If appropriate, you can enter the name of a worksheet, table, chart, etc. that you want to display in the Named Item box.

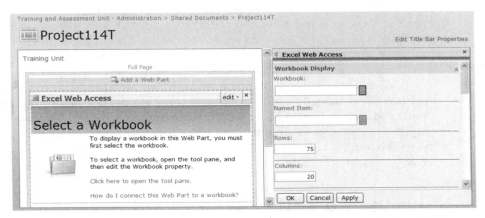

Figure 17-8. Enter the URL or UNC of a workbook to display in the new Web Part Page in the Workbook box in the Web Part tool pane.

6. Adjust the values in the Rows box and/or Columns box to control how many rows and columns will be displayed in each section. You can enter values from 1 to 500, although you should keep in mind that a larger value may result in a smaller font size.

7. Scroll down the tool pane to view the other settings you can customize, such as the type of toolbar and navigation. When you have finished, click OK at the bottom of the Web Part tool pane to close it. To exit Web Part edit mode, click Exit Edit Mode below Site Actions. The workbook will be displayed in Web Part Page Display mode.

Connecting a List View Web Part of a document library or a list to the Excel Web Access Web Part can allow you greater flexibility over how a workbook is displayed. For more information on displaying a workbook this way, see the SharePoint Server 2007 Help and How-to facility.

When you open a workbook in Excel Services, the most recent version of the workbook is loaded and a session will be created. Any changes made to the workbook in the document library after this will not be reflected in your current session. At any time, the same workbook could be opened by many users in multiple sessions or the same user could have the same workbook open in different sessions (using the New Window command in the File menu of Internet Explorer). The session will close when it times out, when you close the browser, or if you open another workbook in the Excel Web Access Web Part.

Excel Web Access will display the worksheet in Normal view or an item like a chart or table in Item view. It also includes a toolbar at the top with menu commands, dropdown lists, and navigation buttons and a Status bar at the top where messages and alerts can be displayed. The Parameter task pane contains parameter labels and text boxes where you can enter values for the parameters.

You cannot edit a spreadsheet in Excel Services, but you can interact with it to carry out tasks like sorting and filtering. If you have the correct permission, you can open the workbook in Excel 2007, either as a normal workbook or as a read-only snapshot. A snapshot is a limited version of the workbook, allowing visible information like cell values, formatting, and objects to be saved; however, details like hidden data, formulas, and connections will be removed.

To open a workbook or snapshot in Excel, click the arrow next to Open menu on the Excel Web Access toolbar (provided that it has not been hidden by the administrator) and click "Open in Excel" or "Open snapshot in Excel." You can also open a snapshot of a workbook from the document library where it is located by pointing to the workbook, clicking the arrow beside it, and selecting Snapshot in Excel. Alternatively, you can select "Edit in Microsoft Excel" to open it in Excel.

Supported and Unsupported Features in Excel Services

Not all Excel features are supported in Excel Services. The following features will be supported when you open a workbook in Excel Services:

- Functions (with a few exceptions)
- Dates
- Excel tables, including headers, total rows, calculated columns, structured references, and styles
- Cells, including values, merged cells, and content overflow
- Defined names and named ranges
- Calculation and recalculation settings
- Charts and PivotChart reports
- Cell and range formatting, conditional formatting (except data bars and icon sets), and number formats
- Connections to external data sources, including OLAP PivotTables
- What-If Analysis tools, including Goal Seek, Solver, scenarios, and data tables
- Consolidation (except in PivotTable reports)

If a workbook contains a feature that is unsupported in Excel Services, it will be prevented from loading. The following features are some of those not supported in Excel Services:

- Visual Basic for Applications (VBA) code, macros, add-ins, and user-defined functions (UDFs)
- Microsoft Excel 4.0 Macro Functions and Microsoft 5.0 dialog sheets
- Form toolbar controls, Toolbox controls, and all Active X controls
- XML maps and embedded smart tags
- Workbooks, worksheets, and ranges with protection and workbooks that have Information Rights Management (IRM)
- Linked or embedded objects or images, inserted pictures, WordArt, shapes, and diagrams and ink features, including drawings, writing, or annotations
- Object Linking and Embedding (OLE) objects and Dynamic Data Exchange (DDE) links
- Workbooks saved with the formulas displayed
- Data validation and dropdown lists
- Web queries and text queries
- Creation of external references (links) to workbooks
- Display and editing of comments
- Digital signatures
- Shared workbooks

To check if a workbook contains any unsupported features, open it in Excel 2007, click the Microsoft Office Button, point to Publish, and select Excel Services. Make sure that the Open in Excel Services checkbox is selected in the Save As dialog box. Excel will attempt to open the workbook in Excel Services and will display an alert if it includes a feature that is not supported.

In some cases workbooks may be displayed differently in the browser than in Excel. Features that will not prevent a workbook from loading but may appear differently on a server include hyperlinks, fonts, charts and PivotChart reports, border styles, fill colors, alignment, and rotation.

Features that will not prevent a workbook from loading but are not supported when displaying a workbook in Excel Services include hyperlinks in charts; the replacement of worksheet column headers by table headers when scrolling; some settings for cell fill patterns, line border styles, or text direction; 3-D graphic effects in charts; embedded charts that have been copied or moved from a worksheet to a chart sheet; some formatting in row and column headers; page layout; and page headers and footers.

Finally, even if a workbook appears the same, sometimes when you interact with it in Excel Services it may behave differently than it would in Excel. Features that may differ include PivotTables and PivotCharts, sorting, filtering, outlining, finding, and selecting. For more information on the differences between using a workbook in Excel and Excel Services, check out the Help facility.

Interacting with Spreadsheets Generated by Excel Services

Excel Services supports most of the formatting and layouts available in Excel 2007; therefore, a spreadsheet viewed in the browser should look much the same as it does in Excel. However, to optimize performance the spreadsheet will be loaded by Excel Services one section at a time. By default, Excel Web Access will display 20 columns and 75 rows on a scrolling page, although these values can be adjusted in the Web Part tool pane (see Figure 17-8). Users can then use paging controls to move between sections or use sheet tabs (as in Excel) to view separate worksheets. If the workbook author selected more than one named item in the Excel Services Options dialog box, you can use the View dropdown lists on the Excel Web Access toolbar (if available) to select a named item to view.

Users accessing a spreadsheet through Excel Services can do more than just view the data. Depending on the spreadsheet and the permissions that have been set, they can also sort, filter, and pivot the data and, if available, open the file in Excel 2007 to allow further manipulation of the data. Other things users will be able to do in the browser include expanding and collapsing outlines, setting parameters, refreshing external data, recalculating the worksheet, and finding values within a worksheet.

If a spreadsheet in Excel Services contains a table or filters, users will be able to execute and update sorts and filters with the exception of sorting and filtering by color. Users can also interact with PivotTables from within the browser and can carry out tasks such as sorting, filtering, and expanding and collapsing levels. Most of these functions operate in a similar manner to Microsoft Office Excel 2007.

To change the value of any of the parameters in a workbook and carry out what-if type analysis, you can use the Parameters task pane. This displays a list of the parameters in alphabetical order, using the defined name for the cell, along with a box where you can change the value. If a comment was added when the name was defined, this will be displayed as a ScreenTip when you hover the mouse over the parameter name. To remove all the values in the Parameters task pane so that you can enter new values, click Clear at the bottom of the task pane. When you have finished changing parameter values, click Apply at the bottom of the task pane to view the results. Any changes you make can only be viewed by you and will not be saved when you close the workbook.

> **NOTE** If the Parameters task pane is not available, the spreadsheet author did not define any parameters or has disabled parameter modification.

Editing a Workbook Published in Excel Services

You can make changes to a workbook you have published in Excel Services at any time using Microsoft Excel 2007. The entire workbook is always opened in Excel, allowing you to make changes to any part of the content. For example, you may want to change the parts of the spreadsheet that users can view or the cells that are editable. When you save the workbook again, any changes that you have made will be reflected on the server. To edit a workbook published in Excel Services, follow these steps:

1. Open the workbook either in Excel or in the browser by doing either of the following:
   - To open the workbook in Excel, click the Microsoft Office Button and click Open (or press Ctrl+O). In the File name box, type the URL of the server and the path of the file and click Open.
   - To open the workbook in the browser, type the URL of the server in the Address bar of the browser, open the document library that contains the file, click the down arrow next to the workbook, and select Edit in Microsoft Office Excel from the menu that appears.
2. Make the changes required to the workbook, ensuring that you name any cells you intend to define as parameters.
3. Click the Microsoft Office Button, point to Publish, and select Excel Services.
4. In the Save As dialog box, click the Excel Services Options button and make any changes required to what users will be able to access in the Show tab. If you want to change the cells that can be edited, select the appropriate cells in the Parameters tab.
5. Click OK to close the Excel Services Options dialog box and click Save to commit the changes you have made.

Removing a Workbook Published to Excel Services

If you no longer want to make a workbook available on Excel Services, you can delete it from the SharePoint document library using either Excel or the browser. To delete a workbook using Excel, click the Microsoft Office Button and select Open (or press Ctrl+O). Click My Network Places and then double-click the name of the server that the workbook is saved to. Double-click on the document library containing the workbook, select the workbook, and click Delete (or press the Delete key).

To delete the workbook using the browser, type the URL of the server in the Address bar of the browser and open the document library containing the workbook. Click the down arrow beside the workbook that you want to delete and select Delete from the dropdown menu.

Location of Popular Excel 2003 Commands in Excel 2007

Command	Excel 2003 Location	Excel 2007 Location
New, Open, Print	File menu Standard toolbar	Microsoft Office Button
Close, Exit Save As	File menu	Microsoft Office Button
Save	File menu Standard toolbar Quick Access toolbar	Microsoft Office Button
Save As Web Page	File menu	Microsoft Office Button ➤ Save As ➤ Other Formats and choose Web Page or Single File Web Page in "Save as type" box
Save Workspace	File menu	View tab, Window group
Permission	File menu Standard toolbar	Microsoft Office Button ➤ Prepare ➤ Restrict Permission
Page Setup Print Area ➤ Set Print Area/ Clear Print Area	File menu	Page Layout tab, Page Setup group Page Layout tab, Sheet Options group (Dialog Box Launcher)
Print Preview	File menu Standard toolbar	Microsoft Office Button ➤ Print
Send to Mail Recipient (As Attachment)	File ➤ Send to	Microsoft Office Button ➤ Send ➤ Email

Continued

Command	Excel 2003 Location	Excel 2007 Location
Properties	File menu	Microsoft Office Button ➤ Prepare
Undo, Redo	Edit menu Standard toolbar	Quick Access toolbar
Cut, Copy, Paste	Edit menu Standard toolbar	Home tab, Clipboard group
Office Clipboard	Edit menu	Home tab, Clipboard group (Dialog Box Launcher)
Paste Special, Paste as Hyperlink	Edit menu	Home tab, Clipboard group, Paste menu
Fill, Clear	Edit menu	Home tab, Editing group
Delete	Edit menu	Home tab, Cells group
Delete Sheet	Edit menu	Home tab, Cells group, Delete menu
Move or Copy Sheet	Edit menu	Home tab, Cells group, Format menu
Find, Replace, Go To	Edit menu	Home tab, Editing group, Find & Select menu
Links	Edit menu	Data tab, Connections group, Edit Links
Normal, Page Break Preview, Full Screen	View menu	View tab, Workbook Views group
Formula Bar	View menu	View tab, Show/Hide group
Header and Footer	View menu	Insert tab, Text group
Comments	View menu	Review tab, Comments group, Show All Comments
Custom Views	View menu	View tab, Workbook Views group
Zoom	View menu	View tab, Zoom group
Cells, Rows, Columns, Worksheet	Insert menu	Home tab, Cells group, Insert menu
Chart	Insert menu Standard toolbar	Insert tab, Charts group
Symbol, Object	Insert menu	Insert tab, Text group
Page Break	Insert menu	Page Layout tab, Page Setup group, Breaks ➤ Insert Page Break
Function	Insert menu	Formulas tab, Function Library group, Insert Function

Command	Excel 2003 Location	Excel 2007 Location
Name	Insert menu	Formulas tab, Defined Names group
Comment	Insert menu	Review tab, Comments group, New Comment
Picture submenu, Clip Art, From File, From Scanner or Camera, AutoShape	Insert menu	Insert tab, Illustrations group
Picture submenu, WordArt	Insert menu	Insert tab, Text group
Picture submenu, Organization Chart Diagram	Insert menu	Insert tab, Illustrations group, SmartArt
Hyperlink	Insert menu Standard toolbar	Insert tab, Links group, Hyperlink
Cells, Row, Column Sheet submenu, Rename, Hide, Unhide, Tab Color	Format menu	Home tab, Cells group, Format menu
Sheet submenu, Background	Format menu	Page Layout tab, Page Setup group
AutoFormat	Format menu	Home tab, Styles group, Format as Table
Conditional Formatting	Format menu	Home tab, Styles group
Style	Format menu	Home tab, Styles group, Cell Styles
Spelling, Research	Tools menu Standard toolbar	Review tab, Proofing group
Error Checking, Formula Auditing	Tools menu	Formulas tab, Formula Auditing group
Share Workbook, Track Changes, Protection	Tools menu	Review tab, Changes group
Goal Seek, Scenarios	Tools menu	Data tab, Data Tools group, What-If Analysis menu
Options	Tools menu	Microsoft Office Button Excel Options
Sort, Filter	Data menu	Home tab, Editing group, Sort & Filter menu Data tab, Sort & Filter group
Subtotals, Group and Outline	Data menu	Data tab, Outline group
Validation	Data menu	Data tab, Data Tools group, Data Validation

Continued

Command	Excel 2003 Location	Excel 2007 Location
Table	Data menu	Data tab, Data Tools group, What-If Analysis menu
Text to Columns Consolidate	Data menu	Data tab, Data Tools group
PivotTable and PivotChart Report	Data menu	Insert tab, Tables group, PivotTable menu
Import External Data submenu, New Web Query	Data menu	Data tab, Get External Data group, From Web
Import External Data submenu, Data Range Properties	Data menu	Data tab, Connections group, Properties
List submenu, Create List	Data menu	Insert tab, Tables group, Table
List submenu, Resize List	Data menu	(Table Tools) Design tab, Properties group, Resize Table
List submenu, Total Row	Data menu	(Table Tools) Design tab, Table Style Options group
List submenu, Convert to Range	Data menu	(Table Tools) Design tab, Tools group
List submenu, Publish List	Data menu	(Table Tools) Design tab, External Table Data group, Export menu
List submenu, View List on Server	Data menu	(Table Tools) Design tab, External Table Data group, Open in Browser
List submenu, Unlink List	Data menu	(Table Tools) Design tab, External Table Data group, Unlink
Chart Type	Chart menu	(Chart Tools) Design tab, Type group, Change Chart Type
Source Data, Add Data	Chart menu	(Chart Tools) Design tab, Data group, Select Data
Chart Options, Add Trendline	Chart menu	(Chart Tools) Layout tab, Analysis group
Location	Chart menu	(Chart Tools) Design tab, Location group, Move Chart
3-D Views	Chart menu	(Chart Tools) Layout tab, Background group, 3-D Rotation

Command	Excel 2003 Location	Excel 2007 Location
New Window, Arrange, Compare Side by Side With, Hide, Unhide, Switch, Freeze Panes,	Window menu	View tab, Window group
Format Painter	Standard toolbar	Home tab, Clipboard group
Sum	Standard toolbar	Home tab, Editing group
Sort Ascending, Sort Descending	Standard toolbar	Home tab, Editing group, Sort & Filter menu Data tab, Sort & Filter group
Font, Font Size, Bold, Italic, Underline, Border, Fill Color, Font Color	Formatting toolbar	Home tab, Font group
Align Left, Align Center, Align Right, Merge and Center, Increase Indent, Decrease Indent	Formatting toolbar	Home tab, Alignment group
Currency, Percent Style, Comma Style, Increase Decimal, Decrease Decimal	Formatting toolbar	Home tab, Number group
Format Report	PivotTable menu (on PivotTable Toolbar)	(PivotTable Tools) Design tab, PivotTable Styles group
PivotChart	PivotTable menu	(PivotTable Tools) Options tab, Tools group
Refresh Data	PivotTable menu PivotChart menu (on PivotChart Toolbar)	(PivotTable Tools) Options tab, Data group
Offline OLAP, Property Fields	PivotTable menu	(PivotTable Tools) Options tab, Tools group, OLAP Tools menu
Hide	PivotTable menu	Right-click row/column cell context menu
Select submenu, Label, Data, Label and Data, Entire Table, Enable Selection	PivotTable menu	(PivotTable Tools) Options tab, Actions group, Select menu
Group and Show Detail submenu, Hide Detail, Show Detail	PivotTable menu	(PivotTable Tools) Options tab, Active Field group, Active Field menu
Group and Show Detail submenu, Group, Ungroup	PivotTable menu	(PivotTable Tools) Options tab, Group group

Continued

Command	Excel 2003 Location	Excel 2007 Location
Formulas submenu, Calculated Field, Calculated Item, Solve Order, List Formulas	PivotTable menu PivotChart menu	(PivotTable Tools) Options tab, Tools group, Formulas menu
Order submenu, Move to Beginning, Move Up, Move Down, Move to End	PivotTable menu	Right-click cell context menu, Move fly-out menu
Field Settings	PivotTable menu PivotChart menu	(PivotTable Tools) Options tab, Active Field group
Subtotals	PivotTable menu	(PivotTable Tools) Design tab, Layout group
Sort and Top 10	PivotTable menu	(PivotTable Tools) Options tab, Sort group Right-click cell context menu, Filter fly-out menu
Table Options Options	PivotTable menu PivotChart menu	(PivotTable Tools) Options tab, PivotTable group, Options
Show Pages	PivotTable menu	(PivotTable Tools) Options tab, PivotTable group, Options ➤ Show Report Filter Pages

Selecting Data in a PivotTable Report

To Select . . .	Do This . . .
All items in a field	Point to the top edge of the field until the mouse pointer becomes a down arrow and click.
Item labels, values, or labels and values	Select the items and choose the Options tab. In the Actions group, click the arrow beside Select. Choose Labels and Values, Values, or Labels as required from the menu.
All occurrences of a single item in a field	Point to the top edge of a column field item until the mouse pointer becomes a down arrow, or point to the left edge of a row field item until the mouse pointer becomes a right arrow, and then click.
One occurrence of an item in a field	Point to the top edge of a column field item until the mouse pointer becomes a down arrow, or point to the left edge of a row field item until the mouse pointer becomes a right arrow. Click repeatedly (taking care not to double-click) until you have selected only the items that you want (the number of clicks required will depend on the number of row or column labels and the position of the item within those labels).
Multiple items in a field	Point to the top edge of a column field item until the mouse pointer becomes a down arrow, or point to the left edge of a row field item until the mouse pointer becomes a right arrow. Click repeatedly (taking care not to double-click) until you have selected only the items that you want (the number of clicks required will depend on the number of row or column labels and the position of the item within those labels). Shift-click or Ctrl-click to select multiple items in the same field. To remove an item from the selection, hold down the Ctrl key and click the item.

Continued

To Select . . .	Do This . . .
Subtotals and totals	Point to the top edge of a subtotal or total in a column label until the mouse pointer becomes a down arrow, or point to the left edge of a subtotal or total in a row label until the mouse pointer becomes a right arrow. Click once to select all the totals for the label; click again to select only the current subtotal or total.
Entire PivotTable report	Select the Options tab and in the Actions group, click the arrow beside Select. Click Entire PivotTable in the menu. Alternatively, select a cell in the PivotTable and press Ctrl+A.

TIP If the mouse pointer does not change to an arrow when you position it at the top or left of a field or label, go to the Options tab and, in the Actions group, click the arrow beside Select and make sure that Enable Selection is selected.

Index

Numbers

0 symbol, number format code for, 76–77

3-D column chart, description of, 233

3D formulas, using functions as, 197

3D SUM function, entering, 196

3-D Views command, location of, 382

" " (double quotes) symbol, number format code for, 77

Symbols

– (negation) operator, example of, 188

- (subtraction) operator, example of, 188

symbol, number format code for, 76–77

value in formulas, removing, 191

error
  meaning of, 191
  resolving, 287

% (percent) symbol, number format code for, 76

% (percentage) operator, example of, 188

& (concatenation) operator, example of, 188

() (parentheses), influencing order of precedence for operators with, 190

* (asterisk) symbol
  number format code for, 77
  using with text filters, 96

* (multiplication) operator, example of, 188

, (comma)
  number format code for, 76
  reference operator, 189

/ (division) operator, example of, 188

/ (slash) symbol, number format code for, 76

: (colon) reference operator, example of, 189

? (question mark)
  number format code for, 76
  using with text filters, 96

@ (at) symbol, number format code for, 77

\ (backslash) symbol, number format code for, 77

^ (exponentiation) operator, example of, 188

_ (underscore) prefix
  number format code for, 77
  as prefix for names, 53

+ (addition) operator, example of, 188

< (less than) operator, example of, 189

<= (less than or equal to) operator, example of, 189

<> (not equal to) operator, example of, 189

= (equal to) operator, example of, 188

= (equals sign)
  using with Formula AutoComplete feature, 192
  using with formulas, 41

> (greater than) operator, example of, 188

>= (greater than or equal to) operator, example of, 189

X

X in red circle, appearance next to digital signature, 313

X Y chart, description of, 234

XFD column, explanation of, 2

.xlam format, explanation of, 22

.xlsm format, explanation of, 22

.xlsx format, explanation of, 22

.xltm format, explanation of, 22

.xltx format, explanation of, 22

XML binary file format, availability of, 22

XML formats, availability of, 22

XNPV (net present value) financial function, explanation of, 204

Y

YEAR function, using, 214–215

years
entering as two digits, 213
format code for, 79

Z

Zoom command, using, 356, 380

Zoom slider, displaying in Status bar, 12

"I learned to use a computer in the third grade."

So, why do all these books treat me like I've never turned on a computer?

I want to learn what's new or unique about an application or technology to maximize my time and get to the next level.

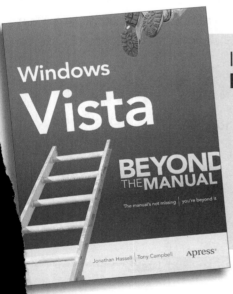

Introducing the **Beyond the Manual** series:

- Written for experienced computer users who must command the latest technology
- Quickly and concisely teaches what you need to excel
- High-density, low-fluff text in a well-referenced, well-organized book

You Need the Companion eBook

Your purchase of this book entitles you to buy the companion PDF-version eBook for only $10. Take the weightless companion with you anywhere.

We believe this Apress title will prove so indispensable that you'll want to carry it with you everywhere, which is why we are offering the companion eBook (in PDF format) for $10 to customers who purchase this book now. Convenient and fully searchable, the PDF version of any content-rich, page-heavy Apress book makes a valuable addition to your programming library. You can easily find and copy code—or perform examples by quickly toggling between instructions and the application. Even simultaneously tackling a donut, diet soda, and complex code becomes simplified with hands-free eBooks!

Once you purchase your book, getting the $10 companion eBook is simple:

❶ Visit **www.apress.com/promo/tendollars/**.

❷ Complete a basic registration form to receive a randomly generated question about this title.

❸ Answer the question correctly in 60 seconds, and you will receive a promotional code to redeem for the $10.00 eBook.

2560 Ninth Street • Suite 219 • Berkeley, CA 94710

eBookshop

ASP**Today**

A**press**
THE EXPERT'S VOIC

Offer valid through 9/19/07.